Lecture Notes in Computer Science 3063

Commenced Publication in 1973
Founding and Former Series Editors:
Gerhard Goos, Juris Hartmanis, and Jan van Leeuwen

Springer
Berlin
Heidelberg
New York
Hong Kong
London
Milan
Paris
Tokyo

Albert Llamosí   Alfred Strohmeier (Eds.)

Reliable Software Technologies - Ada-Europe 2004

9th Ada-Europe International Conference
on Reliable Software Technologies
Palma de Mallorca, Spain, June 14-18, 2004
Proceedings

Springer

Volume Editors

Albert Llamosí
The University of the Balearic Islands
Department of Mathematics and Computer Science
Carretera de Valldemossa km 7.5, 07122 Palma de Mallorca, Spain
E-mail: llamosi@uib.es

Alfred Strohmeier
Swiss Federal Institute of Technology in Lausanne
Software Engineering Laboratory
1015 Lausanne EPFL, Switzerland
E-mail: alfred.strohmeier@epfl.ch

Library of Congress Control Number: 2004105048

CR Subject Classification (1998): D.2, D.1.2-5, D.3, C.2-4, C.3, K.6

ISSN 0302-9743
ISBN 3-540-22011-9 Springer-Verlag Berlin Heidelberg New York

Springer-Verlag is a part of Springer Science+Business Media

springeronline.com

© Springer-Verlag Berlin Heidelberg 2004
Printed in Germany

Typesetting: Camera-ready by author, data conversion by PTP-Berlin, Protago-TeX-Production GmbH
Printed on acid-free paper   SPIN: 11008385   06/3142   5 4 3 2 1 0

Foreword

The Ninth International Conference on Reliable Software Technologies, Ada-Europe 2004, took place in Palma, Spain, June 14–18, 2004. It was sponsored by Ada-Europe, the European federation of national Ada societies, and Ada-Spain, in cooperation with ACM SIGAda. It was organized by members of the University of the Balearic Islands (UIB).

As in past years, the conference comprised a three-day technical program, during which the papers contained in these proceedings were presented, along with vendor presentations. The technical program was bracketed by two tutorial days, when the attendees had the opportunity to catch up on a variety of topics related to the field, at both introductory and advanced levels. Furthermore, the conference was accompanied by an exhibition where vendors presented their products for supporting reliable-software development.

Invited Speakers

The conference presented four distinguished speakers, who delivered state-of-the-art information on topics of great importance, both for now and for the future of software engineering:

- S. Tucker Taft, SoftCheck Inc., USA
  Fixing software before it breaks: using static analysis to help solve the software quality quagmire
- Martin Gogolla, University of Bremen, Germany
  Benefits and problems of formal methods
- Antoni Olivé, Polytechnical University of Catalonia, Spain
  On the role of conceptual schemas in information systems' development
- Stephen Vinoski, IONA Technologies in Waltham, USA
  Can middleware be reliable?

We would like to express our sincere gratitude to these distinguished speakers, well known to the community, for sharing their insights with the conference participants.

Submitted Papers

A large number of papers were submitted, from as many as 15 different countries. The program committee worked hard to review them, and the selection process proved to be difficult, since many papers had received excellent reviews. Finally, the program committee selected 23 papers for the conference. The final result was a truly international program with authors from Australia, Austria, China, Czech Republic, France, Germany, India, Portugal, Spain, the UK, and the USA, covering a broad range of software technologies: static analysis, testing, real-time systems, scheduling, distributed systems, formal methods, critical systems, UML, XML, fault tolerance and middleware, language issues, teaching and Ravenscar.

Tutorials

The conference also included an interesting selection of tutorials, featuring international experts who presented introductory and advanced material in the domain of the conference:

- Jean-Pierre Rosen, *Developing a Web server in Ada with AWS*
- Matthew Heaney, *Programming with the Charles container library*
- Guillem Bernat, *Probabilistic worst case execution time analysis*
- Mário A. Alves, *No pointers, great programs*
- Alfred Strohmeier, *Requirements analysis with use cases*
- Peter Amey and Roderick Chapman, *Practical experiences of safety and security-critical technologies*
- Bruce Lewis and Ed Colbert, *Developing fault-tolerant, time-critical systems with AADL, UML and Ada*
- Ben Brosgol, *Real-time Java for Ada programmers*

Acknowledgements

Many people contributed to the success of the conference. The program committee, made up of international experts in the area of reliable software technologies, spent long hours carefully reviewing all the papers and tutorial proposals submitted to the conference. A subcommittee comprising Dirk Craeynest, Albert Llamosí, Erhard Ploedereder, M.-Ribera Sancho, Alfred Strohmeier and Tullio Vardanega met in Barcelona to make the final paper selection. Some program committee members were assigned to shepherd some of the papers. We are grateful to all those who contributed to the technical program of the conference.

We would also like to thank the members of the organizing committee, with special thanks to Javier Miranda, whose dedication was key to the preparation of the attractive tutorial program and to Miquel Mascaró-Portells, who did a great job in preparing the Web pages and all the Internet facilities. Also to Dirk Craeynest, who worked hard to make the conference prominently visible and Peter Dencker who was in charge of the conference exhibition. Erhard Plödereder and Janet Barnes played an important role in the financial assessment and the liaison with Ada-Europe.

A great help in organizing the submission process and the paper reviews was the START Conference Manager, provided graciously by Rich Gerber.

Finally, we would like to express our appreciation to the authors of the papers submitted to the conference, and to all the participants who helped in achieving the goal of the conference, providing a forum for researchers and practitioners for the exchange of information and ideas about reliable software technologies. We hope they all enjoyed the technical program as well as the social events of the Ninth International Conference on Reliable Software Technologies.

June 2004   Albert Llamosí
                                                                  Alfred Strohmeier

Organizing Committee

Conference Chair

Albert Llamosí, *University of the Balearic Islands, Spain*

Program Co-chairs

Albert Llamosí, *University of the Balearic Islands, Spain*
Alfred Strohmeier, *Swiss Fed. Inst. of Technology Lausanne, Switzerland*

Tutorial Chair

Javier Miranda, *University of Las Palmas de Gran Canaria, Spain*

Exhibition Chair

Peter Dencker, *Aonix GmbH, Germany*

Publicity Chair

Dirk Craeynest, *Offis, Belgium*

Local Organization Co-chairs

Miquel Mascaró-Portells, *University of the Balearic Islands, Spain*
Gabriel Fontanet, *University of the Balearic Islands, Spain*

Ada-Europe Conference Liaison

Laurent Pautet, *ENST, France*

Program Committee

Alejandro Alonso, *Universidad Politécnica de Madrid, Spain*
Ángel Álvarez, *Universidad Politécnica de Madrid, Spain*
Lars Asplund, *Mälardalens Högskola, Sweden*
Neil Audsley, *University of York, UK*
Janet Barnes, *Praxis Critical Systems Limited, UK*
Pierre Bazex, *IRIT, France*
Guillem Bernat, *University of York, UK*
Johann Blieberger, *Technical University Vienna, Austria*
Maarten Boasson, *University of Amsterdam, The Netherlands*

Table of Contents

Invited Papers

Benefits and Problems of Formal Methods 1
Martin Gogolla

On the Role of Conceptual Schemas in Information Systems Development   16
Antoni Olivé

An Overview of Middleware 35
Steve Vinoski

Static Analysis

Static Deadlock Detection in the Linux Kernel 52
Peter T. Breuer, Marisol García Valls

Extracting Ada 95 Objects from Legacy Ada Programs 65
Ricky E. Sward

On the Tree Width of Ada Programs 78
Bernd Burgstaller, Johann Blieberger, Bernhard Scholz

Distributed Systems

The Chance for Ada to Support Distribution and Real-Time in
Embedded Systems... 91
Juan López Campos, J. Javier Gutiérrez, Michael González Harbour

PolyORB: A Schizophrenic Middleware to Build Versatile Reliable
Distributed Applications 106
Thomas Vergnaud, Jérôme Hugues, Laurent Pautet, Fabrice Kordon

Event Language for Real-Time On-the-Fly Control According to the
Initial Requirements... 120
Stepan P. Nadrchal

Real-Time Systems

Implementing Execution-Time Clocks for the Ada Ravenscar Profile 132
*Juan Zamorano, Alejandro Alonso, José Antonio Pulido,
Juan Antonio de la Puente*

Extending the Capabilities of Real-Time Applications by Combining
MaRTE-OS and Linux... 144
  Miguel Masmano, Jorge Real, Ismael Ripoll, Alfons Crespo

Supporting Deadlines and EDF Scheduling in Ada 156
  Alan Burns, Andy J. Wellings, S. Tucker Taft

Reflection and XML

OpenAda: Compile-Time Reflection for Ada 95 166
  Patrick Rogers, Andy J. Wellings

XML4Ada95 Accessing XML Using the DOM in Ada95................ 178
  Zdenko Vrandečić, Daniel Simon

Testing

A Randomised Test Approach to Testing Safety Critical Ada Code 190
  *Sukant K. Giri, Atit Mishra, Yogananda V. Jeppu,
  Kundapur Karunakar*

Good Random Testing.. 200
  Kwok Ping Chan, Tsong Yueh Chen, Dave Towey

Teaching Real-Time Systems Around a Digital Model Railroad
Platform Using Ada... 213
  *Bárbara Álvarez, Juan A. Pastor, Francisco Ortiz, Pedro Sánchez,
  Pedro Navarro*

Critical Systems Modeling

High Integrity Ada in a UML and C World.......................... 225
  Peter Amey, Neil White

Ada Meets Giotto.. 237
  Helge Hagenauer, Norbert Martinek, Werner Pohlmann

High-Integrity Interfacing to Programmable Logic with Ada 249
  Adrian J. Hilton, Jon G. Hall

Scheduling

Dynamic Ceiling Priorities: A Proposal for Ada0Y 261
  *Jorge Real, Alan Burns, Javier Miranda, Edmond Schonberg,
  Alfons Crespo*

Mixing Scheduling Policies in Ada................................ 273
  *Agustín Espinosa Minguet, Ana García-Fornes,
  Vicente Lorente Garcés, Andrés Terrasa Barrena*

Implementing an Application-Defined Scheduling Framework
for Ada Tasking 283
  Mario Aldea, Javier Miranda, Michael González Harbour

Application Programming Interfaces

A Theory of Persistent Containers and Its Application to Ada 297
  Mário Amado Alves

Shortcuts: A Critical Look 309
  Matthew Heaney

Vector Processing in Ada 321
  Franco Gasperoni

Author Index 333

Benefits and Problems of Formal Methods

Martin Gogolla

University of Bremen, Computer Science Department
Database Systems Group, D-28334 Bremen, Germany
gogolla@informatik.uni-bremen.de

Abstract. Formal methods for software development have been discussed for decades. This paper will try to explain when and under what circumstances formal methods and languages in general and the Object Constraint Language (OCL) in particular can be employed in a beneficial way. The success of using a formal approach is highly influenced by the expectations and pre-requisite knowledge of the developers, the role the formal support in the development process is given, and of course by the used tools.

1 Introduction

Formal methods (FMs) for software development have been discussed for decades. The enormous spectrum ranges from naive mathematical set theory over various approaches for model or property oriented specification to newer developments like the Object Constraint Language (OCL) being an integral part of the Unified Modeling Language (UML). People's opinions on formal methods are naturally determined by their experience and knowledge on the subject. In the literature, many positive and also negative views on FMs have been expressed [Hal90,BH95a,BH95b,Gla96,HB96,KDGN97,Sch00].

The aim of this paper is (A) to give a brief introduction and overview on the terminology of formal methods, (B) to shortly debate the various statement papers on formal methods in the light of benefits and problems, and (C) to discuss in this context our own formal method, namely the support the UML Specification Environment USE [RG00] provides for the OCL [WK03].

The structure of the rest of this paper is as follows. Section 1 recites Bjorner's view of important concepts within formal methods. Section 2 repeats the central statement of various position papers on FMs and gives a structuring for the statements collected. Section 3 sets some of those statements into the context of our own work on OCL. Section 4 finishes the paper with a few concluding remarks.

A. Llamosí and A. Strohmeier (Eds.): Ada-Europe 2004, LNCS 3063, pp. 1–15, 2004.

2 Terminology

For central notions relevant within the software development process in the context of formal methods, we follow the definitions and explanations by Bjorner [Bjo98].

Method: A set of principles for selecting and applying techniques and tools in order effectively to analyze and synthesize an effective artifact, here software.

Formal method (FM): A set of principles for formal specification and design calculi techniques.

Design calculi: A set of proof or specification transformation rules.

Formal specification: Describes a model in a comprehensive and consistent way. It is expressed in a formal language. A model can be given, e.g., for an application domain, for a requirement, for a software architecture, or for a program organization.

Formal language: Specifies at meta-level (A) a syntax, (B) a (possibly model-oriented, e.g., denotational or structural operational) semantics, and (C) a proof system.

Tools for design calculi: Aspects (A) and (B) allow for tools that support input, editing, syntactic and abstract interpretation processing of specifications. Aspect (C) allows for tools that support reasoning (automated theorem proving, mechanically assisted proofs) about specifications.

Formal development: All specifications are formal. All proof obligations have been identified and formally proved using the proof system.

Rigorous development: All specifications have been expressed in the formal specification language and relevant theorems have been formally expressed, but the reasoning processes have referred to model-theoretic properties of the modeled domain, requirements or software.

Systematic development: All specifications have been expressed in the formal specification language and reasonable relations between development steps have been informally reasoned.

3 Myths, Myths, and Other Beliefs

Properties of and opinions on formal methods (FMs) have been discussed in the literature for quite a while. In this section we shortly recite and try to structure the work done in:

- "Seven Myths of Formal Methods" [Hal90]
- "Seven More Myths of Formal Methods" [BH95a]
- "Ten Commandments of Formal Methods" [BH95b]
- "Formal Methods are a Surrogate for a More Serious Software Concern" [Gla96]

- "Impediments to Industrial Use of Formal Methods" [HB96]
- "Why Are Formal Methods Not Used More Widely?" [KDGN97]
- "Why Doesn't Anyone Use Formal Methods" [Sch00]

In [Hal90] seven so-called myths of FMs are expressed, and this list is extended by another seven myths in [BH95a]. The claim of these 'Myths' papers is that these statements about FMs are often expressed but that these statements do not hold. The 'Ten Commandments' paper [BH95b] is written to help in the application of FMs in an industrial setting, and the intended audience includes both developers and users of FMs. The 'Beliefs' paper and the 'Impediments' papers both look at FMs from a more critical perspective and frankly point to weak points of FMs. The 'Criteria' paper [KDGN97] mainly looks at FMs from the software development point of view and discusses the relationship between FMs and the software development cycle and its phases. The 'Aspects' paper [Sch00] states requirements for what FMs should be able to do and which properties they should have.

The tables in Fig. 1 and Fig. 2 repeat the central statements of the mentioned papers. The reader is invited to go through these statements. But be warned: Some of the short statements have been distilled by the author of this paper (in particular for [Gla96,HB96]) and might not find acceptance by the original authors.

All these papers express certain statements relevant in the context of FMs. We have classified these statements into seven topics: General criticism, Development, Understanding, Tools, Properties, People, Application domain. Independent of whether the paper is inclined positively and negatively towards FMs the addressed statements represent central points about FMs. The tables in Fig. 1 and Fig. 2 show our statement classification and the corresponding statements from the respective papers. Interestingly, a number of statement topics is addressed in more than one paper. Let us shortly motivate and explain our classification (in the reverse order as opposed to the tables).

Application domain: Some statements concern the application domain or the applicability for FMs. Historically, FMs have many origins in the area of proving program correctness and were used in safety-critical applications, but they might be used in a different scope (not merely for program proving) and in all other application fields.

People: A second class of statements deals with people involved in the development process. It seems to be important that for successful use of FMs developers are well-trained and experts are available.

Properties: Another group of statements expresses properties with respect to computer science principles. FMs seem to have to follow the principles of imperative programming and object-oriented development.

Tools: FMs must be accompanied by tools just as programming languages are supported by compilers. However, the tools must be embedded well into the

General criticism	Belief-1: FMs are underdefined [Gla96]
	Belief-2: FMs are underevaluated [Gla96]
	Belief-3: FMs inhibit software malleability [Gla96]
	Belief-5: FMs will not lead to any breakthrough in software productivity/quality [Gla96]
	Impediment-2: Researchers worked on toy examples and industrially irrelevant problems [HB96]
	More Myth-5: FMs are not required [BH95a]
Development - General	Commandment-02: Thou shalt formalize but not over-formalize [BH95b]
	Commandment-08: Thou shalt not be dogmatic [BH95b]
	Criterion-01: Coverage: Describe all of an application or operate with other notations [KDGN97]
	Criterion-02: Integration with other components [KDGN97]
	Criterion-03: Group development: Combine efforts of several people [KDGN97]
	More Myth-7: FMs people always use FMs [BH95a]
Development - Other Methods	Commandment-05: Thou shalt not abandon thy traditional development methods [BH95b]
	More Myth-3: FMs mean forsaking traditional engineering design methods [BH95a]
Development - Cost	Commandment-03: Thou shalt estimate costs [BH95b]
	More Myth-1: FMs delay the development process [BH95a]
	Myth-5: FMs increase the cost of software development [Hal90]
Development - Evolution	Aspect-4: Specifications must live [Sch00]
	Criterion-04: Evolution of specification and ease its change [KDGN97]
Development - Quality	Commandment-07: Thou shalt not compromise thy quality standards [BH95b]
	Commandment-09: Thou shalt test, test, and test again [BH95b]
Development - Design	Criterion-06: Compatibility with design tools [KDGN97]
	Criterion-07: Compatible with design methods [KDGN97]
	Criterion-08: Communicate desired system characteristics to designers [KDGN97]
	Criterion-09: Facilitate design process [KDGN97]
Development - Implementation	Criterion-10: Implementation performance [KDGN97]
	Criterion-11: Support for unit testing in implementation phase [KDGN97]
Development - Maintenance	Criterion-12: Maintenance comprehension [KDGN97]
	Criterion-13: Maintenance changes [KDGN97]

Fig. 1. Statements - General criticism, Development

Understanding	Aspect-1: Specifications should be easy to understand [Sch00]
	Belief-4: FMs are not readable [Gla96]
	Commandment-01: Thou shalt choose an appropriate notation [BH95b]
	Commandment-06: Thou shalt document sufficiently [BH95b]
	Criterion-05: Usability: Annotate specifications [KDGN97]
	Myth-6: FMs are unacceptable to users [Hal90]
Tools	Aspect-5: Specifications must be supported by tools [Sch00]
	Aspect-6: Specification tools must be compatible and interoperable [Sch00]
	Aspect-7: Specifications must be easily portable and available [Sch00]
	Impediment-1: Existing tools are not production-quality [HB96]
	Impediment-3: Build-it-and-they-will-come - Research is often ignorant of industry challenges [HB96]
	More Myth-2: FMs are not supported by tools [BH95a]
	More Myth-6: FMs are not supported [BH95a]
Properties	Aspect-2: Specifications should be state-oriented [Sch00]
	Aspect-3: Specifications should support abstraction, subtyping and modularization [Sch00]
	Commandment-10: Thou shalt reuse [BH95b]
People	Aspect-8: Specification building must be taught [Sch00]
	Commandment-04: Thou shalt have a FMs guru on call [BH95b]
	Myth-4: FMs require highly trained mathematicians [Hal90]
Application domain	More Myth-4: FMs only apply to software [BH95a]
	Myth-1: FMs can guarantee that software is perfect [Hal90]
	Myth-2: FMs are all about program proving [Hal90]
	Myth-3: FMs are only useful for safety-critical systems [Hal90]
	Myth-7: FMs are not used on real, large-scale software [Hal90]

Fig. 2. Statements - Understanding, Tools, Properties, People, Application domain

development process and offer useful features for everyday practical work. It is not important support fancy theoretical frameworks.

Understanding: A major topic seems to be the understanding (or perhaps better the understandability) of FMs. A clear notation and means for documentation are expressed as fundamental.

Development: We have classified a huge group of statements under the topic 'Development' and have structured it again into: General remarks, Relationship to other (informal or semi-formal) methods, Cost, Evolution, Quality, and Development phases.

General criticism: The last, most critical but also most unspecific group of statements concerns general criticism. In our view, the most serious statement in this group is the one about software malleability. However, this may be just the other side of the possibility of enhanced quality through FMs.

We do not claim that the given classification is the only one or that the assignment of statements to topics is mandatory. The purpose of the tables is to stimulate discussion. In fact, one can view at the tables from inside or outside of FMs: In the inside view, an FM tool developer can use the table topics as a checklist and ask herself what relationships exist between her tool and the respective topic; in the outside view, a possible FM user can ask the methodologist or the tool developer about the connection between each topic and the method or tool.

4   OCL versus Statements on Formal Methods

OCL [OMG03,WK03] as part of the standardized UML has been developed as a language especially suited for object-oriented development. It has a Java-resp. C++-like syntax and claims to be easily applicable by regular developers. On the one hand, OCL is scientifically well-studied (see, e.g., the proceedings of the UML conference or the papers on the OCL workshops or [RG01,GR01] among many other interesting papers), on the other hand commercial tutorials and seminars are available for OCL. Commercial as well as university tools are around [TRF03]. OCL has been used extensively in the development of the UML 1.X and UML 2.X metamodels for expressing structural restrictions.

The basic idea of OCL is that merely diagrams as given by the graphical part of UML are not enough for a precise system description. Textual additions and tightenings in a formal language are necessary for avoiding ambiguities. OCL has emerged from practical needs to sharpen and tighten UML class diagrams, i.e., to formulate structural restrictions. Later OCL was also employed for pre- and postconditions of operations and in other UML diagrams, for example for guards in statechart diagrams.

However, OCL is not a classical formal specification language. Thus OCL does not have the burden of a classical formal method, but OCL as it stands today does also not have the rich background of a classical formal method (and a very high degree of acceptance within the classical formal methods community).

In the rest of this section we will discuss how some selected FM statements relate to OCL and in particular how they relate to our UML/OCL animation tool UML Specification Environment USE [RG00].

4.1 Thou Shalt Choose an Appropriate Notation

OCL expressions usually rely on a given class diagram formulated within UML. Thus the syntactic context, i.e., the classes, their attributes, operations, and associations, for OCL invariants and pre- and postconditions is determined graphically in an easy understandable way.

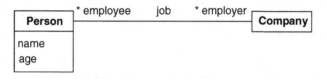

Fig. 3. UML Class Diagram

OCL now allows a short, condensed notation offering good possibilities for documentation of constraints. Let us consider the following invariant requiring that employed people are at least 18 years old which needs the class diagram sketched in Fig. 3.

```
context Person inv asEmployeeAtLeast18:
  employer->notEmpty implies age>=18
```

The mathematical content of the invariant could be stated as follows, but be aware that this mathematical formulation somewhat hides the context, the class Person, and does not mention the constraint name.

$$(\forall p : Person) (employer(p) \neq \emptyset \Rightarrow age(p) \geq 18)$$

Above we mentioned 'condensed notation' and 'documentation'. By condensed notation we mean that OCL knows implicit variables and implicit quantifiers and by documentation we refer to the possibility of specifying constraint names. Thus in the above invariant there an implicit universally quantified variable `self:Person` and, for example, the expression `age` is equivalent to `self.age`. In fact, the complete invariant is also equivalent to the following more verbose OCL expression.

```
context Company inv asEmployeeAtLeast18:
  Person.allInstances->forAll(self:Person |
    self.employer->notEmpty implies self.age>=18)
```

The body of the constraint explicitly introduces a universal quantification with a corresponding variable. This body expression is independent of its context, i.e., it does not use an implicit reference to self. Therefore in this case any context may be used, even the class Company which is not referenced with the constraint body. The usefulness of such shortcuts become important and apparent if one has longer constraints and not short ones like the above one. Be warned: One may be tended to underestimate the simple OCL feature to specify invariant names; this feature is a very useful, although trivial OCL feature; if you have OCL descriptions with, say 50 invariants, and you animate the specification short reference to satisfied and violated invariants is essential.

Another useful OCL feature is flattening of nested collections. For example, if you have an employee ada and you want to have the names of ada's colleagues, i.e., the name of the employees which work in a company for which ada works, you simple write ada.employer.employee.name which has the type Bag(String). Note that the type of the subexpression ada.employer.employee is flattened from Bag(Set(Person)) to Bag(Person).

4.2   Specifications Should Support Abstraction

FMs support abstraction because they allow to ignore irrelevant implementation details. Such abstract descriptions often allow you to formulate your problem in a descriptive way by expressing only the desired properties, not yet an operational solution. However, with regard to executability the operational solution often has more attractive properties than the abstract, descriptive solution.

Consider the following example for describing the root function on the real numbers. The first solution, rootSpec, formulates the function in OCL using pre- and postconditions. The central requirement is that the difference between the number from which the root is to be calculated and the returned result multiplied with itself is below a given precision.

```
rootSpec(arg:Real,precision:Real):Real
context Root::rootSpec(arg:Real,precision:Real):Real
  pre   paramsOk: 0<arg and 0<precision and precision<=1
  post resultOk: (arg-result*result).abs<=precision and result>0
```

The root function may also be described in OCL in an operational way as a function returning a value. Note however, that the following description for the OCL function rootImpl is just one under many other implementations which satisfy the above specification with pre- and postconditions.

```
rootImpl(arg:Real,precision:Real):Real=
  rootImplAux(arg, precision,
             if arg>=1 then 1.0 else arg endif,
```

```
               if arg>=1 then arg else 1.0 endif)
rootImplAux(arg:Real,precision:Real,low:Real,high:Real):Real=
  let new:Real=(low+high)/2 in
  if (arg-new*new).abs<=precision
    then new
    else rootImplAux(arg,precision,
                     if new*new<arg then new else low endif,
                     if new*new<arg then high else new endif)
  endif
```

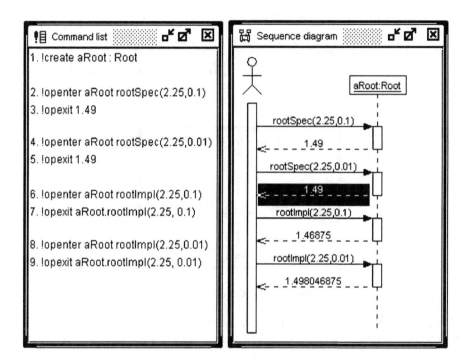

Fig. 4. Executing RootSpec and RootImpl

In Fig. 4 we have displayed part of a USE animation of the two functions in form of a UML sequence diagram. Even the descriptive specification with pre- and postcondition may be animated by providing explicit return values which are checked against the postcondition. The USE animation does use colors to draw special attention to particular points. The black-and-white inverted return arrow is displayed in USE in red. This indicates that the postcondition is not satisfied. In this case the provided return value 1.49 is not close enough to the correct result 1.5 under the given precision 0.01.

4.3   Specifications Must Be Supported by Tools

Let us think of a simple traffic light application where one controller is responsible for four traffic lights in north, south, west, and east directions on a street crossing, and each traffic light is operated by one controller. Consider the UML class diagram for the controller and the traffic lights in Fig. 5 and the corresponding object diagram in Fig. 6. Does the object diagram meet the class diagram?

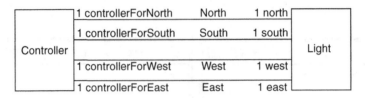

Controller	1 controllerForNorth	North	1 north	Light
	1 controllerForSouth	South	1 south	
	1 controllerForWest	West	1 west	
	1 controllerForEast	East	1 east	

Fig. 5. UML Class Diagram for Traffic Light

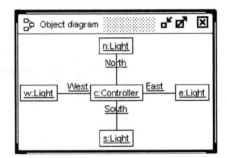

Fig. 6. UML Object Diagram

The multiplicities in the class diagram are not consistent with the object diagram! Consider the traffic light n. The class diagram requires that each traffic light is connected by the association North to one controller, which is true for the traffic light n. But it also requires this for the association South, West, and East. And this is not fulfilled for the traffic light n. In fact, this error can be found in one of my own papers. I did not check the 'obviously' true statement that the object diagram is consistent with the class diagram with our USE tool. The multiplicities are too restrictive. On the controller side they have to be changed to 0..1.

In fact, one of main advantages and tasks of formal methods is that tools can reveal such design errors early in the development. Tools allow you to have on the one hand a general frame of your application world, in this case the class diagram with the multiplicities, and on the other hand concrete scenarios of your application world, in this case the object diagram. And the tools must check the consistency between the two.

4.4   Specifications Must Live

Continuing the traffic light example, if one changes the multiplicities on the controller side to 0..1, it becomes allowed that traffic lights can exist which are not connected to any controller. Therefore, one should demand that for each traffic light exactly one of the four associations has to be established. Now OCL offers many alternatives to formulate this requirement.

```
context Light inv oneController_A:
  (controllerForNorth->size)+(controllerForSouth->size)+
  (controllerForWest ->size)+(controllerForEast ->size) = 1

context Light inv oneController_B:
  Bag{controllerForNorth,controllerForSouth,
      controllerForWest, controllerForEast}->size = 1

context Light inv oneController_C:
  Bag{controllerForNorth,controllerForSouth,
      controllerForWest, controllerForEast}->
  select(c|c.isDefined())->size = 1

context Light inv oneController_D:
  (controllerForNorth->size=1) xor (controllerForSouth->size=1) xor
  (controllerForWest ->size=1) xor (controllerForEast ->size=1)

context Light inv oneController_E:
  ( (controllerForNorth->size=1) and (controllerForSouth->size=0) and
    (controllerForWest ->size=0) and (controllerForEast ->size=0) ) or
  ( (controllerForNorth->size=0) and (controllerForSouth->size=1) and
    (controllerForWest ->size=0) and (controllerForEast ->size=0) ) or
  ( (controllerForNorth->size=0) and (controllerForSouth->size=0) and
    (controllerForWest ->size=1) and (controllerForEast ->size=0) ) or
  ( (controllerForNorth->size=0) and (controllerForSouth->size=0) and
    (controllerForWest ->size=0) and (controllerForEast ->size=1) )
```

Apart from the above five formulations, one can build further variations: Alternatives B' and C' with Set instead of Bag in B and C; alternatives D' and E' with .isDefined() instead of ->size=1 and .isUndefined() instead of ->size=0 in D and E. Thus we end up with nine possibilities. Which of these are equivalent? Which represent the semantics we want to express?

Formal methods need and require tools. These tools have to be based on the formal semantics of the formal specification language. But such tools are also highly needed in order to handle the inherent complexity of formal specification languages in order to understand the language constructs. One has to play around with alternatives, one has to see and feel how different formulations behave different: Specifications must live.

4.5   Thou Shalt Test, Test, and Test again

Let us continue the traffic light example by extending the class Light with a display attribute signal:String and an operation showsGreen():Boolean = signal='G' or signal='YG'. Furthermore three constraints restrict the possible snapshots or object diagrams.

```
context Light inv R_G_YG:
  signal='R' or signal='G' or signal='YG'
context Controller inv northSouth_WestEast_Coincide:
  north.signal=south.signal and west.signal=east.signal
context Controller inv northWest_Different:
  north.signal<>west.signal
```

The aim of the present considerations is to check whether, under the above assumptions, the danger of a crash is present, i.e., whether it is possible to construct a snapshot satisfying the following invariant.

```
context Controller inv crashPossible:
  north.showsGreen() and west.showsGreen()
```

To this aim, we design a special purpose procedure generate constructing snapshots by generating a controller and four traffic lights, by establishing the appropriate links, and by assigning attribute values.

```
procedure generate()
var theController:Controller, theLights:Sequence(Light);
begin
theController:=Create(Controller);
theLights:=CreateN(Light,[4]);
Insert(North,[theController],[theLights->at(1)]);
Insert(South,[theController],[theLights->at(2)]);
Insert(West,[theController],[theLights->at(3)]);
Insert(East,[theController],[theLights->at(4)]);
[theController.north].signal:=Try([Sequence{'R','G','YG'}]);
[theController.south].signal:=Try([Sequence{'R','G','YG'}]);
[theController.west].signal:=Try([Sequence{'R','G','YG'}]);
[theController.east].signal:=Try([Sequence{'R','G','YG'}]);
end;
```

This snapshot or test case generation procedure is embedded into the script shown below and is called after the invariant crashPossible has been dynamically added to the present invariants. Our test case generator responds with the sequence of commands that generate the snapshot where all invariants hold. In the concrete example we see that the given invariants do not guarantee that two adjacent traffic lights, here the north and west one, do not show green at the same time.

```
use> gen load traffic.invs
     Added invariants: Controller::crashPossible
use> gen start ... generate()
use> gen result
     Random number generator was initialized with 7686.
     Checked 45 snapshots.
     Result: Valid state found.
     Commands to produce the valid state:
     !create Controller1 : Controller
     !create Light1,Light2,Light3,Light4 : Light
     !insert (Controller1,Light1) into North
     !insert (Controller1,Light2) into South
     !insert (Controller1,Light3) into West
     !insert (Controller1,Light4) into East
     !set Light1.signal = 'G'
     !set Light2.signal = 'G'
     !set Light3.signal = 'YG'
     !set Light4.signal = 'YG'
```

Proceeding this way, formal methods support test case development. They may be used for test case design nicely because formal methods identify the distinguishing cases clearly as equivalence classes where certain formulas do hold or do not hold. Thus test cases can be generated in an automatic way.

This completes our in-depth discussion of the selected statements on formal methods. We have looked only at five typical statements from the comprehensive list, but we think that really all statements make a concern for formal methods in general and for our USE tool in particular.

5   Conclusion

In this paper we have recaptured central notions from formal methods, structured statements from papers estimating the value of formal methods and put some of these statements into the context of our USE tool.

The essence we have drawn from studying all these statement about formal methods is that the success of a formal method is not determined so much by its nice mathematical properties. We think the success is determined by the tools and in particular by the everyday usability of the tool. One aspect we see underdeveloped in formal method tools is the aspect of documentation possibilities (at least in our USE tool). And the tools and an underlying development method including a tight connection to other parts of the software development process must be documented and explained well. This helps that other people (not the developer of the formal method) can use the approach in a beneficial way. In our understanding, this is what the Build-it-an-they-will-come statement refers to.

On the other hand, working on the Build-it-an-they-will-come front and on the documentation front is scientifically a bit dangerous: If you submit a paper on many small improvements of the previous version of your tool, referees usually underestimate the contribution of this work and give preference to newer, fancier ideas which however are 'not yet' supported by a tool. So working in this direction with a pure research background must be considered well.

Acknowledgments. Thanks to Alfred Strohmeier for initiating the work on this papers. Arne Lindow has provided fruitful comments on draft versions of this paper.

References

[BH95a]   Jonathan P. Bowen and Michael G. Hinchey. Seven More Myths of Formal Methods. *IEEE Software*, 12(4):34–41, July 1995.

[BH95b]   Jonathan P. Bowen and Michael G. Hinchey. Ten Commandments of Formal Methods. *IEEE Computer*, 28(4):56–63, April 1995.

[Bjo98]   Dines Bjorner. Formal Methods in the Twentyfirst Century: An Assessment of Today - Predictions for the Future. In *Proc. Int. Conf. Software Engineering (ICSE'1998)*, 1998. Not included in the official proceedings.

[Bow04]   Jonathan P. Bowen. Virtual Library - Formal Methods. http://vl.fmnet. info, 2004.

[Cha98]   Pierre Chapront. Ada+B: The Formula for Safety Critical Software Development. In Lars Asplund, editor, *Proc. Reliable Software Technologies: Ada Europe (RST'1998)*, pages 13–18. Springer, Berlin, LNCS 1411, 1998.

[CW96]   Edmund M. Clarke and Jeanette M. Wing. Formal Methods: State of the Art and Future Directions. *ACM Computing Surveys*, 28(4):626–643, 1996.

[Gau01]   Marie-Claude Gaudel. Testing from Formal Specifications, a Generic Approach. In Dirk Craeynest and Alfred Strohmeier, editors, *Proc. Reliable Software Technologies: Ada Europe (RST'2001)*, pages 35–48. Springer, Berlin, LNCS 2043, 2001.

[Gla96]   Robert L. Glass. Formal Methods are a Surrogate for a More Serious Software Concern. *IEEE Computer*, pages 19–19, April 1996.

[GR01]   Martin Gogolla and Mark Richters. Expressing UML Class Diagrams Properties with OCL. In Tony Clark and Jos Warmer, editors, *Advances in Object Modelling with the OCL*, pages 86–115. Springer, Berlin, LNCS 2263, 2001.

[Hal90]   J. Anthony Hall. Seven Myths of Formal Methods. *IEEE Software*, 7(5):11–19, September 1990.

[HB96]   C. Michael Holloway and Ricky W. Butler. Impediments to Industrial Use of Formal Methods. *IEEE Computer*, pages 25–26, April 1996.

[KDGN97]   John C. Knight, Colleen L. DeJong, Mathew S. Gibble, and Luís G. Nakano. Why Are Formal Methods Not Used More Widely? In C. Michael Holloway and Kelly J. Hayhurst, editors, *4th NASA Langley Formal Methods Workshop*, pages 1–12, 1997. NASA Langley Research Center, Report CP 3356.

[OMG03]   OMG, editor. *OMG Unified Modeling Language Specification, Version 1.5.* OMG, March 2003. OMG Document formal/03-03-01, www.omg.org.

[RG00]   Mark Richters and Martin Gogolla. Validating UML Models and OCL Constraints. In Andy Evans and Stuart Kent, editors, *Proc. 3rd Int. Conf. Unified Modeling Language (UML'2000)*, pages 265–277. Springer, Berlin, LNCS 1939, 2000.

[RG01]   Mark Richters and Martin Gogolla. OCL - Syntax, Semantics and Tools. In Tony Clark and Jos Warmer, editors, *Advances in Object Modelling with the OCL*, pages 43–69. Springer, Berlin, LNCS 2263, 2001.

[Sch00]   Wolfram Schulte. Why Doesn't Anyone Use Formal Methods. In W. Grieskamp, T. Santen, and B. Stoddart, editors, *Proc. Int. Conf. Integrated Formal Methods (IFM'2000)*, pages 297–298. Spinger, Berlin, LNCS 1945, 2000.

[TRF03]   A. Toval, V. Requena, and J.L. Fernandez. Emerging OCL Tools. *Software and Systems Modeling*, 2(4):248–261, 2003.

[vL01]   Axel van Lamsweerde. Building Formal Requirements Models for Reliable Software. In Dirk Craeynest and Alfred Strohmeier, editors, *Proc. Reliable Software Technologies: Ada Europe (RST'2001)*, pages 1–20. Springer, Berlin, LNCS 2043, 2001.

[WK03]   Jos Warmer and Anneke Kleppe. *The Object Constraint Language: Precise Modeling with UML*. Addison-Wesley, 2003. 2nd Edition.

On the Role of Conceptual Schemas in Information Systems Development

Antoni Olivé

Universitat Politècnica de Catalunya
Dept. Llenguatges i Sistemes Informàtics
Jordi Girona 1-3, 08034 Barcelona (Catalonia)
olive@lsi.upc.es

Abstract. In the literature, the role of Conceptual Schemas (CS) and conceptual modelling in Information Systems (IS) development is not well established. On the other hand, there is some confusion over the relationships between CSs and similar concepts such as domain model, domain knowledge, functional specifications and ontologies. This paper tries to shed light on these issues. We show that a CS is the knowledge needed by an IS to perform its functions. We then analyse the possible roles of CSs in the IS architecture, which range from specification to explicit software component. We also show the role of CSs in the context of the recent OMG's MDA. The paper focuses on ISs, but most of the conclusions may apply to the general field of software.

1 Introduction

The term "conceptual schema" was coined in the early 70's in the database field [1]. In this field, a schema describes which kinds of concrete facts are contained in the database and which constraints and rules they must conform to [4]. There are at least three kinds of schemas: internal, external and conceptual. An internal schema is a description of the data as seen by the "machine". An external schema is a description of the data as seen by the "programmer". A conceptual schema was defined as "the enterprise view's of the structure it is attempting to model in the data base" [1].

The ISO report [11] elaborated on the objectives, roles, form and content of the conceptual schemas, in the general context of information systems. One of the report's important conclusions was the well-known 100% principle : "All relevant general static and dynamic aspects, i.e. all rules, laws, etc. of the universe of discourse should be described in the conceptual schema. The information system cannot be held responsible for not meeting those described elsewhere, including in particular those in application programs".

Twenty years after the ISO report, the term "conceptual schema" is not well established yet in the literature. There is some confusion over the relationships between conceptual schemas and concepts such as domain model, domain knowledge, functional specifications or ontologies. There is some confusion also over the role of conceptual schemas in the development of information systems.

A. Llamosí and A. Strohmeier (Eds.): Ada-Europe 2004, LNCS 3063, pp. 16–34, 2004.

This paper tries to shed light on the above issues. In the next section, we study the nature of the relationship between a conceptual schema and its information system. We show that a conceptual schema has two main components: the domain conceptual schema and the functionality specification. In Section 3, we analyse the relationship between conceptual schemas and ontologies. In Section 4, we study the relationships between conceptual schemas, requirements and specifications. We study also the roles conceptual schemas may play in the system architecture. Section 5 comments on the roles of conceptual schemas in other aspects of system development. Finally, Section 6 gives the conclusions.

Most of the ideas presented here have appeared elsewhere. The originality of the paper is the attempt to knit different ideas with the objective of identifying the nature of conceptual schemas and their roles in information systems development, and also to show the correspondence with related terms. The paper focuses on ISs, but most of the conclusions may apply to the general field of software. On the other hand, a large number of software systems can be characterized as information systems [22].

2   Information Systems Functions and Conceptual Schemas

In this section, first we review the main functions of ISs, and then we analyse the knowledge required by a particular IS to perform these functions. We use as example an elevator control system (based on [12, 40]). The system has to control a set of three elevators serving a building with ten floors. The details will be introduced where they arise.

2.1   Functions of an Information System

Information systems can be defined from several perspectives. For the purposes of conceptual modelling, the most useful one is that of the functions they perform. According to this perspective, an IS performs three main functions [26]:
-   *Memory*: To maintain a consistent representation of the state of a domain.
-   *Informative*: To provide information about the state of a domain.
-   *Active*: To perform actions that change the state of a domain.

The memory function is passive, in the sense that it does not perform anything that directly affects users or the domain, but it is required by the other functions, and it constraints what these functions can perform. Examples in our system are the representation of the existing elevators and their current position and state, the outstanding requests, etc.

In the informative function, the system responds to query events. Query events may be external or generated. External query events are explicit requests for output. Generated query events occur when a generating condition is satisfied. In both cases, the system does not change directly the state of the domain. The answer may be information about the state of the domain, controlling commands to devices, etc. In our example, each cage has a location indicator that shows the current position of the cage. One function of the elevator control system is to display in that indicator the last floor visited by the cage. The function is informative. In this case, the system has to generate a query event when a cage visits a floor. The answer to this event must be the number of the floor just visited.

With the active function, the system performs actions that change the state of the domain when a generating condition is satisfied. In the elevator control system, an example of active function is the issue of commands to a cage motor. These commands change the state (idle, moving) and direction (up, down) of an elevator.

2.2 Knowledge Required by an Information System

To be able to perform the above functions, an IS requires some general knowledge about its domain, and knowledge about the functions it must perform. In the following, we summarize the main pieces of knowledge required by each function [26].

If the memory function of an IS has to maintain a representation of the state of the domain, then the IS has to know the entity and relationship types to be represented, and their current population. Some ISs may require to know that population also at some or all past time points. The entity and relationship types of interest are general knowledge about the domain, while their (time-varying) population is particular knowledge.

In conceptual modelling, we call Information Base (IB) the representation of the state of the domain in the IS. A non-temporal IB represents only the current state of the domain, while a temporal one represents also the state of the domain at any past time.

In our elevator control system, among the entity types that must be represented there are: *ElevatorCage*, *Floor*, *Button* (with subtypes *FloorButton* and *ElevatorButton*) and *Door* (see Figure 1). Examples of relationship types may be: The current floor and state of each elevator cage, the floor corresponding to each button, etc.

The representation of the state in the IB must be consistent. This is achieved by defining a set of conditions (called integrity constraints) and requiring that the IS satisfies them at any time. Such integrity constraints are general knowledge about the domain. One example may be the constraint "at any time, the elevator can be at most at one floor".

The domain state is not static. Most domains change through time, and therefore their state change too. When the state of a domain changes, the IB must change accordingly. There are several kinds of state changes. If they are caused by actions performed in the domain, then they are called external domain events. If they are caused by actions performed by the IS itself, then they are called generated domain events. The IS must know the types of the possible domain events and the effect of each instance on the IB. This is also general knowledge about the domain.

An example of external event type is *Arrival*. An instance occurs when a cage depresses an arrival sensor located in a floor, close to the home position at the floor. The meaning is that the cage arrives at a floor. The effect is that the elevator is now at the floor given by the event.

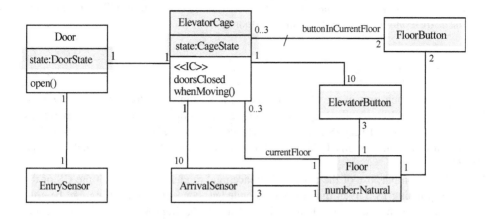

Fig. 1. Fragment of the Conceptual Schema of an elevator control system, in the UML.

If the informative function has to produce output on users request, then the IS must know the possible query event types and the output it has to produce. On the other hand, if there are generated query events then the IS must know the generating condition and the event to generate when it is satisfied. Note that this knowledge is not about the domain, but about the functions required to the IS. For example, the generating condition of the cage location indicator display is the occurrence of an *Arrival*, and the output to produce is to display the number of the corresponding floor.

In general, in order to perform the informative function the IS needs an inference capability that allows it to infer new knowledge. The inference capability requires two main elements: derivation rules and an inference mechanism. A derivation rule is general knowledge about a domain that defines a derived entity or relationship type in terms of others. The inference mechanism uses derivation rules to infer new informa- tion.

An example of derived relationship type is the association between *ElevatorCage* and *FloorButton* shown in Figure 1. An instance *(c,b)* of this association represents the fact that the current floor of cage *c* is the floor corresponding to button *b*. The derivation rule states that "cage *c* is located at the floor of button *b* if the current floor of *c* is the same as the floor corresponding to *b*".

If, in the active function, the IS has to generate domain events when a generating condition is satisfied, then the IS must know this condition and the event to generate when it is satisfied. Note again that this knowledge is not about the domain, but about the functions required to the IS.

One of the tasks that the elevator control system must perform is to issue the com- mands to open and close the doors of the elevators. When an elevator is closing its doors, if its entry sensor detects a *Pass* domain event, the system must open the doors again. In this case, the generating condition is the occurrence of a *Pass* event when the corresponding elevator is closing its doors.

2.3 Conceptual Schemas

The first conclusion of the above discussion is that in order to perform its required functions, an IS must have some knowledge about its domain and about the functions it has to perform. Every IS encodes knowledge about some domain [6; 35, p.417+]. In the information systems field, such knowledge is called the Conceptual Schema[1] (CS).

The main purpose of the activity of conceptual modelling is to elicit the CS of the corresponding IS. Given that a CS is knowledge, conceptual modelling can be considered as a specialization of the field of Knowledge Representation to information systems[2].

On the other hand, given that any useful IS includes some knowledge about its domain and its functions, we arrive easily to the conclusion that conceptual modelling is an essential activity of information systems development [37].

The CS must always exist. The only option designers have is about its form: it may be mental (exists only in the designers' heads) or explicit. An explicit CS is written in some conceptual modelling language, such as the UML [30]. We will see that in some development contexts, explicit CSs are mandatory, and that in the other contexts explicit CSs are very useful.

In all cases, an explicit CS documents the common understanding that users, analysts, and designers have about the domain and the functions imposed to the IS [21, 25]. This is a widely-recognized and important role for explicit CSs, but we will see that it is not the only one they may play in IS development.

2.4 Components of Conceptual Schemas

We have seen that the CS of an IS includes two kinds of knowledge: about its domain and about the functions it must perform. The former is called the Domain Conceptual Schema (DCS) and the latter the Functionality Specification (FS). Every piece of knowledge in the CS is part of either the DCS or the FS. We can then say that the DCS and the FS are the two components of a CS, and represent this by:

---

[1] The term *conceptual model* is often used instead of conceptual schema. However, we prefer to keep the distinction between conceptual model, conceptual schema and information base, analogously to the distinction between data model, database schema and database instance done in the database field.

[2] We adopt here the definition given in [32, p.157]: "The object of **knowledge representation** is to express knowledge in computer-tractable form, such that it can be used to help agents to perform well".

Conceptual schema = Domain Conceptual Schema + Functionality Specification[3]

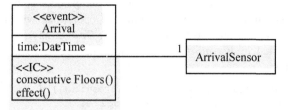

Fig. 2. Definition of external event type *Arrival*, in the UML.

The DCS defines the knowledge about the domain, independent of the IS. For example, the facts "there are elevators and floors", or "the doors of an elevator may be open, closing or closed" are part of the DCS. Such facts are true of the domain and independent of the existence of an elevator control system.

The FS defines:
- The entity and relationship types of the DCS that are represented in the IS.
- The types of the query events the IS has to respond to, and the generating condition of the generated query events.
- The generating conditions of the generated domain events.

For example, the fact "when an elevator is closing its doors, if the system receives a *Pass* event, then the system must issue a command to open the doors" is part of the FS.

The distinction DCS/FS is not new. It has been mentioned in, among others, [24, 7]. The pioneering work was probably [12, ch.1] with the fundamental principle: "…the developer must begin by modelling this reality (the real world), and only then go on to consider in full detail the functions which the system is to perform".

2.5 Conceptual Schemas in the UML

In the UML, a DCS consists mainly of:
- A taxonomy of entity types.
- For each entity type, a set of attributes.
- A taxonomy of *n*-ary associations, for each *n*, if there are one or more *n*-ary associations in the schema. Almost all schemas have several binary associations.
- A set of integrity constraints over the state of the domain. Some of them have a graphical representation, or a particular language construct. More general constraints may be defined formally using the OCL language [29].
- A set of domain event types, with their constraints and the definition of their effect on the IB. This knowledge can be defined by pre and postconditions of operations and/or by state transition diagrams.

---

[3] There is an interesting analogy between this expression and the expression "Algorithm = Logic + Control" in logic programming [19].

Figure 1 shows a fragment of the CS of our elevator control system. As an example of integrity constraint consider "when the cage of an elevator is moving, its doors must be closed". Constraints can be represented as operations with the stereotype <<*IC*>> [27]. These operations must return the value *True* at any time. In this case, the operation is hosted in *ElevatorCage* and called *doorsClosedWhenMoving*. The OCL specification is:

```
context ElevatorCage::doorsClosedWhenMoving() : Boolean
   body: state = CageState::moving implies
         door.state = DoorState::closed
```

Figure 2 shows a domain event type: *Arrival*. An instance of *Arrival* reports that a cage has arrived at a floor at a given time. Domain event types may be defined as ordinary types, but stereotyped as <<event>>. An integrity constraint of *Arrival* is *consecutiveFloors*, which requires that a cage goes from a floor to the next one, either above or below. The formal specification of the corresponding constraint operation is:

```
context Arrival::consecutiveFloors() : Boolean
   body:
   let newFloor : Natural = arrivalSensor.floor.number in
   let oldFloor : Natural =
            arrivalSensor.elevatorCage.currentFloor.number in
      newFloor = oldFloor + 1 or newFloor = oldFloor - 1
```

The effect of an instance of *Arrival* is that the cage is now at a different floor. This effect is achieved by means of the operation *effect*, whose specification is:

```
context Arrival::effect()
   post: arrivalSensor.elevatorCage.currentFloor =
         arrivalSensor.floor
```

On the other hand, an FS consists mainly of:

- The delimitation of the relevant fragment of the DCS. That is, the set of entity types, attributes and associations that must be represented in the IS, their constraints and the relevant domain event types.

- The derivation rules of the entity types, attributes and associations that must be derived.

- A set of query event types, with their constraints and the definition of the output to be produced.

- A set of generating conditions, and the definition of the query or domain events that must be generated when the conditions are satisfied. This knowledge must be defined by pre and post conditions of operations and/or by state transition diagrams.

For example, consider the active function "If a *Pass* event is received while a door is closing, the system will issue immediately an *OpenDoors* event". Figure 3 shows the relevant fragment of the CS. Here, the generating condition is "a *Pass* event is received while a door is closing" and the event to be generated is an instance of *OpenDoors*. In this case, the generating condition can be expressed as part of the effect of event *Pass*:

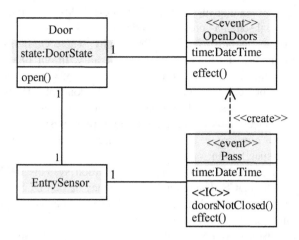

Fig. 3. Definition of external domain event types *OpenDoors* and *Pass*, in the UML.

```
context Pass::effect()
  post: if entrySensor.door.state@pre = DoorState::closing
          then od.oclIsNew() and
               od.oclIsTypeOf(OpenDoors) and
               od.time = CurrentTime and
               od.door = self.entrySensor.door
          else True
          endif
```

The effect of *Pass* is to generate a new instance of *OpenDoors*, with the corresponding values for the occurrence time and door. We assume that once an event has been generated, it effect takes place immediately. In this case, the effect of *OpenDoors* may be:

```
context OpenDoors::effect()
  post: door.state = DoorState::opened and
        door^open()
```

That is, the state of the door is now *opened*, and the operation *open()* in *Door* is invoked. The purpose of this operation is to issue the open command to the corresponding physical door.

3 Ontologies

The term "ontology" is frequently used in agent-oriented ISs, as well as in other fields related to AI. Ontologies are a basic component of the Sematic Web [2]. It is interesting to analyse the meaning of "ontology" in these fields, and to compare it with that of our "conceptual schema" presented in the previous section.

The term "ontology" is borrowed from Philosophy, where Ontology is the branch that deals with the nature and the organization of reality. In our fields, we make the fundamental assumption that a domain (reality) consists of objects and the relationships between these objects, which are classified into concepts. The set of concepts (entity and relationship types) used in a particular domain is a *conceptualisation* of that domain. Such conceptualisation may be implicit (e.g. existing only in someone's head) or explicit. An *ontology* is an explicit specification of a conceptualisation [9]. Ontologies must be specified in some language.

We can then conclude easily that, in the information systems field, an ontology corresponds closely to a DCS. The main difference may be that DCSs include also the concept of domain event (and their effects), while most current ontologies are restricted to the structural part of schemas.

The above conclusion may be reinforced if we analyse the constructs provided by current ontology languages and see what kind of knowledge they may define. To this end, in what follows we review briefly the basic features of one of the most prominent ontology languages, the OWL (Ontology Web Language) [39] and compare them with those provided by UML at the conceptual level. We use an example taken from [39]; its equivalent representation in the UML is shown in Figure 4.

Classes. In OWL, the basic domain concepts are classes (entity types). An example of class definition is *WineDescriptor* (in what follows, many non-essential syntactical details are omitted):

```
<Class WineDescriptor />
```

Most classes are defined as subclasses of existing ones, using the *subClassOf* constructor. For example, the definition of *Wine*:

```
<Class Wine>
  <subClassOf PotableLiquid/>
</Class>
```

A class may be defined via a direct enumeration of its members, using the *oneOf* constructor. For example, *WineColor*:

```
<Class WineColor>
  <subClassOf WineDescriptor/>
  <oneOf Collection>
    <Thing White/>
    <Thing Rose/>
    <Thing Red/>
  </oneOf>
</Class>
```

Individuals. In OWL, it is possible to describe the instances of classes. In conceptual modelling, the instances of entity types appear in the IB rather than in the conceptual schema itself.

Properties. A property is a binary relation. Two types of properties are distinguished: *datatype* properties (attributes) and *object* properties (associations). For example:

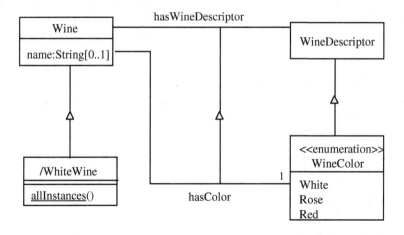

Fig. 4. Fragment of a wine ontology in the UML.

```
<ObjectProperty HasWineDescriptor>
  <domain Wine/>
  <range WineDescriptor/>
</ObjectProperty>

<DatatypeProperty name>
  <domain Wine/>
  <range String/>
</DatatypeProperty>
```

A property can be defined to be a specialization of an existing property, using the *subPropertyOf* construct. For example, *hasColor* is a subtype of *hasWineDescriptor*:

```
<ObjectProperty hasColor>
  <subPropertyOf  hasWineDescriptor/>
  <range WineColor/>
</ObjectProperty>
```

Integrity constraints. It is possible to define several constraints on properties. Some of them are cardinality constraints. For example, the *name* datatype property (shown before) is functional:

```
<DatatypeProperty name>
  <type FunctionalProperty/>
</DatatypeProperty>
```

Or the cardinality of *hasColor* is exactly one:

```
<ObjectProperty hasColor>
  <cardinality 1/>
</ObjectProperty>
```

Properties of individuals. In OWL, it is possible to describe properties of particular individuals. In conceptual modelling, the instances of attributes and associations appear in the IB rather than in the conceptual schema itself.

Complex classes. In OWL, a class can be defined in terms of others, using the basic set operators of intersection, union and/or complement (derivation rules). For example, *WhiteWine* is exactly the intersection of the class *Wine* with the set of things that are white in color:

```
<Class WhiteWine>
  <intersectionOf Collection>
    <class Wine/>
    <Restriction>
      <onProperty hasColor/>
      <hasValue White/>
    </Restriction>
  </intersectionOf>
</Class>
```

In summary, an OWL ontology may include classes, properties and their instances, as well as class definitions and property constraints. Therefore, an OWL ontology corresponds to the combination of a DCS and its IB (sometimes called knowledge base).

4 The Role of Conceptual Schemas in the System Architecture

In this section, we review the different roles CSs may play in the specification and architectural design of the IS.

4.1 Requirements, Specifications, and Conceptual Schemas

In the literature, it is not difficult to find different, and often contradictory, definitions of the terms "requirement" and "specification". If we want to relate our conceptual schemas with those terms we need to choose some basis. To this end, in this paper we will consider first Jackson's definitions [13, 14, 10] and then the conventional ones.

Requirements concern the environment into which the IS will be installed. The environment is the part of the world with which the IS will interact. A requirement R is a condition over the events and the states of the environment that we wish to make true by installing the IS. In the elevator control system, a requirement may be that "an elevator should go to the floor that the passengers want".

A specification S is a condition over the events and states of the environment such that if the IS satisfies S then R will be satisfied too. For example, a specification in the elevator control system is that "when a button is pressed an elevator should come to the floor as requested".

In general, the events and states involved in R are different from those involved in S. If satisfaction of S must ensure satisfaction of R, the environment must have a set of properties E such that S and E entail R. Examples of environment properties are that "when a passenger wants to go to a floor, he presses the corresponding button", or that "if an elevator is at floor n it can go only to floor $n+1$ or $n-1$". The formal definition of R, S and E, and the proof of the satisfaction of R, can be done only if we have a formal definition of the states and events of the environment.

In our terms, the environment is the domain. The description of the events and states of the environment, as well as its properties E (also called domain knowledge or domain model), is the DCS. The specification S corresponds to the FS. The requirements R can be expressed as conditions over the states and events described in the DCS.

The (formal) proof that S and E entail R lies outside the field of conceptual modelling. However, if a methodology or a project requires that proof as part of the system development, then the CS must be explicit.

The conventional definitions of the terms "requirement", "specification" and related ones are given in many places. We adopt here those of [36]. A "software requirement specification" is a document that describes each of the essential requirements and the external interfaces. Requirements are classified as functional and nonfunctional. A functional requirement specifies a function that a software system must be capable to perform, while a non-functional one specifies how the software will do a function. Therefore, in this terminology, a CS is basically the formal specification of the software functional requirements.

4.2 Abstract Architecture

The ISO report [11, 16] proposed an abstract architecture of an IS, shown in Figure 5. The architecture is functionally equivalent to the one proposed by ANSI/SPARC [1]. Our interest here for this architecture is twofold: it highlights the central role of the CS, and it allows us to discuss the possible roles of CSs in the architectures of ISs [26].

An *external schema* is a form of representation of the state of the domain, and an *external database* is a virtual representation of the state of the domain in that external schema. Besides a form of representation, external schemas include aspects of manipulation of this form, like the language used to ask queries or to communicate external events. In general there are several external schemas for a given domain, and it is not possible to single out one that satisfies all possible users and all possible uses. External schemas are defined in terms of the conceptual schema. The *external processor* is the architectural component that interacts with users. These processors receive the messages from users, translate them into the language of the conceptual schema and forward them to the information processor.

The *information processor* is the component that handles the messages originated by the users, and that performs the active function that has been delegated to the system. In particular, if a message reports an external event, then the information proces-

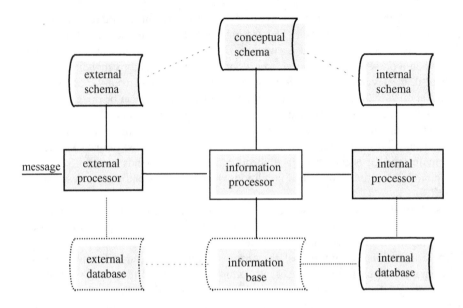

Fig. 5. ISO Abstract Architecture of an Information System.

sor applies the corresponding effect function and checks that the resulting state is consistent. In order to perform these tasks, the information processor needs to access and manipulate the state of the domain. What is most natural for the information processor is to use a representation based on the conceptual schema, which is the IB. However, the IB is virtual, since it does not exist physically within the system.

The *internal schema* is the form of representation of the state of the domain used internally by the system, and the *internal database* is the representation of the state in that schema. The internal database is the only one that has a physical existence. The internal schema includes also the set of operations that may be invoked on the database. The *internal processor* receives the commands issued by the information processor, and executes them, possibly accessing the internal database. In order to perform its task, the internal processor needs to know the internal schema, including its correspondence with the conceptual schema.

Modern architectures of ISs are layered, with three layers: presentation, domain and data management. The equivalent to the external processor is located in the presentation layer, that of the information processor in the domain layer, and that of the internal processor is in the data management layer.

In the abstract architecture described above, the CS is an architectural component. Unfortunately, this is not the case in most concrete architectures, where the CS is diffused among the code in the three layers. In the following, we review the attempts that have been made to develop architectures in which the CS (either partially or in total) is a component. Naturally, if the CS is an architectural component, then the CS must be explicit.

4.3 The Knowledge Representation Hypothesis

Before delving into the details of the role of CSs in the architecture of ISs, it is interesting to observe their role in the architecture of AI systems, and specifically in knowledge-based systems. Recall that, in our terminology, a knowledge base is the CS and the corresponding IB. It is widely accepted that the architecture of knowledge-based systems must include explicit knowledge bases. This methodological assumption was captured by B. Smith [3, p. xiv] as the Knowledge Representation Hypothesis:

"Any mechanically embodied intelligent process will be comprised of structural ingredients that:

a) we as external observers naturally take to represent a propositional account of the knowledge that the overall process exhibits, and

b) independent of such external semantical attribution, play a formal but causal and essential role in engendering the behaviour that manifests that knowledge".

According to this hypothesis, an IS with the abstract architecture shown in Figure 5 must be considered an "intelligent process", since (a) the CS and the IB are structural ingredients that represent the general and state domain knowledge that the process exhibits; and (2) these ingredients play an essential role in the behaviour of the system.

4.4 Knowledge Independence

An approach to the architectural design of ISs which is close to the abstract architecture shown in Figure 5 is called "knowledge independence". The approach has been originated in the database field [5, 38]. It is said that a design exhibits *knowledge independence* when most of the semantics of the domain is encoded in program-independent forms, shared by all programs.

Traditionally, a database system provides data independence (i.e. the ability to define the data structure and to manage data independently from the application itself). Knowledge independence extends data independence with the ability to manage rules governing the data, independently from the application. In database systems, knowledge independence is achieved by expressing knowledge in the database schema, as constraints, deductive and active rules.

Therefore, knowledge independence means that (most of) the CS is an architectural component, similar to the one in the abstract architecture, and that the database management system is the information processor.

However, in general, the model and language of the database schema are not well-suited for the CS of an IS. On the other hand, current database management systems provide only limited capabilities for constraints, deductive and active rules, which are not sufficient for representing all knowledge that includes a full CS.

4.5   Conceptual Schema = Domain Layer

There is an approach to the architectural design of ISs that advocates the use of the CS as the domain layer [8]. The approach is called *domain-driven design*. The idea is that if the CS is executable in the platform in which the IS is implemented, then the CS can be the domain layer. The objective is that the domain layer is literally the CS, without any mapping between both.

The rationale of the approach is that when the CS and the domain layer differ, the value of explicit CSs decrease. The mapping from the CS to the domain layer may be complex. On the other hand, changes that emerge during the development effort may need to be applied to both the CS and the design. The same may happen during IS maintenance or evolution. Some organizations or projects find that maintaining any mapping between the CS and the design is not cost effective. The practical result is that often the CS gets abandoned soon after coding starts [20]. The ideal solution is, of course, to equate the CS with the domain layer.

To make such a close correspondence of CS and design possible, it is essential to use languages that serves both purposes. The approach assumes that object-oriented programming languages such as Java are adequate for both purposes.

The approach works well when it is acceptable to express the CS in the implementation language. In general, this is not the case [7; 23, p. 472]. CSs need to represent knowledge declaratively, while it must be represented procedurally in the domain layer. For example, dynamic and multiple classification or state transition diagrams do not have a literal representation in object-oriented programming languages. Different language constructs and different languages are needed in the CS and in the domain layer.

4.6   Model Driven Architecture

In general, CSs do not map literally to the domain layer. It is an important design task to transform a CS into a domain layer in a specific implementation platform. Usually, the transformation is done manually. However, in many cases the transformation could be automatic.

The goal of the OMG's Model Driven Architecture (MDA) is to make that transformation as automatic as possible [28, 18]. The MDA defines an approach to system specification that separates the specification of system functionality from the specification of the implementation of that functionality on a specific technology platform.

In the MDA there are two kinds of models: Platform Independent Models (PIM) and Platform Specific Models (PSM). The PIMs provide formal specifications of the structure and behaviour of the system that abstracts away technical details. In our terminology a CS is a PIM. The PSMs specify the system in terms of the implementation constructs that are available in one specific implementation technology. Both PIMs and PSMs can be expressed in the UML.

One of the key features of MDA is the notion of mapping. A mapping is a set of rules and techniques used to transform a model into another one. A PIM to PSM mapping is used when the PIM is sufficiently refined to be projected to the execution infrastructure. The projection is based on the platform characteristics. Going from the CS to a domain layer in the J2EE platform is an example of PIM to PSM mapping.

In the MDA, maximizing automation of the CS to domain layer mapping is a goal expected to be achieved in many cases. Complete automation (including code generation) means that conceptual modelling languages take on the role of implementation languages, analogous to the way that third-generation programming languages displaced assembly languages [33]. Note that for this automation to be possible the CS must be explicit. As a by-product we get that the CS is permanently up-to-date.

5   Other Roles of Conceptual Schemas in System Development

In the previous section we have seen that CSs play a crucial role in the specification of ISs and in their architecture. In addition to this, CSs play important roles in other aspects of IS development. In the following, we briefly review some of the roles that have been documented in the literature.

Lexicon. A CS defines the names of the entity and event types, attributes, roles, associations and states. These names are the lexicon of terms to be used in the application and its documentation. As the interface is developed, the software coded, and the documentation written, the CS can be consulted to ensure that terms are used consistently throughout [17].

Use cases. The detailed description of use cases and scenarios should use the terms defined in the CS [17]. Among other things, this ensures consistency when describing several use cases concurrently [15, p. 150].

User Documentation. A CS is the basis for the documentation team to write the user documentation. Important parts of the users' manual are a translation of the functionality described in the CS, written in end-user terms [17; 34, p. 206+].

Design of user interface. The user interface should be designed after the conceptual schema has been designed. Use cases can then be rewritten at the level of the user-interface design [17].

Program understanding. Program understanding is an essential part of all software maintenance and enhancement activities. Understanding concerns both *what* a program does (the problem it solves) and *how* it does it (the programming language constructs that express the solution). The source code is not sufficient to understand what a program does. A CS can give the reader a set of expected constructs to look for in a program [31].

6 Conclusions

We have shown that in order to perform its required functions, an IS must embody some general knowledge about its domain and about the functions it has to perform. That knowledge is called the CS. We have seen that a CS includes two kinds of knowledge: the DCS and the FS. The purpose of the activity of conceptual modelling is to elicit the CS of the corresponding IS. Conceptual modelling is an essential activity of information systems development.

We have related the conceptual schemas with the ontologies studied in agent-oriented ISs and other fields related to AI. We have seen that such ontologies correspond closely to our DCSs. The conclusion has been reinforced with an analysis of the constructs provided by the OWL.

Likewise, we have related the conceptual schemas with the concepts of domain knowledge, domain model and functional specification, as used in the requirements engineering field. We have seen that a CS is the formal specification of the functional requirements, and that a DCS is the domain model or domain knowledge.

We have analysed in detail the roles of CSs in the IS architecture. We have seen that the roles range from specification to explicit software component. The ideal solution would be to equate the CS with the domain layer, but this is not possible with the current implementation languages. In the medium term, the envisaged solution in the OMG's MDA approach is to automate the mapping from a CS to the implementation languages.

The CS of an IS must always exist. The only option designers have is about its form: a CS may be mental or explicit. Currently, the explicit form is mandatory in some development contexts, and convenient in the others. In the near future, if the MDA's promises are fulfilled, explicit CSs will become mandatory in most development contexts.

Acknowledgements. I wish to thank the GMC group (Jordi Cabot, Jordi Conesa, Dolors Costal, Xavier de Palol, Cristina Gómez, Anna Queralt, Maria-Ribera Sancho, Ruth Raventós and Ernest Teniente) for many useful comments to previous drafts of this paper. This work has been partially supported by the Ministerio de Ciencia y Tecnologia and FEDER under project TIC2002-00744.

References

1. ANSI/X3/SPARC. "Interim Report from the Study Group on Database Management Systems". FDT Bulletin of the ACM, 7(2), 1975.

2. Berners-Lee, T.; Hendler, J.; Lassila, O. "The Semantic Web". Scientific American, May, 2001.
3. Brachman, R. J; Levesque, H.J. (Eds). Readings in Knowledge Representation. Morgan Kaufmann, 1985.
4. Bubenko, J.A.jr. "Information Modeling in the Context of System Development". Proc. IFIP 1980, North-Holland, 1980, pp. 395-411.
5. Ceri, S.; Fraternali, P. Designing Database Applications with Objects and Rules. The IDEA Methodology. Addison-Wesley, 1997, 579 .
6. Chandrasekaran, B.; Josephson, J.R.; Benjamins, V.R. "What Are Ontologies, and Why Do We Need Them?". IEEE Intelligent Systems, January/February 99, pp. 20-26.
7. Daniels, J. "Modeling with a Sense of Purpose". IEEE Software, January/February 2002, pp. 8-10.
8. Evans, E. Domain-Driven Design. Tackling Complexity in the Heart of Business Software. Addison-Wesley, 2003.
9. Gruber, T.R. "Toward Principles for the Design of Ontologies Used for Knowledge Sharing". In N. Guarino and R. Poli, (Eds.), International Workshop on Formal Ontology, Padova, Italy. August 1993.
10. Gunter, C.A.; Gunter, E.L.; Jackson, M.; Zave, P. A Reference Model for Requirements and Specifications. IEEE Software, May/June 2000, pp. 37-43.
11. ISO/TC97/SC5/WG3 Concepts and Terminology for the Conceptual Schema and the Information Base, J.J. Van Griethuysen (ed.) March 1982.
12. Jackson, M. System Development. Prentice Hall, 1983, 418 p.
13. Jackson, M. The meaning of requirements. Annals of Software Engineering, 3(1997), pp. 5-21.
14. Jackson, M.; Zave, P. Deriving Specifications from Requirements: an Example. Proc. ICSE'95. IEEE Computer Soc. Press, pp. 15-24.
15. Jacobson, I.; Booch, G.; Rumbaugh, J. The Unified Software Development Process. Addison-Wesley, 1999, 463p.
16. Jardine, D.A. Concepts and Terminology for the Conceptual Schema and the Information Base. Computers & Standards 3 (1984), pp. 3-17.
17. Johnson, J.; Henderson, A. "Conceptual Models: Begin by designing what to design". Interactions, Jan-Feb. 2002, pp. 25-32.
18. Kleppe, A.; Warmer, J.; Bast, W. MDA Explained. The Model Driven Architecture: Practice and Promise. Addison-Wesley, 2003, 170 p.
19. Kowalski, R. "Algorithm = Logic + Control". Comm. ACM, 22(7), 1979, pp. 424-436.
20. Letbridge, T.C.; Singer,J.; Forward, A. "How Software Engineers Use Documentation: The State of the Practice". IEEE Software, Nov/Dec 2003, pp. 35-39.
21. Loucopoulos, P. Conceptual Modeling. In [22], pp. 1-26.
22. Loucopoulos, P.; Zicari, R. (Eds). Conceptual Modeling, Databases and CASE: An Integrated View of Information Systems Development. Wiley, 1992.
23. Martin, R.C. Agile Software Development. Principles, Patterns and Practices. Prentice Hall, 2003, 529 p.
24. Mylopoulos, J. "The Role of Knowledge Representation in the Development of Specifications". Proc IFIP-86, North-Holland, 1986, pp. 317-319.
25. Mylopoulos, J. "Conceptual Modeling and Telos". In [22], pp. 49-68.
26. Olivé, A. "An Introduction to Conceptual Modeling of Information Systems". In Piattini, M.; Díaz, O. (Eds.) Advanced Database Technology and Design. Artech House, 2000, pp. 25-57.

27. Olivé, A. "Integrity Constraints Definition in Object-Oriented Conceptual Modeling Languages". Proc. ER 2003, LNCS 2813, pp. 349-362, 2003.
28. OMG. "Model Driven Architecture (MDA)". Document number ormsc/2001-07-01. 2001.
29. OMG. OCL:Object Constraint Language 2.0. OMG Document ad/2003-01-07. 2003.
30. OMG. UML 2.0 Superstructure Specification. Doc ptc/03-08-02, 2003.
31. Rugaber, S. The use of domain knowledge in program understanding. Annals of Software Engineering, 9 (2000), pp. 143-192.
32. Russell, S.; Norvig, P. Artificial Intelligence. A Modern Approach. Prentice-Hall, 1995, 932 p.
33. Selic, B. "The Pragmatics of Model-Driven Development". IEE Software, September/October 2003, pp. 19-25.
34. Sommerville, I.; Sawyer, P. Requirements Engineering. John Wiley & Sons, 1997, 391 p.
35. Sowa, J.F. Knowledge Representation. Logical, Philosophical and Computational Foundations. Brooks/Cole, 2000, 594p.
36. Thayer, R.H.; Thayer, M.C. "Glossary". In Standards, Guidelines, and Examples on System and Software Requirements Engineering. IEEE Computer Society Press, 1990, pp. 501-572.
37. Tryfona, N.; Jensen, C.S. "Using Abstractions for Spatio-Temporal Conceptual Modeling". Proceedings of the 2000 ACM Symposium on Applied Computing, pp. 313-322.
38. Vieille, L. "From Data Independence to Knowledge Independence: An on-going Story". Proc. of the 24th VLDB Conf, New York, 1998, pp. 650-654.
39. W3C. "OWL Web Ontology Language Guide". http://www.w3.org/TR/2003/CR-owl-guide-20030818/
40. Wieringa, R.J. Design Methods for Reactive Systems. Morgan Kaufmann, 2003, 457 p.

An Overview of Middleware

Steve Vinoski*

IONA Technologies, Waltham MA 02451, USA
vinoski@iona.com
http://www.iona.com/hyplan/vinoski/

Abstract. For a variety of reasons, middleware has become a critical substrate for numerous distributed applications. Middleware provides portability, protects applications from the inherent complexities of networking and distribution, supplies generally useful horizontal services (such as directory services, security, and transactions), and shields developers from system-level concerns so they can focus on the logic of their applications. This paper presents an overview of middleware, including its origins, its fundamental aspects, the different evolutionary paths it has taken, the effects that middleware standards have had on that evolution, and where middleware appears to be headed in the future.

1   Introduction

The term "middleware" refers to software that resides between an application and the operating system, network, or database underneath it. Middleware has evolved from simple beginnings—hiding database and network details from applications—into sophisticated systems that handle many important details for distributed applications. Today, middleware serves as a critical part of numerous applications and systems, even in traditionally cautious and exacting vertical industries such as telecommunications, finance, insurance, manufacturing, and government.

The fact that middleware exists at all is rather unsurprising. Its reason for being is to provide a layer between an application and its underlying platform that helps protect the application from the details and quirks of that platform [1]. In essence, it separates concerns by providing useful abstractions that help reduce coupling between software layers. Separating concerns is important; just as operating systems keep users from having to understand the inner workings of their computing hardware just to be able to run applications, middleware keeps developers from having to be experts in specialized areas (such as networking, distributed systems, security, transactions, and fault tolerance) just so they can build robust and reliable applications.

This paper provides overview of the origins, history, fundamentals, and the various evolutionary paths of middleware. It concludes with a discussion of the directions in which middleware is likely to evolve in the future.

---

* The author would like to thank Douglas C. Schmidt and Michi Henning for their helpful reviews of drafts of this paper.

A. Llamosí and A. Strohmeier (Eds.): Ada-Europe 2004, LNCS 3063, pp. 35–51, 2004.

2 Middleware Origins

Numerous developments over the history of computing have contributed to modern-day middleware, but its origins can be found in on-line transaction processing (OLTP). In the early 1960s, for example, American Airlines and IBM jointly created the SABRE airline reservation system. This system enabled American to handle their airline reservations on mainframe computers, replacing a system based largely on human agents keeping track of flight reservations on paper index cards, thereby vastly increasing the scalability, reliability, and correctness of their reservation system. Today, the SABRE spin-off is worth more than the airline itself [2].

Though technically not middleware, the original SABRE system provided the foundations for the separation of transaction processing (TP) support from both the application and the operating system. IBM's experiences with SABRE and with developing other reservation systems with other airlines led them in the late 1960s and early 1970s to create several OLTP systems. One of these was the Airline Control Program (ACP), later renamed to the Transaction Processing Facility (TPF). TPF is an operating system built specifically to manage high volumes of transactions for applications. IBM also produced the Customer Information Control System (CICS) [3] and the Information Management System (IMS), which were generally the first systems known as TP monitors [4]. Because of their exceptional reliability, TPF, CICS, and IMS are still in use today for many mission-critical OLTP systems. In the decades that have followed the introduction of these first TP monitors, numerous other successful TP monitors for a variety of different platforms have been developed, including BEA's Tuxedo [5] and Digital Equipment Corporation's Application Control and Management System (ACMS).

TP monitors generally manage computing resources on behalf of transactional applications, and provide services such as database connection management, load balancing, and process monitoring on their behalf. General-purpose operating systems also manage computing resources for applications, but they do so at a basic level and usually provide little assistance, if any, for specific styles of applications. TP monitors, on the other hand, are tuned to provide management and services specifically for transactional applications. Many of the application services that modern middleware provides, as well as the resource management functions it performs, can trace their origins to features of TP monitor systems.

Over time, computing systems have evolved from centralized mainframes to decentralized distributed systems, and along the way they have become increasingly heterogeneous. Heterogeneity is inherent in distributed systems not only because of the never-ending march of technology (which creates continual change as systems are updated and replaced), but also because creation and administration of decentralized systems is itself also decentralized. As a result, different parts of the network will over time consist of different types of machines, operating systems, and applications, and the rate of upgrades and replacements for these components will often differ in various parts the network. This is obviously true of the Internet, due to its immense size, but this phenomenon also occurs even in small enterprise computing systems that consist of only tens of machines.

As computing systems have become more diverse and heterogeneous, middleware has come to the rescue, restoring a sort of "virtual homogeneity" to the system. When middleware is developed to be portable to a wide variety of platforms, it can provide the same common interfaces and services to applications regardless of where they might execute. It is not uncommon, for example, for the same middleware package to provide the same interfaces and services to embedded applications, applications that run on desktop systems, and to mainframe applications, despite the tremendous differences in these underlying platforms.

3   Middleware Fundamentals

The general role of middleware is to abstract away the details of underlying facilities and platforms, thereby isolating applications from them. Just as networking protocol stacks can be decomposed into multiple layers, such as the physical, data-link, network, transport, session, presentation, and application layers, so too can middleware be decomposed into the multiple layers [1] shown in Figure 1.[1] Host infrastructure middleware (such as Java Virtual Machines and ACE [6,7]) provides mechanisms to create reusable event demultiplexing, interprocess communication, concurrency, and synchronization objects. Distribution middleware (such as CORBA [8] and Java RMI [9]) defines higher-level distributed programming models. The reusable APIs and objects of these models automate and extend the native OS mechanisms encapsulated by host infrastructure middleware so that applications can invoke operations on target objects without hard-coding dependencies on their location, programming language, OS platform, communication protocols and interconnects, or hardware. Common middleware services (such as directory, transaction, security, and event services) augment distribution middleware by defining higher-level domain-independent reusable services that allow application developers to concentrate on programming business logic, without the need to write the "plumbing" code required to develop distributed applications via lower-level middleware directly. Finally, domain-specific middleware services are tailored to the requirements of particular domains, such as telecommunications, e-commerce, health care, process automation, or aerospace.

Regardless of which layers of middleware are used, good middleware not only makes applications more reliable by shielding them from unnecessary complexity, but it also can make them more scalable. In particular, for applications that must scale well (*e.g.*, in terms of numbers of systems, numbers of simultaneous users, or numbers of requests or operations), middleware reduces the complexities that tend to arise in several areas. These areas are described below.

---

[1] Figure 1 is provided courtesy of Douglas C. Schmidt.

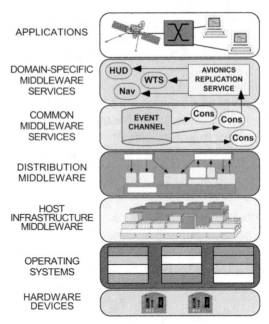

APPLICATIONS

DOMAIN-SPECIFIC
MIDDLEWARE
SERVICES

COMMON
MIDDLEWARE
SERVICES

DISTRIBUTION
MIDDLEWARE

HOST
INFRASTRUCTURE
MIDDLEWARE

OPERATING
SYSTEMS

HARDWARE
DEVICES

Fig. 1. Middleware Layers in Context

3.1   Communication Support

Most middleware-based systems involve distribution, where applications interact with each other and with distributed services over a network. Modern operating systems typically support network programming interfaces (such as sockets), but these are usually low level and complicated to use. Middleware shields application developers from the complexity of low-level network programming details [6].

There are primarily two forms of middleware-based inter-application distributed communication: *remote procedure call* (RPC) [10] and *messaging*. Each of these is described in further detail below.

Remote Procedure Call. The work on structured programming in the 1970s and 1980s made developers aware of the importance of properly modularizing their applications [11]. Developers grew to understand the benefits of properly dividing their applications into procedures so as to encapsulate units of work. The quality of a procedure was judged by its cohesiveness—the higher, the better—and how minimal its coupling was to its callers and to any procedures it called.

A procedure call reflects a change in computing context, and an RPC is simply the result of abstracting that change in context beyond the limits of a single CPU. RPC allows an application, called the *client*, to invoke services provided by a separate application, called the *server*, via what appears in the client source code to be just an ordinary procedure call. Remote procedures can reside within servers running on the same machine as the client but in separate processes, or they can reside on a wholly separate machine across the network.

The intent of RPC is to hide from the client the details of the distributed aspects of invocations of remote procedures. Some of these details include the following:

- *Data transfer.* A procedure normally has one or more parameters and might also return a value. Passing these values over a network between the client and the server requires that they be converted from their programming language representation into a form suitable for network transmission. Conversion from a programming language representation into a network transmission form is called *marshaling*, and the opposite conversion is called *demarshaling* or *unmarshaling*.

There are numerous complexities and subtleties associated with marshaling. For example, exchanging data between little-endian and big-endian systems requires byte swapping. Some protocols require marshaled data to be aligned in certain ways, such as 4- or 8-byte boundaries. Marshaling complicated data structures, such as cyclic graphs, requires the marshaling subsystem to ensure that graph nodes are marshaled only once when sending, and that links between nodes are properly reconstituted upon demarshaling.

One of the goals of RPC is to provide the client with the illusion that all of its procedure calls, even the remote ones, are just normal invocations made within its own address space. Marshaling must therefore be transparent to the application.[2] Middleware normally achieves this transparency by hiding the marshaling behind stubs or proxies [12] that it supplies to the application. A client invoking a remote procedure actually invokes a local proxy, which in turn performs the marshaling and network operations required to send the request to the actual remote procedure in the server. The local proxy also turns the server's remote response into a normal local procedure call return.

- *Network programming.* To invoke a remote request, one or more network messages must be sent from the client application to the remote server application hosting the target procedure. These messages must contain not only the marshaled data expected by the remote procedure, but must also contain enough information to allow the server application to determine precisely which of its procedures is the target of the invocation. These messages also normally contain header information that indicates the type of message being sent (*e.g.*, a request, a reply, an error, etc.). Together, the header, the information about the target, and the marshaled data make up all the information needed to perform the RPC. The rules regarding which sequences of message types are allowed between sender and receiver (*e.g.*, a receiver may send only a reply or an error in response to a request) collectively define the *RPC protocol.*

RPC protocols can be run over both connection-oriented and connection-less network protocols. Since RPC requires strict request-response semantics, however, when it is performed over connectionless protocols, such as the User Datagram Protocol (UDP), the middleware must take care of dealing with lost

---

[2] Note, however, that complete local/remote transparency is not possible, *cf.* [13] and the discussion of networking failures on page 41.

and duplicate packets, packet ordering issues, etc., to shield applications from these networking details. For this reason, most modern middleware communications rely on connection-oriented protocols, typically the Transmission Control Protocol (TCP), to avoid handling the low-level networking details associated with UDP.[3] UDP is useful, however, for tasks where lost or duplicate packets are acceptable, such as some forms of logging and event communication.

To actually make an RPC, of course, one or more network transmissions of some sort must occur between the client and server. Middleware that uses connection-oriented transmission protocols must hide all the details of establishing connections from the application. This is normally done by having the application provide some sort of *network handle* to the middleware when it invokes an RPC. The handle contains enough networking information, such as the host and port of the remote target application, to allow the middleware to connect properly. Such connections can either be established *implicitly*, where the middleware transparently creates the connection when the application first invokes a remote procedure using that handle, or *explicitly*, where the application calls a specific middleware API to establish the connection.

For server applications making their procedures available for remote invocation, network programming is even harder. Not only must such applications listen for connections and establish them when requested, but they must be able to do this for numerous callers. Writing scalable and robust server-side code that can handle many simultaneous connections and requests from clients, without unduly sacrificing performance, requires a great deal of expertise. Numerous publications document the details of this expertise [6,14].

Since the APIs offered by operating systems for network access tend to be extremely low-level and obtuse, network programming is quite tedious and error-prone. Polluting applications with these kinds of calls can mean that the application logic is intermixed with networking logic, making the application as a whole very brittle, hard to maintain, and unreliable. Middleware alleviates this issue and restores reliability by taking care of connection establishment and management in a manner that is largely transparent to the application.

• *Failures.* Distribution introduces chances for *partial failure* into a networked application. Unlike a monolithic application that executes in a single address space, where failure is either all or nothing, distributed applications often fail partially. For example, a client application might invoke an RPC, but the machine hosting the server application might fail while the client is waiting for a response. Alternatively, the network between the client and server might partition while the client is waiting. In cases like these, parts of the overall distributed application are left running while other parts have failed. Determining such failure modes and recovering from them can be extremely hard.

Due to partial failure, RPC protocols must provide the ability for the client and server middleware to indicate errors to each other. For example, if in making

---

[3] In fact, middleware that attempts to support reliable connection-oriented communications over UDP ends up essentially reimplementing TCP.

a request the client middleware somehow violates the RPC protocol, the server must be able to indicate this in an error reply. Middleware must also be able to set timeouts to prevent an application from hanging in the event of a networking problem or a problem with another associated distributed application.

Sometimes middleware can shield applications from the errors inherent in distributed computing. For example, should a transient condition arise in a network that causes a remote invocation to fail, the middleware can sometimes hide this from the application by simply transparently retrying the invocation. If the condition has somehow been corrected in the interim, the retry could succeed, with the result that the application is blissfully unaware that any error ever occurred.

Unfortunately, hiding errors in this manner is not always possible. For example, consider the case where a client invokes an RPC on a server. If a partial failure occurs that prevents the client middleware from knowing whether the server actually executed the procedure call or not, the client middleware must inform the client application that the invocation failed because the target remote procedure might not be *idempotent*, *i.e.*, invoking it more than once might have deleterious effects, such as making multiple withdrawals from a bank account where only one was intended. In cases like these, the middleware has no choice but to return error conditions to the application because only the application can know whether it is safe to retry the operation (unless the middleware has included explicit support for marking remote procedures as being idempotent). Since there is little overlap between the failure modes of local procedure calls and RPCs, local calls and RPCs cannot transparently be treated as being the same [13]. If applications are not properly coded to handle these types of error conditions, their reliability will suffer.

In terms of these three areas that RPC addresses—data transfer, network programming, and failures—note that other approaches that have evolved from RPC, specifically distributed object approaches and remote method invocations, are very similar to RPC, as they too aim to hide these same details. RPC and distributed objects differ mainly in their programming models, in much the same way that C differs from C++.

Messaging. While RPC approaches try to hide network programming details from the application developer as much as possible, messaging takes almost the opposite approach: messaging systems tend to directly and explicitly expose their presence and their APIs to applications. Messaging approaches do not mimic programming language procedure calls or method invocations. Messaging applications therefore need not bother trying to pretend that they are confined to a single address space. Instead, they specifically target inter-application communication.

Messaging APIs tend to be minimal, typically providing a queueing abstraction that applications use to put messages onto and get messages from a queue. Messaging systems often do not provide marshaling support, meaning that applications must perform their own message formatting and interpretation.

Unlike RPCs, which are inherently *synchronous* because they cause the client to wait until the server responds, messaging is *asynchronous*— often called "fire and forget"—because applications simply post messages to queues and continue processing without waiting synchronously for a response. Asynchrony has the primary advantage of providing *loose coupling* because applications work with queues, not directly with other applications. In a client-server system, if a client calls a server that happens to be down, the client is in trouble, as there is little it can do to continue operating correctly. In a messaging system, conversely, messages can be stored persistently in queues until applications become available to retrieve them.

It is possible to implement RPC-like semantics in a messaging system, and vice-versa. For example, RPC can be achieved in a messaging system via the use of two queues, one for request messages and one for replies, while messaging-like semantics can be integrated with RPC systems by implementing queues behind asynchronous proxies.

3.2   Concurrency Support

Many middleware-based applications must be highly scalable, typically in terms of numbers of requests or messages processed per second. This requires maximizing the amount of concurrency in the system, so that it can continously operate on as many tasks as possible at the same time. Middleware systems employ a variety of techniques and patterns to enhance concurrency [14]. For example, employing multiple threads within a server process allows middleware communication subsystems to maximize both the handling of network connections and the handling of requests and messages that arrive on those connections. Depending on the server application characteristics, performance and scalability can depend heavily on the connection handling and request dispatching facilities that the middleware provides.

In addition to multi-threading, concurrency can also involve multiple processes. For example, running only a single instance of a heavily-used server is usually unacceptable not only because of limited throughput, but also because failure of that process means that the service becomes completely unavailable. Running concurrent process replicas allows middleware to balance request load among the replicas, thus providing better service to calling applications. It also allows middleware to divert incoming requests from a failed replica to a live one. Diverting requests in this manner is called *failover*. Quality middleware can perform load balancing and failover transparently for calling applications.

Due to the inherent difficulty of concurrent programming, some middleware systems try to hide its complexities. These approaches usually take the form of frameworks [7] based on patterns [14] that impose rules about what actions applications are allowed to take within certain contexts. Sometimes these rules disallow explicit application invocations of threading APIs, thus allowing the underlying middleware to completely control how the overall application utilizes threading. Such approaches can work for simple applications, but they are usually too inflexible for systems of even moderate complexity.

3.3   Common Middleware Services

In addition to leveraging the communication and concurrency support described above, distributed applications also typically use middleware services to address concerns that are independent of any particular application domain. Some of the most common middleware services are described below.

- *Directory services* allow applications to look up or discover distributed resources. For example, naming services allow applications to find resources based on their names, while trading services provide for discovery based on various resource properties. Directory services avoid the need to hard-code network addresses and other communication details into applications, since hard-coding them would result in a very brittle and hard-to-maintain system that would break anytime host addresses changed or applications were moved to new hosts. Directory services are often federated, meaning that the services are not centralized and are instead implemented across a number of hosts and linked to form a coherent distributed service.

- *Transaction services* help applications commit or roll back their transactions. Such services are critically important in distributed transactional systems, such as those used for financial applications or reservations systems. Middleware for this domain typically takes the form of distributed transaction managers that create and coordinate transactions together with resource managers that are local to each node involved in the transaction.

- *Security services* provide support for authentication and authorization across a distributed system. Such services often coordinate across multiple disparate security systems, supplying single sign-on capabilities that manage credentials transparently across the underlying systems on behalf of applications.

- *Management services* help monitor and maintain systems while they are running, typically in production. Each application in the distributed system is able to log error, warning, and informational messages regarding its operation via a distributed logging service, and to raise alerts to monitoring systems to notify system operators of problems.

- *Event services* allow applications to post event messages for reception by other applications. These can form the basis for the management alerts described above, or for any general publish/subscribe system. In RPC-style systems, event services allow for looser coupling between applications, and can even provide messaging-like persistent queueing capabilities.

- *Persistence services* assist applications with managing their non-volatile data. There are a variety of approaches to providing persistence for applications. Some are oriented around relational databases, others around object-oriented databases, and still others around non-typical datastores such as persistent key-value pairs or even plain text files. Regardless of which approach is used, middleware persistence abstraction layers hide these underlying storage mechanisms from applications.

• *Load balancing* services direct incoming requests or messages to appropriate service application replicas capable of best handling the request at that point in time. Typically, balancing services track the load of individual service replicas and transparently forward each request or message to the particular replica that is least loaded.

• *Configuration services* add flexibility to applications by allowing middleware capabilities to be modified or augmented non-programmatically, often through management consoles. This type of service allows application behavior, performance, and scalability to be modified and tuned without requiring the application to be recompiled. In some cases, for example, an application can have its security or transactional capabilities enabled or disabled entirely via configuration.

The fact that middleware platforms supply such services relieves applications from having to supply them for themselves. Many of these services, especially those related to security and transactions, require significant expertise and resources to develop correctly. Applications that depend on such services can be smaller, easier to develop, and more flexible, but ultimately their reliability and robustness are only as good as that of the services they rely on.

4   Middleware Evolution

The evolution of middleware has been influenced by numerous developments and standards efforts. Some of these are described in the following sections.

4.1   Early Influences

As described above in section 2, middleware evolved out of early OLTP systems. Along the way, it has also been heavily influenced by programming language developments and by the proliferation of computer networks. By and large, many of today's middleware mechanisms (such as concurrency approaches and process control) have evolved from TP monitors, while middleware abstractions (such as interface definition languages and proxies) have evolved mainly from the area of programming languages.

The influence of programming languages on middleware is not surprising. Developing middleware applications has never been easy, and as a result much effort has been invested in developing abstractions at the programming language level to help ease the development of such applications. Abstractions such as RPC and its descendant, distributed objects, both resulted directly from programming language research and development.

Systems such as Apollo's Network Computing Architecture (NCA) [15], Sun's Remote Procedure Call standard [16], and the Open Software Foundation's Distributed Computing Environment (DCE) [17] are all examples of successful RPC-oriented middleware that has been used for significant production applications. The success of these RPC systems was relatively limited, however, due in large part to their accidental complexity. In particular, the fact that they were tied mostly to the C programming language made them accessible only to expert developers.

4.2   Distributed Objects and Components

At the same time these systems were being productized in the 1980s and early 1990s, significant research was occurring in the area of distributed objects. Distributed objects represented the confluence of two key areas of information technology: distributed systems and object-oriented (OO) design and programming. Techniques for developing distributed systems focus on integrating many computing devices to act as a coordinated computational resource. Likewise, techniques for developing OO systems focus on reducing software complexity by capturing successful patterns and creating reusable frameworks based on encapsulation, data abstraction, and polymorphism. Significant early distributed object-based and OO systems included Argus [18], Eden [19], Emerald [20], and COMANDOS [21].

As a result of research on these and other distributed object systems, combined with an evolution of the TP monitor into the concept of an "object monitor," the Common Object Request Broker Architecture (CORBA) was created by the Object Management Group (OMG) in 1991 [8]. CORBA is arguably the most successful middleware standard ever created. Just as a TP monitor controls and manages transactional processes, an object monitor, or *object request broker* (ORB), controls and manages distributed objects and invocations on their methods. A number of commercial, research, and open source ORBs have been implemented in the years since CORBA was first published. On top of these implementations, thousands and thousands of middleware applications have been successfully built and deployed into production. Today, CORBA-based applications serve as critical elements of systems in a wide variety of industries, especially telecommunications, finance, manufacturing, and defense.

From a technical point of view, the success of CORBA is due largely to the balance it provides between flexibility and stringency. CORBA is fairly stringent with respect to the definition of its object model and its invocation rules. Beyond that, it provides a great deal of flexibility for applications, allowing them to be built in a variety of ways. For example, it allows for applications to be built using generated code (in the form of object proxies) based on object interface definitions, which can provide for very high-performance systems, or built using dynamic approaches that can adapt to any object interface, which enables slower but extremely flexible applications. CORBA also supports both RPC and messaging approaches, the latter through asynchronous proxies as well as through notification and event services. Adding to this flexibility is the fact that CORBA APIs are available in a variety of programming languages, including C, C++, Java, Python, COBOL, and PL/I. This flexibility is critical, given the fact that CORBA is most often used for integration "glue" between disparate systems. CORBA's flexibility has allowed it to be used in an extremely wide variety of applications.

CORBA directly addresses heterogeneous distributed systems using a layered architecture like the one shown in Figure 1. Unfortunately, handling heterogeneous systems sometimes requires approaches that represent the lowest common denominator of the individual systems involved. Indeed, this has been a common criticism of CORBA. For example, the CORBA Interface Definition Language (IDL) has similarities to C++, yet it excludes common OO features, such as method overloading, because of the difficulty of mapping them to non-OO languages such as C [22]. The fact that CORBA objects are defined in IDL—but implemented in an actual programming language—means that the developer is faced with a constant "impedance mismatch" between CORBA constructs and the native constructs of the implementation language. This impedance mismatch can add complexity to the development of CORBA applications [23].

Due to the limitations and trade-offs that dealing with heterogeneity requires at the application development level, some distributed system designers have opted to instead create platforms that are specific to a given programming language. For example, developers using Java Remote Method Invocation (RMI) [9] use normal Java constructs and approaches when developing RMI applications.

4.3   Enterprise Application Integration

While the evolution of distributed objects in the 1990s was marked by significant efforts to establish standards such as CORBA, the evolution of messaging-oriented middleware was practically devoid of standards efforts. In fact, today's most popular messaging systems, such as IBM MQ Series and TIBCO Rendezvous, are proprietary. Even so, messaging systems were widely deployed during this time, primarily because of the loose coupling they afforded, their ease of development with respect to RPC and distributed object systems, and the ease with which they allowed connections to be established between disparate systems.

In the mid to late 1990s, Enterprise Application Integration (EAI) evolved from message-oriented middleware. EAI is characterized as hub-oriented communication between disparate systems, where adapters convert the native formats of the systems being connected into the canonical protocols and formats of the EAI hub.

4.4   Component Models and Web Services

In the late 1990s, the growing popularity of Java, the explosive growth of the World Wide Web (WWW), and lessons learned from CORBA and messaging middleware were all combined to form the Java 2 Enterprise Edition (J2EE) [24], a comprehensive component middleware platform. J2EE provides support for numerous application types, including distributed objects, components, web-based applications, and messaging systems. For example, it includes Enterprise Java Beans (EJB), which essentially provide a simpler form of the most common CORBA object approaches while adding support for message-driven beans. It also includes a variety of other middleware approaches: servlets and Java Server Pages (JSP) for building web-centric systems, JDBC[4] for database access, Java Message Service (JMS) for messaging support, and the Java Connector Architecture (JCA) for EAI-like functionality. J2EE aimed to introduce some simplicity into the middleware arena, especially with its heavy use of deployment descriptors and other configuration approaches that serve to separate deployment concerns from the actual application code. Unfortunately, despite its features and its homogeneous nature, J2EE remains quite complex. As a result, most uses of J2EE involve only JSPs or servlets and JDBC.

Throughout the development of CORBA, J2EE, and proprietary messaging systems, Microsoft was busy developing its Common Object Model (COM) [25] distributed objects system. COM was seen mainly as a competitor to CORBA, but it was specific to the Windows platform.[5] The main contribution COM made to the overall middleware picture—or more specifically, the tools that were built above COM—was ease of use. Even developers using simple programming languages, such as Visual Basic, could leverage COM's features and support, using them to easily create practical and working distributed applications.

In 1999 and 2000, the Web's influence on middleware started to become readily apparent with the publication of the initial version of SOAP [26]. Initially dubbed the *Simple Object Access Protocol*,[6] SOAP was the result of trying to create a system-agnostic protocol that could be used over the Web and yet still interface easily to non-SOAP middleware, including CORBA, COM, J2EE, and messaging middleware systems.

The introduction of SOAP spawned a new middleware category called *Web Services* [27]. In 2000 and 2001, the development of the SOAP standard in the World Wide Web Consortium (W3C) enjoyed an unprecedented level of industry support. Seemingly every vendor, large and small, was unified behind the creation of the SOAP standard. Given the 1990s "middleware wars" between between J2EE, CORBA, and COM, and between RPC and messaging, the unified support for SOAP was indeed groundbreaking. At the time, it seemed that SOAP and Web Services might finally provide the basis for broad industry agreement on middleware standards, and that ubiquitous application interoperability

---

[4] JDBC originally stood for "Java Database Connectivity." It is now a trademark of Sun Microsystems.

[5] Efforts to port COM to other operating systems besides Windows were made, but they never achieved commercial success.

[6] "Simple Object Access Protocol" was a poor name, given that SOAP is neither simple nor object-oriented. This name was eventually dropped in favor of the name *SOAP*.

and portability would soon follow. Not surprisingly, this was not to be, given the substantial inter-company political and business conflicts in this market. Despite broad agreement around SOAP and the Web Services Description Language (WSDL), which is used to define Web Services interfaces [28], significant disagreements remain over what Web Services are and how they are best applied [29,30].

5   The Future of Middleware

Web Services are clearly the immediate future of middleware. This does not mean, however, that Web Services will displace older approaches, such as J2EE and CORBA. Rather, Web Services complements these earlier successful middleware technologies.

Initial Web Services developments were heavily RPC-oriented, and were touted as possible replacements for more complicated EJBs or CORBA objects. However, the performance profile of Web Services is such that they are often several orders of magnitude slower than CORBA when used for fine-grained distributed resource access. As a result, the use of Web Services for RPC systems is now considered much less significant than using them for document-oriented or message-oriented systems.

Rather than trying to replace older approaches, today's Web Services developments are instead oriented around middleware integration [31], thereby adding value to existing messaging, J2EE, and CORBA middleware systems. WSDL allows developers to abstractly describe Web Service interfaces while also defining the concrete *bindings*—the protocols and transports—required at runtime to access the services. For example, projects such as the Apache Web Services Invocation Framework (WSIF; http://ws.apache.org/wsif/) aim to allow applications to access Web Services transparently via EJB, JMS, JCA, or as local Java objects. This move towards integration allows services implemented in these different technologies to exposed as Web Services and made available to a variety of client applications. Middleware integration is truly the sweet spot for Web Services applications for the foreseeable future.

Web Services standardization efforts continue, with various standards bodies working on standards for security, transactions, addressing, orchestration, choreography, reliable messaging, business processes, and management. Unfortunately, these standardization efforts are currently splintered across a number of standards bodies. Still, even splintered standards efforts are usually better than none. For example, because EAI has no associated standards, Web Services are quickly moving to wholly displace EAI because customers view standards as affording them at least some degree of freedom from vendor lock-in. EAI thus appears to be a middleware evolutionary dead end.

Middleware also has a bright future for distributed real-time and embedded (DRE) systems [32] This domain is traditionally extremely conservative because of the stringent requirements for predictability, size, and performance in DRE systems. The construction of middleware suitable for such systems is now well understood and standardized (*e.g.*, via the Real-time CORBA and Real-time Java specifications), meaning that middleware benefits are now available for DRE systems. This, combined with continuing advances in hardware such as higher data bus and CPU clock speeds, smaller circuits, and larger memory capacities, promises to advance the capabilities of many real-time and embedded systems and allow DRE techniques to be applied to new areas.

Another recent middleware development, grid technology [33], is attempting to provide distributed infrastructure for "utility computing." The goal of grid technology is to create a computing grid that is as ubiquitous and invisible as the power grid. Users of grid middleware infrastructure hope to take advantage of continuous increases in compute power, network speed, and storage capacities to make distributed access to computing resources easier and faster. Companies such as IBM, HP, and Sun are working hard to achieve grid computing because they view it as a way to sell their next generation of high-end compute servers. Work is also being done to unite grid approaches with Web Services technologies to create the Open Grid Services Architecture (OGSA) [34], which promises to make grid distributed services available via Web Services interfaces.

Grid technologies count on the existence and ubiquity of very high speed networks to minimize latency when accessing remote resources. As a result, the potential for success of grids is currently unclear, as such networks are still under development in research testbeds and are not yet ubiquitously available in the commercial sector.

Commercial-off-the-shelf (COTS) middleware platforms have traditionally expected static connectivity, reliable communication channels, and relatively high bandwidth. Significant challenges remain, however, to design, optimize, and apply middleware for more flexible network environments, such as self-organizing peer-to-peer (P2P) networks, mobile settings, and highly resource-constrained sensor networks. For example, hiding network topologies and other deployment details from networked applications becomes harder (and often undesirable) in wireless sensor networks since applications and middleware often need to adapt according to changes in location, connectivity, bandwidth, and battery power. Concerted R&D efforts [35] are therefore essential to devising new middleware solutions and capabilities that can fulfill the requirements of these emerging network technologies and next-generation applications.

6   Concluding Remarks

This paper has presented a broad overview of middleware, describing its evolution from transaction processing systems into RPC systems, message queuing systems, distributed object systems, and web-based service applications. Covering the entire middleware spectrum would require significantly more pages than this format allows, but this paper has attempted to accent the most significant developments in the history of middleware and show the effects of those developments on middleware evolution. Due to its separation of concerns, middleware will continue to provide performance, scalability, portability, and reliability for applications while insulating them from many accidental and inherent complexities of underlying operating systems, networks, and hardware.

References

1. R. Schantz and D. Schmidt. "Middleware for Distributed Systems: Evolving the Common Structure for Network-centric Applications," *Encyclopedia of Software Engineering*, Wiley and Sons, 2002.
2. C. Zook and J. Allen. "Growth Outside the Core." *Harvard Business Review*, 81(12), December 2003, pp. 66–73.
3. B. Yelavich. "Customer Information Control System—An Evolving System Facility." *IBM Systems Journal*, 24(3/4), 1985, pp. 264–278.
4. P. Bernstein and E. Newcomer, *Principles of Transaction Processing*, Morgan Kaufmann, 1997.
5. J. Andrade, T. Dwyer, S. Felts, M. Carges, *The Tuxedo System: Software for Constructing and Managing Distributed Business Applications*, Addison-Wesley, 1996.
6. D. Schmidt and S. Huston, *C++ Network Programming, Vol. 1: Mastering Complexity with ACE and Patterns*, Addison-Wesley, 2002.
7. D. Schmidt and S. Huston, *C++ Network Programming, Vol. 2: Systematic Reuse with ACE and Frameworks*, Addison-Wesley, 2003.
8. Object Management Group. "The Common Object Request Broker: Architecture and Specification (CORBA)," OMG document number 91-12-1, 1991.
9. Javasoft, "Java Remote Method Invocation—Distributed Computing for Java, a White Paper," available online at
   `http://java.sun.com/marketing/collateral/javarmi.html`.
10. A. Birrell and B. Nelson. "Implementing Remote Procedure Calls," *ACM Transactions on Computer Systems*, 2(1), February 1984, pp. 114–122.
11. D. Parnas, "On The Criteria To Be Used In Decomposing Systems Into Modules," *Communications of the ACM*, 15(12), 1972, pp. 1053–1058.
12. E. Gamma, R. Helm, R. Johnson, J. Vlissides, *Design Patterns: Elements of Reusable Object-Oriented Software*, Addison-Wesley, 1995.
13. J. Waldo, G. Wyant, A. Wollrath, S. Kendall, "A Note on Distributed Computing." Technical Report SMLI TR-94-29. Sun Microsystems Laboratories, Inc, 1994.
14. D. Schmidt, M. Stal, H. Rohnert, F. Buschmann, *Pattern-Oriented Software Architecture, Vol. 2: Patterns for Concurrent and Networked Objects*, John Wiley & Sons, Ltd, 200.
15. L. Zahn, T. Dineen, P. Leach, E. Martin, N. Mishkin, J. Pato, & G. Wyant, *Network Computing Architecture*, Prentice-Hall, 1990.
16. Sun Microsystems, "RPC: Remote Procedure Call Protocol Specification," Technical Report RFC-1057, Sun Microsystems, Inc., June 1988.
17. W. Rosenberry, D. Kenney, and G. Fischer. 1992. *Understanding DCE*, O'Reilly and Associates, Inc.
18. B. Liskov, "The Argus Language and System," In M. Paul and H.J. Siegert, editor, Distributed Systems—Methods and Tools for Specification, Lecture Notes in Computer Science no. 190, Springer Verlag, 1985, pp. 343–430.
19. G. Almes, A. Black, E. Lazowska and J. Noe, "The Eden System: A technical Review," *IEEE Transactions on Software Engineering*, SE-11(1), 1985, pp. 43–59.
20. A. Black, N. Hutchinson, E. Jul, H. Levy, and L. Carter. "Distribution and Abstract Types in Emerald," *IEEE Transactions on Software Engineering*, SE-13(1), 1987, pp. 65–76.

21. C. Horn and S. Krakowiak. "Object Oriented Architecture for Distributed Office Systems." In ESPRIT '87: Achievements and Impact, North-Holland, 1987.
22. S. Vinoski. "Toward Integration: It's Just a Mapping Problem," *IEEE Internet Computing*, 7(3), May/June 2003, pp. 88–90.
23. M. Henning. "A New Approach to Object-Oriented Middleware," *IEEE Internet Computing*, 8(1), 2004, pp. 66–75.
24. Sun Microsystems. *J2EE 1.4 Platform Specification*. Available online at `http://java.sun.com/j2ee/`, November 2003.
25. D. Box, *Essential COM*, Addison-Wesley, 1998.
26. World Wide Web Consortium (W3C). 2003. "SOAP Version 1.2." Available online at `http://www.w3.org/TR/SOAP/`.
27. E. Newcomer, *Understanding Web services: XML, WSDL, SOAP, and UDDI*, Addison-Wesley, 2002.
28. World Wide Web Consortium. "Web Services Description Language(WSDL) Version 2.0 Part 1: Core Language," W3C Working Draft, 10 November 2003, available online at `http://www.w3.org/TR/wsdl20/`.
29. S. Vinoski, "Toward Integration: Web Services Interaction Models, Part 1: Current Practice," *IEEE Internet Computing*, 6(3), May/June 2002, pp. 89–91.
30. S. Vinoski. "Toward Integration: Web Services Interaction Models, Part 2: Putting the 'Web' Into Web Services," *IEEE Internet Computing*, 6(4), July/Aug 2002, pp. 90–92.
31. S. Vinoski, "Toward Integration: Integration With Web Services," *IEEE Internet Computing*, 7(6), Nov/Dec 2003, pp. 75–77.
32. D. C. Schmidt and F. Kuhns, "An Overview of the Real-time CORBA Specification," *IEEE Computer Magazine*, 33(6), June 2000, pp. 56–63.
33. I. Foster, "The Grid: A New Infrastructure for 21st Century Science," *Physics Today*, 55(2), February 2002, available online at `http://www.aip.org/pt/vol-55/iss-2/p42.html`.
34. I. Foster, C. Kesselman, J. Nick, S. Tuecke, "Grid Services for Distributed System Integration." *IEEE Computer*, 35(6), June 2002, pp. 37–46.
35. *IEEE Network* Special Issue on Middleware Technologies for Future Communication Networks, Edited by D. Schmidt, G. Blair, and A. Campbell, Vol 18, No. 1, January/February 2004.

Static Deadlock Detection in the Linux Kernel

Peter T. Breuer and M. García Valls

Universidad Carlos III de Madrid

Abstract. This article describes a C code static analyser that detects misuse of spinlocks in the Linux kernel. Spinlock misuse is difficult to detect by testing, relatively common, and leads to runtime deadlocks in the Linux operating system kernel on multiprocessor architectures.

1 Introduction

The Linux operating system kernel currently deploys on 15 different architectural platforms, ranging from embedded ARM systems through Sun SPARC to the ubiquitous IBM PC. As distributed, the kernel source now comprises some 3.5 million lines of code. The code is mostly C, plus some assembler. Of this total, some 85% is architecture-independent, and the remaining 15% provides low-level support for the various architectures, including the multiprocessor support. The latter importantly comprises assembler level implementations for the "spinlock" primitives: lock, and unlock. Spinlocks are the discretionary mutual exclusion mechanism of choice in the kernel. A spinlock will keep other kernel threads out of a spinlocked region of code while that code is being executed.

A spinlock is a busy wait on a counter in the spinlock structure in memory. When that counter drops to zero, the busy loop simultaneously exits and sets the counter to one via machine code that achieves the required atomicity in a multiprocessor context. Setting the counter is called "locking" or "taking" the spinlock, and no other thread of control can take the spinlock via the lock primitive while the counter remains set. A thread which tries will spin in a busy loop until the counter is reset. To "unlock" or "release" the spinlock, the counter is (atomically) set to zero again by the same thread of control that took the spinlock.

The spinlock mechanism is effective for guarding short stretches of code that do not call other routines and which take a very short time to process, because it is faster to spinlock the other processor out, and take the penalty of spinning the processor uselessly until the short stretch of code has been processed, than it would be to select and swap in some other code and context for the other processor to execute meanwhile. But spinlocks are easy to accidentally misuse.

Spinlocks can give rise to runtime deadlocks in various ways. For example, attempting to take the same spinlock again while already within a spinlocked region of code is a deadlock. The processor will spin in the busy loop within the spinlock lock call, waiting for itself to release its own spinlock, which it will never do. Linux spinlocks are by design not recursive; that is, they do lock against a

A. Llamosí and A. Strohmeier (Eds.): Ada-Europe 2004, LNCS 3063, pp. 52–64, 2004.

thread of execution taking the very same spinlock that it has already taken. One reason for this design decision is the extra operational overhead of the accounting that would be required for recursive spinlocks. Another reason is the process-engineering argument that non-recursive spinlocks make coding errors easier to find, because they can cause deadlocks much more easily. Both arguments have historically been prominent in debates over spinlocks on the Linux kernel mailing list, the principal communication channel among kernel developers, so they should be accepted. Whatever the rationale for it, the decision has been in force since multiprocessor support was first introduced into the Linux kernel, and as a result, Linux spinlocks are non-recursive.

It is certainly the case, however, that there are some debugging mechanisms that can be activated in the kernel that can detect spinlock deadlocks at runtime. In order to enable these mechanisms, the kernel has to be compiled in debugging mode for spinlocks, and with certain watchdog functions and monitors included. But in practice, these detection mechanisms are rarely used by authors – often authors will be unaware of their existence, or will not have a multiprocessor platform on which to test. They are also often not used simply because they require recompiling the whole kernel and extra drivers in an inconvenient and binary incompatible way. And of course the mechanisms only detect spinlock deadlocks that occur, not those that do not occur during the testing. In practice, deadlocks are encountered not by the authors who might be able to apply the debugging techniques, but by users, who are not able to apply them.

Even recursive spinlocks would not liberate the kernel from runtime deadlocks through many of the common mistakes of coding or design. For a counter-example, it suffices to consider two threads which take each others spinlocks. For example, given two spinlocks A and B, and two threads, if thread 1 takes spinlock A then B (while still under A) on one processor, and thread 2 takes spinlock B then A (while still under B) on another processor, there is a small deadlock window. The deadlock occurs if thread 1 takes A, then thread 2 takes B before thread 1 does. In that situation thread 1 (and the processor it occupies) spin waiting for B to be released, but thread 2 (and its processor) spin waiting for A to be released, and neither can progress.

The latter deadlock is relatively easy to evoke via coding errors, because different authors may decide to take two common spinlocks in a different order. But there are still easier and more common deadlocks – which will be described later in this article. All in all, the kernel source code is rife with hazard for authors in the multiprocessor setting, but at least some of the hazards can be reliably detected by code analysis - a virtual "dry run" that can detect possible deadlocks through the appropriate abstract interpretation [6] of the kernel C code. This article describes

1. a prototype tool which detects certain types of deadlock in the kernel code, and
2. the several different deadlock mechanisms detected and the technique used to detect them.

Parsing the kernel C code creates some difficulties of its own. The variant of C used in the Linux kernel is not ANSI C but "Gnu C", an extension of ANSI C the syntax of which is only well-documented by the code of the Gnu C compiler itself, and these particular extensions make a single token lookahead (1TLA) parse particularly difficult. (The Gnu C compiler code is freely available under the conditions of the General Public License (GPL) version 2 from the Free Software Foundation (FSF). The Linux kernel code is heavily dependent on several of the Gnu extensions, notably "__attribute__" modifiers for variables and functions, and the "__asm__" assembler inserts, so it is impossible to avoid treating the Gnu C extensions. A top-down unbounded lookahead C parser [1] for Gnu C based on a context-free grammar was rapidly developed as the basis for the syntax analyser (development time for the grammar was about 3 man-weeks, comprising 24 revisions, for 844 lines of code and 59 grammar productions).

The principal algorithms of this paper are presented in Section 2, as implemented in the present prototype analyser. Examples of use are given in Section 3. Section 4 discusses future planned extensions which detect more types of coded deadlocks.

2   Sleep under Spinlock

The most common mistake leading to deadlock in kernel programming is rescheduling a running thread while it holds a spinlock. This is also called "sleeping under spinlock". "Scheduling" refers to removing the thread from the processor, and passing control to another thread of execution instead. In this situation, the only thread that will release the spinlock is not running. If another thread tries to take the spinlock, it will busy-wait on the spinlock in the processor, keeping the owner thread out and preventing any further progress.

The only hope is for the owner thread to be brought back in by an interrupt or to be brought back in by the process scheduler on another processor, and release the spinlock. But it may well be the case that interrupts are being held off, or that all processors too rapidly become occupied by threads spinning on the blocked spinlock. This is the case if the spinlock is ubiquitously used in the kernel, such as the I/O spinlock for example (in the 2.4 series kernels, there is a single global I/O spinlock).

"Scheduling" is often called "sleeping" because from the thread's point of view it looks as though it has gone to sleep for a while. The common way of causing a thread to sleep is to call one of the many kernel functions with "sleep" or "wait" in their name (or simply, call "schedule()"). That works by directly or indirectly causing the thread to be scheduled out of the processor.

Thus sleep under spinlock happens when the author calls a function that sleeps while still holding a spinlock. To avoid the possibility, experienced kernel authors try never to hold a spinlock over any stretch of code that calls any other function at all. But they can be deceived by macros, and by some common exceptions – some kernel functions are intended to be called under spinlock and this encourages the occasional call under spinlock. The standard kernel end_request function (which is used to signal that processing of a kernel read/write request has completed) is perhaps the most common example – it is intended to be called with the I/O spinlock held. The existence of such conventions and the occasional changes to them that take place can cause sufficient confusion that sleep under spinlock does occur often in practice. Usually, the author has called some function under spinlock that was at one time safe to call under spinlock (because it did not sleep) and the function has since been altered so that it now does sleep. Simply asking for or freeing kernel heap memory is enough to allow a function to sleep. So the replacement in the code of a statically preallocated structure by one obtained from the heap on first demand is enough to provoke this kind of error. Semi-formally:

Definition 1. *It is said that a kernel function* may sleep *if, informally,*

1. *it is one of a certain set of basic kernel functions, including, among others, kmalloc, kfree, schedule, interruptible_sleep_on, interruptible_sleep_on_timeout, down, down_interruptible; or*
2. *it calls a function that may sleep.*

To make the following discussion easier, we will use the term "piece of code" in a formally defined way:

Definition 2. *A* piece of code *here means a linear sequence of (semicolon terminated) statements.*

A "statement" may be a labelled statement, switch statement or conditional, for or while or do loop, a goto, continue, break or return, an inline assembler statement, a block of statements, an expression used as a statement (including an assignment or function call), or an empty statement (semicolon). Gotos and returns indicate termination of a linear code sequence, and may only appear at the end of a sequence, or at the end of a block within the sequence.

We say that a piece of code may sleep when its set of execution paths includes a call to a function that may sleep. Formally:

Definition 3. *A* piece of code *may sleep if it contains a call to a kernel function that may sleep.*

A piece of code will take and release spinlocks along its execution paths. A section that begins with a lock call is spinlocked until the following unlock call:

Definition 4. *It is said of a piece of code that it is* spinlocked *(once) if, informally,*

1. *it begins with a call to one of a certain set of basic kernel functions (the* spinlock *functions), including, among others, spin_lock, spin_try_lock, spin_lock_irqsave, read_lock, write_lock, write_lock_irqsave, read_lock_irqsave; and*

2. *it does not contain a call to any of a certain distinct set of basic kernel functions (the* spinunlock *functions), including, among others,* spin_unlock, spin_unlock_irq, spin_unlock_irqrestore, read_unlock, write_unlock, read_unlock_irqrestore, write_unlock_irqrestore.

A spinlocked piece of code begins with a spinlock call and thereafter has an excess of at least one spinlock call over spinunlock calls throughout its length. That is to say, at least one spinlock is actively held through all its execution paths.

Definition 5. *A piece of code may sleep under spinlock if it is both spinlocked and may sleep.*

A function may sleep under spinlock if its body contains a piece of code that may sleep under spinlock.

A well-formed piece of kernel code will have balanced spinlock and spinunlock calls. In the region under spinlock, the definitions above make a call to a function that may sleep computably a "sleep under spinlock", as will be detailed below.

In the absence of gotos a compositional analysis suffices. Gotos are not common in the kernel code, but they do occur. As to whether they should be treated or ignored, it is a question of how accurate and in what direction the analysis should err on the side of, and that question will be dealt with later. In the following paragraphs we present three syntactic computations, $N[\ldots]$, $R[\ldots]$, $B[\ldots]$, which together determine the spinlock imbalance in a piece of *structured* code, if there is any imbalance. They respectively represent the spinlock imbalance through to a *normal* exit (falling off the end of a piece of code), through to a *return* statement, and to a *break* statement.

This analysis is based on a generic 3-phase programming logic [2,3]. The logic binds a pre-condition for execution, a post-condition, and an exception-condition to every imperative statement. In the present case, the except-condition represents the state on break out from the normal sequential programming flow via a continue, break or similar imperative. The post-condition represents the state on reaching the end of a piece of code.

Given that n is the spinlock call imbalance measured to a certain point in the code, $N[\ldots]_n$ is the function that measures the imbalance that has been attained by time of the normal exit that occurs through control falling off the end of the piece of code. While-loops and the continue and break statements they may contain will in a few paragraphs time be treated by recursion through computations with B and R, but here first of all for expositional purposes is an *approximate* stand-alone computation with N alone. Alternatively, it may be regarded as a computation that supposes that there are no continues and breaks within loops. The difference between it and the (refined) computations that follow is in the treatment of loops:

$$N[a; b; \ldots; z;]_n = N[b; \ldots; z;]_{N[a;]_n} \tag{1}$$
$$N[spinlock(\ldots)]_n = n + 1$$

$$N[spinunlock(\ldots)]_n = n - 1$$
$$N[\text{if } (a) \ b; \text{ else } c;]_n = \max(N[b;]_n, N[c;]_n)$$
$$N[\text{while } (a) \ b;]_n = \max(n, N[b;]_n * \infty)$$
$$N[a = b;]_n = n$$
$$N[f(a, b, \ldots, z);]_n = n$$

The computation on expressions (apart from assignments and function calls used as statements) is suppressed in the above. In Gnu C, expressions can be a sequence of statements ($\{a; b; \ldots z; \}$) in parentheses and braces, so the computation on expressions need not be completely trivial, but the result of the computation on expressions will always be zero in practice, so we represent it as such above. Incidentally, the value of such a "statement expression" (a block of code in parentheses and braces) is that bound to the last statement in the sequence of statements, which can be and usually is a simple expression.

The reason that function calls are evaluated as zero above is that functions are normally already balanced as a whole with respect to spinlock calls, so there will be no imbalance imported by a function call. If there were an imbalance, the error, and it is a coding style error, would already have been flagged by the spinlock imbalance calculation on the function concerned. But of course different spinlock imbalance values than zero can be assigned to particular functions, if necessary. The spinlock call itself is an example of such.

On any other statements than those listed explicitly above in (1), the computation evaluates as *NaN* (Not a Number). That is true of particular of continue and break statements and returns. The convention is that *NaN does not count in a max and combines to form another NaN in a sum.* This means that paths leading to an early continue or break or return are not counted in the $N[\ldots]$ calculation. Only those paths which reach and fall off the end of the code are counted in $N[\ldots]$.

Modulo the obvious provisos due to possible invisible aliasing in C (a spinlock call can be invisible if a renamed pointer to the function is used instead):

Proposition 6. *The computation (1) above overestimates the imbalance in spinlock calls over a piece of code, if there exists any.*

It is an *abstract interpretation* [6] of structured C code into the domain of integers.

In particular, the $N[\ldots]$ measure (1) across a *loop* whose body is unbalanced is infinite. This is in order to make the abstract interpretation across loops always correct – it is not known a priori how often the loop will cycle, so any positive imbalance must be overestimated to infinity. In normal circumstances a loop body will be balanced, because a spinlock will be taken and released during every turn through the loop. However, the following form is common when the test must be made under spinlock, and it always evaluates (inappropriately) to infinity under the computation above. It is an infinite loop with a conditional break-out:

```
spinlock(...);
while (1) {
    ...
    if (...) {
        spinunlock(...);                                    (*)
        break;
    }
    ...
}
```

This example makes it clear that the pieces of code in the loop leading inevitably to a break out of the loop should not be counted in the loop body, since they cannot repeat, but without a full control-flow analysis it is difficult to determine which pieces of code should be counted and which should not. That is why the N calculation given above in general needs refinement in order to be useful. In the following it is refined making use of the promised B and R calculations. The approach simplifies particularly if we make a simplifying assumption:

Assumption 1. *There is at most one spinlock imbalance in any code considered, and it is positive (i.e. more spinlock than spinunlock calls).*

Then it is not necessary to overestimate loop imbalances out to infinity, because if the imbalance is in the loop it will be counted as one and not masked by other contributions elsewhere – since they will all be zero –, and if it is elsewhere, then the loop contribution will not mask it because the loop contribution will be zero. In particular, the spinlock call imbalance in an infinite while loop can be calculated looking along the paths to an exceptional *break* exit from the loop, calculated using the $B[...]$ computation given in the following paragraphs.

$$N[\text{while } (1) \ b;]_n = B[b;]_n \tag{$1'$}$$

and in the more general case:

$$N[\text{while } (a) \ b;]_n = N[\text{while } (1) \ \{\text{if } (\tilde{\ }a) \text{ break}; \ b; \}]_n = B[\text{if } (\tilde{\ }a) \text{ break}; \ b;]_n$$

The calculation $(1')$ amounts to supposing that each while-loop is traversed exactly once, thus treating it like an if-statement. The formal statement that this calculation suffices is:

Proposition 7. *Under the simplifying assumption of only at most one spinlock call imbalance, the computation $(1')$ elaborated by $(2,3)$ in the following paragraphs overestimates the imbalance of spinlock calls if there is any.*

The modified calculation gives the example code fragment $(*)$ an evaluation of zero, which is correct. The loop evaluates as -1, since there is a spinunlock call on the way out of it, and there is a spinlock call before the loop, which counts as $+1$. The $B[\ldots]$ (break) calculation on the loop discards the branch that does not lead to the break, leaving only the -1 on the break path.

Picking out the code sequences which lead to a break within a structured loop is done by the parser. The imbalance to an exceptional exit via break is given in full by the following computation:

$$B[a; b; \ldots; z;]_n = \max(B[a]_n, B[b; \ldots; z]_{N[a;]_n}) \qquad (2)$$
$$B[\text{if } (a)\ b; \text{else } c;]_n = \max(B[b;]_n, B[c;]_n)$$
$$B[\text{break};]_n = n$$

Any other statement than those listed simply gets the value NaN (Not a Number), and by convention, $\max(x, NaN) = x$. So a code path that does not terminate in a break is simply not counted here.

In similar style, the following computation calculates the spinlock call imbalance along a path leading to a return statement:

$$R[a; b; \ldots; z;]_n = \max(R[a]_n, R[b; \ldots; z]_{N[a;]_n}) \qquad (3)$$
$$R[\text{if } (a)\ b; \text{else } c;]_n = \max(R[b;]_n, R[c;]_n)$$
$$R[\text{while } (a)\ b;]_n = R[b;]_n$$
$$R[\text{return } a;]_n = n$$

and any other statement gets the value NaN.

This gives the spinlock imbalance in a function definition: it is $R[b;]$ where $b;$ is the body of the function. If the function has a void return type, then it may be necessary to add an extra return at the end of the code body before processing. The main point of the (slightly contorted) computations above, is, however, that they can be carried out in a side-effecting way, as stated below:

Proposition 8. *The subscript n in the computations for N, B and R above represents the spinlock imbalance at the start of the code that corresponds to the argument of N, B, R.*

It suffices to apply R to a function body, and maintain the count n, starting from 0. As the code is deconstructed syntactically by the recursion, the computation (of all three measures at once) moves down various code paths, incrementing and decrementing n. Those paths leading to an if-statement one of whose branches leads to a return and the other to a break, for example, will still be traversed exactly once by the calculation, which will then split into sub-calculations for the two branches. The sub-calculations may eventually be discarded (if for example, the top-level calculation is an N and neither branch from the if-statement terminates "normally"), but the value of n at any point on the linear sequence leading to the if-statement will not change as the calculation progresses.

Proposition 9. *Sleep under spinlock is detected when a call to a function that sleeps is made at a point in the code where the value of n in the computation above for the spinlock imbalance is positive.*

What to do about gotos? The approach described can be extended to deal with any finite number of labelled statements that are the target of gotos. But once gotos become an influential factor in the evaluation of code, the situation is already desperate for the code! Their use in the Linux kernel is generally restricted to code for state-machines, in which the jumps are all similar to the cases in a switch. However there are other occasions where they are difficult to treat. One approach is to perform a full analysis along those execution paths that lead forwards, discarding the backwards-going paths. Another approach is to treat each labelled statement as the start of an (interior) subroutine and gotos as calls to that subroutine, at which point the analysis given so far in this paper applies.

3   Example

The following code comes from the request-handling routine of a network-adapted version of Alessandro Rubini's sbull device, a simple block device that stores data in a block of reserved memory and returns it on request. The code deals with the queue of requests sent by the kernel to the device.

```
while(1) {
    INIT_REQUEST;   /* returns when queue is empty */

    /* Which "device" are we using? */
    device = sbull_locate_device (CURRENT);
    if (device == NULL) {
        end_request(0);
        continue;
    }

    /* Perform the transfer and clean up. */
    wake_up_interruptible(&cli);
    interruptible_sleep_on(&dbr);
    spin_lock(&device->lock);
    status = sbull_transfer(device, CURRENT);
    spin_unlock(&device->lock);
    end_request(status);
}
```

Among the dangerous coding practices in this code is that it calls a routine, sbull_transfer, under spinlock, so that routine must not sleep. However, the whole routine here is itself called under spinlock – the global kernel "I/O" spinlock, and it is indeed essential that the end_request routine be called with that spinlock held. There is no call to unlock the I/O spinlock here, so it is held throughout, so the interruptible_sleep_on routine (which, as the name implies, does sleep) is implicitly being called under the I/O spinlock!

Running the prototype code analyser over the 592 lines (16K characters) of the sbull driver code, it first of all expands the code to 28165 lines (34K characters) by pulling in the following #include header files, and their #includes, and expanding the macros:

```
#include <linux/config.h>
#include <linux/module.h>
#include <linux/sched.h>
#include <linux/kernel.h>  /* printk() */
#include <linux/slab.h>    /* kmalloc() */
#include <linux/vmalloc.h> /* vmalloc() */
#include <linux/fs.h>      /* everything... */
#include <linux/errno.h>   /* error codes */
#include <linux/timer.h>
#include <linux/types.h>   /* size_t */
#include <linux/fcntl.h>   /* O_ACCMODE */
#include <linux/hdreg.h>   /* HDIO_GETGEO */
#include <asm/system.h>    /* cli(), *_flags */
#include <asm/uaccess.h>   /* access_ok() */
#include <linux/blk.h>
#include "sbull.h"         /* local definitions */
#include <linux/blkpg.h>   /* blk_ioctl() */
```

The analyser detects over 10000 references to functions and local variables in the expanded code, which it resolves down to base definition locations, and it finds six new inline functions in the #include chain that can sleep:

```
smb_lock_server  is sleepy because it calls down
lock_parent      is sleepy because it calls down
double_down      is sleepy because it calls down
triple_down      is sleepy because it calls down
double_lock      is sleepy because it calls double_down
lock_super       is sleepy because it calls down
```

and identifies three functions in the sbull driver that can sleep, of which the first is the function whose code body is largely quoted above:

```
sbull_request   is sleepy because it calls interruptible_sleep_on
sbull_init      is sleepy because it calls kfree
sbull_cleanup   is sleepy because it calls kfree
```

It identifies no "sleep under spinlock" errors. Without knowing that the sbull request function is called under the I/O spinlock, the analyser has nothing to flag, but it does notice that the routine can sleep. If the request function code is itself altered by interchanging just two lines so that it reads (line numbers added at left, lines 418 and 419 are the interchanged pair):

```
        . . .
416     /* Perform the transfer and clean up. */
417     wake_up_interruptible(&cli);
418     spin_lock(&device->lock);
419     interruptible_sleep_on(&dbr);
        . . .
```

then the analyser spots the problem and flags it:

```
***
*** sleep under spinlock at file="sbull.c" about line=419
***
```

(the location is sometimes approximate for implementational reasons).

4   Other Spinlock Coding Errors

In this section deadlock detection techniques not yet implemented in the proto-type analyser are discussed.

There are two further common coding errors by authors leading to deadlock in the Linux kernel:

1. taking a spinlock again while still under the same spinlock;
2. taking two different spinlocks in different orders, one under the other.

The algorithm of the last section can be altered to indicate *which* spinlock, given a suitable classification method, is currently active at any point in the code. But finding out that a called function takes a particular spinlock is *type* information.

The information on which spinlocks are taken by a function can be collected in the same way as information on whether a function sleeps or not is collected – by looking for instances of spinlock calls within the body, but taking note of the parameter to the spinlock call and constructing different counts for the different objects referenced. There are generally two types of object to which the parameter resolves:

(i)   the address of a global, itself a spinlock structure;
(ii) the address of a spinlock field in a structure passed by address as a parameter to the function.

What can be said in the later case is usually "the function takes a spinlock referenced in field x of the first parameter to the function", or similar. The "first parameter" will usually be a structure representing the whole device to a device driver, or some other equally pivotal object for the code module in question.

There are two typing techniques that can be applied to the spinlocks encountered:

(a) type as object – using the built-in resolution capabilities of the analyser to resolve spinlock references back to an original, also extending the resolution mechanism to trace back through function call parameters;
(b) sub-classing the spinlock type – assigning a special type to the spinlock field in a given structure type, and modify the type mechanism of C so that functions are determined to have the following kind of extra trait (italics):

> `int f(*A,...)` *takes spinlock of type* `*A_lock,` `...;`

The case (i), global spinlock references, is handled well enough via the mechanism (a), aliasing in C notwithstanding. A modified spinlock imbalance calculation can determine if a call to a function that takes a spinlock x is made while the spinlock x is already being held.

But, particularly when resolving spinlock references back through function parameters in function calls, the technique is not guaranteed to detect a real error even when it is there. That is because opaque aliasing in C can easily hide the identity of the spinlocks. If an error is detected, however, then it is guaranteed to be real. That is, false negatives are possible, but not false positives.

In the case (ii), spinlocks chiefly passed through the fields of structs passed by reference, the technique (b) may be more suitable. A modified spinlock imbalance calculation can determine if a call to a function that takes a spinlock of type t is ever made while a spinlock of type t is being held.

This test does not necessarily represent a real programming error when it triggers, but if there is a real error, then this analysis technique detects it. That is, false positives are possible, but there are no false negatives. Together, the two tests are very informative.

Detecting inconsistent uses of spinlock A under spinlock B versus spinlock B under spinlock A is a question of typing the spinlocks, so that they get the following kind of extra trait (italics):

> `spinlock &lo->lock` *is used under spinlock* `&io_lock`, ...;

This is a call graph, and it can be constructed as the spinlock calls are encountered during a run of a modified spinlock imbalance counting algorithm, one that counts per-spinlock. If the spinlock call graph contains a cycle, then there is a possible deadlock in the code. The technique gives no false positives, but does allow false negatives, through opaque C aliasing.

This technique can also be adapted to work with types. It suffices to note the calls of which type of spinlock under which other type of spinlock:

> `spinlock *A_lock` *is used under spinlock* `*B_lock`, ...;

In that case the results will show false positives, but no false negatives.

5   Source Code

Source code for the prototype C analyser discussed in this article can be found at `ftp://oboe.it.uc3m.es/pub/Programs/c-1.0.tgz`. The code was released under GPL on the Linux kernel mailing list in March 2003. In an earlier correspondence, Linus Torvalds had stated to one of the authors of the present paper that it was his aim also to produce such an analyser. The publication of the code excited comment from at least one other group aiming at analysing kernel C code. David Wagner remarked that the group were producing an alpha release of their own design [5] (MOPS – MOdelchecking Programs for Security properties, see `http://www.cs.berkeley.edu/~daw/mops/` – is a modelchecker which checks for violation of certain "defensive programming" rules in C code).

6   Summary

This article has described a C code static analyser which detects code authoring abuses that lead to certain types of deadlock in the Linux operating system kernel on multiprocessor architectures. An example run has been illustrated.

This is deliberately a "cheap" implementation of a formal method that adds an assurance of safety to Linux kernel code. It is intended to be widely accessible – it requires no special tool support, just a C compiler and Makefile. The underlying thinking here is that it is much more important in the context of open source to be 1% useful to 10,000 authors, than to be 100% useful to only 10 of them. It does not matter if there are better techniques "out there" because they are neither cheap (in the appropriate sense, whether it be financial or intellectual investment) nor widely available in the Linux context. It is important to set an extremely low entry barrier for the use of a formal method in that context.

References

1. P.T. Breuer and J.P. Bowen. A PREttier Compiler-Compiler: Generating higher order parsers in C. *Software — Practice & Experience*, 25(11):1263–1297, November 1995.
2. P.T. Breuer, N. Martínez Madrid, L. Sánchez, A. Marín, and C. Delgado Kloos. A formal method for specification and refinement of real-time systems. In *Proc. 8'th EuroMicro Workshop on Real Time Systems*, pages 34–42. IEEE Press. July 1996. L'aquilla, Italy.
3. P.T. Breuer, C. Delgado Kloos, N. Martínez Madrid, A. López Marin, L. Sánchez. A Refinement Calculus for the Synthesis of Verified Digital or Analog Hardware Descriptions in VHDL. *ACM Transactions on Programming Languages and Systems (TOPLAS)* 19(4):586–616, July 1997.
4. P.T. Breuer. A Formal Model for the Block Device Subsystem of the Linux Kernel. In *Proc. 5th International Conference on Formal Engineering Methods, ICFEM 2003*, pages 599-619. J.S. Dong and J. Woodcock (Eds), Springer-Verlag, LNCS 2885. Singapore, 5-7 Nov. 2003.
5. Hao Chen and David Wagner. MOPS: An infrastructure for examining security properties of software. In *Proc. Ninth ACM Conference on Computer and Communications Security (CCS-9)*. Washington DC, 18-22 November 2002.
6. P. Cousot and R. Cousot, Abstract interpretation: A unified lattice model for static analysis of programs by construction or approximation of fixpoints, In *Proc. 4th ACM Symposium on the Principles of Programming Languages*, pages 238–252, 1977.
7. E.S. Raymond. *The Cathedral and the Bazaar*, Cambridge: O'Reilly & Associates, 1999.
8. A. Rubini. *Linux Device Drivers*. O'Reilly, Sebastopol CA, Feb. 1998.

Extracting Ada 95 Objects from Legacy Ada Programs

Ricky E. Sward

Department of Computer Science
U.S. Air Force Academy, CO 80840
719-333-7664
ricky.sward@usafa.af.mil

Abstract. Maintaining legacy code can be challenging and time consuming. As code reaches the point where it becomes hard to maintain, developers may wish to convert from code designed using structured analysis and design techniques into code designed using the object-oriented analysis and design methodology. This paper describes one method, Parameter-Based Object Identification (PBOI) that uses information about parameters passed between sub-programs to extract objects and classes from legacy code. The PBOI method is applied to legacy Ada code with examples showing how objects and classes are extracted and built using Ada 95 programming constructs. Transformations that preserve the functionality of the legacy code are used to extract the Ada 95 code.

1 Introduction

As programs age and continue through their maintenance phase, they often become *legacy code* that is a challenge to maintain and update. At times, even small changes to the code can have far reaching effects on the entire system. Because of the paradigm shift from imperative to object-oriented, code that was developed using structured analysis and design is not easily transformed into objects and classes. Legacy imperative code must be reverse engineered to some higher level of abstraction and then forward engineered into the object paradigm.

This paper describes work that is being done to re-engineer legacy imperative Ada code into objects and classes in Ada 95 code. This re-engineering is accomplished using the Parameter-Based Object Identification (PBOI) methodology developed by Sward [7]. Sward showed that the transformations in the PBOI methodology preserve the functionality of the original legacy code [7]. Instead of relying on extensive test suites, a formal proof was presented to show that the extracted object design is functionally equivalent to the legacy code. The original PBOI methodology was based on a generic imperative model (GIM) intermediate language instead of Ada [8]. The work presented in this paper focuses on applying PBOI to Ada code instead of the GIM. The proof of functional equivalence was done using the GIM, so a new proof for Ada is needed and is left as future work. The Ada examples in this paper come from a legacy system that was built to schedule students into workshops. The scheduling system consists of 13 files and 6,196 lines of code.

A. Llamosí and A. Strohmeier (Eds.): Ada-Europe 2004, LNCS 3063, pp. 65–77, 2004.

2   Related Work

There have been several methods presented for extracting objects from legacy imperative code. Liu and Wilde [2] define two such methodologies. Global-Based Object Identification (GBOI) extracts objects from legacy code by grouping the subprograms together that act on the same global variables. Type-Based Object Identification (TBOI) extracts objects by using the data types of the parameters being passed to sub-programs. Lividas and Johnson [3] add a third methodology called Receiver-Based Object Identification (RBOI). This method extracts objects by using the data types of the *out* parameters of sub-programs. Newcomb [4] defines a method for extracting objects from COBOL code that are *functionally faithful* to the legacy code. Ong and Tsai [5] extract objects from FORTRAN code based on the COMMON blocks of data items in the legacy code.

One common weakness of these methods is their reliance on the structure of the imperative legacy code as built by the original programmer. If the programmer has used global variables and data types in the right way, then meaningful objects can be extracted. The PBOI methodology presented in this paper extracts objects using a more extensive view of how data is passed throughout the system. There is no claim that the PBOI methodology extracts semantic objects from the problem domain, nor do any of the previous methods claim this. However, if the object-oriented design is functionally equivalent to the legacy system, then the design is quite valuable. Such a design can replace the legacy system and provide the same functionality while being maintained in the object-oriented paradigm. Unlike the previous methods, a formal proof has been provided by Sward [7] showing that PBOI maintains the functionality.

3   Parameter-Based Object Identification

The overall rational for PBOI is that objects can be recognized in imperative legacy code by examining the parameters that are being passed from one sub-program to another. The parameters are transformed into attributes of objects using specific transformations. Classes that define the attributes of these objects are built and the sub-programs are converted into methods of these classes. Because of the reliance on parameters being passed between sub-programs, the PBOI methodology requires that all data items are either passed as parameters to the sub-programs or declared as local variables. Systems that do not follow this convention must be converted appropriately. This constraint ensures that the main program is the origin of all data items being passed to the called sub-programs. Processing of the legacy code begins with the main program, but each of the sub-programs called from the main program is transformed before the main program is transformed. In addition, any sub-programs that are called by these sub-programs are transformed first creating a depth-first approach to transforming the Ada code. Circular procedure calls and recursion are not allowed placing another constraint on systems to be converted. The depth-first approach of PBOI results in several intermediate designs being merged at different steps of the transformation. The following sub-sections describe the PBOI transformations.

3.1 Taxonomy of Sub-programs

In order to classify and partition the transformations required for each sub-program in a legacy system, a taxonomy of sub-programs was developed. The taxonomy is built on whether or not a sub-program produces data items and on whether or not a sub-program includes procedure call statements that invoke other sub-programs. An Ada sub-program *produces* a data item if that data item appears as an *out* or *in out* parameter of the sub-program. Table 1 shows the taxonomy of sub-programs.

Table 1. Taxonomy of sub-programs

	Produces 0 or 1 data items	**Produces > 1 data item**
Calls 0	Category 2	Category 4
Calls > 0	Category 3	Category 5

Originally, the taxonomy included Category 0 and Category 1 sub-programs that produced zero data items and included zero or more calls, respectively. Because of the similarity between these categories of sub-programs, Category 0 and Category 2 were combined and Category 1 and Category 3 were combined. The following sections discuss the particular categories and give examples of how they are processed using PBOI.

3.2 Category 2 Sub-programs

Category 2 sub-programs produce zero or one data items and call no other programs. If we consider the call structure of a legacy system as a tree, Category 2 sub-programs appear as leaf nodes and are transformed first using PBOI's depth-first approach. To transform these sub-programs, an analogous entity is needed from the object paradigm. In his Object Modeling Technique, Rumbaugh [6] defines a method that produces a value but includes only the target object as a parameter as a *derived attribute*.

```
procedure Deschedule_Student ( Period     : in      Integer;
                  Length    : in      Integer;
                  Name      : in      String_Ten;
                  Scheduled : in out Integer_Array_Type ) is
   End_Period : Integer;
begin
   End_Period := Period + Length - 1;
   for I in Period .. End_Period loop
      Scheduled(I)  := 0;
   end loop;
end Deschedule_Student;
```

Fig. 1. Category 2 sub-program

```
type Class_1 is tagged record
      Period    : Integer;
      Length    : Integer;
      Name      : String_Ten;
      Scheduled : Integer_Array_Type;
end record;

procedure Deschedule_Student ( C_1 : in out Class_1 ) is
   End_Period : Integer;
begin
   End_Period := C_1.Period + C_1.Length - 1;
   for I in C_1.Period .. End_Period loop
      C_1.Scheduled(I) := 0;
   end loop;
end Deschedule_Student;
```

Fig. 2. Class and method for Deschedule_Student

Using this rational, the formal parameters of a Category 2 sub-program are converted into attributes of a class and the sub-program is transformed into a method of that class. For example, Figure 1 shows a Category 2 sub-program. This sub-program is transformed into a class and method as shown in Figure 2. The type Class_1 defines a new class in Ada 95 having four attributes Period, Length, Name, and Scheduled. The method Deschedule_Student now has a single parameter of type Class_1, namely C_1. In the body of the procedure, all accesses to the parameters have been replaced by Ada 95 accesses to attributes of objects. Using this rationale, all Category 2 sub-programs are converted to object-oriented Ada 95 code.

3.3 Category 3 Sub-programs

Category 3 sub-programs produce zero or one data items and call other subprograms. Because of the depth-first nature of the PBOI methodology, the transformation of Category 3 sub-programs analyzes and makes changes to the object-oriented design.

As an example, consider the Category 3 sub-program shown in Figure 3, which calls the Deschedule_Student sub-program shown in Figure 1. The first step in transforming the Category 3 sub-program is to build a temporary class and method that includes the formal parameters from the sub-program as attributes of the class just as was done for Category 2 sub-programs. Figure 4 shows this first, temporary class and method built for the Check_Minimum_Enrollment sub-program. Here, the formal parameters have been replaced by an object, C_2, which is an instance of Class_2. Class_2 currently includes all the formal parameters from the original sub-program as attributes of the class. Each of the references to the parameters has now been transformed into references to the attributes of the C_2 object, for example Enrollment and Length. Also notice that the call to Deschedule_Student has not yet been transformed into the object-oriented design. We will transform the call after adjusting the design as needed.

At this point, four cases are considered in order to update the object-oriented design. These cases are based on whether or not a formal parameter is passed as an actual to a called program and on whether or not an actual parameter has been converted to an attribute of an object or not. These cases determine whether or not an attribute will remain part of a class or is removed. Each of these cases is described in detail in the following sub-sections.

```
procedure Check_Minimum_Enrollment (
      Name            : in       String_Ten;
      Scheduled       : in out Integer_Array;
      Length          : in       Integer;
      Min_Enrollment : in       Integer_Array;
      Enrollment      : in       Integer_Array  ) is
   End_Period      : Integer;
begin
   for Period in 1 .. 10 loop
      if (Enrollment(Period) < Min_Enrollment(Period)) then
         Deschedule_Student (
               Period    => Period,
               Length    => Length,
               Name      => Name,
               Scheduled => Scheduled);
         End_Period := Period + Length - 1;
      end if;
   end loop;
end Check_Minimum_Enrollment;
```

Fig. 3. Category 3 sub-program Check_Minimum_Enrollment

```
type Class_2 is tagged record
      Name             : String_Ten;
      Scheduled        : Integer_Array_Type;
      Length           : Integer;
      Min_Enrollment : Integer_Array_Type;
      Enrollment       : Integer_Array_Type;
end record;

procedure Check_Minimum_Enrollment ( C_2 : in out Class_2  ) is
   End_Period : Integer;
begin
   for Period in 1 .. 10 loop
      if ( C_2.Enrollment(Period) < C_2.Min_Enrollment(Period) ) then
         Deschedule_Student (
               Period    => Period,
               Length    => Length,
               Name      => Name,
               Scheduled => Scheduled);
         End_Period:= Period + C_2.Length - 1;
      end if;
   end loop;
end Check_Minimum_Enrollment;
```

Fig. 4. Initial, temporary class and method

3.3.1 PBOI Case 1

In this first case, an actual parameter in a sub-program call is also a formal parameter of the calling sub-program and the actual parameter has been transformed into an attribute of a class. In this case, we have found an object that is being passed from one sub-program to another, so the object-oriented design is transformed in order to reflect this object properly.

For example, in Figure 4, examine the Length, Name and Scheduled parameters in the call to Deschedule_Student. These are actual parameters in the call to the sub-program that are also formal parameters of the calling sub-program. These parameters have already been transformed into attributes of Class_1 as shown in Figure 2. This indicates that the instance of Class_1 is being passed down through the calling sub-program, so we need to update the design to reflect this. Each of the attributes of Class_1 should remain attributes of Class_1 and be removed as attributes from Class_2. Figure 5 shows this new object-oriented design.

```
type Class_1 is tagged record
       Period    : Integer;
       Length    : Integer;
       Name      : String_Ten;
       Scheduled : Integer_Array_Type;
end record;

type Class_2 is tagged record
       Min_Enrollment : Integer_Array_Type;
       Enrollment     : Integer_Array_Type;
end record;
```

Fig. 5. New object-oriented design

Figure 6 shows the updated Check_Minimum_Enrollment method. Here, a new object instance of Class_1, C_3, is built as a formal parameter of Check_Minimum_Enrollment and any of the attribute references are updated to reflect the correct class. For example, since Length is now an attribute of Class_1, we reference it from C_3 as shown on line 9.

```
1) procedure Check_Minimum_Enrollment (
2)         C_2 : in out Class_2;
3)         C_3 : in out Class_1'Class  ) is
4)      End_Period : Integer;
5) begin
6)      for Period in 1 .. 10 loop
7)          if (C_2.Enrollment(Period)<C_2.Min_Enrollment(Period)) then
8)              Deschedule_Student( C_3 );
9)              End_Period:= Period + C_3.Length - 1;
10)         end if;
11)     end loop;
12) end Check_Minimum_Enrollment;
```

Fig. 6. Updated Check_Minimum_Enrollment

Next, we can replace the call to the Deschedule_Student sub-program with a call to the method in Class_1. We include the instance C_3 as the only parameter in the call to the method, as shown on line 8 of Figure 6. Note that since we want this method to dispatch on the object instance C_2, but not C_3, we must add the 'Class modifier to the declaration of C_3 as shown on line 3 of Figure 6.

3.3.2 PBOI Case 2

In this case for Category 3 sub-programs, an actual parameter in a sub-program call is also a formal parameter of the calling sub-program, but the actual parameter has *not* been transformed into an attribute of a class. Since the parameter appears as a formal parameter in the calling sub-program, it will have been converted temporarily into an attribute, so it is transformed back into a formal parameter of the calling sub-program.

```
procedure Deschedule_Student ( C_1      : in out Class_1;
                               Length : in      Integer);
```

Fig. 7. Contrived version of Deschedule_Student

For example, consider a *contrived* example of the method built for the Deschedule_Student method as shown in Figure 7. In this version of Deschedule_Student, the Length attribute appears as an actual parameter to Deschedule_Student along with the object C_1. Since it was a formal parameter of the Check_Minimum_Enrollment sub-program, the Length parameter was temporarily converted to an attribute of Class_2, as shown in Figure 4. However, since Length in our contrived example is now a parameter to the method Deschedule_Student, we transform the Length attribute back into a formal parameter of the Check_Minimum_Enrollment method. The rationale for this case is that the transformation of the called sub-program has already happened and it was determined at a lower level to move the attribute back to a formal parameter of the method. At the higher level, that decision will be propagated by moving the attribute back to a formal parameter of the calling method as well.

3.3.3 PBOI Case 3

In the third PBOI case, an actual parameter in a sub-program call is not a formal parameter of the calling sub-program. However, the actual parameter has been transformed into an attribute of a class. In this case, the original transformation of the called sub-program resulted in the parameter being transformed into an attribute of a class. At this higher level, we see that the parameter is not being passed down from a parameter in the calling sub-program, but instead is a local variable of the calling sub-program. In this case, we remove the attribute from the class and adjust the object-oriented design to reflect this class properly.

```
type Class_1 is tagged record
      Length     : Integer;
      Name       : String_Ten;
      Scheduled : Integer_Array_Type;
end record;

procedure Deschedule_Student (
      C_1     : in out Class_1;
      Period : in      Integer );
```

Fig. 8. Updated class and method for Deschedule_Student

As an example, consider the class and method built for the Deschedule_Student sub-program presented in Figure 2. Note that the parameter Period is an attribute of Class_1. Also consider the initial, temporary method built for Check_Minimum_Enrollment presented in Figure 4. Note that in Check_Minimum_Enrollment, the variable Period is a local variable of the for loop. This example illustrates the condition for PBOI Case 3 since Period is an attribute of Class_1 but appears as a local variable in the Check_Minimum_Enrollment method. Using the transformation for PBOI Case 3, Period is transformed from an attribute of Class_1 into a parameter of the Deschedule_Student method, as shown in Figure 8.

The Check_Minimum_Enrollment method is updated to reflect the new design by including the proper call to the Deschedule_Student method with Period as an actual parameter to the method. Figure 9 shows this updated method.

```
1) procedure Check_Minimum_Enrollment (
2)         C_2     : in out Class_2;
3)         C_3     : in out Class_1'Class  ) is
4)      End_Period : Integer;
5) begin
6)      for Period in 1 .. 10 loop
7)          if ( C_2.Enrollment(Period) <
8)               C_2.Min_Enrollment(Period) ) then
9)              Deschedule_Student( C_3, Period );
10)             End_Period:= Period + C_2.Length - 1;
11)         end if;
12)     end loop;
13) end Check_Minimum_Enrollment;
```

Fig. 9. Updated Check_Minimum_Enrollment

3.3.4 PBOI Case 4

In this fourth PBOI case, an actual parameter in a sub-program call is not a formal parameter of the calling sub-program, but the actual parameter has not been transformed into an attribute of a class. In this case, there is no change required in the object-oriented design.

For example, consider the updated version of Deschedule_Student as shown in Figure 8. In this method, Period is passed as a parameter and is not an attribute of Class_1. To illustrate, consider the *contrived* example where this updated version is initially considered when transforming Check_Minimum_Enrollment. Here, we see that Period appears in Check_Minimum_Enrollment as a local variable. In this case, Period is a parameter of the called method and is not a formal parameter of the calling sub-program. The conditions of PBOI Case 4 indicate that this is the right decision for the object-oriented design, thus no changes are needed.

In summary, it should be noted that when transforming a Category 3 sub-program each parameter is tested to see which of the four PBOI cases applies to it and that case is applied to that parameter. In this way, each parameter and/or attribute is placed in the desired location in the object-oriented design according to the PBOI method.

3.4 Category 4 Sub-programs

Category 4 sub-programs produce multiple data items, but do not call other sub-programs. For these sub-programs, we use a technique called *program slicing* [10, 9] that *projects* the behavior of a sub-program needed to produce a specific data item. By using program slicing, each Category 4 sub-program is sliced into two or more Category 2 sub-programs, one for each of the data items produced by the Category 4 subprogram. The new slices are then transformed using the PBOI method for Category 2 sub-programs. See [9] for examples of program slicing.

3.5 Category 5 Sub-programs

Category 5 sub-programs produce multiple data items and call other sub-programs. These sub-programs are also split using *program slicing* and produce either Category 2 or Category 3 sub-programs. The new slices are then transformed using the PBOI method for Category 2 or Category 3 sub-programs.

3.6 Converting the Main Program

The final step of the transformation of the legacy system is to convert the main program into the object-oriented design. The main program provides a unique opportunity to transform the object-oriented design that has been built up to this point. The depth-first nature of the PBOI method implies that all the sub-programs in the system will have already been transformed into methods. In order to transform the main program, a single method is built for the main program and any calls to other sub-programs are converted to calls to the corresponding methods. To transform the sub-program calls to method calls, all object instances needed for the method calls must be built in the main program.

Recall that one of the constraints on systems being transformed by the PBOI methodology is that all sub-program variables are either parameters or local variables. This means that the main program is the source of all data items passed to sub-programs in the system. Since the object instances are created from the variables in the original main program, care must be taken not to duplicate these variables in the object-oriented design. At this point, further refinement of the object-oriented design can be performed based on the assumption that any attributes which can be linked to the same main program variable are part of the same object. As part of the refinement, *duplicate object instances* are removed and *overlapping classes* are merged as explained below.

```
-- other code from original main program
C_5 := (Name => Name, Length => Length, Scheduled => Schedule);
C_4 := (Name => Name, Length => Length, Scheduled => Schedule);
-- other code from original main program
```

Fig. 10. Duplicate object instances C_4 and C_5

```
-- other code from original main program
C_6 := (Name => Name, Length => Length, Scheduled => Schedule);
-- other code from original main program
```

Fig. 11. Duplicate object instances removed

Consider Figure 10 where objects C_4 and C_5 are built as instances of Class_1 (shown in Figure 8) and built using the same variables from the main program. Since this introduces duplicate attributes, the declarations of the two objects C_4 and C_5 are replaced by a single instance of Class_1, namely C_6, as shown in Figure 11.

The second transformation that can be done at this point is the *merging of overlapping* classes. Under the assumption that any attributes which can be linked to the same main program variable are part of the same object, a class *overlaps* another class when an instance of each class is built using at least one common variable from the original main program. Merging overlapping classes avoids introducing duplicate attributes into the object-oriented design. Two classes are merged by using the union of the attributes and the methods of the classes to build one new class.

As an example, Figure 12 shows the classes and methods built for two subprograms along with the main program method that includes the instantiations of the required objects. As you can see in Figure 12, both C_10 and C_11 are built using the Num_Students main program variable. According to the assumption that any attributes which can be linked to the same main program variable are part of the same object, Class_3 and Class_4 overlap and are merged. Figure 13 shows the results of merging Class_3 and Class_4 into a new class, Class_5, which includes the union of the attributes from Class_3 and Class_4 as its attributes. It also includes the methods from Class_3 and from Class_4 as its methods. Note that the objects passed to the methods are now instances of Class_5. In the main program method, the two instances C_10 and C_11 have been replaced by a new instance of Class_5, namely C_12, which now passed to the method calls in the main program method.

The transformation of the main program provides a final opportunity to modify the object-oriented design being extracted from the legacy Ada code. Each object needed for the method calls is created, duplicate objects are eliminated and overlapping classes are merged.

4   Using ASIS

The prototype implementation of the PBOI method is being built using the Ada Semantic Interface Specification (ASIS) interface [1]. The AdaSlicer tool [9] used for the program slicing portion of the PBOI method has already been implemented using version 3.15a1 of the GNAT compiler and the ASIS interface.

The built-in procedures in the ASIS implementation provide easy access to complicated Ada programming constructs such as the modes and data types of parameters. For example, the pairings of actual and formal parameters in calls to subprograms are easily accessed using procedures already provided in ASIS. The built-in procedures in ASIS use terminology found in the Ada Language Reference Manual, so learning and using the ASIS interface is straightforward.

```
type Class_3 is tagged record
   Highest_Max  : Integer;
   Num_Students : Integer;
end record;

procedure Gather_Summary_Info_Highest_Max (
      C_8 : in out Class_3 );

type Class_4 is tagged record
   Lowest_Min   : Integer;
   Num_Students : Integer;
end record;

procedure Gather_Summary_Info_Lowest_Min (
      C_9 : in out Class_4 );

procedure Main_Program is
   C_10 : Class_3;
   C_11 : Class_4;
   -- other main program variable declarations
begin
   -- other code from original main program
   C_10 := (Highest_Max=>Highest_Max, Num_Students=>Num_Students);
   Gather_Summary_Info_Highest_Max( C_10 );
   C_11 := (Lowest_Min => Lowest_Min, Num_Students => Num_Students);
   Gather_Summary_Info_Lowest_Min( C_11 );
   -- other code from original main program
end Main_Program;
```

Fig. 12. Classes and methods before merging

```
type Class_5 is tagged record
   Highest_Max  : Integer;
   Num_Students : Integer;
   Lowest_Min   : Integer;
end record;

procedure Gather_Summary_Info_Highest_Max (
      C_8 : in out Class_5 );

procedure Gather_Summary_Info_Lowest_Min (
      C_9 : in out Class_5 );

procedure Main_Program is
   C_12 : Class_5;
   -- other main program variable declarations
begin
   -- other code from original main program
   C_12 := (Highest_Max => Highest_Max, Num_Students => Num_Students,
            Lowest_Min => Lowest_Min);
   Gather_Summary_Info_Highest_Max( C_12 );
   Gather_Summary_Info_Lowest_Min( C_12 );
   -- other code from original main program
end Main_Program;
```

Fig. 13. Classes and methods after merging

One particularly useful feature of ASIS is the ability to traverse from one part of an Ada program to another. For example, given a variable that appears in a statement, a *semantic reference* can be used in ASIS to retrieve the declaration of the variable or the declaration of its data type. The ASIS procedures that provide this semantic link eliminate the need to search the parse tree for the information making ASIS a powerful tool for developing applications.

5   Future Directions

A prototype version of the PBOI methodology has already been implemented based on the generic intermediate language. Currently, only the program slicing tool, AdaSlicer [9], and the Category 2 transformation have been implemented for Ada procedures. It must be expanded to include functions, generics and tasks. In the future, we plan to compare object-oriented designs recovered manually by students against the designs recovered automatically by the PBOI tool. There is currently no semantic value associated with the classes extracted from the legacy Ada code, but future versions will allow the user to input the name of a class. We will also experiment with allowing the user to interact with the design decisions being made during the extraction process. Formal proofs showing that the PBOI transformations preserve the functionality of the legacy code have been done for the GIM [7]. These proofs need to be redone for the transformations of the Ada code. By using formal methods to prove the transformations preserve functionality, a functionally equivalent object-oriented design can be extracted from the legacy Ada code without needing to rely on extensive test suites.

Overall, the PBOI method provides a valuable tool for re-engineering legacy Ada code into objects and classes in Ada 95.

References

[1] *ASIS Basic Concepts.* Retrieved June 3, 2003, from www.acm.org/sigada/wg/asiswg /basics.html, 1998.
[2] Liu, S. S. and N. Wilde. Identifying objects in a conventional procedural language: An example of data design recovery. In *Proceedings of the Conference on Software Maintenance*, pages 266-271, IEEE, Nov 1990.
[3] Lividas, P. E. and T. Johnson. A new approach to finding objects in programs. *Technical Report SERC-TR-63-F.* University of Florida, June 1993.
[4] Newcomb, P. Re-engineering procedural into object-oriented systems. In *Proceedings of the Second Working Conference on Reverse Engineering*, Los Alamitos, CA, Jul 1995. IEEE Computer Society and ACM SIGSOFT.
[5] Ong, C.L. and W.T. Tsai. Class and object extraction from imperative code. *Journal of Object-Oriented Programming*, 6(1):58-68, Mar 1993.
[6] Rumbaugh, J. and M. Blaha. *Object-Oriented Modeling and Design.* Prentice-Hall, Inc., New Jersey, 1991.

[7] Sward, R.E. Extracting Functionally Equivalent Object-Oriented Designs from Legacy Imperative Code. PhD Thesis, Air Force Institute of Technology, Wright-Patterson AFB, OH, Sep 1997.

[8] Sward, R.E. and Hartrum, T.C. Extracting objects from legacy imperative code. In *Proceedings of the 12th IEEE International Conference on Automated Software Engineering*, Incline Village, Nevada, November 1997, pp. 98-106.

[9] Sward, R.E. and A.T. Chamillard, AdaSlicer: A Program Slicer for Ada. *Proceedings of the ACM International SIGAda 2003 Conference*, Dec 2003, San Diego, CA.

[10] Weiser, M. Program slicing. *IEEE Transactions on Software Engineering*, SE-10(4):352-357, July 1984.

On the Tree Width of Ada Programs

Bernd Burgstaller[1], Johann Blieberger[1], and Bernhard Scholz[2]

[1] Institute for Computer-Aided Automation, TU Vienna, Treitlstr. 1–3, A-1040
Vienna, Austria, {blieb,bburg}@auto.tuwien.ac.at
[2] School of Information Technologies, Madsen Building, F09, University of Sydney
NSW 2006, Australia, scholz@it.usyd.edu.au

Abstract. The tree width of a graph G measures how close G is to
being a tree or a series-parallel graph. Many well-known problems that
are otherwise NP-complete can be solved efficiently if the underlying
graph structure is restricted to one of fixed tree width.

In this paper we prove that the tree width of goto-free Ada programs
without labeled loops is ≤ 6. In addition we show that both the use of
gotos and the use of labeled loops can result in unbounded tree widths
of Ada programs.

The latter result suggested to study the tree width of actual Ada programs. We implemented a tool capable of calculating tight upper bounds
of the tree width of a given Ada program efficiently. The results show
that most existing Ada code has small tree width and thus allows efficient automatic static analysis for many well-known problems and – as
a by-product – most Ada programs are very close to series-parallel programs.

1 Introduction

The notion *tree width* has originally been introduced by Robertson and Seymour [RS83]. Intuitively, the tree width of a graph G measures how close G is
to being a tree or a series-parallel graph. In this way the tree width of a tree
equals 1 and the tree width of a series-parallel graph is 2. For more general
graphs the tree width increases more and more.

Many well-known problems that are otherwise NP-complete can be solved
efficiently (i.e. in polynomial time) if the underlying graph structure is restricted
to one of fixed tree width (cf. e.g. [ALS91]). See also [Bod93] for a survey. Our
particular interest in the tree width of Ada programs stems from the fact that a
well-known approach to find the *worst-case execution time (WCET)* of a program
([PK89]) can be determined in linear time if the underlying *control flow-graph
(CFG)* has tree width k. This follows easily from [ALS91] where it is proved
that all graph properties definable in monadic second-order logic (MS) with
quantification over vertex and edge sets can be decided in linear time for classes
of graphs of fixed bounded tree width, because the approach to find the WCET
mentioned above is expressible in MS.

In [Tho98] Thorup presents a measure called k-complexity that is equivalent
to the original definition of tree width given by Robertson and Seymour [RS83].

A. Llamosí and A. Strohmeier (Eds.): Ada-Europe 2004, LNCS 3063, pp. 78–90, 2004.
© Springer-Verlag Berlin Heidelberg 2004

Based on the notion of k-complexity Thorup shows in [Tho98] that goto-free Algol and Pascal programs have control flow-graphs of tree width ≤ 3, that Modula-2 programs have control flow-graphs of tree width ≤ 5, and that goto-free C programs have control flow-graphs of tree width ≤ 6.

In particular, Thorup's definition can be used for implementing a parser for a certain programming language in order to compute actual data on the tree width of existing code. This method has been used by Gustedt, Mæhle, and Telle to study the tree width of actual Java programs [GMT02]. We discuss this method in Section 2.

The impact of Ada's very rich set of language features on the resulting tree width of programs is described in Section 3. A restricted class of Ada programs is shown in Section 4 to have tree width ≤ 6. However, in general, Ada programs turn out to have non-bounded tree width, which is proved in Section 5.

In this way it is of paramount interest to study actual Ada programs to find statistics on their tree width. Implementation details of our tool are described in Section 6; the results of the study are given and discussed in Section 7. We conclude our paper in Section 8.

2 On the k-Complexity of Graphs

The notion of tree width was introduced by Robertson and Seymour [RS83]. It is based on a tree-decomposition of a graph:

Definition 1. *A tree-decomposition of a graph $G = (V, E)$ is defined by a tree $T = (I, F)$ together with a family $\{W_i\}_{i \in I}$ of subsets of V such that:*

1. *$\bigcup_{i \in I} W_i$ is V.*
2. *for all edges $(v, w) \in E$, there exists an $i \in I$ such that $\{v, w\} \subseteq W_i$.*
3. *for all $i, j, k \in I$, if j is on the path from i to k then $W_i \cap W_k \subseteq W_j$.*

The width of the decomposition is $\max_{i \in I} |W_i| - 1$ and the tree-width of G is the minimal width over all tree-decompositions of G.

Thorup [Tho98] introduced k-complexity of a graph and showed that if a graph is k-complex then the tree width of this graph is k and vice versa. The k-complexity of a graph uses the notion of a listing $L = v_1, \ldots, v_n$ that is an ordered set of the vertices.

Definition 2. *Given a graph G, a $(\leq k)$-complex listing is a listing of vertices of G such that for every vertex $v \in V$, there is a set S_v of at most k of the vertices preceding v in the listing, whose deletion from G separates v in G from all the vertices preceding v in the listing. In this case, we say that G is $(\leq k)$-complex. The set S_v is referred to as the* separator set *of v in the listing.*

Figure 1 (a) shows a simple program, a corresponding control flow graph (b) and a listing (c) with its separator sets of the vertices. In the example we have seven control flow nodes. To demonstrate the separator sets we have chosen an arbitrary listing. For this given listing the minimal separator sets can be computed as outlined in Section 4 of Thorup's work [Tho98]. Note that for Definition 2 directed arcs in CFGs have to be replaced with undirected edges.

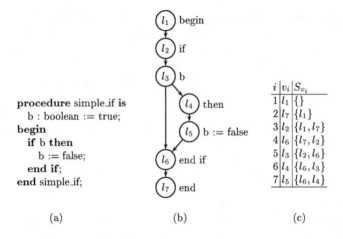

```
procedure simple_if is
    b : boolean := true;
begin
    if b then
        b := false;
    end if;
end simple_if;
```

i	v_i	S_{v_i}
1	l_1	$\{\}$
2	l_7	$\{l_1\}$
3	l_2	$\{l_1, l_7\}$
4	l_6	$\{l_7, l_2\}$
5	l_3	$\{l_2, l_6\}$
6	l_4	$\{l_6, l_3\}$
7	l_5	$\{l_6, l_4\}$

(a)   (b)   (c)

Fig. 1. Example: Simple If-Statement

The importance of k-complexity compared to the original definition of tree width comes from the fact that k-complexity can be computed easily for CFGs based on the syntax of the underlying programming language. In terms of the *Abstract Syntax Tree (AST)* it can be implemented by a simple traversal of the AST.

Definition 3. *Given a graph G, a vertex of the graph and its separator set S_v, we define a S-path from node v to a node $w \in S_v$ to be a path from v to w which does not contain a node $u \in S_v$ ($u \neq w$). Let G_v be a subgraph of G which contains v and all nodes lying on S-paths from v to nodes in S_v. The nodes of S_v themselves are not contained in G_v.*

In Figure 1 node l_4 has separator set $S_{l_4} = \{l_6, l_3\}$. Graph G_{l_4} contains the nodes l_4 and l_5. Note that l_5 has a greater listing number than l_4. It is easy to check that all nodes of Figure 1 fulfill the condition that G_v only contains vertices whose listing number is greater than the listing number of v.

For the remainder of this section we use the program shown in Figure 2 (a) as a running example. For sake of simplicity we address nodes by their listing number and do not specify the mapping between labels and listing numbers anymore. This simple example consists of 10 nodes and, therefore, there are $10! = 3628800$ different listings according to Definition 2. Generating all possible listings in order to determine the minimum choice with respect to k-complexity constitutes a computationally intractable problem for the general case. For this reason Thorup [Tho98] proposes a method for calculating the k-complexity based on the syntax of the underlying programming language. In accordance with Definition 2 this method consists of two steps, namely the derivation of a listing from a given CFG, and the generation of the corresponding separator sets. The following two subsections present an overview of this method. For further details the reader is referred to [Tho98] Section 2.

Derivation of a Listing from a CFG. Each program expressible in a certain programming language can be derived from a starting non-terminal symbol by

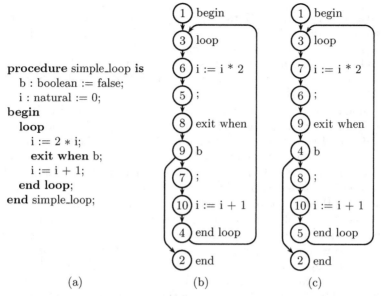

Fig. 2. Example: Simple Loop with Exit Statement

applying a number of productions. Thorup's central idea is to assign numbers to the terminals of a production when it is applied to a sentential. The numbers are assigned from left to right. It is common to assign numbers also to the semi-colons which separate statements from each other [Tho98].

To return to our example (Figures 2 (a) and 2 (b)), the terminal **begin** of the procedure *simple_loop* gets assigned number 1 and the corresponding terminal **end** gets assigned 2. The next production is the one producing the loop statement. Thus the terminal **loop** gets number 3 and the terminal **end loop** gets 4. The next terminal to consider is the semi-colon after the first statement of the loop body; it gets number 5. The first statement itself, namely i := 2 * i, gets assigned 6.

It is not necessary to perform this method on a level deeper than that of "basic" statements such as assignments, null statements, procedure calls and so on. For this method these basic statements are also considered "terminals" of a production. However it turns out that boolean expressions of if-statements or exit statements have to be examined more carefully because the k-complexity is increased if the boolean expression contains short-circuit operators such as **or else** and **and then** [KP98].

Hence the semi-colon after the exit statements gets assigned 7 and the exit statement itself gets 8. After that the condition of the exit statement is examined. Since in our case it consists of an atom only, this atom **b** gets number 9.

The only remaining statement is the assignment after the exit which gets number 10.

It is clear that generating a k-complex listing by this method can be done in time linear in the size of the program.

Generation of Separator Sets. Thorup's method allows for calculating the separator sets during the generation of the k-complex listing as described above. The separator set of a certain statement (node) can be determined from the CFG predecessors and from the CFG successors of the node. Thorup calls these nodes *potential neighbors*. In fact, neighbors are defined for subgraphs the nodes of which are subtrees of the corresponding AST.

The topmost view of our example consists of the terminal **begin**, the loop-statement, and the terminal **end**. The loop statement consist of nodes 3, 6, 5, 8, 9, 7, 10, and 4 (cf. Figure 2 (b)). The potential neighbors of the loop-statement are therefore node 1, which is the CFG predecessor of this statement, and node 2, its CFG successor. Thorup calls neighbors like the first one *in-neighbors* and those of the second kind *out-neighbors*.

In addition there are also *exit*-neighbors. An exit-neighbor is the target node of the exit-statement of a loop if the exit-condition evaluates to *true*.

In the second view of our example (after applying the production that derives the loop body) we find that the exit-neighbor of the statement sequence between **loop** and **end loop** of the loop body is node 2. The in-neighbor of this statement sequence is node 3 and its out-neighbor is node 4.

In the third view (after the production that derives the first statement of the statement sequence) the in-neighbor of node 6 is node 3 and its out-neighbor is node 5.

Similarly the in-neighbor of the exit-statement (nodes 8 and 9) is node 5 and its out-neighbor is node 7.

Traversing the exit-statement we find that the in-neighbor of node 8 is node 5 and its out-neighbor is node 7. The boolean expression in node 9 has in-neighbor 8 and out-neighbor 7.

Finally, the in-neighbor of node 10 is node 7 and its out-neighbor is node 4.

The separator sets can now be determined based on the type of the statement and its neighbors. For an assignment statement the separator set contains its in- and out-neighbors. In this way, node 6 has separator set $S_6 = \{3, 5\}$.

For an exit-statement the corresponding separator set contains its in-, out-, and exit-neighbors. Hence $S_8 = \{5, 7, 2\}$ and $S_9 = \{8, 7, 2\}$.

For a node corresponding to a semi-colon, the separator set contains its in-, out-, and exit-neighbors. For example $S_5 = \{3, 4, 2\}$.

Summing up we conclude that the separator sets can also be determined in linear time by Thorup's method.

Finally we would like to note that more complex programs require the notion of *stop-neighbors* due to the occurrence of return-statements. In terms of the CFG such a return-statement introduces an edge from the **return** to the **end**.

Discussion of Thorup's Method. Thorup's method is well fitted to determine upper bounds of the tree width for certain programming languages. For example Thorup [Tho98] shows that all Modula-2 programs have tree width ≤ 5 and that goto-free C programs have tree width ≤ 6.

For our running example (cf. Figure 2) Thorup's method calculates a tree width of 3. We did a complete enumeration of all possible listings for this example. Of all 3628800 cases 872 produced a tree width of 3 and 3627928 produced a tree width of 2. So in this case Thorup's method only finds an upper bound for the tree-width!

In the following we discuss some other serious drawbacks of Thorup's method.

1. First, it considers *potential* neighbors and not *actual* neighbors. For example a loop without an exit statement (quite common for non-terminating loops in server tasks) will have potential exit-neighbors. But since there is no exit-statement, the statement succeeding the **end loop** cannot be reached. Thus there is no path from the start node to this node. Nevertheless Thorup's method still lists the start node as an in-neighbor for this "dead" node.

   Employing synthesized attributes [ASU88] for the calculation of the neighbors would enable Thorup's algorithm to derive the *actual* neighbors from the *potential* neighbors. However, the only synthesized attribute used is the listing number (cf. [Tho98]).

2. Second, Thorup's method always assumes that all conditions contain short-circuit expressions. Although he shows how the nodes of CFGs can be renumbered if the boolean expressions do not contain short-circuit expressions, his method silently assumes that conditions consisting of a single atom, are short-circuit. This renumbering in general produces listings with smaller separator sets.

   However, Thorup performs renumbering only on a small number of nodes local to the if-statement. In contrast the renumbering below touches almost all nodes of the loop enclosing the exit statement. This kind of renumbering is not mentioned in [Tho98] and shows again that Thorup's method produces upper bounds only.

   If we introduce the renumbering $6 \to 7$, $5 \to 6$, $8 \to 9$, $9 \to 4$, $7 \to 8$, and $4 \to 5$ in our example (cf. Figure 2 (c)), the separator sets change to: $S_7 = \{3, 6\}$, $S_6 = \{3, 4\}$, $S_9 = \{6, 4\}$, $S_4 = \{3, 2\}$, $S_8 = \{4, 5\}$, $S_{10} = \{8, 5\}$, and $S_5 = \{3, 2\}$. Hence the tree width decreases from 3 to 2 by this renumbering. As a side-note we mention that this renumbering also works for more complex exit conditions but the condition must not contain short-circuit expressions.

A simple work-around to get rid of problem (1) is to generate a k-complex listing with Thorup's method, but instead of applying Thorup's neighbor based method use a "greedy" algorithm that calculates the separator set for node v by traversing the paths of graph G_v (Definition 3). This results in a method using time quadratic in the size of the program.

3   Tree Width of Ada Programs

In [Tho98] Thorup studies the following language features that are known to increase the tree width:

- *short-circuit expressions* in conditions of if-statements,
- *multiple returns* from subroutines, and
- *exits* from unlabeled loops.

In addition to the language features studied by Thorup, Ada provides the following features:

```
procedure Ada_Worst_Case is
    A, B, C, D, E, F, G, H, I, J: boolean:= true;
begin
    if A then return;
    end if;
    if not A then raise constraint_error; end if;
    loop
        if B then
            if C or else D then
                if E then return;
                end if;
                exit when F;
                if not A then raise constraint_error; end if;
            else
                if G then return;
                end if;
                exit when H;
                if not A then raise constraint_error; end if;
            end if;
        end if;
        if I then return;
        end if;
        exit when J;
        if not A then raise constraint_error; end if;
    end loop;
    if not A then raise constraint_error; end if;
exception
    when others =>
        return;
end Ada_Worst_Case;
```

Fig. 3. Example: Restricted Ada Program with Largest Possible Tree Width

- *elsif* and *case statements*,
- both *short-circuit expressions* and *non-short-circuit expressions* in a single boolean expression,
- *for-loops* and *while-loops*,
- *multiple exits* from labeled loops,
- *conditional exits* from loops[1],
- *exceptions* and *exception handlers*, and
- *tasks* and *protected objects*.

Thorup's method can be modified to handle elsif- and case-statements correctly.

Conditions containing both short-circuit expressions and non-short-circuit expressions require a delicate treatment but can also be treated correctly.

While-loops that do not interfere with other language features, in general have a tree width of 3 except when their condition is atomic, i.e., does not

---

[1] Thorup uses exit-statements enclosed in if-statements to model conditional exits.

contain any of **not, and, or, and then,** and **or else** statements. In this case their tree width is 2. For-loops also result in a tree width of 2.

Multi-exit loops and their consequences are discussed in Section 5.

Conditional exits are handled as if-statements with an unconditional exit in the then branch.

Since our primary interest is in static program analysis, we do not model the exact dynamic semantics of exceptions. Instead we assume that if an exception is raised, it is handled by the nearest statically enclosing exception handler. Note also that we only model explicitly raised exceptions. We therefore do not account for exceptions raised by the runtime system due to faults such as division by zero or failed subtype range checks.

Nevertheless exceptions give rise to a new kind of neighbors, so-called *raise-neighbors*. The raise-neighbor of a certain statement is the node corresponding to the start of the exception handler of the enclosing block.

Tasks and protected objects are handled correctly, including all different forms of select statements, which are treated like case and if-statements. The abort statement is treated only partially correct. A fully correct treatment would imply that every task must be aware of an abort at any time. We assume that an abort statement is only used to abort the task itself, thus the corresponding CFG has an additional edge from the abort statement to the CFG's end node.

4 The Class of (≤ 6)-Complex Ada Programs

Considering Ada programs without gotos and without labeled loops[2], we know that the tree width of such programs is bounded above by 6. The reason for this is that Ada adds short-circuit expressions, exit statements, multiple return statements and exceptions to series-parallel programs. Since each of these features adds 1 to the tree width, we get 6 as an upper bound for the tree width of these restricted Ada programs. In fact we can construct a program whose tree width assumes the largest possible value. Such a program is shown in Figure 3.

Program `Ada_Worst_Case` is an extension of a program given in [Tho98]. The program studied there contains a 6-clique which is trivially 5-complex. Our program adds an exception handler and raise-statements which – as can be seen easily – results in a 7-clique being contained in the corresponding contracted CFG[3].

Thus we have proved the following theorem.

Theorem 1. *Ada programs without gotos and without labeled loops are of tree width ≤ 6.* □

---

[2] Gotos and labeled loops will be studied in Section 5.

[3] A thorough treatment makes use of Lemma 6 of [Tho98] which allows contracting some nodes of a CFG into one node without increasing the complexity (tree width).

```
procedure non_bounded is
   C1, C2, C3, C4 : boolean := true;
begin
   L1: loop
     L2: loop
       L3: loop exit L1 when C1; exit L2 when C2; exit L3 when C3;
         ≪I≫ loop exit L1 when C1; exit L2 when C2; exit L3 when C3;
               exit when C4; end loop;
         ≪R≫ exit L1 when C1; exit L2 when C2; exit L3 when C3; end loop L3;
       ≪B3≫ exit L1 when C1; exit L2 when C2; end loop L2;
     ≪B2≫ exit L1 when C1; end loop L1;
   ≪B1≫ null;
end non_bounded;
```

Fig. 4. Example: Four Nested Loops

5   The Class of Ada Programs with Non-bounded Tree Width

First of all, Ada has a goto statement. Hence it is possible to write Ada programs whose CFGs contain k-cliques for any k. The tree width of such graphs is $k - 1$ and thus can be arbitrarily large.

In the following we restrict our interest to goto-free Ada programs. Statistics for the usage of gotos in Ada programs have been given by Gellerich et al. [GKP96].

Gustedt et al. [GMT02] find that labeled break and continue statements are responsible for the fact that Java programs result in CFGs of non-bounded tree width. In contrast Ada supports some form of labeled break statement, the exit from a labeled loop, but no continue statement. Anyway, we are able to prove that Ada programs result in CFGs of non-bounded tree width.

Theorem 2. *For any value of $k \geq 0$ there exists a goto-free Ada program with k nested loops such that its control flow-graph has tree width $\geq k + 1$.*

Proof. Figure 4 shows four nested loops with several exits statements which have been labeled to facilitate the proof.

In the following we again apply Lemma 6 proved in [Tho98] which can be used to contract nodes of a CFG into one node without increasing the complexity (tree width).

We will show in the following that the statements I, R, L3, B3, B2, and B1 form a 6-clique, by looking at them in the above order and arguing that each of them is connected to all the ones following it in the given order.

First, the node I is connected to all the other nodes, as the control flows from it to R via the last exit-statement, control flows naturally into I from L3, and for the remaining statements I contains exit-statements targeting that node.

Next, R is connected to L3 as this is the natural flow of control and R contains exit-statements targeting the statements following it in the given order. The argument for the remaining statements follows a similar line of reasoning.

Thus the CFG for the example in Figure 4 contains a 6-clique.

It is easy to prove by induction that this is also true for k nested loops. In this case the statements involved are I, R, L{k-1}, B{k-1}, ... , B2, and B1. These form a $k+2$-clique and the theorem is proved.   □

Corollary 1. *From Theorem 2 it follows that even goto-free Ada programs do not have bounded tree width.*

Because of Corollary 1 it is of paramount interest to study actual Ada programs to find statistics on their tree width. We have thus decided to implement a (slightly modified) version of Thorup's method for Ada and to calculate the tree width of existing Ada code. As a byproduct our study provides insight into how close Ada programs are to series-parallel programs.

6   Implementation Details

In order to calculate Thorup's k-complexity measure, several approaches can be used:

1. Create the CFG for a given program and use a general purpose algorithm that builds the node listings and separator sets for a general CFG [Bod93].
2. Build a parser for the programming language that – as a byproduct – produces node listings and separator sets.
3. Employ dataflow methods to compute node listings and separator sets.
4. Compute node listings and separator sets by use of an AST built by a compiler.

Approach 1 would have needed to implement a general purpose algorithm such as that mentioned in [Bod93] which we considered an error-prone task. So we did not use this approach.

Approach 2 has been proposed by Thorup [Tho98] and followed by Gustedt et al. [GMT02]. Since however Ada's rich set of language features requires some sort of semantic information in order to calculate the separator sets as exactly as possible, we did not employ this approach.

Approach 3 was also considered error-prone. So we did not use it either.

Instead we extended GNAT and used its AST to calculate the node listings. Because of the semantic information present in the AST we were able to compute the separator sets as exactly as possible. In fact we implemented the "greedy" algorithm mentioned in Section 2.

For example consider a simple if statement such as that depicted in Figure 1. As already pointed out in Section 2, Thorup's original work assumes "potential neighbors" for all nodes, which means that many nodes would have separator sets augmented with the targets of potential exit, return, or raise statements. By traversing the AST, however, it is easy to find that no such statements exist in the code. Thus the cardinality of the separator sets turns out to be smaller than the original Thorup approach suggests, which implies that also the tree width of the example is smaller than the Thorup approach finds.

We also implemented Thorup's method of renumbering the nodes if a boolean expression does not contain short-circuit operators. We did not implement the renumbering shown to solve problem (2) in Section 2 for general loop and exit statements; we did, however, implement it for while- and for-loops without exits, which was much easier to do and covers many practically important cases.

For these reasons we still only compute upper bounds for the tree width of Ada programs, but we think – and this is supported by our results – that the calculated tree width is very tight to the actual tree width, which could only have been found by much more effort, both in time used for implementation and in running time of our tool[4].

Our tool calculates the tree width of so-called *units*. The Ada language features that constitute such units are enumerated below:

- (generic) subroutine bodies,
- task bodies,
- entry bodies,
- declare blocks, and
- (generic) package bodies.

Finally we note that all units containing goto statements are ignored by our tool. However, the total number of goto statments we encountered was less than 1000.

7   Results of Study

In the following we describe the Ada projects we have included in our study.

AdaBroker is a set of tools and libraries that can be used to develop CORBA applications in Ada. *AdaCGI* is an Ada95 interface to the "Common Gateway Interface" (CGI). *AdaDoc* is a tool to create documentation from a specification package. *AdaGPGME* is a thin Ada 95 binding to GNUPG Made Easy. *Aflex* is a lexical analyzer written in Ada, *ayacc* is a compiler-compiler also written in Ada. *ASIS* is the GNAT implementation of the Ada Semantic Interface Specification. *BC* is the Ada implementation of the Booch components. *BfdAda* provides an Ada API to use the GNU Binutils BFD library. *CMA* is a Configuration Management Assistant for Ada. *Components* is the implementation of some data-structures. *FSFGNAT* is the Free Software Foundation's version of GNAT. *GLADE* is ACT's implementation of the Distributed System Annex. *GNACK* is an Ada binding for the ORBit Corba ORB. *GNADE* is a project to develop an Ada 95 development environment providing a seamless integration of SQL-based databases into Ada 95. *GNAT* is ACT's Ada Compiler. *GPS* is ACT's GNAT Programming System, an integrated programming environment. *GtkAda* denotes an Ada binding to GTK, the GIMP Toolkit, a graphical library. *GVD* is the GNU Visual Debugger, written in Ada. *Intervals* is an implementation of interval arithmetic in Ada. *JGNAT* is ACT's Ada to Java Byte Code translator. *Libra* is a general library of data structures for Ada95 under Unix-like operating systems. *MaRTE* is the Minimal Real-Time

---

[4]   In general, calculating the tree width of a given graph is NP-complete [ACP87].

Table 1. Tree Width of Ada Applications

Name	Version	No. Units	% tw 5	% tw 4	% tw 3	% tw 2	Avg. TW
AdaBroker	1.0	5644	0.00	0.53	16.99	82.46	2.18
AdaCGI	1.6	84	0.00	1.19	17.86	80.95	2.20
AdaDoc	2.01	240	0.00	0.42	14.17	85.42	2.15
AdaGPGME	0.4.2	25	0.00	0.00	12.00	88.00	2.12
aflex	1.4a	259	0.00	0.39	17.37	82.24	2.18
ASIS	3.15p	4148	0.00	0.96	16.20	82.84	2.18
ayacc	1.1	440	0.00	2.27	24.09	73.64	2.28
BC	20030815	1464	0.00	0.82	12.09	87.09	2.13
BfdAda	0.9	203	0.00	0.00	7.88	92.12	2.07
CMA	—	1129	0.00	3.28	23.29	73.43	2.29
Components	1.2	108	0.00	0.93	23.15	75.93	2.25
FSFGNAT	20020814	9713	0.01	3.12	22.46	74.41	2.28
GLADE	3.15p	4113	0.00	1.09	12.13	86.77	2.14
GNACK	1.1c	733	0.00	0.55	27.56	71.90	2.28
GNADE	1.5.0	1855	0.00	0.11	10.24	89.65	2.10
GNAT	3.15p	9933	0.02	3.16	22.46	74.36	2.28
GPS	1.2.2	10816	0.00	0.92	12.33	86.75	2.14
GtkAda	2.2.0	4574	0.00	0.13	5.79	94.08	2.06
GVD	1.2.5	1408	0.00	1.07	24.43	74.50	2.26
Intervals	1.0	115	0.00	0.00	11.30	88.70	2.11
JGNAT	1.1p	8285	0.01	3.07	21.94	74.98	2.28
Libra	0.2.0	405	0.00	0.25	13.83	85.93	2.14
MaRTE	1.2	1271	0.00	0.55	25.96	73.49	2.27
MAST	1.2.2	1289	0.00	1.32	17.77	80.92	2.20
ORK	2.2b	8021	0.01	3.00	21.61	75.38	2.27
PIWG	—	1319	0.00	0.38	6.52	93.10	2.07
PPlanner	—	162	0.00	0.00	19.14	80.86	2.19
Rail	—	2278	0.00	2.02	28.67	69.32	2.32
Style	—	104	0.00	0.96	15.38	83.65	2.17
Units	1.3	157	0.00	0.00	43.95	56.05	2.43

Operating System for Embedded Applications and *MAST* is the Modeling and Analysis Suite for Real-Time Applications. Both are developed by the Real-Time Group of the Universidad de Cantabria. *ORK* is the open source implementation of the Ravenscar profile. *PIWG* is the Performance Issues Working Group's test suite. *PPlaner* is a Project Planner written in Ada. *Rail* is a small part of a project planning tool for electronic railway interlocking systems (a compiler) implemented by ARC Seibersdorf research. *Style* is an Ada style checker. *Units* is a units of measurement implementation in Ada.

Table 1 shows percentages of how many units have tree widths 2, 3, 4, and 5. No unit had tree width higher than 5. The last column shows the average tree width of the software projects.

It is not surprising that bindings such as GtkAda are at the lower end of the scale because bindings usually only use a small part of Ada's language features.

It is however remarkable that compilers are at the upper end of the results.

Comparing our results with those of [GMT02] for the tree width of Java applications, we see that the smallest average tree width for Java is 2.48 and the largest tree width is 2.94, while the corresponding values for Ada are 2.06 and 2.43, i.e., the largest value for Ada is smaller than the smallest value for Java.

8   Conclusion

In this paper we have proved that in general Ada programs may result in non-bounded tree width. On the other hand, a study of existing Ada code showed that the actual tree width is quite low. Thus, for example, Ada programs can be analyzed very efficiently by static analysis tools.

In addition we have introduced renumbering schemes that allow to derive tighter upper bounds for the tree width of Ada code. This includes for- and while-loops which have not been treated in [Tho98].

Our results cannot be compared directly to those of [GMT02] because the Java study has used the approach of building a parser and ignored exceptions completely. However, on the average Ada programs turned out to have a smaller tree width than Java programs. This is the case even though Ada programmers utilize all flow affecting constructs the language provides.

Acknowledgments. We are grateful to *ARC Seibersdorf research* for handing over part of their railway code for the study.

References

[ACP87]   Stefan Arnborg, Derek G. Corneil, and Andrzej Proskurowski, *Complexity of finding embeddings in a k-tree*, SIAM J. Alg. Disc. Meth. **8** (1987), no. 2, 277–284.

[ALS91]   Stefan Arnborg, Jens Lagergren, and Detlef Seese, *Easy problems for tree-decomposable graphs*, Journal of Algorithms **12** (1991), 308–340.

[ASU88]   Alfred V. Aho, Ravi Sethi, and Jeffrey D. Ullman, *Compilers, Principles, Techniques and Tools*, Series in Computer Science, Addison Wesley, 1988.

[Bod93]   Hans L. Bodlaender, *A tourist guide through treewidth*, Acta Cybernetica **11** (1993), 1–21.

[GKP96]   Wolfgang Gellerich, Markus Kosiol, and Erhard Ploedereder, *Where does GOTO go to?*, Ada-Europe'96 International Conference on Reliable Software Technologies (Montreux, Switzerland), June 1996, pp. 385–395.

[GMT02]   Jens Gustedt, Ole A. Mæhle, and Jan Arne Telle, *The treewidth of Java programs*, Proc. ALENEX'02 - 4th Workshop on Algorithm Engineering and Experiments (San Francisco, CA), LNCS, 2002, pp. 42–51.

[KP98]   Sampath Kannan and Todd A. Proebsting, *Register allocation in structured programs*, Journal of Algorithms **29** (1998), 223–237.

[PK89]   Peter Puschner and Christian Koza, *Calculating the maximum execution time of real-time programs*, The Journal of Real-Time Systems **1** (1989), 159–176.

[RS83]   Neil Robertson and Paul D. Seymour, *Graph minors. I. Excluding a forest*, J. Comb. Theory Series B **35** (1983), 39–61.

[Tho98]   Mikkel Thorup, *All structured programs have small tree width and good register allocation*, Information and Computation **142** (1998), no. 2, 159–181.

The Chance for Ada to Support Distribution and Real-Time in Embedded Systems[*]

Juan López Campos, J. Javier Gutiérrez, and Michael González Harbour

Departamento de Electrónica y Computadores
Universidad de Cantabria, 39005 - Santander, SPAIN
{lopezju,gutierjj,mgh}@unican.es

Abstract. This paper presents a modification of GLADE —the current GNAT implementation of the Ada 95 Distributed Systems Annex (DSA)— to support the development of distributed applications with hard real-time requirements. This modified implementation, that we call RT-GLADE (Real-Time GLADE), is specially suitable for embedded applications composed of a small number of heterogeneous processors and communication networks, because it ensures predictable timing behaviour. A real-time model of the implementation allows the application developer to determine and optimize the overall timing behaviour by applying the corresponding schedulability analysis and priority assignment techniques. This realtime version of GLADE continues to conform to the DSA, so the entire real-time application can be built within the Ada 95 context. To implement RT-GLADE, we provide a priority-based communication network over standard Ethernet that is used to ensure predictable transmission times.

Keywords: Real-Time, Embedded Systems, Distributed Systems, Ada 95, Modelling, Schedulability.

1   Introduction

In the past 20 years the concept and necessity of distribution in computer systems have received increasing attention, and the technology that allows us to make this distribution now offers a wide range of possibilities. We have seen how the distribution paradigms have been developing since the message passing services to the remote procedure calls, to the distributed objects, or more recently, to the distributed components. This need of distribution was included in the Ada 95 standard [16] in its Annex E, no doubt coming from the needs of Ada users. For instance, until the adoption of the Ada 95 standard, only in the ACM SIGADA Ada-Letters series, at least 38 papers appeared regarding distributed systems and Ada in different aspects such as real-time, fault-tolerance, communications, or modelling.

However, the truth is that this Annex has had a minimal impact on the different environments involving the development of distributed applications. We may think of multiple reasons, but perhaps, the most important one is that instead of using the implementation of the Distributed Systems Annex (DSA), Ada developers have

---

* This work has been funded in part by the *Comisión Interministerial de Ciencia y Tecnología* (CICYT) of the Spanish Government under grant number TIC2002-04123-C03-02 (TRECOM), and by the IST Programme of the European Commission under project IST-2001-34820 (FIRST).

A. Llamosí and A. Strohmeier (Eds.): Ada-Europe 2004, LNCS 3063, pp. 91–105, 2004.

always been able to find an alternative that could better adapt to the specific requirements of their application. For example, just for distribution, they could choose changing the programming language to Java, which supports a more modern distribution infrastructure. If they sought integration with software developed in other languages and for different platforms, they could choose the CORBA objects distribution [10]. As far as this last point concerns, there are studies in which some integration strategies between the Ada and CORBA worlds have been discussed and considered [12][15].

But perhaps the most important reason why the DSA has not been widely used is that in the application environment in which Ada is strongest, real-time systems, the DSA does not provide the required timing behaviour predictability and controllability. We think that if the DSA would support distribution of real-time applications, it could be used in those environments in which Ada is chosen as the superior real-time programming language.

The motivation for this paper is to obtain an implementation of the current Annex E that could be used for real-time applications, showing that the changes and additions to the DSA proposed in [6] are viable and complete. The implementation discussed in this paper is targeted at the application environment in which we usually work, which is embedded industrial control systems (robots or visual inspection systems) composed of different distributed processors connected by one or more communication networks, and in which it is necessary to guarantee temporal requirements.

There are a few implementations of the Distributed Systems Annex, that support partitioning and allocation of Ada applications on distributed systems. One of these implementations is GLADE, which was initially developed by Pautet and Tardieu [11][13] and is currently included in the GNAT project, developed by Ada Core Technologies (ACT) [1].

The implementation that we present in this paper is called RT-GLADE (Real-Time GLADE), because it was built by modifying GLADE to enhance its real-time capabilities. The modifications are based on our previous work towards the specification of a distributed real-time annex for Ada [5][6].

In order to develop real-time applications it is also necessary that RT-GLADE has access to communication networks with real-time features. In this paper we integrate into RT-GLADE the real-time network RT-EP [8], which implements a token-passing protocol over standard Ethernet hardware. Another important need in this kind of systems is a real-time operating system. We have implemented RT-GLADE with MaRTE OS [2], which is a real-time operating system that follows the POSIX Minimal Profile [14]. Because MaRTE OS is based on version 3.15p of the GNAT compiler, we have modified the 3.15p version of GLADE, the last public version available, which is compatible with that compiler. Having built all the parts of the system with real-time behaviour —application, Ada run-time system, underlying OS, communications middleware, and communications network—, it is possible to build a model that allows a correct characterization of the timing response [4][9][7].

The paper is organized as follows. First, in Section 2 we present an overview of GLADE to show its architecture and the main characteristics related to the real-time behaviour and the compliance with the DSA. Section 3 presents new capabilities introduced in the RT-GLADE implementation, as well as the subset of the configuration parameters usable for real-time applications. It also shows some details of the communication subsystem that supports real-time requirements. In Section 4 a simple example on how to use RT-GLADE to build an application is shown. Section 5 gives metrics that help in evaluating the benefits of the new implementation. Finally, in Section 6 we draw our conclusions.

2   Ada Distribution and GLADE Overview

Ada 95 [16] defines a distributed system as an interconnection of one or more processing nodes, and zero or more storage nodes, with some communication means among those nodes. It also defines a distributed program as one or more partitions that execute independently in the distributed system. The partitions communicate with each other by exchanging data, using remote subprogram calls and distributed objects. There are two kinds of Ada 95 partitions: active, which can execute in parallel with each other, possibly in a separate address space and possibly in a separate computer; and passive, which have no thread of control of their own, have all their library units preelaborated, and their data and subprograms are accessible to one or more active partitions. The communication between active partitions is made in a standard way using the facilities provided by the Partition Communication Subsystem (PCS). The PCS has a language-defined interface given by the package System.RPC, so an implementation of the PCS can be independent of the compiler and the run-time system.

The DSA leaves some important issues as implementation defined [5][6]. Some of them are very important to develop an implementation that has real-time capabilities. For example, the way in which RPCs are handled, or the priorities at which the task executing an RPC should execute are totally dependent on the implementation. Other implementation-defined issues like the configuration language to describe the distributed system, which may be important from a standardization perspective, are not so important from the real-time point of view.

GLADE is the first industrial-strength implementation of the distributed Ada 95 programming model. The work in [13] proposes GLADE as a framework for developing object-oriented real-time distributed systems. However, [5] and [6] show that there are issues that need to be addressed for a predictable and controllable implementation of the DSA, which are focused on the priority management in the RPC handlers and on the restrictions that have to be observed when configuring the system. Some but not all of these issues were implemented in version 3.15p of GLADE.

GLADE is divided in two major parts [11]:

- GARLIC: the Partition Communication Subsystem, which is primarily composed of the packages System.RPC and System.Garlic and its child packages, containing the heart of the PCS that takes care of network-related system calls, concurrent requests, partition localization and launching, error handling and recovery, etc.

- GNATDIST: the partitioning tool, which is responsible for checking the consistency of a distributed system before building it, calling GNAT with the appropriate parameters to build the needed stubs, configuring the filters that will be used between different partitions, linking the partitions with GARLIC and building the initialization sequence, and building the main program that will launch the whole distributed application on the specified hosts.

Inside GARLIC [3], a pool of *RPC handler* tasks of the type RPC_Handler is created at initialization time to take care of concurrently executing the RPCs on a given partition. This preallocation of tasks is done for the purpose of avoiding the overhead of task creation and destruction at each RPC. If an RPC arrives and all the tasks in the pool are being used by previously issued RPCs, then a new task will be created for the new RPC. The pool of tasks can be configured with the partition attribute Task_Pool of the configuration language, which allows expressing three parameters: the task pool minimum size (number of RPC handlers preallocated and always available), the task pool high size (when an RPC is completed, its RPC handler task is deallocated if the number of task in the pool is greater than this ceiling), and the task pool maximum size (it is a limit to the number of simultaneously active remote calls; if the number of active remote calls is greater than this number, then the request is kept pending until an RPC handler task becomes available).

GLADE also uses dynamic allocation of tasks when a message arrives at the receiver partition of an RPC. Every partition has one or more TCP/IP incoming ports (created from configuration parameters such as the Boot_Location pragma, or the Self_Location partition attribute), and for every incoming port a new task of the type Accept_Handler is created at initialization time, waiting for incoming messages. When a message arrives, this task hands over the processing of the message to another task of the type Connect_Handler, which is found in a second pool of tasks. At initialization time, this pool is empty, and the task is dynamically created in case it is necessary. The Connect_Handler task takes care of processing the message and calling the RPC handler task that executes the subprogram, meanwhile leaving the Accept_Handler free to wait for new incoming messages at the reception port.

Although it is possible to statically allocate the RPC handler tasks, allocation of the Connect_Handler tasks is dynamic and is not appropriate for real-time applications. There needs to be a mechanism for avoiding the dynamic allocation of internal tasks.

The DSA has no provision for expressing the priorities at which the task executing an RPC should execute, nor the priorities of the messages in a communication network. In GLADE 3.15p the concept of priority policy is introduced, with two possible values: Client_Propagated and Server_Declared. The first value provides a simple mechanism to express the execution priority of the RPC that is transparent to the user: the priority of the task invoking the RPC is encoded in the message sent to the receiver partition. Then, in that partition, the RPC handler task that will execute the call reads the priority of the original calling task, which is encoded in the received stream, and sets its own priority to that value. It is known, however, that this is not the optimum priority assignment [5]. The priority policy is set via a configuration pragma (Priority), which means that all the partitions will use the same policy. The Server_Declared value establishes a fixed priority for all the RPC handler tasks in a given partition using a partition attribute (Priority). The original priority of the RPC handler task is set to the maximum level by default, and also returns to this level when the task finishes its work. In [5] we showed that it was possible to achieve better results if the application could specify the initial priority of the RPC handler as well as the priority for each call. In addition, GLADE does not support specifying priorities for the messages in the communication networks.

In GLADE, calls between two partitions allocated in the same processing node are made using the network capabilities, while it would be more efficiently done by using some local protocol that would avoid going through the network.

There are also some aspects in GLADE introducing non uniform overheads that should be minimized in hard realtime systems. For example, once a task of the calling partition has sent a message over the network to make an RPC, it waits for the answer, the RPC reply, on a single entry of a protected object. Every task of the calling partition will be enqueued in the same entry, so, when an RPC reply is processed, it is necessary to determine which task is the 'owner' of the answer. To do this, every task enqueued in the entry is dequeued, and then all the tasks except the one accepting the RPC reply are enqueued again. This implies an unnecessary overhead that is proportional to the number of tasks waiting for an RPC reply.

The Shared_Passive pragma defined in the DSA is used for managing global data shared between active partitions. GLADE's implementation of this pragma is made using operating system files to hold the data corresponding to passive partitions, and it is assumed that the data will be shared using some kind of network file system. However, most implementations of these distributed file systems do not have real-time capabilities, and therefore we will not address support for this pragma in RT-GLADE.

3   RT-GLADE Characteristics

The modifications made to GLADE to support real-time behaviour are mainly focused on the following aspects, that will be described separately in more detail:

- Full application control of the priorities of the RPC handler tasks, and of the messages sent across the network, according to the recommendations given in [5].

- Incorporating a priority-based communication network based on standard Ethernet and a new local protocol to increase the efficiency of the calls into the same processing node.

- Removing the dynamic creation of the tasks at the receiving end of an RPC and improving the wait mechanism for the RPC reply in the calling partition.

- Adapting the configuration of the system to the new real-time capabilities, including the aspects related with the real-time communication networks.

The proposed modification makes the implementation still conform to the current DSA, although a few new interfaces are needed to support the real-time features.

3.1. Priority Management in the Overall System

In order to be able to control the timing behaviour of a real-time application we need some mechanism to specify the priorities for the RPCs that will be executed, as well as for the messages that will be sent across the network.

According to the discussion in [6], we use the type `Global_Priority` defined in package `System.Garlic.Priorities` and representing a value with a global meaning across the distributed system, and we modify that package to make it pure because we need to exchange priorities across the different partitions. We also use the mapping functions defined in `System.Garlic.Priorities.Mapping` that translate between values of this global priority type and values of `System.Priority`. The same naming scheme is used for adding the new mapping functions between the type `Global_Priority` and the priorities of the RT-EP network that we use in our implementation.

In addition, we create the `RPC_Priorities` package, which contains the operations to set the priorities of the outgoing message that is sent by the partition calling an RPC, of the RPC handler task for that particular call, and of the incoming message that is returned by the called partition when the execution of the RPC has finished:

```
with System.Garlic.Global_Priorities;
use System.Garlic.Global_Priorities;
package RPC_Priorities is
   procedure Set
      (RPC_Handler,
       Outgoing_Message,
       Incoming_Message: in Global_Priority);
   procedure Get
      (RPC_Handler,
       Outgoing_Message,
       Incoming_Message: out Global_Priority);
end RPC_Priorities;
```

Procedure `Set` is used to set the priorities used for future RPCs or APCs issued by the calling task, and can be invoked by the user before making the call. These priorities are in effect until `Set` is called again. In this way, the application can specify the priorities of its RPCs either on an individual basis, or by grouping several calls under the same priorities. Initial values for the priorities are set to an intermediate priority level. Procedure `Get` returns the current values of the RPC priorities. The implementation of this package stores the priorities by creating three task attributes using the facilities described in the optional but standard package `Ada.Task_Attributes` [5].

To avoid context switches, we have moved the work done by the `Connect_Handler` tasks into the `Accept_Handler` tasks. Since the underlying communication subsystem implements message queuing there is no message loss using this strategy.

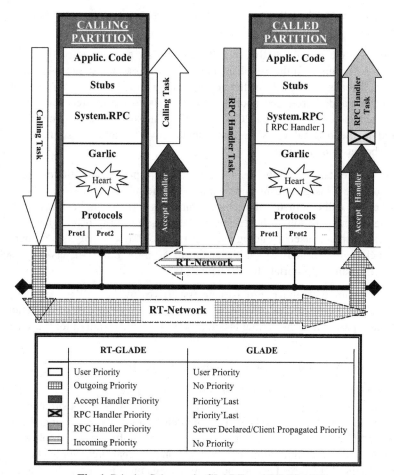

Fig. 1. Priority Schemes in GLADE and RT-GLADE

To avoid the priority inversion that could be caused by the initial priority of the RPC handler tasks of the pool, we let the application configure it by specifying in the configuration file the partition attribute called Priority, of the type Global_Priority. In our implementation we use this attribute to also set the priority of the Accept_Handler tasks.

Fig. 1 shows a typical RPC call and how the priorities are managed in the original GLADE and in our implementation. For the latter, the calling task sets the priority values involved in the RPC: for the outgoing message, the incoming message, and the execution of the RPC in the called partition. Then it executes all the middleware code at its own priority until it sends the request through the real-time network. When the calling task reaches the Do_RPC or Do_APC functions of the System.RPC package, instead of writing the priority of the calling task in the message stream as in the original GLADE, we call RPC_Priorities.Get and we write the RPC_Handler and Incoming_Message priorities into that stream. The priority at which the stream is sent across the network is the `Outgoing_Message` priority (after mapping it to the appropriate type).

Once the message arrives at the called partition, an `Accept_Handler` task (see Subsection 3.3) running at the established priority processes the stream. As part of this processing, it reads the priority of the corresponding RPC handler from the message, selects a free handler from the pool, sets its priority to the desired value, and then awakens the handler passing the RPC stream to it. This strategy saves context switches compared to the original GLADE implementation in which it was the own RPC handler who set its own priority.

The RPC handler task reads the `Incoming_Message` priority and the parameters of the call from the message stream, and then invokes the subprogram associated with the RPC. When the call completes, the return parameters and error indications, if any, are sent to the calling partition at the `Incoming_Message` priority level. Then, the RPC handler task suspends itself by going back into the pool. It's priority is left unchanged because before it will start executing again an `Accept_Handler` task will set its priority to the value appropriate for the new RPC.

When the stream with the return parameters arrives at the calling partition, it is processed at the established priority by an `Accept_Handler` task (see Subsection 3.3) which in turn passes it to the calling task that was suspended waiting for this answer.

3.2. New Communication Features Added to GARLIC

As RT-GLADE uses a network, it is obvious that it is necessary to use one with real-time characteristics. The TCP/IP network provided by GLADE is not suitable for real-time communication. In our RT-GLADE implementation we are using the RT-EP (Real-Time Ethernet Protocol) network [8], which is a software-based token-passing Ethernet protocol for multipoint communications in real-time applications using standard ethernet hardware. This protocol can manage messages up to 1492 bytes long in a single packet, but it is currently being extended to manage larger messages using packet division.

Within the implementation other real-time protocols may be available, so when an RPC is performed, it is necessary to determine the protocol that we are going to use for the communication. Once the protocol has been selected, it is necessary to pass to it the information required to contact the remote partition through the network. This information comprises the node identification where the partition is located, and any other possible information for the protocol chosen, e.g., the destination port as in the GLADE implementation.

RT-EP [8] uses a concept similar to the port, called the reception channel, which is a number used for the purpose of identifying communication endpoints in a given station. To be able to transmit through RT-EP it is necessary to know the MAC address of the destination node, and the RT-EP reception channel number inside that node. We code this information using the partition attribute `Self_Location` and the `Boot_Location` pragma of the configuration language (see Subsection 3.4).

We have defined a new virtual network protocol that we call the Local protocol, which is used to increase the efficiency when making a call to a subprogram belonging to an RCI library unit in a partition located in the same processing node than the calling partition. The use of the Local protocol also avoids a limitation of the RT-EP communication subsystem, which does not allow sending a message to the same node. This protocol is implemented with the same interface as RT-EP [8], also using a reception priority queue for each reception channel defined in the configuration process. A message sent through the Local protocol is enqueued with the priority of the called task, which is the RPC handler priority for the request and the priority of the calling task for the answer. When a message is sent through the Local protocol, neither the Outgoing_Message nor the Incoming_Message priorities are used, because there is no network scheduling involved. Internally, the priority of the calling task is written into the stream in order to enqueue the answer message in the right order.

Once a calling task executing an RPC has checked that the call does not belong to the same partition nor to a partition located in the same node, the implementation has to determine how to contact the remote partition, i.e., which protocol to use. For this purpose, the calling task checks a table with information on which protocol to use for accessing the desired partition. It is not necessary that if, for instance, partition P1 had to contact partition P2 using the RT-EP protocol, partition P2 had to use the same protocol to contact P1. In the configuration process, we use the partition links (see Subsection 3.4) to select the protocol to be used between a calling partition P1 and a called partition P2.

3.3. RPC Receiver Handling

RT-GLADE removes the dynamic task creation of the GLADE implementation for the execution of RPCs simply by configuring the number of RPC handler tasks in the pool to a sufficient number of static tasks, ensuring the execution of all the possible concurrent RPCs. For this purpose, we just set the minimum number of tasks in the pool using the partition attribute Task_Pool. If we want a static pool of tasks, the other two numbers in this attribute (high and maximum sizes) must be set to the same value as the minimum. This also follows the recommendations stated in [6].

The other place of the GLADE implementation with dynamic creation of tasks is the management of the Accept_Handler and Connect_Handler tasks. In RT-GLADE each partition has one Accept_Handler task (and no Connect_Handler task) per reception channel configured in the real-time protocol (currently the Local protocol and RT-EP). These tasks are created at initialization time and are immediately blocked waiting for the reception of messages at their respective reception channels.

In order to avoid the non uniform overhead associated with the use of a unique entry to wait for the RPC replies, we propose using a family of entries. Every task waiting for an RPC reply will be enqueued on a different entry. Before issuing the outgoing message, we determine the identifier of the entry at which the calling task will be enqueued. This identifier is sent with the message and then sent back with the reply to determine which entry is to be serviced. After usage, the entry is freed for subsequent use in some other call. A new configuration parameter is added to specify the number of entries of the protected object.

3.4. RT-GLADE Configuration Parameters

The GNATDIST tool has its own interface for implementing the configuration of a distributed application. This tool reads a ".cfg" file which follows the rules of its Ada-like configuration language. RT-GLADE uses a subset of GLADE's configuration language together with a few extensions. We will summarize which of the GLADE configuration attributes and pragmas are specially relevant to RT-GLADE, which are not used, and which are forbidden:

- The configuration and partition declarations, or setting the main procedure in a partition are the same as in the original tool.

- Pragma Starter has to be set to None, because we want to manually launch the different partitions generated. The reason is that RT-GLADE will be tested on a real-time OS (MaRTE) that does not have the conventional remote shell used by the GLADE launcher. Each MaRTE OS node can automatically upload the partition from a host where the partitions have been created.

- It is not necessary to set the partition attribute Host for every partition. This attribute is related with the remote launching facility that is not used in MaRTE.

- The partition attribute Self_Location is used to configure how a partition can be reached through a communication protocol. Each partition must specify this attribute at least once for every possible location in which the partition can be allocated. The information coded in this attribute is a list of: a protocol name, a processing node identifier, a reception channel identifier, and a list of partitions to which corresponding partition links will be set. A partition link defines the preferred protocol to send messages from the specified partition to the one to which the attribute Self_Location is applied.

  Pragma Boot_Location has to be specified also in order to determine the location of the boot server in which all the partitions have been registered. This boot server is located on the main partition. It contains the same information as Self_Location.

  In order to completely specify the network information an additional file must be written to associate the network addresses (MAC addresses for RT-EP) and the processing node identifiers. The reason for adding this new file is to not overload the configuration file with information that is only relevant to the communication protocols.

- The partition attribute Task_Pool must be configured as described in section 3.3.

- The filtering service is not necessary and, consequently, nor are the bidirectional channels that GLADE implements, which are mainly focused on this service. This part of the configuration is ignored.

- Pragmas or attributes related to the configuration of passive partitions are forbidden. More work has to be done to arrive at a real-time solution for this issue.

- Dynamic aspects associated with the reconnection in GLADE are also forbidden for hard real-time applications due to the difficulties in achieving predictable timing behaviour; they could be used in a future implementation for soft real-time systems.

- The partition attribute `Priority` has been reused to configure the initial priorities of the `Accept_Handler` tasks.

- A new partition attribute called `Max_RPC_Replies` has been added to set the number of entries of the protected object at which the tasks doing an RPC wait for the reply.

4   Usage Example

Fig. 2 shows a simple example of a distributed application composed of two CPUs connected by a network using the RT-EP protocol. The example code is divided into three library units: the main procedure `Remote_Caller`, the RCI package `Calculator`, and a library unit containing the task `Local_Caller_Task`. Each library unit is allocated to a different partition and assigned to a CPU as shown. The main procedure makes an RPC to the `Calculator.Add` function, through the RT-EP protocol. This call must specify the three priorities needed to make an RPC. The `Local_Caller_Task` calls the same function, but because it is located in the same CPU it will use the Local protocol, and therefore only the `RPC_Handler` priority must be specified.

The RT-GLADE configuration file that corresponds both to the distribution and to the way in which the protocols are used is as follows:

```
configuration Configuration_File is
   pragma Starter (None);
   Partition1: partition := (Calculator);
   Partition2: partition := (Remote_Caller);
   Partition3: partition := (Local_Caller);
   procedure Remote_Caller is in Partition2;
   pragma Boot_Location (("RT_EP","CPU1:1"));
   for Partition1'Self_Location use
      ((("RT_EP","CPU2:1"), ("Local","CPU2:1:Partition3")));
   for Partition2'Self_Location use
      (("RT_EP","CPU1:1"));
   for Partition3'Self_Location use
      ((("RT_EP","CPU2:3"), ("Local","CPU2:3:Partition1")));
   for Partition1'Priority use 27;
   for Partition1'Task_Pool use (8, 8, 8);
   for Partition1'Max_RPC_Replies use 4;
end Configuration_File;
```

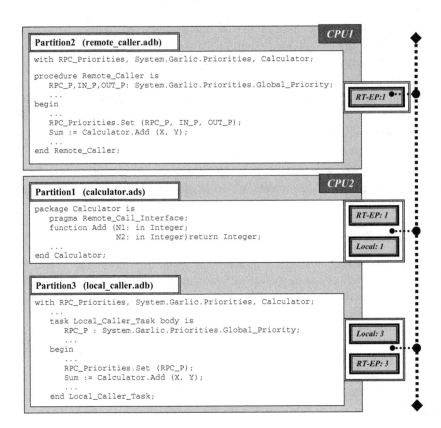

Fig. 2. Simple example using RT-GLADE

The partition attribute Self_Location applied to Partition2 determines that it has two communication protocols (RT-EP and Local) and the channels used. Although in this case it is not necessary to specify a partition link because there is only one network protocol available, Partition2 explicitly requests from Partition1: "if you send a message to me, you have to use the RT-EP protocol and reception channel 2". In this example, it can be seen also that the number of RPC handler tasks in Partition1 is statically established to a value of 8, the initial priority of these tasks and of the accept handlers is set to 27, and the maximum number of simultaneously pending replies is set to four.

5   Evaluation

The real-time modelling of an application using RT-GLADE may be done by using the models described in [8] for RT-EP and [9] for the RPCs. The measurement of the time parameters specified in the model depend on the particular platform and thus their absolute values are not representative. In this section we will show the response times of a simple example that shows how the full control of the individual RPC and message priorities lets us achieve better results than with the two priority models used

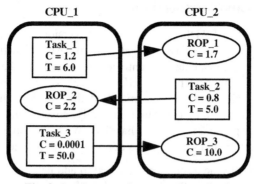

Fig. 3. Architecture of an example application

in the original GLADE. Fig. 3 shows the architecture of a simple application with two processors and three tasks (numbered 1 to 3) executing remote operations (named ROP 1 to 3) in the opposite processor. The worst-case execution times (C) and periods (T) are shown in the figure. The application is divided in two partitions, one for each processor. Task_1 and Task_2 have hard real time requirements with deadlines equal to their respective periods; Task_3 has no real-time requirements, and thus is executed at a low priority level. Time units are in seconds. Since the original GLADE does not consider priorities in the network, we have used a single priority level for all the messages in the network, to make a fairer comparison. The time measurements have been made on the same platform, so that the differences are only due to the priority management scheme.

Table 1 shows the worst-case response times observed for Task_1 and Task_2 with the following priority schemes: RT-GLADE with some specific assignment that is not possible in GLADE; and the two possibilities in GLADE: the Client Propagated model and the Server Declared model, each with different possible priority combinations.

Table 1. Comparison of the different priority schemes

Priority Schemes	Task_1 Prio.	ROP_1 Prio.	Task_2 Prio.	ROP_2 Prio.	Task_1 WCRT (s)	Task_2 WCRT (s)
RT-GLADE	High	Medium	High	Medium	4.26	4.81
Client Propagated	High	High	Medium	Medium	3.34	Unbounded
	Medium	Medium	High	High	8.17	3.44
Server Declared	High	Medium	High	Medium	16.81	6.18
	High	High	Medium	Medium	10.85	Unbounded
	Medium	Medium	High	High	Unbounded	3.44

We can see how the timing requirements of this particular example are only met under RT-GLADE. The results for the Server Declared scheme are especially bad because the remote operation ROP_3 invoked by the lower priority task is forced to execute at the same priority as ROP_1. The unbounded response times are obtained in some cases because the task is unable to complete before its period and work continues to accumulate with increasing response times.

6   Conclusions and Further Work

We have presented RT-GLADE, which is a new version of GLADE, the GNAT implementation of the Ada 95 Distributed Systems Annex, with better real-time capabilities. The new implementation continues to conform to the DSA and is also offered as free software under the GNU licence. To achieve predictable and controllable timing behaviour we have modified the priority scheme used by the implementation to allow the application to fully specify the priorities of the communication messages and of the RPC handlers. We have also eliminated the need for dynamic task creation and some sources of non uniform overheads.

In addition to changes to the middleware, we had to add network services capable of providing real-time behaviour. We have used RT-EP, a real-time protocol based on standard Ethernet hardware. In addition, because some calls to procedures declared as remote may result in calls to the same processing node, a Local protocol has been included for efficiency and generality purposes.

More work needs to be done in the current implementation to remove the unused features of GLADE that are still coded in RT-GLADE. It is also important to change the way in which GLADE starts up the system, in order to make it simpler and more controllable, although the current implementation does not affect the real-time behaviour once the system has been initialized. Finally, as a very specific issue, a mechanism to catch the exceptions raised by an APC would be useful for the applications using RT-GLADE.

In summary, by using RT-GLADE we can build applications that can guarantee meeting their real-time requirements. As a conclusion, we have shown how the changes and additions that we proposed in [6] for the DSA are viable and complete, and can lead to a Real-Time Distributed Systems Annex in Ada with moderate effort. It would be extremely useful for the Ada Language to incorporate these changes and additions to the standard DSA. This extension could facilitate using Ada's distribution services in real-time systems, and would help in keeping Ada as the reference language for real-time systems.

References

[1]   Ada-Core Technologies, Ada 95 GNAT Pro, http://www.gnat.com/

[2]   M. Aldea and M. González. "MaRTE OS: An Ada Kernel for Real-Time Embedded Applications". Proceedings of the International Conference on Reliable Software Technologies, Ada-Europe 2001, Leuven, Belgium, in Lecture Notes in Computer Science, LNCS 2043, May 2001.

[3]   Y. Kermarrec, L. Pautet, and S. Tardieu. "GARLIC: Generic Ada Reusable Library for Interpartition Communication". Proceedings of Tri-Ada'95, Anaheim, California, USA, ACM, 1995.

[4]   M. González Harbour, J.J. Gutiérrez, J.C. Palencia and J.M. Drake. "MAST: Modeling and Analysis Suite for Real-Time Applications". Proceedings of the Euromicro Conference on Real-Time Systems, Delft, The Netherlands, June 2001.

[5]   J.J. Gutiérrez García, and M. González Harbour. "Prioritizing Remote Procedure Calls in Ada Distributed Systems". Proceedings of the 9th International Real-Time Ada Workshop, ACM Ada Letters, XIX, 2, pp. 67–72, June 1999.

[6]   J.J. Gutiérrez García, and M. González Harbour. "Towards a Real-Time Distributed Systems Annex in Ada". Proceedings of the 10th International Real-Time Ada Workshop, ACM Ada Letters, XXI, 1, pp. 62–66, March 2001.

[7]   Jane W. S. Liu. "Real-Time Systems". Prentice Hall, 2000.

[8]   J.M. Martínez, M. González Harbour, and J.J. Gutiérrez. "RT-EP: Real-Time Ethernet Protocol for Analyzable Distributed Applications on a Minimum Real-Time POSIX Kernel". Proceedings of the 2nd International Workshop on Real-Time LANs in the Internet Age, RTLIA 2003, Porto (Portugal), July 2003.

[9]   J. Javier Gutiérrez, José M. Drake, Michael González Harbour, and Julio L. Medina. "Modeling and Schedulability Analysis in the Development of Real-Time Distributed Ada Systems". Proceedings of the 11th International Real-Time Ada Workshop, ACM Ada Letters, Vol. XXII, No. 4, pp. 58–65, December 2002.

[10]   Object Management Group, "Realtime CORBA Joint Revised Submission". OMG Document orbos/99-02-12 ed., March 1999.

[11]   L. Pautet and S. Tardieu, "Inside the Distributed Systems Annex". Proceeding of the Intl. Conf. on Reliable Software Technologies, Ada-Europe'98, Uppsala, Sweden, in LNCS 1411, Springer, pp. 65–77, June 1998.

[12]   L. Pautet, T. Quinot, and S. Tardieu. "CORBA & DSA: Divorce or Marriage". Proc. of the International Conference on Reliable Software Technologies, Ada-Europe'99, Santander, Spain, in Lecture Notes in Computer Science No. 1622, pp. 211–225, June 1999.

[13]   L. Pautet and S. Tardieu. "GLADE: a Framework for Building Large Object-Oriented Real-Time Distributed Systems". Proc. of the 3rd IEEE Intl. Symposium on Object-Oriented Real-Time Distributed Computing, (ISORC'00), Newport Beach, USA, March 2000.

[14]   IEEE Std. 1003.13-2003. Information Technology -Standardized Application Environment Profile- POSIX Realtime and Embedded Application Support (AEP). The Institute of Electrical and Electronics Engineers.

[15]   Scott Moody. "Object-Oriented Real-Time Systems Using a Hybrid Distributed Model of Ada 95's Built-in DSA Capability (Distributed Systems Annex-E) and CORBA". Proceedings of the 8th International Real-Time Ada Workshop, ACM Ada-Letters, XVII, 5, pp. 71–76, September-October 1997.

[16]   S. Tucker Taft, and R.A. Duff (Eds.). "Ada 95 Reference Manual. Language and Standard Libraries". International Standard ISO/IEC 8652:1995(E), in LNCS 1246, Springer, 1997.

PolyORB: A Schizophrenic Middleware to Build Versatile Reliable Distributed Applications

Thomas Vergnaud[1], Jérôme Hugues[1], Laurent Pautet[1], and Fabrice Kordon[2]

[.] GET-Télécom Paris – LTCI-UMR 5141 CNRS
46, rue Barrault, F-75634 Paris CEDEX 13, France
{thomas.vergnaud,jerome.hugues,laurent.pautet}@enst.fr
[.] Université Pierre & Marie Curie, Laboratoire d'Informatique de Paris 6/SRC
4, place Jussieu, F-75252 Paris CEDEX 05, France
fabrice.kordon@lip6.fr

Abstract. The development of real-time distributed applications requires middleware providing both *reliability* and *performance*. Middleware must be *adaptable* to meet application requirements and integrate legacy components. Current middleware provides only partial solutions to these issues. Moreover, they newer address all of them. Thus, a new generation of middleware is required. We have introduced the *schizophrenic middleware* concept as an integrated solution to build versatile reliable distributed applications. PolyORB, our implementation of schizophrenic middleware, supports various distribution models: CORBA (Common Object Request Broker Architecture), SOAP (Simple Object Access Protocol), DSA (Ada 95 Distributed System Annex), Message Passing (an adaptation of Java Message Service to Ada 95) and Web Server paradigm (close to what AWS offers). In this paper, we describe the implementation of PolyORB and provide a summary of our experience regarding the issues mentioned above.

1 Introduction

The term "middleware" designates a piece of software that eases both development and deployment of distributed applications. It handles basic functions to distribute applications in heterogeneous environments. Offered services are for example transport protocol, remote execution, addressing, data marshalling, etc.

Distributed systems use classical distribution paradigms like message passing (MP), remote subprogram call (RPC), distributed objects (DOC) or shared memory (DSM). The community has defined several distribution models which propose a combination of these paradigms. DOC can be implemented using CORBA or RMI (Remote Method Invocation). DSA (Distributed Systems Annex for Ada 95) provides several paradigms like RPC, DOC and DSM. Distribution models also lead to many variations. CORBA or DSA define asynchronous remote method invocation. Middleware classically implements one distribution model.

The choice for a distribution model or for a list of distribution mechanisms is driven by the application requirements; a correct (or incorrect) choice may

A. Llamosí and A. Strohmeier (Eds.): Ada-Europe 2004, LNCS 3063, pp. 106–119, 2004.

dramatically impact design and performances [Mul93]. The growing demand for distribution functions in a wide range of systems (embedded, mobile or real-time systems) increases the multiplication of distribution models with some specific variations.

Each application comes with its specific needs and takes advantage of one distribution model. But all these applications (possibly based on heterogeneous distribution models) have to interoperate one with another. Middleware usually handles interoperability between heterogeneous hardware or operating systems. In the context of heterogeneous components interactions, middleware has to propose a new form of interoperability on which this paper focuses e.g. an interoperability between distribution models. This property is summarized as *Middleware to Middleware* interaction (M2M) [Bak01].

Designing from scratch specific middleware for a variant of distribution model, driven by particular application requirements, would be too expensive. A better approach consists of designing general middleware that can be *tailored* to the specific application needs. This saves both time and money.

Configurable or generic middleware provides a first efficient solution to tailor these distribution platforms so that they meet the application needs: TAO [SC97] can be configured to address real-time concerns, and Jonathan [DHTS98] can be personalized for various distribution models. But such middleware does not provide interoperability between existing components based on different distribution models. Yet this issue cannot be discarded since distributed systems now commonly reuse legacy components.

We have introduced the *schizophrenic middleware* concept [QPK01] as a global solution to both configurability to meet application requirements, adaptability of distribution mechanisms and interoperability between distribution models. It also provides support for execution determinism and formal verification. PolyORB [PQK+01], our implementation of such middleware, is a proof of concept.

The aim of this paper is to describe the schizophrenic concepts and the associated architecture. We study the PolyORB implementation and demonstrate the viability of such middleware. We first give an overview of configurable and generic middleware, and of the interoperability issues. Then we introduce the schizophrenic middleware concept and the current status of PolyORB, and the distribution models it supports. Finally we study the performances of PolyORB, compared to other middleware solutions.

2 Middleware Adaptability and Interoperability: An Overview

Few projects directly focus on the design of middleware. They define architectures and building blocks to facilitate middleware modification and adaptation. Very few others focus on interaction between systems developed with different distribution models.

In this section, we analyze the design principles of *configurable* and *generic* middleware. We describe several architectures which provide these properties. We also present the difficulties to enforce interoperability between different distribution models.

2.1   Configurable Middleware

Configurable middleware enables an application to select actual components and specific run-time policies that address its requirements for a single distribution model.

TAO: *The ACE ORB* (TAO) is a free configurable ORB based on the *ACE* (Adaptive Communication Environment) communication and synchronization library. TAO supports CORBA real-time features. It controls the scheduler policy to enforce real-time properties or to satisfy Quality of Service requirements. It is highly dedicated to avionics, multimedia or simulation applications. TAO architecture is based on design patterns [GHJV94]. It can be configured with the appropriate components to address a specific application domain and to ensure performance, determinism or scalability properties. TAO provides an IDL (Interface Description Language) compiler that optimizes the generated stubs and skeletons depending on user requirements.

2.2   Generic Middleware

Generic middleware extends the configurability concept in order to adapt middleware to the distribution model required by the application. It defines canonical components and architecture which are extended or *personalized* to support the given distribution model. In other words, a generic middleware is instantiated according to a distribution model to create a *personality*.

Quarterware: This C++ middleware [SSC98] defines a restricted set of components. These components may be extended or specialized to implement a specific distribution model. This process has been successfully applied to the COR-BA, RMI and MPI (Message Passing Interface) models. Quarterware's components embody typical middleware functions specified as design patterns. Their specialization are supposed to be fast and efficient. Unfortunately, this middleware is not an open source software and it is not possible to evaluate its reuse code ratio or its performances.

Jonathan: This architecture emphasizes on a core system, Jonathan, and its *personalities*. Jonathan [DHTS98] is a Java framework of configurable components and abstract interfaces. Current implementation provides a CORBA personality (*David*), a RMI personality (*Jeremie*) and specialized personalities for multimedia systems.

Generic middleware can be instantiated to meet the application needs; however, the development of a new personality implies the engineering of a significant amount of code. For instance, as Jonathan is mostly based on abstract interfaces, personalities like David and Jeremie reuse only 10% of the generic code.

2.3   Interoperability between Distribution Models

Legacy components usually rely on multiple heterogeneous technologies. This includes heterogeneous distribution models. Hence, software reusability may rise interoperability issues, leading to M2M concern described in section 1.

Typical solutions involve middleware nodes communicating one with another through ad hoc gateways. CIAO [Qui99] provides static gateways between COR-BA and DSA nodes; CORBAWeb [MGG96] follows the same principles by providing dynamic gateways between CORBA and Web clients. This approach requires a gateway between each pair of middleware paradigm.

Other solutions like *Java/HPC++* [BDV+98] rely on the choice of a *common exchange protocol*. Then only one translator between each middleware paradigm and this common protocol is necessary.

These solutions are interesting: they isolate the components interaction issue. This allows the developer to reuse legacy components. However, the use of intermediate entities requires a significant translation work; it impacts the performances of the whole distributed system. This may not offer sufficient performances.

3   Schizophrenic Middleware

Configurable and generic middleware ease middleware adaptation. However they lack flexibility: configurable middleware provides adaptation hooks to abide to application constraints; generic middleware is a solution to tailor to a distribution model. Interoperability between different middleware types is often dealt as a separate issue.

We claim that an architecture combining configurability, genericity but also interoperability capabilities into a common middleware architecture is sufficient to address both application and distribution model requirements. This requires an architecture that emphasizes on separation of concerns. We now present this architecture.

3.1   Decoupling Functionalities

Schizophrenic middleware refines the definition and role of personalities introduced by Jonathan. It proposes *application-level* and *protocol-level* personalities, and a *Neutral Core Middleware* (NCM). The latter allows for the interaction between multiple personalities, as shown on figure 1.

Application personalities: They constitute the adaptation layer between application components and middleware through a dedicated API or code generator. They register application components within the NCM; and they interact with it to enable the exchange of requests between entities at the application-level.

Protocol personalities: They handle the mapping of personality-neutral requests (representing interactions between application entities) onto messages transmitted through a communication channel.

Requests handled by a protocol personality originate from three sources. Application entities produce requests to be sent to other nodes of the distributed application and convey them to the protocol personality through an application personality and the NCM. Requests also come from other application nodes and are received by the protocol personality. At last, they also come from another protocol personality through the NCM: in this case the application node acts as a proxy performing protocol translation between third-party nodes.

The Neutral Core Middleware (NCM): It acts as an adaptation layer between application and protocol personalities. It manages execution resources and provides the necessary abstractions to transparently pass requests between protocol and application personalities in a neutral way. It is completely independent from both application and protocol personalities: this enables the selection and interaction of any combination of application and protocol personalities.

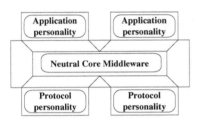

Fig. 1. Schizophrenic architecture

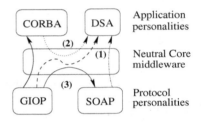

Fig. 2. PolyORB personalities interactions

Figure 2 summarizes the different ways various personalities can exchange requests through the neutral core middleware. This naturally leads to interoperability: entities registered to an application personality are available to any client using a middleware for which the corresponding protocol personality exists (1), or to another collocated application or protocol personalities (2, 3); the NCM acts as a gateway between inter-operating personalities. Hence, this architecture separates three main concerns in middleware: protocol-side, application-side and internals.

Personalities implement a specific aspect of a distribution model. The NCM enables the presence and interaction of multiple collocated application and protocol personalities within the same middleware instance, leading to "schizophrenia".

3.2   Services

Personalities and the NCM are built on top of seven basic services that embody key steps in client/server interactions (e.g. RPC or Distributed Objects). We now present these services through an example: the interaction between a DSA client and a CORBA server using the SOAP protocol (figure 3).

Each entity is given a unique identifier within the entire distributed application using the *addressing* service (1). This is used by the client to get a reference on a server entity. Then the NCM uses the *binding* service (2) and creates a binding object. It provides mechanisms to establish and maintain associations between interacting objects and the resources that support this interaction (e.g. a socket, a protocol stack).

Then request parameters are translated into a representation suitable for transmission over network, using the *representation* service (3). A *protocol* (4) is implemented for transmissions between the client and the server nodes, through the *transport* (5) service, which establishes a communication channel between the two nodes. Then the request is sent and unmarshalled by the server.

Upon the reception of a request, the middleware instance ensures that a concrete entity implementing objects is available to execute the request, using the *activation* service (6). Finally, middleware assigns execution resources to process every incoming request, using the *execution* service (7).

Middleware main loop handles the coordination of these different services and ensures correct propagation of data flow within the middleware node.

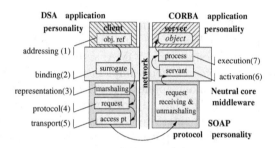

Fig. 3. Invocation request path

Middleware may also provide advanced services which are optional for some personalities. They implement facilities and high-level APIs that ease the development or deployment of a distributed application.

The *naming* service provides association between a reference on an entity and a symbolic name, e.g. CORBA COS Naming or the Ada Distributed System Annex internal naming scheme. The *interface repository* services provide a metadata describing the interface of application entities and the types they define. This provides mechanisms to implement the CORBA Interface Repository. The *termination* service determines consensus on whether a distributed application has completed its task or not. Such a service is useful in a DSA implementation. The *shared data* service provides transparent access to data shared by different nodes in a distributed application. Such a service is also present in the DSA specification. The *synchronization* service provides mechanisms to coordinate actions of different nodes (e.g. distributed mutexes).

Then basic and advanced services are combined to build a middleware instance; this enables a precise adaptation to application requirements. We now describe our ongoing work on PolyORB, our implementation of schizophrenic middleware.

4   PolyORB: Implementation of a Schizophrenic Middleware

PolyORB is our free software implementation of schizophrenic middleware, in Ada 95. It is released under the GNAT Modified GPL licence [PQK+01]. PolyORB is now stable software and entered industrialization process. In this section, we detail PolyORB implemented personalities and Neutral Core Middleware.

These implementations reuse components from GLADE [PT00], our implementation of the Distributed System Annex for GNAT; AdaBroker, our implementation of CORBA; AWS [Obr03] components for Web applications; and XML/Ada [Bri01].

4.1   Application Personalities

PolyORB supports different distribution models, implemented as application personalities: Distributed Object with CORBA and DSA; Remote Procedure Call with DSA; Message Passing with MOMA; and Web applications with AWS.

CORBA: We reuse some elements implemented for the AdaBroker ORB to produce a CORBA-compliant application personality. This personality provides an IDL-to-Ada compiler that supports most IDL constructs, except for fixed-point numbers, abstract interfaces and object by value. It also provides a communication system that supports static and dynamic invocation and implements the Portable Object Adapter (POA). Moreover, CORBA application personality provides some CORBA COS Services: COS Naming, COS Event, COS Time and the Interface Repository.

Distributed System Annex: The implementation of the DSA application personality was facilitated because of the know-how acquired during the development of GLADE. The implementation of this personality carried on the partial rewriting of the GNAT compiler so that PolyORB neutral core middleware and protocol personalities act as a communication system for the distributed system annex. The DSA personality supports Annex E specification. Some of the advanced services introduced in GLADE such as termination, bootstrap servers will be ported to PolyORB in a near future.

Message Passing: MOMA (Message Oriented Middleware for Ada) provides message passing mechanisms through an Ada 95 implementation of the well-known Sun's Java Message Service (JMS) [SUN99]. JMS is a standardized API for common message passing models; it keeps the distribution layer implementation-defined. We focused directly on MOM distribution logic and defined MOMA as an application personality. As for DSA, PolyORB NCM and protocol personalities act as a communication system. Our MOM architecture supports typical MOM primitives like 1-to-1 and 1-to-N message exchanges. Those are implemented using a *servant*-like pattern: clients invoke specific methods on MOMA objects to exchange messages.

Web Server: The Web Server personality provides the same API as the Ada Web Server project (AWS) [Obr03]. It allows for the implementation of web services, web server applications, or classical web pages. AWS-based servers allow the programmer to directly interact with incoming or outgoing HTTP (HyperText Transfer Protocol) and SOAP requests. We have implemented a *servant*-like pattern to enable servers creation; request manipulation is done through a wrapper on PolyORB's internals. The AWS personality provides the basic functionalities of the original AWS; other functionalities are facilities to ease data manipulation. They will be incorporated in future releases.

4.2   Protocol Personalities

Protocol personalities provide support for data exchange. PolyORB supports GIOP (General Inter-Orb Protocol) for all-purpose requests, MIOP (Multicast Inter-Orb Protocol) for multicast and SOAP for Web Services.

GIOP: GIOP is the transport layer of the CORBA specifications. AdaBroker provided a basis for the implementation of GIOP. This personality implements GIOP versions from 1.0 to 1.2 along with the CDR (Common Data Representation) representation scheme to map data between the neutral core layer and CDR streams. GIOP is a generic protocol for which we provide several instances. IIOP (Internet Inter-Orb Protocol) supports synchronous request semantics over TCP/IP. MIOP [OMG03] instantiation of GIOP enables group communication over IP multicast. DIOP (Datagram Inter-Orb Protocol) relies on UDP/IP communications to transmit one-way requests only.

SOAP: SOAP protocol [W3C03] enables the exchange of structured and typed information between peers. It is a self-describing XML document [W3C00] that defines both its data and semantics. Basically, SOAP with HTTP bindings is used as a communication protocol for Web Services. PolyORB's SOAP personality reuses code from AWS, and takes advantage from the XML self-describing properties to propose a direct mapping between SOAP and neutral requests.

4.3   Neutral Core Middleware

Neutral Core Middleware is the heart of PolyORB. It provides a basic implementation for most middleware services defined in section 3.2. Besides, it implements different APIs and patterns on top of which distribution facilities are built. Finally, it provides hooks to register and to configure application or protocol personalities.

These components are designed to maximize code reuse, performance and configurability. For instance, PolyORB tasking constructs can be adjusted to application requirements. It supports No Tasking, Full Tasking but also Ravenscar run-time [DB98]. Moreover, tasking policies may be defined to precisely control tasks allocation to process requests. It reuses notions introduced in GLADE and

AdaBroker and define different policies: *thread pool, thread per session, thread per request.*

Moreover, the NCM eases to proof determinism of key middleware elements. Hence, the Ravenscar tasking run-time enables determinism of concurrency patterns. Static and dynamic perfect hash tables [DKM$^+$94] enable $O(1)$ lookup time in dictionaries.

5   Experiments and Validation

This section illustrates PolyORB capabilities and efficiency to assess its usability as a distribution platform to develop complete applications. We first address its compliance to strict specifications; we then discuss code reuse and performance issues.

5.1   Interoperability and Compliance to Standards

Middleware specifications strictly prescribe the components on top of which a distributed application may be built, e.g. protocols, API. Strict compliance to these norms is required to ensure interoperability with other products.

We first verified compliance at the protocol level: transport of request must enable communication with other middleware.

CORBA/IIOP: We verified interoperability using the IIOP instantiation of GIOP with other CORBA-based middleware, C++ implementations: omniORB, TAO; Java implementations: Jonathan and OpenORB. Our tests verify data transfer consistency for various types as defined by the OMG IDL: simple, aggregate and complex ones.

CORBA/MIOP: We tested interoperability with TAO implementation of MIOP: messages were correctly broadcasted and then received by TAO and PolyORB nodes.

SOAP: We tested interoperability with AWS clients and servers built on top of AWS original implementation. We verified data transfer consistency.

Then, we verified compliance at the application level: implemented API or generated code must verify a defined semantics and run-time properties:

CORBA: The OMG defined in [OMG01] how CORBA specifications are to be translated into Ada 95. We implemented these recommendations and verified correctness on typical CORBA examples. Besides, the implementation of the COS[1] Naming, COS Event and the Interface Repository stressed our implementation. Let us note that this mapping is currently under revision; adjustments may be required.

DSA: We used the *Ada Conformity Assessment Authority* test suite to validate our implementation of the Distributed System Annex. We removed the conformity tests of obsoleted features like the compliance to `System.RPC` which is no longer normative in Ada0Y (paragraph E.4.20). We pass all tests but two.

---

[1] COS: Common Object Service

The missing tests are related to variable-length types, and will be added in a near future.

AWS & MOMA: These two personalities rely on specific and not normalized interfaces. We verified on selected examples that the application nodes behaved correctly.

These different tests demonstrate that PolyORB provides a stable implementation of various distribution models, compliant to industrial standards.

Fig. 4. Code reuse in PolyORB and Jonathan

	Client	omniORB	TAO	PolyORB
Server				
omniORB		1.382s	3.310s	1.869s
TAO		N/A	2.986s	2.498s
TAO TP		N/A	3.361s	3.865s
PolyORB		1.785s	3.576s	2.056s
PolyORB TP		3.340s	5.053s	3.602s

Fig. 5. Execution time for 10,000 requests

5.2 Code Reuse

Code reuse ratio provides a measure of the reusable functional key components provided by middleware. Figure 4 shows a measure of the SLOCs present in comparable applications. We computed Source Lines Of Code (SLOCs) of the generic core and personalization specific code between PolyORB and Jonathan, for which source code is freely available. The measures have been done using SLOCCount [2].

We considered two distinct configurations: "ORB", using CORBA/GIOP personalities; and "RPC" comparing DSA/GIOP for PolyORB and RMI for Jonathan.

A raw analysis demonstrates that PolyORB NCM represents a significant part — more than 66 % — of the distribution infrastructure; Jonathan core and sets of abstract interfaces represent around 10 %. PolyORB's numbers demonstrate that the NCM provides key building blocks to implement middleware. This clearly reduces the need to write large portions of code when adapting PolyORB to meet the needs of an application. Hence, PolyORB facilitates the development of new personalities. This has been verified when implementing AWS, MIOP and MOMA: PolyORB provides generic abstractions to build different distribution models.

5.3 Code Efficiency

PolyORB novel architecture enables great configurability, genericity and interoperability. These are interesting properties when developing or deploying a dis-

---

[*] from David A. Wheeler, http://www.dwheeler.com/sloccount/

tributed application. However, middleware implementations should have acceptable performance as well. Thus, we benchmarked PolyORB against typical and configurable middleware to assess impact of its architecture on performances.

We compared the execution time for PolyORB configured with CORBA/GIOP personalities; and two very distinct C++ CORBA ORB: omniORB and TAO. omniORB (from AT&T Labs) is known for its strict compliance to CORBA specifications and its efficiency. TAO advertises its configurability and reliability properties.

PolyORB relies on dynamic mechanisms. In order to have coherent measurements sets, we tested against other dynamic clients and servers, i.e. CORBA Dynamic Interface Invocation (DII) clients and CORBA Dynamic Skeleton Interface (DSI) servers. We measure the time required to execute 10, 000 requests. Each request "echoes" an unsigned long parameter.

Figure 5 summarizes our measurements. omniORB uses its default settings, TAO and PolyORB denotes no tasking configuration of middleware, TAO Thread Pool (TP) and PolyORB TP are full tasking configurations of middleware, using a thread pool of four threads.

We note that TAO DSI cannot interoperate with omniORB DII clients, indicated by "N/A" in the table; this is a known bug. PolyORB competes with these two platforms. In thread pool mode, PolyORB has similar performance compared to TAO, better performance in mono tasking — nearly 30 %. omniORB is the fastest ORB, performance loss factor ranges from 1.3 to 2.4. The main explanation to this significant difference with omniORB is its over-optimized architecture that in return limits configurability.

5.4   Towards Reliability of Distribution Middleware

Building reliable software is a complex task, more specifically when it comes to distributed applications. Middleware tends to be used as COTS[3] components in mission critical applications. However, the integration of COTS components raises new issues to ensure reliability or to certify applications [Bud03]. Hence, developer requires precise knowledge on component behavior and properties.

At the implementation level, PolyORB enforces determinism. The use of selected algorithms and patterns as well as of the Ravenscar profile (section 4.3) ensure determinism of the basic elements of the implementation.

Then we contemplated the formal verification of our architecture. Schizophrenic middleware provides a comprehensive description of its architecture built around different well-defined services. Middleware functions are delegated to specific services. This enables separate verification of its components.

In [HPK03], we proposed a roadmap to middleware verification. The middleware main loop coordinates all functions within a middleware node. We identified this loop as the most critical component of middleware. Then, we defined and modelled it using Petri Nets. This allows us to formally verify qualitative prop-

---

[3] COTS: Commercial Off-The-Shelf

erties on the behavior of this component such as the bounds of buffers or the appropriate use of critical sections.

The other middleware services and components are less complex entities. They implement well known patterns, or simply manipulate data: they do not directly rely on constructions that may lead to faulty execution. We plan to gradually verify them. The combination of these different results is a first step towards formal verification of middleware. This provides inputs to assess properties and then to prove reliability.

PolyORB properties and performances make it a possible choice to develop distributed applications. PolyORB provides configurability and genericity which does not impede performance. Besides, PolyORB relies on strong engineering methods. The formal verifications of qualitative properties ensure middleware reliability. These are first steps to ensure the usability of PolyORB to build reliable distributed applications.

6   Conclusion

The diversity of application requirements leads to different distribution models, and then middleware implementations adapted to a specific context. Thus, distributed application engineering requires adaptable middleware to fit a wide range of applications. This paper discussed about adaptable middleware design and implementations.

First, we identified several requirements on middleware architecture: adaptability to application needs, interoperability between heterogeneous components, reliability.

Then, we discussed existing solutions. Configurable middleware allows for fine adaptation to application needs, but is restricted to a given distribution model. Generic middleware defines abstract interfaces that are to be instantiated to meet the specific needs of the application; however this implies engineering of a large portion of code for each instantiation. Interoperability between heterogeneous middleware is often addressed separately. This slows down the performances of the whole system.

We introduced *schizophrenic middleware* as a comprehensive solution to distributed applications engineering. Schizophrenic middleware solves both configurability, genericity and interoperability concerns. Schizophrenic middleware extends the concept of middleware personalities to permit several collocated personalities to inter-operate within the same middleware instance. We defined *application* personalities and *protocol* personalities, all bound to a *Neutral Core Middleware*.

Our implementation PolyORB, which is available under a free software license, demonstrates the validity of the schizophrenic concepts. We developed personalities for SOAP and protocols associated to GIOP. We also developed personalities for CORBA, DSA, Message Passing (MOMA) and Web (AWS) middleware types.

Finally, we analyzed PolyORB implementation. We detailed its compliance to industrial specifications, and discussed its interoperability with other middleware implementations. We discussed code reuse, and indicated how PolyORB design eases the implementation of new distribution models. PolyORB's benchmarks show that it competes with other well-known implementations, yet it offers more adaptation capabilities. We also discussed reliability issues: PolyORB relies on strict engineering and design methods that help to prove its reliability. We are currently modelling key elements of middleware to formally prove their reliability in specific use cases. This will provide more information on middleware reliability.

PolyORB current development focuses on stringent determinism and real-time properties of distribution middleware, as well as the implementation of real-time middleware specifications such as RT-CORBA.

References

[Bak01]   S. Baker. Middleware to middleware. In *Proceedings of the 3rd International Symposium on Distributed Objects and Applications (DOA'01)*, September 2001.

[BDV⁺98]   F. Breg, S. Diwan, J. Villacis, J. Balasubramanian, E. Akman, and D. Gannon. Java/RMI performance and object model interoperability: Experiments with Java/HPC++ distributed components. In *Proceedings of Workshop on Java for High-Performance Network Computing*, pages 91–100, May 1998.

[Bri01]   E. Briot. *XML/Ada: a full XML suite*, 2001.

[Bud03]   T. J. Budden. Decision Point: Will Using a COTS Component Help or Hinder Your DO-178B Certification Effort. *STSC CrossTalk, The Journal of Defense Software Engineering*, November 2003.

[DB98]   B. Dobbing and A. Burns. The Ravenscar tasking profile for high integrity real-time programs. In *Proceedings of SigAda'98*, Washington, DC, USA, November 1998.

[DHTS98]   B. Dumant, F. Horn, F. Dang Tran, and J-B. Stefani. Jonathan: an open distributed processing environment in java. In *Proceedings of the IFIP International Conference on Distribut ed Systems Platforms and Open Distributed Processing*, 1998.

[DKM⁺94]   M. Dietzfelbinger, A. Karlin, K. Mehlhorn, F. Meyer, H. Rohnert, and R. E. Tarjan. Dynamic perfect hashing: upper and lower bounds. *SIAM Journal on Computing*, 23(4):738–761, August 1994.

[GHJV94]   E. Gamma, R. Helm, R. Johnson, and J. Vlissides. *Design Patterns: Elements of Reusable Object-Oriented Software*. Addison Wesley, Massachusetts, 1994.

[HPK03]   J. Hugues, L. Pautet, and F. Kordon. Refining middleware functions for verification purpose. In *Monterey Workshop on Software Engineering for Embedded Systems: From Requirements to Implementation*, Chicago, IL, USA, September 2003.

[MGG96]   P. Merle, C. Gransart, and J-M. Geib. CORBAWeb: A generic object navigator. *Computer Networks and ISDN Systems*, 28(7-11):1269–1281, 1996.

[Mul93]   S. Mullender. *Distributed Systems*. ACM, 1993.

[Obr03]   P. Obry. Ada Web Server (AWS) 1.3, 2003.

[OMG01]   OMG. *Ada Language Mapping Specification, v1.2*. OMG, October 2001. OMG Technical Document formal/2001-10-42.

[OMG03]   OMG. *unreliable Multicast InterORB Protocol specification*. OMG, January 2003. OMG Technical Document ptc/03-01-11.

[PQK* 01]   L. Pautet, T. Quinot, F. Kordon, J. Hugues, and T. Vergnaud et al. Polyorb, 2001. http://libre.act-europe.fr.

[PT00]   Laurent Pautet and Samuel Tardieu. GLADE: a Framework for Building Large Object-Oriented Real-Time Distributed Systems. In *Proceedings of the 3rd IEEE International Symposium on Object-Oriented Real-Time Distributed Computing (ISORC'00)*, Newport Beach, California, USA, June 2000.

[QPK01]   T. Quinot, L. Pautet, and F. Kordon. Architecture for a reuseable object-oriented polymorphic middleware. In *Proceedings of PDPTA'01*, Las Vegas, USA, June 2001.

[Qui99]   T. Quinot. CIAO: Opening the Ada 95 distributed systems annex to CORBA clients. In *Ada France 1999*, Brest, France, September 1999.

[SC97]   D. Schmidt and Christ Cleeland. Applying patterns to develop extensible and maintainable ORB midd leware. *Communications of the ACM, CACM*, 40(12), 1997.

[SSC98]   A. Singhai, A. Sane, and R. Campbell. Quarterware for Middleware. In *Proceedings of ICDCS'98*. IEEE, May 1998.

[SUN99]   SUN. Java Message Service (JMS), 1999.

[W3C00]   W3C. *Extensible Markup Language (XML) 1.0*, 2000. W3C recommandation.

[W3C03]   W3C. *Simple Object Access Protocol (SOAP) 1.2: primer*, june 2003. W3C recommandation.

Event Language for Real-Time On-the-Fly Control According to the Initial Requirements

Stepan P. Nadrchal

DCIT Ltd., Jose Martiho 2/407, Prague
and Department of Software Engineering, Charles University, Prague
nadrchal@dcit.cz

Abstract. The paper describes a logical language (called ECL) based on Duration Calculus (DC) for the description of the requirements and behaviour of distributed and/or real-time systems. Purpose of the language is to check the behaviour of the computer base system according to the requirements written by DC in the maintenance time of the system. Furthermore, the language supports simulation of the system behaviour in the development time. The language is supported by a multipurpose tool - the EC-console, which was developed by the author in the period 1998 to 2002.

EC-console was designed to support the whole software life-cycle. It can be used to:
- define requirement conditions,
- perform simulation tests,
- check and control the running system on-the-fly.

The first part of the paper describes the concept of the language ECL; the next part presents how the conditions written in DC are mechanically translated to the ECL, and the last one presents the recent utilization of the language during the software development process.

1 Introduction

The research presented in this paper focused on the design and implementation of a formal language that could be used throughout the life-cycle of a real-time distributed system, starting with the requirements capture, modelling and simulation, through the design up to the production and maintenance support. Presented research emphasizes the integration of a formal logical language used for requirement specification and requirement correctness verification to all parts of computer-base system life cycle including the maintenance time.

We decided to build up the language upon the Duration Calculus (DC). DC is a well-tried calculus with available provers (e.g. [5]). Nevertheless, requirement description written for the correctness checking cannot be utilized for checking, if the developed system accomplishes them. Furthermore, neither DC nor interval logic or its descendants are designed to describe and check the conditions necessary in a wide

A. Llamosí and A. Strohmeier (Eds.): Ada-Europe 2004, LNCS 3063, pp. 120–131, 2004.

distributed system. Calculi were created in the time when software systems were not built with successive permanent modifications according to the fast-change business requirements. Contemporary checking system should be able to check the system on-the-fly to control its behaviour in the real world with the influence of constant changes of the system environment and system itself.

In this paper we present an Event Clause Language (ECL) that was developed during our research. The main characteristics of the language are:
- ECL is a stand-alone logical language based on evaluating conditions written in the form of logical clauses in comprehensible way. Clauses can be used by slightly trained developers without detailed knowledge of the logic
- Evaluation of clauses is fast enough to allow on-the-fly checking of the system in the runtime
- A model written in ECL can adopt extensions or modifications according to the changes of described system or its environment
- The expression power of the language goes beyond calculi and algebras oriented to the timing of real-time system and enables description of various kinds or requirements, including description of a system nodes communication or planning of resources.

Briefly, the major differences of ECL against its ancestors are the universality of the language and the possibility to check requirements on-the-fly during the run of the monitored system.

2 ECL Language

This section informally describes ECL. This paper does not provide a detailed and formal description that was published in [3].

ECL is based on Timed CSP [4], which is an extension of Communicating Sequential Process (in literature is sometimes called process algebra). The framework of both Timed CSP and ECL is founded on two basic objects: events and processes. Behaviour of systems may be viewed by way of events representing process changes and their interaction among themselves and with the environment. CSP is founded on a number of process composition operators, each of which describes a distinct behaviour pattern. The operators are based on the well-understood algebraic laws.

ECL adheres to the concepts of Timed CSP. Events with time stamps describe processes and their states. A sequence of timed events describes the system behaviour equally as in CSP. ECL clauses describe relation between processes through assertions about the set of events. ECL follows the logical concept of clauses but clusters them in the structure of classes for accurate description of object reality whilst CSP (like other logical languages) does not structure the description in this way.

Joining of the logical concept inherited from Timed CSP with the structural approach common in the programming languages enables to define algorithms from the logical description of the system constraints. This is the main distinction of the ECL from duration calculus, interval logic or CSP. A description of conditions can be used directly to build an application monitoring the developed system or even work as a console of a system.

2.1 Informal Introduction to the ECL

At the beginning of a system development is a detailed system description of requirements, conditions and observations of characteristics of the maintained and co-operating environment. We use the following requirements describing intensive care unit to introduce ECL:

Req. 1: A delay at least of 2 minutes should be between consecutive blood pressure measurements.

Req. 2: Blood pressure has to be controlled each 5 minutes.

Req. 3: If pulse decreased under 40 per minute, heart stimulator has to start with the frequency 55 pulses per minute not later than after 20 s.

The environment behaviour and the interface between the system and its environment have to be described as precisely as the system itself. The following assertions are examples of such an environment description:

Req. 4: Patient's pulse must be checked each minute (i.e. at least once in 2 minutes and not more frequently than 2 times in a minute).

Req. 5: The blood pressure should be checked at least 5 times during half an hour.

The EC language focuses on the description of dependencies between events. Each event describes a change of the state of the system. New data or signals coming from the environment also represent a change of state. In a similar way, if there was a continuous data or control flow from the environment to the system and its value significantly changed it also changes the state of the system. (A value changes significantly if the system has to react to the change.)

All assertions in ECL are described by *clauses*. The clause describes relations between events according to the time in which they occurred and information stored in the global variables. Clause can also modify the value of a global variable or generate a new event. The events, which represent changes of the system, are represented by symbol $\{e, x_1,...,x_n,t\}$ where e is the name of the event, x_i are parameters which describe the change of the state and t represents a time point when the event had been raised.

The Req. 1 and Req. 2 may be described by the following simple clause:

$$\{pulse\_control, t1\} \ \& \ \{pulse\_control, t2\}$$
$$-> t2 - t1 < 5 \text{ min} \ \& \ t2 - t1 > 2 \text{ min} \qquad \text{(c1)}$$

Symbol $\{pulse\_control, t_i\}$ describes that event *pulse control* has been raised at the time t_i. We suppose, that the event informs about testing of the pulse. Simply told, clauses (c1) checks that a time interval between two controls of the pulse is at least 30 seconds and no more than 2 minutes.

The following sections present, how requirements Req. 1 and Req. 2 are described and checked in ECL. The start and the end of the measurement are significant changes of the manometer represented by events *manometer_start* and *manometer_end* (abbreviated to *m_s* and *m_e*, when necessary).

Fig.1 presents events and clause evaluation on the time axis.
The following clause describe Req. 1:

$$\{m\_e, t1\} \ \& \ \{m\_s, t2\} \ \& \ t2 > t1 \ -> \ t1+2 \ min \geq t2 \qquad (c2)$$

Note that symbols & and | represent connectives $\wedge$ and $\vee$. Likewise in DC, clause does not explicitly define that there is no event *manometer_start* between two used events and that tested events arose successively. The validity of clauses is defined upon a sequence of external events. Events are used in the order as they arose and each event can be used for the successful evaluation of each clause only once. The validity of a clause is checked each time when it might change. The evaluation time points are marked *ev1,..., ev4* at Fig.1. The clause is evaluated in the time when an event, which is used by the clause, arises.

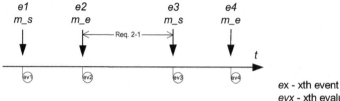

ex - xth event
evx - xth evaluation of a clause
m_s (m_e) - manometer_start (end)

Fig.1. Evaluation of clause (c2)

The oldest from the sequence of raising events are used for the evaluation of the clause. Each event is used for a successful evaluation only once. The rule is valid not only for a clause as a whole but also for each sub-clause. Table 1 shows how the events are used during the evaluation of (c2).

It may be proved that the event *e1* would never be successfully used for the clause evaluation. Futhermore, the condition t2 > t1 in the clause is necessary only because of the unused event e1. To remove e1 at start we can write a clause as follows:

$$(\{m\_s, t\} \ \& \ \neg \ \{m\_e, t1\}) \ | \ (\{m\_e, t1\} \ \& \ \{m\_start, t2\} \ ->$$
$$t1+2 \ min >= t2 \qquad (c3)$$

Although the Req. 1 and the Req. 2 look similarly, there is an important difference. If the Req. 2 was described by the clause

$$\{m\_s, t1\} \ \& \ \{m\_s, t2\} \ -> \ t1 + 5 \ min >= t2 \qquad (c4)$$

only each second interval is being checked. Although it might be sufficient in some cases, it is not what we expected. Furthermore, we check whether intervals between two manometer runs are not larger than 5 minutes. Such a check does not protect the patient against a manometer failure! If the manometer failed it does not raise a new event and so the clause will not fail because there would not be two events with an interval over 5 minutes between them.

Following clauses check that the manometer ran at least once within each 5 minutes since monitoring started. The symbol @{*clause_name, parameters, time_of_raising*} used in the clauses is called *event generator*. If used in a clause, it raises a new internal event that can be accepted by any clause of the model.

Table 1. Sequence of steps of the evaluation of clause (c2)

Ev	Sequence of events	Evaluation description	Result
ev 1	e1: {m_s, t}	Clause {m_e,t1} & {m_s,t2} fails because there is no event *manometer_end* in the sequence and the clause does not match up with it	True (the first operand of the implication is false)
ev 2	e1: {m_s, t}, e2: {m_e, t+$\square_1$}, $\square_x$ > 0	Clause is not valid because t2 > t1, i.e. t > t+$\square_1$ is not true	True
ev 3	e1: {m_s, t}, e2: {m_e, t+$\square_1$}, e3: {m_s, t+$\square_1$+$\square_2$}, $\square_x$ > 0	Clause is evaluated successfully in case that $\square_2$ > 2 minutes. The events e2 and e3 are used for the evaluation and removed from the sequence	True
ev 4	e1: {m_s, t}, e4: {m_e, t+$\square_1$+$\square_2$+$\square_3$}, $\square_x$ > 0	The first operand of the implication is not evaluated successfully for the same reason as in the evaluation ev2	True

Warning in the case that event *manometer_start* does not arise in the right time is given by clause (c7). An internally generated event _START is raised automatically at the start of the run of the monitored system and is used for the initial setting of the model.

$$\{\_START, t\} \; -> \; @\{m\_s\_test, t+5min+\square\} \tag{c5}$$
$$\{m\_s, t\} \; -> \; @\{m\_s\_test, t+5min\} \tag{c6}$$
$$\{m\_s\_test, t1\} \; -> \; \{m\_s, t2\} \; \& \; t2 \square t1 \tag{c7}$$

The term x + $\square$ represents a time point after x and is defined as:

$$\square y : (y > x \Rightarrow (y = x + \square \square \; y > x + \square))$$

Clause (c5) initialises the model by generating the first internal event *manometer_start_test*. The event is generated with the raising time t + 5 minutes and therefore it is not included in the sequence of event immediately but after 5 minutes.

Clause (c6) generates a new testing event *manometer_start_test* after each raising of the event *manometer_start*.

Clause (c7) is evaluated after each arrival of the clause *manometer_start* or the clause *manometer_start_test*. The clause is not successfully evaluated after *manometer_start* arises because the left implication operand is false. When *manometer_start_test* arises, the clause checks whether *manometer_start* had arisen before that. If not, the clause fails and can evoke an emergency action like "call hospital staff".

The example described how to check the reaction time of the monitored system. We focused on this part of the usage of the ECL because it is critical for transformation of the conditions from DC to ECL. Nevertheless, usage of ECL is not limited on time requirements. The monitored events can include also parameters, which describe how the monitored value changed. Values received by clauses can be kept in the global variables and can be used consecutively. Clauses are not evaluated as stateless logical formulas but in the context of global variables and upon a list of unused events.

The next example presents how Req. 4 is tested. *g_meass_c* is a global variable representing how many times the pulse has been tested within the last 5 minutes.

$$\{\_START, t\} @ \{m\_s, t1\} -> @\{check\_pr, t+30 \text{ min}\} \tag{c8}$$

$$\{manometer\_start, t\} -> g\_meass\_c := g\_meass\_c + 1 \tag{c9}$$

$$\{check\_pr, t\} -> g\_meass\_c >= 5 \ \& \ \{m\_s, t1\} \ \& \ \{m\_s, t2\} ->$$
$$g\_meass\_c := g\_meass\_c - 1 \ \& \ @\{check\_pr, t2+30 \text{ min}\} \tag{c10}$$

The implementation of ECL can define as many functions as necessary, e.g. a mathematical or goniometrical function, a text processing function, etc. The ECL definition is limited to the description of operators working with time point and time point differences. It defines predicates for compartment of time points and time point differences and for finding the last (predicate *max*) and the first (predicate *min*) time point from a set of them.

As was shown above, one requirement is often described by several clauses. Clauses mutually cooperate by sharing information in global variables and raising events, which are handled by another clause. Except that, a clause can call directly another clause or itself recursively. Thanks to that, clauses can be used for definition of new functions.

Furthermore, a clause can check the result of evaluation of another clause. Note that a failure of the evaluation of a clause does not necessarily mean that something is wrong. Each requirement has defined the clause, failure of which represents a failure of the requirement. The failure of a clause that does not represent any requirement is not significant.

3   From DC to ECL

In this chapter we shall show how conditions written in DC can be mechanically rewritten to the ECL notation. As an example, we use a familiar example description of conditions of gas burner, first described in [6]. We don't describe syntax of DC, which can be found elsewhere , e.g. in [2]. The following example illustrates principles of DC.

3.1 Introduction to DC

The computer system checks whether the flame is on or off using data from a flame detector. The control system manages a gas valve, which can be opened or closed. The gas burner is heating while the flame burns and idles otherwise. Before the gas burner starts to heat, there is a short time, when gas flows but the burn does not flame. Hence, there is an unavoidable time interval when gas leaks. To prevent an explosion, this time interval must not be too long and time interval between them should be sufficient to prevent the accumulation of gas. Let us suppose that the ventilation is sufficient to remove gas after a leak before gas leaks again, and that gas does not leak more than one twentieth of the elapsed time and that time over which the system is observed should be at least one minute.

DC describes conditions using two state variables G, F $\square$ *Time* $\square$ {0, 1}; *Time* is a set of non-negative reals and state expression L $\square$ *Time* $\square$ {0, 1} as follows

$$G(t) = 1 \text{ iff the gas is flowing}$$
$$F(t) = 1 \text{ iff the flame is burning}$$
$$L \square G \square \ F$$

The formalized expression of the requirement is:

$$(e \square b) \square 1\min \Rightarrow 20 \int_b^e L(t)dt \ \square (e \square b) \qquad \text{(Req)}$$

For any time interval [b,e], b $\square$e. $\int_b^e L(t)dt$ is a measure for the duration of the time interval [b,e], b $\square$e.

When the requirement is used during the design of the checking computer system it is described in decisions, which the system should fulfil and thence meets the requirement. In our example, the system controls gas valve and so it can guarantee the time when the gas flows and when not. Descriptions can be expressed as follows:

$$\square c,d : b \square c \square d \square e \square((\square t : c < t < d \square L(t) = 1) \Rightarrow (d \square c) \square 1\sec) \qquad \text{(D1a)}$$

$$\square c,d : b \square c \square d \square e \square L(c) \square (\square t \square c < t < d \square \ L(t)) \square L(d)$$
$$\Rightarrow (d \square c) > 30\sec \qquad \text{(D2a)}$$

The decision says that any gas leak in the period when the gas must not leak should be stopped within one second.

DC formulas are built up from state variables SV = {X, Y, Z,...}, symbol *l* representing length of an interval, function and predicates letter, symbol *true*, logical connectives and a modality operator $\frown$. Further, DC defines the following abbreviations:

$$\Diamond D \cong true^\frown (D^\frown true) , \text{ reads: for some subinterval } D$$
$$\square D \cong \neg\Diamond(\neg D) , \text{ reads: for all subinterval } D$$
$$\lceil P \rceil \cong \int P = l \wedge l > 0$$
$$\lceil \ \rceil \cong l = 0$$

The last abbreviations concern the notion of duration. They represent interval duration and duration of the empty interval. The abbreviation $\lceil P \rceil$ is true on a non-point interval when the state expression P is equal to 1 in the entire interval. $\lceil\,\rceil$ is true only for the point interval.

Descriptions (D1a) and (D1b) in DC are written as follows:

$$\square(\lceil L \rceil \Rightarrow l \le 1) \tag{D1b}$$

$$\square((\lceil L \rceil ^\frown \lceil \neg L \rceil ^\frown \lceil L \rceil) \Rightarrow l > 30) \tag{D2b}$$

The formulas (D1b) and (D2b) describes Requirement (Req) which can be described in DC notation as follows:

$$(\text{D1b} \wedge \text{D2b}) \Rightarrow \text{Req}$$

The formulas (D1b) and (D2b) describes Requirement (Req) which can be described in DC notation as follows:

$$(\text{D1b} \,\square\, \text{D2b}) \Rightarrow \text{Req}$$

The role of DC is to prove that the implication is correct, i.e. that the fulfilment of (D1) and (D2) by the gas burner system in any time interval is sufficient to meet (Req).

3.2 Rewriting of DC Formulas to ECL Clauses

In this section, the mechanism of translation of DC formulas to ECL is described. The first part presents how (D1) from the example above is translated and the second part presents common transcription rules.

The description (D1) says that the duration of L is shorter than one second. The state variables G and F represent the state of the gas burner and the change of their values represents the change of the system state .

ECL represents any change of the system by events informing about the change. Thence for each state variable, we define an event informing about the change. For lucidity, the names of events are derived from the names of state variables and the value of the parameter is *false* or *true* and represents the value of the state variable.

The event symbols {g, *true*, t} and {g, *false*, t} represent the change of the state of the variable G to a new value true or false. State expression $G \,\square\, F$ is rewritten:

$$\{g, gx, t1\} \,\&\, \{f, fx, t2\} \;\text{->}\; gx = true \;\&\; \quad fx = true \tag{c11}$$

From now on we will use the following abbreviation (both for *false* and *true*):
{x, *true*, tx1} $\square$ {x, gx, tx1} & gx = true

Condition $fx = true$ can be rewritten to the $fx = false$. However, we should check that only last change of the state variable is considered and that the event does not represent older change of the state. That is why expression should be written as follows:

$$(\{g, true, t1\} \,\&\, \{f,\ false, t2\} \ -> \ @\{l, true, \max(t1,t2)\}) \mid$$
$$(\{g, x1, t1\} \,\&\, \{g, x2, t2\} \,\&\, t1 > t2 \ -> \ @\{g, x1, t1\}) \mid$$
$$(\{f, x1, t1\} \,\&\, \{g, x2, t2\} \,\&\, t1 > t2 \ -> \ @\{g, x1, t1\}) \tag{c12}$$

The first line of (c12) generates an event informing that state expression L started. The two next lines check whether two events about the change of the state were raised. In that case only the last one is saved for the next clause evaluation and the first one is forgotten. Exactly told, the second part of (c12) processes all possible changes of the state expression that are not processed by the condition described by the first line.

The description (D1) requires that the state L cannot last longer than one second, i.e. the state should change within one second:

$$(\{l, true, t1\} \,\&\, \{l, false, t2\} \,\&\, t2 > t1 \ -> \ t2 < t1 + 1sec) \mid$$
$$\{l, false, t1\} \tag{c13}$$

The failure of evaluation of (c13) means, that (D1) was violated. Clause (c12) generates the event g informing that state L occurred, but we need another clause informing that state L finished. The clause informing about the end of the state is derived from the negation of L:

$$L\square\ (G\square\ F)\square\ G\square F$$

The clause describing L is written as follows:

$$(\{g, false, t1\} \mid \{f, true, t2\} \ -> \ @\{l, false, \max(t1,t2)\}) \mid$$
$$\{g, true, t1\} \mid (\{f, false, t2\} \tag{c14}$$

The first line of (c14) generates an event about the end of L when L is false. However, (c14) does not fail until a new event is raised. The second line of (c14), as well as the second part of (c12), handles the changes not handled by the first part.

The clause (c13) is sufficient if backward checking of descriptions on a running system is required. Nevertheless, the on-the-fly checking, when violation of the condition is detected in the time, when it happens, would be more useful. The following clause (c16) checks (D1) instead of (c13) at the moment, when it fails. The following clauses are based on the same technique, as was described for the clause (c4).

$$(\{l, true, t1\} \ -> \ @\{l\_check, true, t1 + 1sec + \square\}) \mid \{l, false, t1\} \tag{c15}$$
$$(\{l\_check\} \ -> \ (\{l, true, t1\} \ -> \ (\{l, false, t2\} \,\&\, t2 > t1 \ -> \ t2 < t1 + 1sec))) \mid$$
$$\{l, false, t1\} \tag{c16}$$

The second operand of the implication in (D1b), i.e. $l\,\square\,1$, expresses that something must be checked at last after one second. Hence, when L starts, the clause (c15) generates a checking event that raises after one second – which is the interval defined by (D1b). This checking event is raised regardless of the change of the state of the monitored event.

At last, we should initialise the checking system. That means that events representing initial state of the system should be generated. Let us suppose that the system starts with gas stopped and so fire not burning:

$$\{\_START, t\} \rightarrow @\{g, \mathit{false}, t\} \ \& \ @\{f, \mathit{false}, t\} \ \& \ @\{l, \mathit{false}, t1\} \qquad (c17)$$

The clauses (c12) and (c14) – (c17) create together an on-the-fly checking system that checks the run of the burning system according to (D1). The clause (c16) fails and raises a warning in the moment when the (D1) is violated and never else. Note that clauses are evaluated repeatedly every time when state changes or could change.

The model checks whether descriptions (D1) and (D2) are kept by the running system. It does not check whether (Req) is fulfilled by (D1) and (D2). A proof checking correctness of the model should be in DC.

3.3 Rules of Mechanical Transcription of DC

The section summarizes rules, which are used for mechanical translation of requirements written in DC to the ECL. The mechanism can be fully automated for the creation of clauses for backward checking of the system and thence the entire model of requirement described by DC can be mechanically transferred to ECL. Symbol $Trans(\varphi)$ represents the transcript of clause φ written in DC in ECL.

1. *Each change of the state variable or state expression is described by events.* Separate events are defined for the change of state. It can be defined as two different events g_true, g_end or as one event g with parameter (*true, false*).
2. *Initial state should be set.* All state variables and state expressions should have defined initial state in which the system starts. The initial clause, e.g. (c17), raises events corresponding with the initial state of the system.
3. *All state expressions have definition based on State variables or other state expressions, if no recursive of definitions occur.* Definition of the state expression in DC is logic proposition according to state variables. (c11) presents how a proposition is transferred to ECL clause step by step. Briefly, a clause is built up by the following rules:

   $X \equiv \{x, \mathit{true}, t1\} \ ; \ \neg X \equiv \{x, \mathit{false}, t1\}$

   $X \wedge Y \equiv \{x, \mathit{true}, t1\} \ \& \ \{y, \mathit{true}, t2\}$

4. *A formula is transcribed in two steps. In the first step it is transcribed according to the following rules:*

   $\lceil X \rceil \rightarrow \{x, true, t1\} \& \{x, false, t2\} \& t2 > t1$

   $\lceil \neg X \rceil \rightarrow \{x, true, t1\} \& \{x, false, t2\} \& t2 < t1$

   $\lceil X \rceil \frown \lceil \neg X \rceil \rightarrow \{x, true, t1\} \ \& \ \{x, false, t2\} \ \& \ \{x, true, t3\} \ \& \ t2 > t1 \ \& \ t3 > t2$

   $\lceil X \rceil \frown \lceil Y \rceil \rightarrow \{x, true, t1\} \ \& \ \{x, false, t2\} \ \& \ \{y, true, t3\} \ \& \ \{y, false, t4\}$
   $\qquad\qquad\qquad \& \ t2 > t1 \ \& \ t4 > t3 \ \& \ t2 = t3$

   $\Box X \rightarrow \neg\{x, false, t\}$

$\Diamond X \ \Box \ \{x, true, t\}$

$Trans(\Box\Box\Box) \ \Box \ Trans(\Box) \ \& \ Trans(\Box)$

$Trans(\ \Box) \ \Box \quad Trans(\Box)$

$l \ \Box \quad max(t1, \ldots, tn) - min (t1, \ldots, tn)$ where ti, i=1...n are all time points of events. Let us use the symbol $Trans^l(\Box)$ for the result of the 1st step of the transcription. In 2nd step $Trans^l(\Box)$ is supplemented by accepting all unused events:

$$\prod_{\{e_i, y_i, t_i\}}^{i+1\dots n} \Box \ Trans^1(\Box) \ \Box \ Trans^1(\Box) \prod_{\substack{x_1,\dots,x_n \Box \\ \{true, false\}}} \left(\prod^{j+1\dots n}\{e_j, x_j, t_j\} \Rightarrow @^{i=2\dots n}\{e_i, x_j, t_i\} \right) \setminus \prod_{\{e_i, y_i, t_i\}}^{i+1\dots n}$$

Examples of the rule are given e.g. in clauses (c12) or (c16) where the second part was created according to the described rule.

According to the described rule, (D2b) is transcribed to ECL as follows:

$\{l, true, t1\}$ & $\{l, false, t2\}$ & $\{l, true, t3\}$ & $\{l, false , t4\}$ & $t1 < t2$ &
$t2 < t3$ & $t3 < t4$ -> $max(t1, t2, t3, t4) - min(t1, t2, t3, t4) > 30sec$ |
$\{l, false, t1\}$ & $\{l, true, t2\}$ & $\{l, false, t3\}$ & $\{l, true , t4\}$ ->
  $@\{l, true, t2\}$ & $@\{l, false, t3\}$ & $@\{l, true , t4\}$ |
$\{l, false, t1\}$ & $\{l, true, t2\}$ & $\{l, false, t3\}$ & $\{l, false , t4\}$ ->
  $@\{l, true, t2\}$ & $@\{l, false, t3\}$ & $@\{l, false , t4\}$ |... (c18)

As mentioned, transript rules create clauses that check the validity of the system reactively, e.g. when a monitored system raises an event, clause checks whether the requirement is fulfilled. A clause checking that something must happen not earlier than after a given time is evaluated correctly on-the-fly.

On the contrary, a clause checking that the change must happen before a given time is evaluated in the time when the change happens instead of the evaluation in the time when the change is requested. Such clauses should be rewritten using an internally generated event as was illustrated by the clauses (c13) and (c16). The description of rules for active control of duration is beyond the scope of this paper. Nevertheless the recently described rules are sufficient for more simple formulas. A mechanical transcription of complex clauses for on-the-fly checking has not yet been precisely algorithmized and it depends on the human operator support.

4 Conclusion

In our paper we have presented a new logical language for checking of the correctness of the developed computer base system. The strength of the language is in its focus on real time systems where duration of actions should be considered and checked, and for a distributed system where conditions can be checked over many nodes.

As far as we know, no other tool for on-the-fly checking of the system can accept inputs in DC. DC and interval logic variants are well known and used at the beginning of critical projects to test the completeness of the system requirement description. ECL is the second step of the description utilization; it gives an opportunity to check the finished system directly according to the translated system requirements.

Furthermore, ECL is not limited to the checking of requirements. Expression strength of ECL significantly overcomes DC, which is focused on time aspects of the system run. ECL clause can describe any requirement given to the developed system, which can be checked from the deducible changes of the system state.

As had been proved by the developed tool called EC-console, the evaluation of ECL clauses is fast enough (over 600 evaluations of clauses in a second on a low-end 1-processor PC) so that ECL system description may be used directly for maintenance of a complex distributed system. ECL-console can manage the behaviour of system nodes using standard TCP/IP connection with the checked system or other communication channels including emails for the communication with remote nodes that are located behind a firewall that does not allow a direct data channel. The EC-console can serve either as a checking system or as a control centre of a distributed real time system. In that case, an ECL model manages the system behaviour by generating output events that drive the system nodes.

4.1 Further Work

As mentioned above, the transcription of DC is not sufficient for generating clauses for on-the-fly checking of complex formulas. It is sufficient for reactive system checking or for more simple clauses. The following research will be directed to the improvement of rules and the next step should develop fully functional automatic translation machine for the translation of DC model to the ECL model.

Rules for the mechanical transcription of the analysis and design models from the real-time methodology Octopus [1] had been proposed but there is no direct link with any of the recently used CASE tools. The creation of an add-on module to some CASE tool that enable a tight integration of ECL to the software development process is intended to allow a better utilisation of the language for a modelling and a testing of a system under development.

References

1. Awad M., Kuusela J., Ziegler J.: Object–Oriented Technology for Real–Time systems, Prentice Hall, 1996
2. Hansen, M. R., Zhou C.: Lecture Notes on Logical Foundations of Duration Calculus, Department of Computer Science, Technical University of Denmark, 1995
3. Nadrchal S.: Checking and Controlling Distributed and Real Time Systems, Information System Modelling, 2003
4. Nissanke N.: Realtime systems, Prentice Hall, 1997
5. Skakkebaek, J. U., Shankar N.: A Duration Calculus Proof Checker: Using PVS as a Semantic Framework, CSL Technical Report, 1993
6. Sorensen E.V., Ravn A.P., Rischel H, Control Program for gas burner: Part I: Informal Requirements, procos study 1, Technical report, ProCos Rep. ID/DTH EVS2, 1990

Implementing Execution-Time Clocks for the Ada Ravenscar Profile[*]

Juan Zamorano, Alejandro Alonso, José Antonio Pulido, and
Juan Antonio de la Puente

Departamento de Ingeniería de Sistemas Telemáticos (DIT)
Universidad Politécnica de Madrid (UPM), E28040 Madrid, Spain
{zamorano,aalonso,pulido,jpuente}@dit.upm.es

Abstract. The capability to monitor the amount of processor time that is used by real-time tasks is crucial for building real-time systems that are robust with respect to worst case execution time estimations. Execution-time clocks and timers have been proposed to be added to the language in order to support this functionality. Since a wide class of systems which may benefit from this mechanism are likely to use the Ada tasking subset known as the Ravenscar profile, it is important to check that the proposed execution-time clocks can be implemented on top of the simplified run-time systems that are used to support this profile. This paper describes a pilot implementation of execution-time clocks for the ORK kernel, and gives some examples of their possible usage in Ravenscar programs.

1 Introduction

High-integrity real-time systems usually have hard timing requirements, which have to be guaranteed by using an appropriate engineering approach for their design and implementation (see e.g. [1]). Such an approach is usually based on a computation model which enables the temporal behavior of a system to be analyzed and adjusted if necessary.

One well known example of such a computation model is based on fixed-priority scheduling theory and the associated response time analysis methods [2]. The Ada Ravenscar profile [3,4] is a subset of Ada tasking which can be used to develop high-integrity real-time applications which can be analyzed with these techniques. The profile has raised a high interest in the Ada real-time systems community, and has been preliminarily accepted to be included in the next revision of the Ada language standard[1].

Static timing analysis for fixed priority systems requires some temporal attributes, such as task periods, deadlines and execution times, to be known. However, an accurate determination of worst-case execution times (WCET) is very difficult, especially for current processors with such acceleration mechanisms as

---

[*] This work has been supported by the Spanish Ministry of Science and Technology, project no. TIC2002-04123-C03-01.

[·] See AI95-00249 and AI95-00305 on http://www.ada-auth.org/ais.html.

A. Llamosí and A. Strohmeier (Eds.): Ada-Europe 2004, LNCS 3063, pp. 132–143, 2004.

cache memories, segmentation mechanisms and speculative execution [5]. The consequence is that the WCET values that are used in timing analysis may be too optimistic and, actual execution times can occasionally be longer than expected. In order to prevent the erroneous behavior that can arise in such situations —usually called an *overrun*—, the execution time of real-time tasks should be monitored, and overruns should be detected and handled in such a way that the system integrity is not compromised.

Execution-time clocks were first included in the POSIX standard as a mechanism for execution time monitoring. Different ways of adding this kind of mechanism to the Ada language have been proposed and discussed [6], and a prototype implementation has been built on top of MaRTE OS [7]. As a result of all this work, the convenience of having execution-time clocks in Ada has gained widespread acceptance in the real-time community, and a proposal to include them in the next Ada standard has been made to the Ada Rapporteur Group (ARG) [8,9][2]. The proposal is to be included in the Real-time Systems annex, and is not restricted to the Ravenscar profile. Moreover, the application examples included in the proposal make extensive usage of some features that are forbidden in the profile, such as select statements and dynamic priorities. Using execution-time clocks with the Ravenscar profile, however, has a clear interest for the designers of high-integrity real-time systems. A recent paper [10] analyzes some possible usage patterns for an older version of the proposal, concluding that it is indeed a useful mechanism to be used with the profile.

This paper presents a new implementation of execution-time clocks on top of ORK [11], an open-source kernel that implements Ravenscar tasking for the GNAT compilation system, and provides some usage patterns which have been adapted to the version of the proposed interface which is currently under discussion by the ARG. The rest of the paper is organized as follows: section 2 summarizes the current proposal for adding execution-time clocks to Ada. The ORK implementation is described in section 3. Some performance metrics are provided in section 4. Example usage patterns are proposed in section 5. Finally, section 6 contains some conclusions.

2   Execution-Time Clocks in Ada

The current execution-time clock proposal[3] specifies a standard library package, Ada. Real_Time.Execution_Time, with the following definitions:

- A private CPU_Time type, with a set of primitive operations including basic arithmetics and Boolean comparison operators, as well as constructors and selectors, much in the same way as Ada.Real_Time.Time.
- An execution-time clock for each task, which keeps track of the time that has been spent by the system executing that task. The execution-time of a task includes run-time and kernel services executed on behalf of it.
  The current value of a task execution-time clock can be read by means of a Clock function, which returns a CPU_Time value.

---

[*] See AI95-00307 on http://www.ada-auth.org/ais.html.
[*] This paper refers to version 1.9 of AI95-00307.

The proposal also specifies a child package, Ada.Real_Time.Execution_Time. Timers, which defines a Timer type, from which execution-time timers can be declared. Each timer is associated to a task, and thus it is attached to the execution-time clock of that task. Multiple timers can be declared for a task, but the implementation may limit the number of timers associated with a single task.

Timers can be armed and disarmed. A timer can be armed either for an interval (of type Ada.Real_Time.Time_Span) or for an absolute CPU_Time value. In both cases, an access to a protected handler procedure must be provided. When the task execution-time clock has been incremented by the specified interval, or when it reaches the specified absolute value, the handler procedure is called by the run-time system. A minimum value of the ceiling priority of the enclosing protected object is specified in the Timers package. Operations for checking if a timer has expired, and for reading the remaining time for expiration, are also defined. The proposed execution-time mechanisms are indeed compatible with the Ravenscar profile, as they do not use any of its restricted features:

- Execution-time clocks and timers can be used with library-level task and protected objects, as restricted by the profile. They require the Ada.Task_Identification package, which is indeed allowed by the Ravenscar profile.
- Execution time handlers are protected procedures which can indeed be declared within library-level protected objects with zero or one protected entry, if necessary.

The only remaining issue is the use of an access procedure parameter to specify the handler in a timer Arm operation. However, the profile does not forbid the use of access procedure parameters, and while there may be some reasons for excluding them from high-integrity systems, we shall assume that limited use of this feature is acceptable at least in a wide range of Ravenscar applications.

3   Ravenscar Implementation of Execution-Time Clocks and Timers

Implementing execution-time clocks in a Ravenscar kernel has some advantages over a full Ada implementation. The fact that the task model is static and the kernel is comparatively simple and small obviously enables a simpler implementation. As a proof of concept, an implementation of execution-time clocks on top of ORK is described in this section. In particular, the reported implementation is targeted to ERC32-based computers. ERC32 is a radiation-hardened implementation of the SPARC V7 architecture which has been adopted as a standard by the European Space Agency (ESA).

Execution-time clocks and real-time clocks are conceptually very similar. In both cases, time is kept by counting the number of clock ticks. The only meaningful difference is that in the former case, time only advances for a task while it is running. In other words, the value of an execution-time clock represents the execution-time spent by a task since its start. As a consequence, there should be one such clock for each task in the system.

On the other hand, multiple timers could exist for each task. However, this feature is not useful in Ravenscar programs, where select statements are forbidden. As we shall see in section 5, all the programming patterns that we have identified for execution-time clocks under the Ravenscar restrictions use only a timer per task. In the proposed implementation, we have enforced this restriction in order to make the implementation simpler.

The next paragraphs describe the main implementation steps which have been carried out in order to add execution-time support to ORK.

3.1   Execution-Time Clocks

The implementation of execution-time clocks in ORK is based on the implementation of the real-time clock [12]. ORK uses an efficient way to implement the real-time clock, based on having the clock value split into two parts. The least significant part is kept in a hardware periodic timer. The most significant part is stored in memory and incremented by the timer interrupt handler. The period of the timer can have a relatively high value, which implies a low interrupt handling overhead. The time resolution depends only on the clock frequency that drives the hardware timer. When Ada.Real_Time.Clock is called, both parts are used to provide a time value with a high resolution. Time is represented internally in the kernel as an integer count of ticks.

The implementation of the execution-time clock in ORK follows a similar scheme. Task control blocks are augmented with two new fields. The first one is the value of the real-time clock when the task was last dispatched for execution (TDT, or *task dispatch time*). The second field is the value of the execution time when the task was last preempted or suspended (TET, *task execution time*). The time values in both fields are represented as integer counts of ticks, which is consistent with the representation of real-time as above described.

When a context switch occurs, the following operations are performed:

- For the task leaving the CPU, compute the elapsed time since the task started running, and add this value to the accumulated execution time: TET := TET + (Kernel.Time.Clock - TDT);
- For the task entering the CPU, store the current real-time clock value into the task dispatch time field: TDT := Kernel.Time.Clock;

  Calls to Execution_Time.Clock are handled as follows:

- If the invoked clock belongs to the running task, then the returned value is obtained by computing the time elapsed since the task started running and adding this value to the accumulated execution time: Clock := TET + (Kernel.Time.Clock - TDT);
- If the clock belongs to another task, then it is enough to return the value of TET field: Clock := TET;

3.2   Timer Objects

As previously stated, a maximum of one timer per task is supported. This limit enables static storage allocation to be used, and is also consistent with the Ravenscar profile requirements for static allocation of tasks and protected objects.

A timer object is implemented as a record with the following fields:

- Task identifier: the owner of the timer.
- Expiration time: the absolute execution-time at which the timer expires, in CPU ticks.
- Armed: Boolean flag, set to true when the timer is armed.
- Handler: access to the protected procedure which is to be called upon timer expiration.

3.3   Timer Operation

Fundamentals. The implementation of execution-time timers is based on that developed for absolute delays in ORK [12], which can be summarized as follows:

- All timing events —pending delays— are kept in a single delay queue, which is ordered by absolute expiration time. Every time the delay queue is modified, a single-shot hardware timer is programmed to interrupt after a real-time interval which is the difference between the expiration time of the first event in the queue and the current value of the real-time clock.
  Since the Ravenscar profile forbids all kinds of abort and select statements, delay events cannot be removed from the queue before the delay expires. This restriction also helps keeping the implementation simple.
- When the hardware timer expires, it issues an interrupt. The interrupt handler removes one or more tasks from the delay queue, adds them to the ready queue, and restarts the hardware timer provided there are more pending events in the queue.

The ERC32 computers to which ORK is primarily targeted have only one hardware one-shot timer. This means that the same hardware timer must be used for delays and execution-time timers. Therefore, each time there is a change in either the head of the delay queue or the expiration-time of the active task execution-time timer, both values are compared and the hardware timer is restarted to interrupt after an interval which is the minimum of:

- the difference between the absolute (real) expiration time of the first event in the delay queue and the current value of the real-time clock, and
- the difference between the absolute (execution) expiration time of the execution-time timer and the current value of the task execution-time clock.

Figure 1 shows an example of the hardware timer management.

Arming Timers. Execution-time timers can be armed in two ways:

- Relative time: the absolute expiration time value is computed by adding the relative execution-time interval to the current value of the task execution-time clock, and stored in the armed timer object.
- Absolute time: the execution-time value is directly stored in the armed timer object.

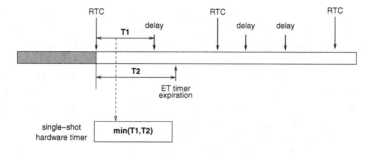

Fig. 1. One-shot timer use.

If the requested expiration time is greater than the current value of the task execution-time clock, the timer is armed (or re-armed, if it was already armed). Otherwise, the timer is said to be expired, and the appropriate handling actions are executed.

When a timer is armed the following actions are performed:

– Compute the expiration-time of the timer in CPU ticks.
– Reload the one-shot hardware timer if needed, i.e. if the timer which is being armed belongs to the running thread and expires before the the head of the delay queue.

Disarming Timers. Disarming a timer is quite a simple operation. It is only required to set the Armed flag to false and reload the one-shot timer if needed, i.e. if it was programmed for the expiration time of the disarmed timer.

Context Switches. When there is a context switch before the hardware timer expires, it has to be re-programmed taking into account the expiration time of the execution-time timer belonging to the new running task —if armed— as explained above.

3.4   Notification of Timer Expiration

An interrupt from the hardware timer may signal the expiration of an absolute delay or an execution-time timer. In the first case, the delay and ready queues are updated as above explained, and the timer is reprogrammed. Alternatively, if the interrupt signals the expiration of an execution-time timer, the associated protected procedure handler has to be called.

The Ravenscar profile allows a simple implementation of the handler call, taking into account that it prescribes the locking policy to be Ceiling_Locking. ORK uses this feature to prevent that an interrupt is accepted by the processor as long as the active priority of the running task is equal or greater than the priority of the interrupt. When this happens, the interrupt remains pending until the active priority of the running task becomes lower than the priority of the interrupt, and only then the interrupt is recognized. This means that an interrupt handler can never be blocked waiting for a protected object to become free. As a result, protected interrupt handlers can be directly used as low level interrupt handlers.

In ORK, protected handlers are called from the kernel interrupt routines, including also some prologue and epilogue code. A similar scheme is used for calling protected handler procedures upon expiration of execution-time timers. Handlers are directly called from the hardware timer low-level interrupt service routine in the kernel, without any need for any intermediate code. Of course, this implementation requires Min_Handler_Ceiling to be greater or equal than the priority of the hardware timer interrupt, which is System.Interrupt_Priority'First + 12 for ERC32 computers. It should be noticed that previous proposals of execution-time clocks for Ada[4] did not allow this implementation, because the ceiling priority of the protected object containing the timer handler was System.Priority'Last, which had as a consequence the need for an additional intermediate task [13].

3.5   External Interrupts

In the implementation described, the execution time of external interrupts is put on the running task, which is not correct in most cases. In order to avoid this undesirable effect. the value of real-time clock can be read as soon as the interrupt is recognized, and it back again just before returning to the interrupted task, i.e. in the preamble and epilogue of the interrupt service routine (ISR). The difference between both readings equals the execution time of the interrupt service routine and the user interrupt handler, if any. This value has to be subtracted from the accumulated execution time field (TET) of the running task in order to leave interrupt servicing time out of the accounted execution time of application tasks. It should be noticed that the clock must be read carefully from inside an interrupt routine. Otherwise, race conditions may arise if the hardware periodic timer interrupts are masked [12].

Properly taking into account the effect of external interrupts in execution-time timers is more complex. If the running task has an armed timer, and the hardware one-shot timer is programmed for the related expiration timing event, the hardware timer has to be stopped in the preamble, and restarted back in the epilogue, of the interrupt service routine. It must be noticed that the corresponding timing event will be delayed, and the expiration time (ET) has to be computed again. The new expiration time (ET) equals the previous one plus the execution time of the external interrupt (computed, as before, from two real-clock readings at the beginning and the end of interrupt servicing). Therefore, the closest timing event may have changed, and thus the delay queue has to be explored again. As a result, the hardware timer may have to be programmed in the epilogue with a different timing event, i.e. a closer absolute delay.

If the hardware timer is armed because the closest events is the expiration of an absolute delay, the hardware timer need not be stopped or restarted. In such cases, it is enough to correct the TET value of the interrupted task as above explained.

[.] See e.g. AI95-00307, rev 1.6 on http://www.ada-auth.org/ais.html.

These operations could be easily done if a dedicated one-shot timer were available for execution-time timers. In this case it would be enough to read the clock and stop the dedicated timer in the preamble of the ISR, and to read the clock and start the dedicated timer in the epilogue. The accumulated execution time of the interrupted task (TET) should be also updated, as before. Unfortunately, this is not the case for currently available ERC32 computers, which requires the only one available one-shot timer to be used for both absolute delays and execution-time timers.

4   Metrics

Table 1 shows significant run-time metrics for the described implementation, expressed in clock cycles. The GNAT run-time library (GNARL) uses one nanosecond resolution for all time types. In order to keep consistent with this choice, the same value (1 ns) has been used for Ada.Real_Time.Execution_Time.CPU_Time'Small in this implementation of execution-time timers.

In previous ORK versions the Kernel.Time.Time type was implemented as an integer number of nanoseconds, in order to avoid conversions between this type and the time types of GNARL. However, conversions between ticks and nanoseconds had still to be made for reading or writing the registers of the hardware timers. We have found that there is a clear gain in implementing Kernel.Time.Time as an integer number of ticks, because the speed-up of operations with clocks and timers is large enough to compensate the required conversions between the kernel and GNARL time types. As an example, the context switch overhead was reduced from 300% to 60% by this change in representation. It must be said that the ERC32 (SPARC V7) has no multiply or divide instructions, but just a multiplication step instruction. This explains the speed-up when using only integer arithmetic operations.

5   Applications

The execution-time clock proposal (AI95-00307) includes several examples of usage, but all them require full Ada tasking support, as they make use of asynchronous transfer of control or dynamic priorities. A set of Ravenscar-compliant

Table 1. Execution-time metrics in processor clock cycles.

Run-time metric	Time in	
	ns	ticks
Ada.Real_Time.Execution_Time.Timer.Arm	3251	1000
Ada.Real_Time.Execution_Time.Clock	942	171
Context Switch Overhead	1551	300
Notification Lateness	1898	802

NOTE: The context switch time without execution-time support is 523 clock cycles.

templates for detecting and handling overruns using execution-time clocks was provided in a recent paper [10], but they use a previous version of the proposed interface. This section includes updated versions of the templates, which can be used in Ravenscar-compliant applications built on top of the ORK kernel.

5.1 Handled Overrun Detection

This is an example of a periodic task that can detect execution-time overruns and handle them locally. The code of the example is given in program 1:

```
-- Program 1: Handled overrun detection

with Ada.Real_Time, Ada.Real_Time.Execution_Time;
use type Ada.Real_Time.Time, Ada.Real_Time.Time_Span,
        Ada.Execution_Time.CPU_Time;

task Periodic_Handled is
   pragma Priority(...);
end Periodic_Handled;
                                                                    10
task body Periodic_Handled is
   Next_Start : Ada.Real_Time.Time := Ada.Real_Time.Clock;
   Budget    : constant Time_Span := Ada.Real_Time.Microseconds(500);
   Period    : constant Time_Span := Ada.Real_Time.Milliseconds(100);
   Limit     : Ada.Real_Time.Execution_Time.CPU_Time;
begin
   loop
      Limit := Ada.Real_Time.Execution_Time.Clock + Budget;
      Do_useful_work;
      if Ada.Real_Time.Execution_Time.Clock > Limit then            20
         -- budgeted execution time exceeded
         Handle_the_error;
      end if;
      Next_Start := Next_Start + Period;
      delay until Next_Start;
   end loop;
end Periodic_Handled;
```

This a simple scheme, but it has the disadvantage that the overrun is only detected when task finishes its useful work, which may be too late and might compromise the behavior of other tasks in the system. A more elaborate scheme which overcomes this problem follows in the next section.

5.2 Supervised Overrun Detection

The second example (program 2) uses a timer and a supervisor task to detect the overrun when it happens. A protected object is used to synchronize the supervisor task with the timer expiration.

-- Program 2: Supervised overrun detection

```ada
with Ada.Real_Time,
     Ada.Real_Time.Execution_Time, Ada.Real_Time.Execution_Time.Timers
     Ada.Task_Identification;
use type Ada.Real_Time.Time, Ada.Real_Time.Time_Span,
     Ada.Real_Time.Execution_Time.CPU_Time;

task Periodic_Supervised is
   pragma Priority(...);                                                  10
end Periodic_Supervised;

task Supervisor is
   pragma Priority(...);
end Supervisor;

protected Control is
   pragma Priority(...);
   -- must be >= Ada.Real_Time.Execution_Time.Timers.Min_Handler_Ceiling
   entry Wait_Overrun;                                                    20
   procedure Signal_Overrun;
private
   Expired : Boolean := False;
end Control;

task body Periodic_Supervised is
   My_Id : aliased Task_Identification.Task_Id :=
     Periodic_Supervised'Identity;
   My_Timer : Ada.Real_Time.Execution_Time.Timers.Timer (My_Id'Access);
                                                                          30
   Next_Start : Ada.Real_Time.Time := Ada.Real_Time.Clock;
   Budget   : constant Time_Span := Ada.Real_Time.Microseconds(500);
   Period   : constant Time_Span := Ada.Real_Time.Milliseconds(100);
   Limit    : Ada.Real_Time.Execution_Time.CPU_Time;
begin
   loop
     Ada.Real_Time.Execution_Time.Timers.Arm
       (My_Timer, Budget, Control.Signal_Overrun'Access);
     Do_useful_work;
     Ada.Real_Time.Execution_Time.Timers.Disarm(My_Timer);              40
     Next_Start := Next_Start + Period;
     delay until Next_Start;
   end loop;
end Periodic_Supervised;

task body Supervisor is
begin
   loop
     Control.Wait_Overrun;
     Handle_the_error;                                                   50
   end loop;
end Supervisor;
```

This example leaves unsolved the question of how to handle overruns once detected. Some possible recovery schemes are proposed in earlier publications (see e.g. [10]).

6 Conclusions

The previous sections describe the implementation in ORK, and some usage schemes, of execution-time clocks as specified in the current proposal for including this mechanism in the future revision of the Ada standard. The work takes advantage of the Ravenscar profile restrictions, which enable a simple, efficient implementation of the execution-time functionality. We also believe that the ideas behind the ERC32 implementation can be easily translated to other platforms, such as the ORK version for embedded PC architectures.

An unsolved question is how to handle an overrun when working under the Ravenscar profile restrictions. Dynamic priorities, and select and abort statements are forbidden, which leaves few options to handle overrun situations. System reset and safe stop procedures are common options, but no reconfiguration is possible under the static design schemes favored by the Ravenscar profile definition.

References

1. Vardanega, T.: Development of on-board embedded real-time systems: An engineering approach. Technical Report ESA STR-260, European Space Agency (1999) ISBN 90-9092-334-2.
2. Burns, A.: Preemptive priority based scheduling: An appropriate engineering approach. In Son, S., ed.: Advances in Real-Time Systems. Prentice-Hall (1994)
3. Burns, A., Dobbing, B., Romanski, G.: The Ravenscar profile for high integrity real-time programs. In Asplund, L., ed.: Reliable Software Technologies — Ada-Europe'98. Number 1411 in LNCS, Springer-Verlag (1998)
4. Burns, A., Dobbing, B., Vardanega, T.: Guide for the use of the Ada Ravenscar profile in high integrity systems. Technical Report YCS-2003-348, University of York (2003)
5. Puschner, P., Burns, A.: A review of worst-case execution time analysis. Real-Time Systems **18** (2000) 115–128
6. Aldea, M., González-Harbour, M.: Extending Ada's real-time systems annex with the POSIX scheduling services. Ada Letters **XXI** (2001) 20–26 Proceedings of the 10th International Real-Time Ada Workshop, Las Navas, Ávila, Spain, September 2000.
7. Aldea, M., González-Harbour, M.: MaRTE OS: An Ada kernel for real-time embedded applications. In Strohmeier, A., Craeynest, D., eds.: Reliable Software Technologies — Ada-Europe 2001. Number 2043 in LNCS, Springer-Verlag (2001) 305–316
8. González-Harbour, M., Vardanega, T.: Report of session: Current real-time AIs. Ada Letters **XXIII** (2003) 22–23 Proceedings of the 12th International Real-Time Ada Workshop (IRTAW 12).
9. Burns, A., Vardanega, T.: Report of session: Generating new AIs. Ada Letters **XXIII** (2003) 93–95. Proceedings of the 12th International Real-Time Ada Workshop (IRTAW 12).
10. de la Puente, J.A., Zamorano, J.: Execution-time clocks and Ravenscar kernels. Ada Letters **XXIII** (2003) 82–86

11. de la Puente, J.A., Ruiz, J.F., Zamorano, J.: An open Ravenscar real-time kernel for GNAT. In Keller, H.B., Ploedereder, E., eds.: Reliable Software Technologies — Ada-Europe 2000. Number 1845 in LNCS, Springer-Verlag (2000) 5–15

12. Zamorano, J., Ruiz, J.F., de la Puente, J.A.: Implementing Ada.Real_Time.Clock and absolute delays in real-time kernels. In Strohmeier, A., Craeynest, D., eds.: Reliable Software Technologies — Ada-Europe 2001. Number 2043 in LNCS, Springer-Verlag (2001) 317–327

13. Dobbing, B., de la Puente, J.A.: Session: Status and future of the Ravenscar profile. Ada Letters **XXIII** (2003) 55–57 Proceedings of the 12th International Real-Time Ada Workshop (IRTAW 12).

Extending the Capabilities of Real-Time Applications by Combining MaRTE-OS and Linux[*]

Miguel Masmano, Jorge Real, Ismael Ripoll, and Alfons Crespo

Department of Computer Engineering (DISCA)
Universidad Politécnica de Valencia, Spain
{mmasmano,jorge,iripoll,alfons}@disca.upv.es

Abstract. This paper presents two different ports of the MaRTE operating system to work jointly with the Linux system on the same processor. The first port enables MaRTE OS to be executed as a regular Linux kernel module; this port enhances the MaRTE OS environment with all the Linux facilities while keeping the real-time performance of the original MaRTE kernel.
The other development presented is the Linux user-mode MaRTE OS, which is a port of MaRTE to be executed as a single standard Linux process.
These two ports greatly improve and simplify the use of MaRTE.

1 Introduction

The importance and significance of embedded systems is increasing as well as their complexity and the range of application. This is supported by an increasing degree of heterogeneity and networking, and working with a large variety of information sources to interact with sensors and actuators. Now, many embedded systems are large in size and include several sensors, actuators and computing elements. Examples of large embedded systems include industrial controllers, flight control systems, robotic systems and vehicle control. Examples of small embedded systems include cell phones, car engine controllers, smart sensors, and smart cards.

There exist a huge number of commercial and academic Real-Time Operating Systems (RTOSs) that provide different kinds of services to develop embedded systems. Some of them play an important role in the real-time field (VxWorks, LynxOS, QNX, RTEMS, MaRTE OS, RTLinux, etc.). A comparison of their functionalities and services can be found in [1]. Some of them correspond to open-source projects and provide the sources of the RTOS like RTEMS, MaRTE OS and RTLinux.

Although Linux was designed as a general purpose operating system, the Linux community has been working to adapt it to real-time and embedded systems. RTLinux is an example of how Linux can be used for real-time applications by adding an executive to the Linux kernel that provides real-time services, whilst Linux is seen as a thread. Moreover, Linux can improve its real-time capabilities with the addition of several patches [2,3] to reduce the latency of the Linux kernel and allow using it for soft real-time applications. A good example of the synergy of RTLinux and Linux for hard and soft real-time applications can be found in [4] where the Linux thread is executed as a

---

[*] This work has been supported by the European Commission OCERA project: IST-2001-35102.

A. Llamosí and A. Strohmeier (Eds.): Ada-Europe 2004, LNCS 3063, pp. 144–155, 2004.
© Springer-Verlag Berlin Heidelberg 2004

constant bandwidth server (CBS) at the RT-Linux level, providing a guaranteed use of the CPU. This approach allows to implement resource management at the Linux level.

Moreover, the Linux kernel itself provides the drivers for a large number of devices, it is relatively simple to develop new drivers and it is possible to run Linux on several hardware platforms. The combination of small and powerful real-time kernels, like MaRTE OS and Linux, can be a good approach to develop embedded systems with hard and soft real-time constraints, and with access to a wide range of services.

MaRTE OS [5] is a real-time kernel for embedded applications developed at the *Universidad de Cantabria* that follows the Minimal Real-Time POSIX.13 subset, providing both C and Ada interfaces. On the other hand, in the OCERA project [6], the POSIX interface of RTLinux has been completed and it has made it possible to port Ada applications to RTLinux [7].

In this paper we try to combine the advantages of MaRTE OS and the Linux kernel to provide an execution environment that is adequate to implement hard and soft real-time applications. By virtualising the hardware, it is possible to run a kernel like MaRTE OS beneath the Linux kernel, as RTLinux does, or as a Linux process, for testing purposes. This approach facilitates the use of Ada for hard and soft real-time applications, as well as applications with both kinds of requirements.

This paper is organised as follows. Section 2 describes in detail the MaRTE OS and RTLinux approaches, comparing their advantages and drawbacks. Section 3 describes the hardware virtualisation needed to run MaRTE OS as a kernel module or as a Linux process. Finally, Section 4 provide our conclusions.

2   MaRTE OS and RTLinux-GPL: Two Different Approaches for Real Time Kernels

2.1   MaRTE OS Overview

Before MaRTE OS was developed, most existing POSIX real-time operating systems were commercial systems that did not provide their source code —or required confidentiality agreements—, and the freely available OSs were not POSIX-compliant, e.g. RTEMS [8] or the first versions of RTLinux [9]. For these reasons it was necessary to produce a new kernel from scratch, completely designed to follow the POSIX model. This kernel, called MaRTE OS, is suitable for the development of real-time applications and also as a research tool where new features can be tested.

MaRTE OS (Minimal Real-Time Operating System for Embedded Applications) is a real-time kernel for embedded applications that follows the Minimal Real-Time POSIX.13 subset, providing both Ada and C POSIX interfaces. Most of its code has been written in Ada with some C and assembly parts.

As shown in figure 1, MaRTE OS has been designed in two well-defined parts: the kernel and the hardware abstraction layers.

The kernel, which has been completely written in Ada, implements the POSIX functionality through the Florist library[1] and it also provides a basic, standard C library. The

---

[1] Florist (Florida State University/Forest) is a GPL binding of the POSIX (IEEE Standard 1003.5b-1996) standard operating system functions

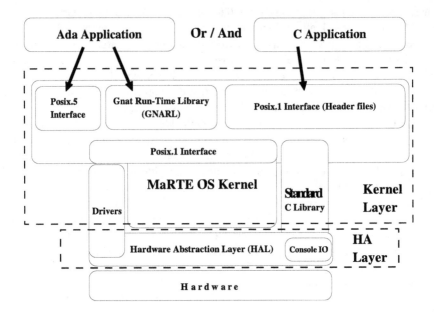

Fig. 1. The MaRTE OS architecture

kernel system calls can be directly used by C applications or indirectly —through the GNAT run-time system— by Ada applications.

The low-level, hardware-specific code is located in the Hardware Abstraction Layer (HAL). The MaRTE OS HAL only supports the hardware that is relevant to real-time performance, i.e., interrupt management, clock and timer management, context switch and basic port access facilities. Since MaRTE OS does not use virtual memory, neither paging nor segmentation are required. On system boot, virtual memory is not activated.

2.2   RTLinux-GPL Overview

Linux was initially designed as a general purpose OS, mainly for use as a desktop OS. Once Linux became more popular, it started to be used in server machines. Kernel developers added multiprocessor support, management of large amounts of memory, efficient handling of large numbers of running processes, etc. Nowadays, Linux is a full-featured, efficient (good throughput) OS, but with little or no real-time performance.

There are two different approaches to provide real-time performance in a Linux system:

1. To modify the Linux kernel to make it a kernel with real-time characteristics. For this purpose, the kernel needs to be:

   Predictable: This requires to improve the internal design to use efficient and time-bounded algorithms. For example, a fast scheduler.

Responsive: The kernel needs to be preemptable in order to interrupt (or postpone) the servicing of a low priority process when a high priority process becomes active and requires to use the processor.

Real-time API: Real-time applications have special requirements not provided by the classic UNIX API. For example, POSIX real-time timers, message queues, special scheduling algorithms, etc.

2. To add a new operating system (or executive) that takes the control of some hardware subsystems (those that can compromise the real-time performance) and that gives Linux a virtualised view of the controlled devices.

RTLinux was the first project to provide real-time in Linux using two separate OSs: Linux as the general purpose OS and a newly developed executive running beneath Linux. The RTLinux internal structure can be divided into two separate parts: 1) a hardware abstraction layer, and 2) the executive operating system.

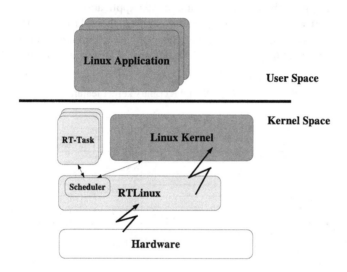

Fig. 2. The RTLinux-GPL architecture

The RTLinux HAL [2] is in charge of the hardware devices that conflict with Linux (interrupt controller and clock hardware). This layer provides access to these hardware devices to both the RTLinux executive and Linux in a prioritised way. Hardware virtualisation is achieved by directly modifying the Linux kernel sources applying a patch file. These changes do not replace the hardware drivers by virtual drivers but prepare

---

[2] The mechanism to intercept hardware access off a general purpose OS to implement a real-time layer is covered by U.S. Patent No. 5,995,745, titled: "ADDING REAL-TIME SUPPORT TO GENERAL PURPOSE OPERATING SYSTEMS". The owner of the patent permits the use of the patented method if the software is released under the General Public License (GPL). For more details read "The RTLinux Open Patent License, version 2.0" [10]

the kernel, adding hooks, to dynamically replace the drivers. The code that actually vir-
tualises the interrupt and clock devices are two separate kernel modules [3]: rtl.o and
rtl_timer.o.

Currently, there are several Linux projects that use this (or a similar) approach:
Real-Time Application Interface (RTAI), Adaptive Domain Environment for Operating
Systems (ADEOS) and RTLinux-GPL. The work presented in this paper has been based
on the code of the RTLinux-GPL project. In what follows, RTLinux-GPL will be referred
to as RTLinux for short.

The RTLinux executive implements a partial Minimal Real-Time POSIX.13 interface. The executive is highly customisable. It has been implemented in a modular way
that permits to dynamically load into the system the parts of the API that are used by the
application. In addition, several parts of the code are surrounded by conditional prepro-
cessor directives that allow to tailor the final RTLinux executive even more, by using a
graphical interface.

Support for Ada in RTLinux is provided through RTLGNAT [7]. RTLGNAT is a port
of the GNAT compiler that allows to compile Ada applications as RTLinux modules.
Since RTLinux was not directly designed to support the Ada programs, it needs to
duplicate tables to store system information (e.g., thread and mutex information, etc.).

Table 1 summarises the main differences between RTLinux and MaRTE OS.

Table 1. MaRTE OS and RTLinux kernel features

	MaRTE OS	RTLinux-GPL
API	POSIX	POSIX like (Not Completely POSIX)
Supported languages	Ada, C	Ada, C, C++
Ada support	Native	Needs RTLGNAT
Written in	Ada, Assembly, C	Assembly, C
Architectures	i386	i386, PPC, ARM
Development environment	Cross	Native
Footprint using Ada	800 KB approx.	800 KB approx. + Linux kernel size
Footprint using C	800 KB approx.	120 KB approx. + Linux kernel size
Communications	RS232, Ethernet	RS232, Ethernet,
Inter-Task	Shared-Memory	RTFifos, Shared-Memory
Debugging	Cross GDB, Event tracer	GDB, Event tracer
Supported by	MaRTE OS's authors	Mailing list
License	GPL	GPL, Comercial
Graphics support	No	Yes (throught Linux)
Drivers	Nowadays there exists a small number of drivers	Hundreds of device drivers (provided by the Linux Kernel)

3   Extending the Capabilities of MaRTE OS

MaRTE OS is an ideal choice for developing embedded, hard and/or soft real-time
applications in Ada, C or both.

---

[3] A Linux kernel module is a piece of code that can be loaded and unloaded into the kernel upon
demand.

However, MaRTE OS is a recent product, currently at the beginning of its development, and it almost does not provide device drivers nor other capabilities like networking. Moreover, it is currently supported only in the x86 architecture. This section describes the two methods we have explored to improve the usability of MaRTE OS: 1) using the RTLinux approach for executing *MaRTE OS as a Linux module*; and 2) modifying the MaRTE OS kernel to be executed as *Linux user application*.

3.1   Running MaRTE OS as a Linux Kernel Module

The general idea is to use the same approach used by RTLinux (and the same code, since it is an open source project under GPL), but replacing the RTLinux API by the MaRTE OS executive. This way of executing MaRTE greatly simplifies the use of MaRTE applications since no rebooting is needed to re-run.

Most of the port work has focused on adapting the MaRTE HAL to use the RTLinux HAL. Also minor changes have been done to the kernel code of MaRTE. The following is a more detailed description of the port work.

Virtual interrupt manager. This part of the HAL has been directly taken from the RTLinux HAL. This code is composed of a patch to be applied to the Linux kernel sources and a kernel module. The only difference with the original code is the addition of an integer counter to count number of nested interrupts, in order to call the MaRTE OS scheduler properly (on the return from a non-nested interrupt routine if scheduling has been marked as pending). The functionality provided is to deliver real interrupts to MaRTE OS and software (emulated) interrupts to the Linux kernel. Hardware interrupts are first handled by MaRTE OS, who then reissues to the Linux kernel the interrupts that must be processed by Linux. The virtual interrupt manager system offers the following interface:

– For MaRTE OS:

  - To install/uninstall an interrupt handler. These functions allow MaRTE OS to install/uninstall interrupt handlers for handling real interrupts. They also allow MaRTE OS to deal with exceptions.
  - To enable/disable interrupts. These functions are directly translated into the STI and CLI processor instructions.
  - To send virtual interrupts to the Linux kernel. MaRTE OS can generate virtual interrupts.

– For the Linux kernel:

  - Install/Uninstall an interrupt handler. These functions allow the Linux kernel to install/uninstall interrupt handlers for dealing only with virtual interrupts but they do not allow to manage real ones.
  - Enable/Disable interrupts. These functions enable/disable virtual interrupts. The Linux kernel does not have to be allowed to enable/disable real interrupts because this could produce priority inversion problems.

Virtual hardware timer. This implementation is completely based on the RTLinux implementations. No modifications have been done to the original code. The functionality of the virtual timer is to send a periodic virtual timer interrupt to the Linux kernel every 10 milliseconds. It also offers a timer interface to MaRTE OS.

- For MaRTE OS:
  - To get the current time.
  - To set the timer to produce a timer interruption.
- For the Linux kernel:
  - To emulate the timer hardware by delivering a clock interrupt every 10 milliseconds. No Linux code has been changed.

Providing the necessary kernel symbols. The Linux kernel module loader assumes that several symbols are defined in the module:

- init_module(): when a Linux kernel module is loaded this is the first function to be executed. It is invoked by the loader and is in charge of initialising virtual devices and the MaRTE OS kernel.
- cleanup_module(): this function removes device drivers and stops the MaRTE OS kernel.
- KERNEL_LICENSE, KERNEL_VERSION, MODULE_AUTHOR, etc. are not mandatory, but recommended.

MaRTE OS's HAL. The new version of the MaRTE HAL (called **linux_x86 HAL**) contains the new interrupt and clock drivers, taken from RTLinux code (including the above explained modifications), and the I/O port access as well as the context switch of the original MaRTE HAL.

Virtual processor. Besides sharing interrupt and clock devices, MaRTE and Linux also have to share the processor. The first and simpler solution is to run the Linux kernel (jointly with Linux applications) as the background [4] task of MaRTE OS. This is the same strategy used by RTLinux. This solution forces to modify the MaRTE OS kernel layer, which is not hardware dependent. The modification affects the Idle task body. The following listing shows The previous Idle_Task_Body:

```
function Idle_Task_Body (Arg : System.Address)
                        return System.Address is
begin
   while True loop
      null;
   end loop;
   return System.Null_Address;
end Idle_Task_Body;
```

---

[4] A more flexible solution, but also more complex, is to schedule the Linux kernel using a constant bandwidth server [4]

and this is the modified code:

```
function Idle_Task_Body (Arg : System.Address)
                        return System.Address is
   procedure Enable_Linux_Thread;
   pragma Import (C, Enable_Linux_Thread, "enable_linux");
begin
   Enable_Linux_Thread;
   return System.Null_Address;
end Idle_Task_Body;
```

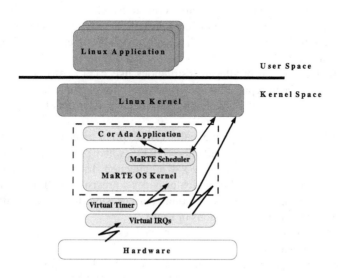

Fig. 3. MaRTE compiled as a Linux kernel module

In addition, a single function of the MaRTE C libraries (the exit() function) has been modified. Figure 3 summarises the modifications done to the x86 hardware abstraction layer.

3.2   Running MaRTE OS as a Linux User Application

In this second port, the hardware abstraction layer of MaRTE has been replaced by a new HAL, different to the previous port (MaRTE/LKM) that provides the same API to the MaRTE kernel but works on top of the Linux kernel as a regular Linux process. In this environment (MaRTE/LUP, for short), it is not possible to provide hard real-time performance since we are constrained by the limited real-time capabilities of Linux. On the other hand, since Linux processes are executed with many security restrictions, an erroneous application will not hang the computer. It is much easier and faster to develop and debug applications in this safe environment, where the developer can compile and safely run the application in the same computer.

As a consequence, running MaRTE OS as a Linux user application is a powerful combination to develop and test the logical correctness of applications. And once the application is ready, the same application code can be compiled with either the original MaRTE OS code to be deployed in a stand-alone machine, or with the MaRTE OS Linux module to work jointly with Linux.

This port is just a replacement of the MaRTE OS HAL with a new one: the Linux HAL. Following is a description of the main issues raised during the implementation of the new Linux HAL.

Interrupt manager. MaRTE interrupts are mapped into UNIX signals. This means that MaRTE/LUP applications (as other Linux processes) do not have the view of interrupts. Instead, signals are the only events to which a handler can be attached. For example, when the MaRTE OS kernel installs an interrupt handler for the timer interrupt, it is the Linux HAL who will actually install the timer handler by providing a hook to SIGALRM.

Privileged intructions. All privileged instructions like `cli()`, `sti()`, `out()`, `in()` and so on, have been replaced with virtual ones. For example the `cli()`, `sti()` instructions do not actually enable/disable processor interrupts but enable/disable process signals.

Timer driver. Two different implementations of a virtual timer have been done. The first one uses the High Resolution Timers (HRT) [5], which provides the POSIX timers API with a precision of 1 μsec in the x86 architecture. The second implementation uses the System V `itimer` API which provides a precision of 10 ms. The second implementation was done for compatibility reasons, since the System V timers API is available by default in all versions of Linux.

I/O devices. The console has been implemented using the standard `read()` and `write()` "C" functions.

Initialisation. A wrapper `main()` function initialises the MaRTE OS virtual timer and executes the `iopl()` [6] Linux system call for allowing MaRTE applications to access all the I/O ports and also to directly execute `sti` (setting interruptions) and `cli` (clearing interruptions) processor instructions.

Next is a list of all the Linux system calls used to implement the Linux HAL:

- I/O functions: `write`, `read`, `iopl`, `open`, `close`.
- Unix standard funcions: `exit`, `getuid`.
- POSIX Signals functions: `sigaction`, `pause`.
- Timing functions: (System V) `setitimer`; (POSIX) `timer_settime`, `timer_create` and `timer_delete`.

The MaRTE context switch code as well as the port access functions of the new Linux HAL are the same as in the original HAL. It is important to note that the whole MaRTE OS jointly with the MaRTE application are executed as a single Linux process: it is MaRTE who internally implements concurrency.

---

[5] HRT is a contribution to the Linux kernel, distributed as a patch file for kernel 2.4.x and which will be included in the next release of Linux (2.6.x).

[6] `iopl()` changes the I/O privilege level

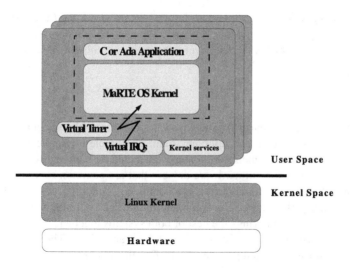

Fig. 4. MaRTE OS as a Linux user mode application

As shown in figure 4, this port requires a small number of changes, allowing us to port new versions of MaRTE OS in a few hours.

Like any other Linux user applications, with this port the MaRTE executive (MaRTE + application) gains the capability to invoke directly all the Linux system calls and, of course, all the services of the standard Linux C library, providing them all the Linux facilities, e.g. network, disk, access to all device drivers, and so on.

Nevertheless this port was not done with that aim since MaRTE applications which use Linux services or other Linux facilities could be incompatible with other MaRTE versions, for example the fork() system call will work in MaRTE/LUP but the result of that call will not be the same in a MaRTE/LKM program.

However, there exist cases where the use of Linux services is justified, for example when a new network is being developed for MaRTE; it would interesting to test applications which need this new stack with the Linux stack first and afterwards with the new stack MaRTE.

The main advantage of this port is, basically, the capability to test any MaRTE application in a memory protected enviroment with only one machine, a Linux box, before running them in the actual MaRTE target.

This approach also provides the capability of debugging any application and even the MaRTE Kernel through a Linux debugging tool (e.g., gdb).

Obviously, when running a MaRTE application as a Linux executable one can not expect the same timing behaviour as will be achieved in a final (purely MaRTE) version.

In summary, the advantages are access to the Linux services, memory protection and the possibility of using well-known debugging tools. Once the application has been tested in this framework, a MaRTE version can be compiled and run with all the timing properties of the MaRTE OS.

Another interesting use for this port, besides the previous one (as a test plataform) is for academic purposes. Students can use a whole POSIX compliant real-time OS (without real-time guarantees in the development phase) with only a Linux box.

4   Conclusions

The work presented in this paper is directed towards combining the advantages of MaRTE OS and Linux to provide an execution environment suitable for applications with hard and/or soft real-time requirements. MaRTE is well suited for hard real-time applications, but lacks drivers to cope with hardware devices that are common to modern real-time applications. On the other hand, Linux is a complete, general-purpose OS, but cannot provide real-time performance. The combination of these operating systems by means of hardware virtualisation brings the best of both systems together.

We have shown two ways of combining MaRTE and Linux. The first one is to run MaRTE beneath Linux, which provides MaRTE with full control of hardware, running at a higher priority than Linux. This approach provides hard real-time guarantees for the MaRTE application. The second combination is to run the MaRTE application as a regular Linux process, which fits very conveniently in the first stages of implementation, where the logical correctness of the application can be comfortably tested, without the need for frequent rebooting.

For this work to be possible, the design of MaRTE has been of key importance: its clean architecture, with two well-defined layers, has helped enormously to implement the two ports hereby presented.

Another possibility —to be explored in the future— is to use both approaches at the same time, with the hard real-time part of the application running at the highest priority, beneath the Linux kernel, and the soft real-time parts running as Linux processes. The communication between these parts can be achieved by means of real-time FIFOs (available as Linux modules) or shared memory.

As a final conclusion, this approach facilitates the use of Ada for both hard and soft real-time applications.

References

1. Ripoll, I., Pisa, P., Abeni, L., Gai, P., Lanussea, A., Saez, S., Privat, B.:   RTOS Analysis. OCERA Deliverable.   http://www.ocera.org/archive/deliverables/ms1-month6/-WP1/D1.1.html (2002)
2. Ingo Molnar: Linux Low Latency Patch from Multimedia Applications. http://people.redhat.-com/mingo/lowlatency-patches/ (2000)
3. MontaVista: Preemption Patch for the Linux Kernel. http://www.linuxdevices.com/articles/-AT4185744181.html (2000)
4. L. Marzario, G. Lipari, P. Balbastre, P. Mendoza and A. Crespo: A new reclaiming algorithm for server-based real-time systems. In: Proceedings of the Real-Time System Sysmposium, Work-in-progress Session. Cancun. Mexico. (2003)
5. Aldea, M., González-Harbour, M.: MaRTE OS: An Ada Kernel for Real-Time Embedded Applications. Volume 2043. (2001) 305–316

6. OCERA: Open Components for Embedded Real-Time Applications. European IST programme 35102. http://www.ocera.org (2002)
7. M. Masmano and J. Real and I. Ripoll and A. Crespo: Running Ada on Real-Time Linux. In: J. P. Rosen, A. Strohmeier (Eds): Proceedings of 8th Reliable Software Technologies - Ada-Europe 2003, Toulouse, France, June 16-20, 2003. Lecture Notes in Computer Science. Volume 2655., Springer Verlag (2003) 322–333
8. OAR: RTEMS. Real-Time Operating System for Multiprocessor Systems. http://www.rtems.com (1997)
9. Barabanov, M.: A Linux-based Real-Time Operating System. Master's thesis, New Mexico Institute of Mining and Technology, Socorro, New Mexico (1997)
10. FSMLabs: The RTLinux Open Patent License, version 2.0. http://fsmlabs.com/products/rtlinuxpro/rtlinux_patent.html (1999)

Supporting Deadlines and EDF Scheduling in Ada

Alan Burns[1], Andy J. Wellings[1], and S. Tucker Taft[2]

Department of Computer Science
University of York, UK
{burns,andy}@cs.york.ac.uk
SofCheck, USA
stt@sofcheck.com

Abstract. Scheduling policies are of crucial importance to real-time systems. Ada currently gives full support to the most popular policy, fixed priority dispatching. In this paper we argue that the language should be extended to support another common paradigm, Earliest Deadline First (EDF). A proposal is described that uses standard priorities and the priority ceiling protocol for protected objects.[1]

1 Introduction

One of the major features of Ada 95 is its support for fixed priority scheduling. A complete and consistent model is provided that allows this common dispatching approach to be used in real industrial applications. The model is also retained in the Ravenscar subset [3]. Ada does not however restrict itself to this single paradigm; it allows other dispatching policies to be defined. Unfortunately without the force of the language definition, new policies have not been introduced by vendors or specified in any secondary or de facto standards.

The current ISO process of considering amendments to the language allows the dispatching rules of Ada to be expanded. For example, an Ada Issue (AI) on non-preemptive (fixed priority) scheduling has already been agreed by WG9 (the ISO working group responsible for the language standard). This required some rewording of the ARM (sections D.2.1 and D.2.2).

Much more is now understood about scheduling than was the case when the original Ada definition was created. If Ada is to remain a viable language of choice in the real-time domain it would benefit from an increase in its expressive power in this area. Indeed, significant advances would help reassert Ada's prominence.

The literature on scheduling methods implies that Ada could be expanded in three areas:

- Support for new paradigms, eg. Earliest Deadline First (EDF).
- Support for combining paradigms.
- Support for user-defined paradigms.

---

[1] This work has been supported by the Commission of the European Communities under contract IST-2001-34140 (The First Project).

A. Llamosí and A. Strohmeier (Eds.): Ada-Europe 2004, LNCS 3063, pp. 156–165, 2004.

In this paper we consider the first two of these areas. The use of dynamic priority assignment (and other language features) does support a certain level of user-defined scheduling, including coverage for some new paradigms. However we feel that direct support, via definitions in Annex D, will increase the likelihood of implementations becoming available, will standardize on the approaches, and show the continuing development of Ada. For a detailed discussion on adding user-defined schedulers to Ada see the proceedings of the 11th International Real-Time Ada Workshop (IRTAW) [10].

2   Support for Deadlines

Earliest deadline first (EDF) is a popular paradigm as it has been proven to be the most efficient scheme available. If a set of tasks is schedulable by any dispatching policy then it will also be schedulable by EDF. To support EDF requires two language features:

- representation of deadline for a task,
- representation of preemption level for a protected object.

The first is obviously required; the second is the EDF equivalent of priority ceilings and allows protected objects to be 'shared' by multiple tasks [1] (see next two sections).

A deadline is usually defined to be *absolute* if if refers to a specific (future) point in time; for example there is an absolute deadline on the completion of this paper of 1st Feb 2004 (presumable at 23:59:59). A *relative* deadline is one that is anchored to the current time: "I have one week to finish this paper". Obviously if the current time is known then a relative deadline can be translated into an absolute one. Repetitive (periodic) tasks often have a static relative deadline (for example 10ms after release) but will have a different absolute deadline every time they are released. The EDF scheme is correctly expressed as *earliest absolute deadline first*.

It is an anomaly that Ada's support for real-time does not extend as far as having a direct representation for 'deadline', but the task attribute features or equivalent does allow a deadline attribute to be assigned. The following gives a suitable package for the support of deadlines.

```
with Ada.Task_Identification;
   use Ada.Task_Identification;
with Ada.Real_Time;
package Ada.Deadlines is
  subtype Deadline is Ada.Real_Time.Time;
  Default_Deadline : constant Deadline :=
    Ada.Real_Time.Time_Last;
  procedure Set_Absolute_Deadline(
    D : Deadline;
    T : Task_ID := Current_Task);
  procedure Set_Relative_Deadline(
    R : Ada.Real_Time.Time_Unit;
    T : Task_ID := Current_Task);
  function Get_Deadline(
    T : Task_ID := Current_Task)
```

```
    return Deadline; -- returns absolute deadline
end Ada.Deadlines;
```

The meaning of the operations of this package should be clear, examples of use are given later in this paper. Note all tasks are given a deadline - if one has not been explicitly set then Time_Last (the far distant future) is given as the default.

A pragma will also be needed to give an initial relative deadline to a task to control dispatching during activation.

A program can manipulate deadlines, and even catch a deadline overrun via the asynchronous transfer of control (select-then-abort) feature:

```
loop
  select
    delay until Deadlines.Get_Deadline;
  then abort
    -- code
  end select;
  -- set next release condition
  -- and next absolute deadline
end loop;
```

3   Baker's Preemption Level Protocol for Protected Objects

One of the major feature improvements that Ada95 provided was the introduction of the protected object. Although the rendezvous is a powerful synchronization and communication primitive, it does not easily lead to tight scheduling analysis. Rather a more asynchronous scheme is desirable for real-time applications. The protected object (a form of monitor) provided this form of communication. With this construct, and the use of a fixed priorities for tasks and a priority ceiling protocol for protected objects, it is possible to predict worst-case completion times for tasks.

With standard fixed priority scheduling, *priority* is actually used for two distinct purposes:

– to control dispatching
– to facilitate an efficient and safe way of sharing protected data.

The latter is known as the priority ceiling protocol. What Baker [1] proposed in his stack-based protocol is to use two distinct notions for these policies:

– earliest deadline first to control dispatching[2],
– preemption levels to control the sharing of protected data.

With preemption levels (which is a very similar notion to priority) each task is assigned a static preemption level, and each protected object is assigned a ceiling value that is the maximum of the preemption levels of the tasks that call it. At run-time a newly released task, τ_1, can preempt the currently running task, τ_2, if and only if:

---

[2] His paper actually proposes a more general model of which EDF dispatching is an example.

– Absolute deadline of τ_1 is earlier (i.e. sooner) than deadline of τ_2
– Preemption level of τ_1 is higher than the preemption of any locked protected object.

With this protocol it is possible to show that mutual exclusion (over the protected object on a single processor) is ensured by the protocol itself (in a similar way to that delivered by fixed priority scheduling and ceiling priorities). Baker also showed, for the classic problem of scheduling a fixed set of periodic tasks, that if preemption levels are assigned according to each task's relative deadline then a task can suffer at most a single block from any task with a longer deadline. Again this result is identical to that obtained for fixed priority scheduling. Note preemption levels must be assigned inversely to relative deadline (the smaller the relative deadline, the higher the preemption level).

Although EDF scheduling results in higher resource usage and Baker's protocol furnishes efficient data sharing between tasks, certain forms of analysis and application characteristics are more complex then the fixed priority equivalent. However response time analysis, for example, does exist for EDF scheduling [9,11].

4   Supporting EDF Scheduling in Ada

Clearly, as currently defined, Ada does not support EDF scheduling and hence new facilities must be added; however any new functionality should be minimum and it is desirable for fixed priority and EDF scheduling to work together (see Section 5). To this end the current proposal does not attempt to define a new locking policy but uses the existing ceiling locking rules without change. Priority, as currently defined, is used to represent preemption levels. EDF scheduling is defined by a new dispatching policy.

```
pragma Task_Dispatching_Policy(EDF_Dispatching);
```

With Ada95, dispatching is defined by a model that has a number of ready queues, one per priority level. Each queue, for the standard model, is ordered in a FIFO manner. Tasks have a base priority (assigned by pragma `Priority` and changed, if desired, by use of `Dynamic_Priority.Set_Priority`). They may also have a higher active priority if they inherit such a value during, for example, a rendezvous or execution within a protected object. Preemptive behaviour is enforced by requiring a context switch from the current running task if there is a higher priority non-empty ready queue. This is known, within the Reference Manual, as a *Dispatching Point*. At any dispatching point the current running task is returned to its ready queue and another task (or indeed the same task if appropriate) is taken from its ready queue and executed. It should be noted that this is an abstract model of the required behaviour; an implementation does not need to deliver the required semantics in this way. This also applies to the new model defined below.

To illustrate the different dispatching behaviours described in this paper, consider the small task set illustrated in Table 1. There are five tasks (A, B, C, D, E) and three protected objects (X, Y, Z). Each task has a deadline equal to period and priorities have been assigned (optimally) by the rate monotonic priority algorithm [8] (in Ada the larger the integer, the higher the priority). Once computation times are known (estimated) and

Table 1. An Example System with five Tasks and three Protected Objects

Name	Period (tasks)	task use of protected objects / protected objects used by tasks	Priority / Ceiling Priority
A	10	X	5
B	12	Y	4
C	15	X	3
D	20	X,Y,Z	2
E	50	Y,Z	1
X		A,C,D	5
Y		B,D,E	4
Z		D,E	2

system overheads measured/calculated then fixed priority response time analysis can be carried out [5].

Each of the five tasks will have the same structure/pattern, for example:

```
task A is
   pragma Priority(5);
end A;

task body A is
  Next_Release: Ada.Real_Time.Time;
begin
  Next_Release := Ada.Real_Time.Clock;
  loop
      -- code, including call(s) to X
    Next_Release := Next_Release +
        Ada.Real_Time.Milliseconds(10);
    delay until Next_Release;
  end loop;
end A;

protected X is
  pragma Priority(5);
  -- definitions of subprograms
  private
  -- definition of internal data
end X;
```

Fixed priority preemptive dispatching is designated by the use of the appropriate configuration pragma:

```
pragma Task_Dispatching_Policy(FIFO_Within_Priorities);
```

4.1   The Rules of EDF Dispatching

The basic preemption rule given earlier for Baker's protocol, whilst defining the fundamental behaviour, does not give a complete model. For example, it is necessary to define what happens to a newly released task that is not entitled to preempt. A complete model, within the context of Ada's ready queues, is defined by the following rules:

1. All ready queues are ordered by Deadline (shorter absolute deadline implies closer to the head of the ready queue).
2. Execution within a protected object occurs at the ceiling priority of that object (i.e. the existing rule).
3. Whenever a task, τ, becomes runnable it is placed on the highest non-empty ready queue R such that Deadline of τ is less than the deadline of the task at the tail of queue R and base priority of τ is greater than R. If no such R exists τ is added to the ready queue for Priority'first (i.e. the lowest priority ready queue).

Note the base priority of a task is not directly used to control dispatching; and its active priority is determined by the state of the other runnable tasks when it is released. With this model, a task's active priority may indeed be less than its base priority.

As rule 3 is perhaps not intuitive, some examples will be needed to explain its role. First consider the situation when no protected objects exist. Here all released tasks will always be placed on the ready queue for Priority'first. This is the only queue that will ever have tasks on it. It is ordered by deadline and hence will furnish EDF scheduling. A second simple case is when a task is released when no protected objects are 'locked'. Here again all runnable tasks are on Priority'first and the newly released task takes its place appropriately on this queue.

Now consider the situation of a task (S) executing inside a protected object, with ceiling priority P, when a newly released task (T) arrives. The current priority of S is the higher ceiling level of the protected object and so at this dispatching point S is on the ready queue for level P. Two cases are possible; T should, or should not, preempt S.

Case 1

If T should preempt S then it must have a shorter deadline than S and a base priority higher than P. It is placed on the ready queue for level P, but is in front of S as it has a shorter deadline. It thus executes before S.

Case 2

If T should not preempt S then it is placed on the ready queue at level Priority'first and S continues to execute. Task T could fail this preemption test for two reasons which gives rise to two sub-cases.

Case 2a. T has a longer deadline than S. Here EDF rules clearly state that S should run before T. Even when S leaves the protected object and its priority falls to Priority'first it will continue to execute.

Case 2b. T had a lower preemption level but a shorter deadline. Here the locking rules do require S to continue executing, but as soon as it leaves the protected object it will be added to the ready queue for Priority'first behind T and hence T will now preempt. Although T has the earlier deadline it suffers a short period of 'deadline inversion'. This is unavoidable but is limited to this single occurrence by the protocol.

Returning to the case in which T does preempt S and hence is executing at priority P, if one or more tasks become runnable they will either be placed in the Priority'first queue or the P queue. If the P queue is appropriate then the task must have a shorter deadline than S and hence be in front of S on that queue. Task S will not run again until all these other tasks (on queue P) have left the system (become unrunnable for whatever reason). If any of these tasks while executing calls a protected object then it must be of a higher priority than P (as its base priority is higher than P). A new ready queue is now in use for this new level (say P_2) and the behaviour is repeated at level P_2 as it was for P. Indeed newly arrived tasks can, depending on their parameters, be placed at level P_2, P or Priority'first.

It should be clear from this description that the tail of any ready queue (apart from that at level Priority'first) will be a task executing within a protected object. Indeed this tail position is the only possible place for such tasks. It is also straightforward to see that mutual exclusion over protected objects is maintained. Task S while executing within the protected object can only be preempted by a task with a strictly higher base priority. This task cannot call the protected object without violating the ceiling protocol.

4.2   An Important Constraint

The above rules and descriptions are, unfortunately, not quite complete. The ready queue for Priority'first plays a central role in the model as it is, in some senses, the default queue. If a task is not entitled to be put in a higher queue, or if no protected objects are in use, then it is placed in this base queue. Indeed during the execution of a typical program most runnable tasks will be in the Priority'first ready queue most of the time. However the protocol only works if there are no protected objects with a ceiling at the Priority'first level. Such ceiling values must be prohibited but this is not a significant constraint. Ceilings at this level are rare (all user tasks would need to have priority Priority'first) and the use of Priority'first + 1 will not have a major impact. Indeed a common practice is to set any ceiling at maximum usage + 1.

4.3   Example Task Set

Returning to the task set given in Table 1, if EDF dispatching is required (perhaps to make the system schedulable) then very little change is needed. The Priority levels of the task and protected objects remains exactly the same. The task's code must, however, now explicitly refer to deadlines:

```
task A is
   pragma Priority(5);
   pragma Deadline(10); -- gives an initial relative
           -- deadline of 10 milliseconds
end A;

task body A is
  Next_Release: Ada.Real_Time.Time;
begin
  Next_Release := Ada.Real_Time.Clock;
  loop
     -- code, including call(s) to X
    Next_Release := Next_Release +
       Ada.Real_Time.Milliseconds(10);
    Deadlines.Set_Deadline(Next_Release +
       Ada.Real_Time.Milliseconds(10);
    delay until Next_Release;
  end loop;
end A;
```

Note that as soon as the deadline is reset then the task has its new deadline and, therefore, is likely to be preempted before it executes the delay until statement. However, as its deadline approaches, it will be rescheduled in time to iterate around the loop. As this is a common pattern it would be useful to directly support a 'delay and set deadline' primitive.

Finally the dispatching policy must be changed:

```
pragma Task_Dispatching_Policy(EDF_Dispatching);
```

4.4   Rendezvous and Other Considerations

The above considerations have concentrated on the use of protected objects for task communications. This is because their use is more appropriate for real-time systems. A new dispatching policy must nevertheless be complete in the sense of being well defined for other language features. There are a number of places where priority inheritance is defined in the tasking model of Ada. The rendezvous and task activation being two of them. A rendezvous is defined to take place at the maximum priority of the two tasks involved. If the highest priority task is the second one to 'arrive' at the rendezvous then this is straightforward. However if the highest priority task must block waiting for its rendezvous partner then this could compromise the model. Consider task T executing at priority P in the earlier discussion. If it now blocks at a rendezvous entry call, then it must loose this active Priority P when it next executes (S may have disappeared by this time). Indeed it would be wrong for the task subsequently executing the accept statement to inherit priority P. For this reason any task, when it blocks, must have its active priority assigned to Priority'first.

There are other places, such as task activation that have priority inheritance. It is not proposed here that any form of *deadline inheritance* is used. The preemption level protocol is sufficient.

5   Mixed Dispatching Systems

All the above descriptions have assumed that EDF dispatching is an alternative to fixed priority dispatching. The current language change however goes further and allows mixed systems to be defined. Following the approach advocated by Burns et al [4], the system's priority range can be split into a number of distinct non-overlapping bands. In each band a specified dispatching policy is in effect. So, for example, there could be a band of fixed priorities on top of a band of EDF with a single round robin level for non-real-time tasks at the bottom.

Obviously to achieve this, the properties assigned above to level Priority'first would need to be redefined for the base of whatever range is used for the EDF tasks. Also rules need to be defined for tasks communicating across bands (via protected objects or rendezvous), and for tasks changing bands (via the use of Dynamic_Priorities.Set_Priority). These rules are being defined for the language amendment.

With the example given earlier it would be possible to define a mixed system if, for example, tasks A and B were critical whilst tasks C, D and E were not:

```
pragma Task_Dispatching_Policy(Priority_Specific);

pragma Priority_Policy(FIFO_Within_Priority, 5, 4);

pragma Priority_Policy(EDF_Dispatching, 3, 1);
```

The two integer parameters indicate upper and lower priorities of the band.

There are also usage paradigms in the real-time area that run all tasks in an EDF queue but then move any 'hard' task to a higher fixed priority if there is any danger of its deadline being missed [7,6,2]. Such algorithms would be simple to achieve with the facilities defined in this paper.

6   Conclusion

EDF scheduling is the policy of choice in many real-time systems, particularly those that are less critical and where minimising resource usage is critical (for example, mobile embedded systems and multi-media applications). The proposal described in this paper (and in the AI being considered for inclusion in the language standard) shows how full support for EDF can be achieved in a manner fully compatible with the current language model. Preemption Level control over the use of Protected Objects is achieved with no change to the ceiling locking policy. The inclusion of EDF and mixed scheduling within the Ada language significantly increases the expressive power, usability and applicability of the language. It is a strong indication of the continuing relevance of Ada.

Although the Ravenscar profile prescribes FIFO_Within_Priority, it would be possible to define a very similar scheme with EDF_Dispatching. All the restriction of Ravenscar could equally be applied to a constrained EDF scheme.

References

1. T.P. Baker. Stack-based scheduling of realtime processes.*Real-Time Systems,* 3(1), March 1991.
2. G. Bernat and A. Burns. Combining (n m)-hard deadlines with dual priority scheduling. In *Proceedings of 18th IEEE Real-Time systems symposium. San Francisco, CA,* December 1997.
3. A. Burns, B.Dobbing, and T. Vardanega. Guide for the use of the Ada Ravenscar Profile in high integrity systems. Technical Report YCS-2003-348, University of York, Department of Computer Science, 2003.
4. A. Burns, M. Gonz´alez Harbour, and A.J. Wellings. A round robin scheduling policy for Ada. In *Reliable Software Technologies, Proceedings of the Ada Europe Conference,* volume LNCS 2655, pages 334–343. Lecture Notes on Computer Science, Springer Verlag, 2003.
5. A. Burns and A. J. Wellings. *Real-Time Systems and Programming Languages.* Addison Wesley Longman, 3rd edition, 2001.
6. A. Burns and A.J. Wellings. Dual priority scheduling in ada 95 and real-time posix. In *Proceedings of the 21st IFAC/IFIP Workshop on Real-Time Programming, WRTP'96,* pages 45–50, 1996.
7. R.I. Davis and A. J. Wellings. Dual priority scheduling. *In Proceedings Real-Time Systems Symposium,* pages 100–109, 1995.
8. C.L. Liu and J.W. Layland. Scheduling algorithms for multiprogramming in a hard real-time environment. *JACM,* 20(1):46–61, 1973.
9. J.C. Palencia and M. Gonz´alez Harbour. Response time analysis for tasks scheduled under edf within fixed priorities. In *Proceedings of the 24th IEEE Real-Time Systems Simposium, Cancun, Mxico,* pages 200–209, 2003.
10. M. Aldea Rivas and M. Gonz´alez Harbour. Application-defined scheduling in Ada. In J.L Tokar, editor, *Proceedings of the 11th International Real-Time Ada Workshop,* pages 77–84. ACM Ada Letters, 2002.
11. M. Spuri. Analysis of deadline scheduled real-time systems. Technical Report RR-2772, INRIA, 1996.

OpenAda: Compile-Time Reflection for Ada 95

Patrick Rogers[1] and Andy J. Wellings[2]

[1]Ada Core Technologies
rogers@gnat.com
[2]University of York, York, UK
andy@cs.york.ac.uk

Abstract. This paper introduces OpenAda, a compile-time reflective facility supporting full Ada that is similar to OpenC++ and OpenJava. We explain the general concepts of reflection, including compile-time reflection, introspection, and intercession, and then describe how the compiler is dynamically extended to perform user-defined translations. We then describe the compiler's support for introspection and intercession and provide a complete (though relatively simple) demonstration of use. This example illustrates certain limitations inherent to the implementation that we explain, along with the work-arounds provided.

Keywords: Reflection, compiler, tools, Ada language

1 Introduction

"Computational reflection" is defined as the ability of a computational process to reason about, and manipulate, a representation of itself [5, 11]. The program's act of observing and reasoning about itself is known as "introspection". Manipulation of itself – its representation, its execution state, indeed, its very meaning – is known as "intercession". Both aspects require an encoding of the program's representation as well as its execution state; the provision of this encoding is known as "reification"[1]. Once reified, previously implicit or hidden implementation artefacts become accessible to users.

Software based on reflective facilities is structured into distinct levels: the *baselevel* and one or more *metalevels*. The baselevel addresses the functional requirements of the application. The metalevels represent and control the baselevel. As such, the metalevels are responsible for the non-functional aspects of the system. The differences in these levels can be illustrated in terms of a stage production: the baselevel is everything seen by the audience; the considerable activity off-stage occurs in the metalevels [3]. A protocol is defined for how entities in the metalevels are used to introspect and intercede. This protocol is, therefore, known as a Metaobject Protocol (MOP). The MOP includes the interfaces these entities define, the expected sequence of invocations, the order of invocations, and so forth.

---

[1] To "reify" is to make concrete that which is otherwise abstract or not "real".

A. Llamosí and A. Strohmeier (Eds.): Ada-Europe 2004, LNCS 3063, pp. 166–177, 2004.

The metalevel and baselevel are causally related: modification of one affects the other. This relationship may be achieved by making the actual baselevel implementation available to the metalevel, such that changes by the metalevel are automatically effective at the baselevel. To the degree that the implementation is made available, everything in the implementation and application – the syntax, the semantics, and the run-time data structures – is "opened" to the programmer for modification via the metalevels.

Such fundamental malleability may seem radical. One could argue, however, that reflective programming is in fact evolutionary, in terms of ever-later binding times, with dynamic dispatching provided by object-oriented programming languages as one of the intermediate points [6]. The later binding in this case is provided by the ability of the metalevel to intercept the baselevel operations, such as function calls and value references, and to then perform arbitrary activities. For example, the metalevel code could perform sophisticated processing in support of non-functional aspects such as distribution, concurrency, or fault tolerance.

The extreme flexibility and malleability of reflective programming languages are clearly advantageous. However, the idea behind reflection is not that systems should be designed with flexibility in mind; any such mechanisms would be limited by the designer's foresight and the range of the mechanisms provided. For example, an operating system that allows the scheduling policy to be replaced has addressed flexibility of scheduling but not flexibility of memory management (to pick one arbitrarily). In contrast, a reflective facility opens essentially everything to modification. The *user* is then free to decide what to change based on application-specific criteria. In the context of programming languages, Kiczales et al. describe a programming language "design space" populated by languages at discrete points [3]. Reflection makes it possible to move a given language within the design space toward the optimum language for a given application. The ability to optimise in ways and for reasons wholly unforeseen by the designer is the greatest advantage of reflective systems.

We have implemented a reflective compiler fully supporting Ada 95. The following sections describe the compiler's operation and user interface. Specifically, section two introduces the notion of "open compilers" that form the basis of compile-time reflective compilers. Section three then explains how such a compiler is extended dynamically at run-time to perform user-defined translations. Sections four and five describe the introspection and intercession facilities. Section six provides a complete example. We discuss limitations in section seven. The paper is then summarized in section eight.

2 Compile-Time Reflection

The inefficiencies incurred from reflection, especially with interpretive implementations, are significant. Some fully-interpretive reflective programming language implementations degrade performance by a factor of 10 to 1000 over non-reflective languages with optimizing compilers. Hybrid (i.e., interpreted-compiled) approaches improve the situation but still exhibit overhead of a factor of ten [7].

There are techniques for interpretive implementations that attempt to address the performance issue but they do not entirely remove the overhead. These inefficiencies have led to "open compilers" that allow users to change the language's semantics without necessarily incurring performance penalties [4]. In these compilers the internals, including parsing, the data structures, semantic analysis, and so forth, are reified such that new functionality and even new syntax may be added to the language. Such changes are achieved by subclassing these reified internal classes. This approach has been available for Smalltalk for many years. Smalltalk has even been extended with this approach to handle a (small) subset of Ada 95 [9].

The concept exemplified by open compilers is movement of the entire reflective programming model back to the point of compilation; the resulting metaobject protocol is referred to as a "compile-time MOP". With such a MOP the metalevel code only runs during compilation: the metalevel code controls compilation of the program and, thereby, albeit indirectly, run-time behaviour [1].

An alternative to reifying the compiler internals is to have the translation driven by a single "translator" metaclass. A metaclass is, in this approach, a specialization of a predefined translator. OpenC++ introduced this concept [2]. The input source code contains an annotation that controls the translation. In this case the annotation requests a specific metaclass to perform the translation. As a result, the metaclass can be said to customize the translation of the input source code rather than customizing the compiler's internals.

Given these facilities, metalevel programmers can produce reusable metaclasses that address the non-functional aspects of an application without cluttering the base-level code addressing the functional aspects. Furthermore, with a compile-time MOP no performance penalty need be imposed.

OpenAda is our compile-time reflection facility for Ada 95 using the "translating metaclass" approach. The similarity of the name to OpenC++ (and OpenJava) is not a coincidence – OpenAda operates and is used in very much the same manner. In particular, OpenAda produces translated Ada code under the control of a user-defined metaclass, much like OpenC++ produces translated C++. The difference in this regard is that we do not then call a standard C++ compiler to convert the C++ code into object code; we leave that step to the user.

3   Dynamically Extending the Compiler

A fundamental concept of a translating metaclass compiler is that the compiler extends itself dynamically by loading the metaclass specified by the user in the base-level source code. Once extended the compiler translates the remaining baselevel code under the control of that metaclass.

OpenAda source code is distinct from standard Ada source code only because an additional implementation-defined pragma exists to identify the metaclass translator. The pragma annotates the original source, much like Intrigue and OpenC++. In OpenC++ the annotation is an extra bit of syntax (the word "metaclass") that identifies the metaclass to perform the translation. In OpenAda the annotation is the pragma "Metaclass".

The pragma is placed in the source file before the compilation unit to which it applies. The first parameter specifies the name of the target program unit and, typically, a type declared within that unit. The compiler verifies that the specified unit (and perhaps type) exists within the compilation. The second parameter specifies the name of the translator metaclass. Any other parameters are optional; their interpretation is entirely defined by the specific metaclass loaded.

The OpenAda compiler reacts to the presence of the pragma by loading the specified translating metaclass and removing the pragma from the internal representation. The compiler then traverses this representation using the loaded metaclass to control translation by dynamically dispatching to the metaclass' overridden primitive operations. Then, if pragma Metaclass has not been reinserted by the translation, the internal representation is simply printed to a file, completing execution. Otherwise the representation is again traversed using the newly loaded metaclass translator indicated by the reinserted pragma. The process continues until no pragma Metaclass is encountered. Fig. 1 depicts the extension approach.

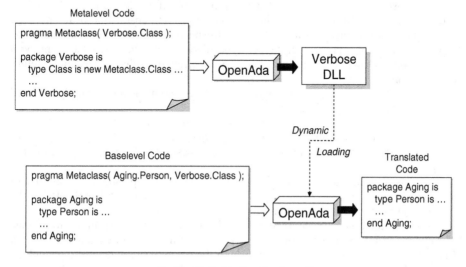

Fig. 1. Extending the Compiler

The target type Aging.Person will be translated by the metaclass Verbose.Class. This is the baselevel code indicated in Fig. 1. Strictly speaking, the translation target need not be a class; it can be any compilation unit because Ada includes more than classes. For example, *clients* of the translated types may also require translation and these need not be classes themselves.

Users create dynamically loadable metaclasses by deriving from an OpenAda base type named OpenAda.Meta.Class and processing the resulting metaclass source code with the OpenAda compiler. In this case only

one parameter (naming the translation target) is specified to pragma Metaclass. This is the metalevel code shown in Fig. 1. Using a default metaclass, the compiler converts the source into a DLL (or shared object for Unix machines). When the compiler encounters the name of the metaclass in the baselevel occurrence of pragma Metaclass it locates the corresponding DLL and dynamically loads it. Translation is then under the control of the metaclass represented by the DLL. (Obviously the metaclass must be processed by the compiler prior to any baselevel references.) The translated code ultimately produced is standard Ada 95.

4 Introspection

Any introspection facility is inherently language-dependent. OpenAda is naturally designed for the Ada language, including the way Ada represents classes. We describe the resulting interfaces of the OpenAda system in this section.

4.1 Reifying Classes

Following in the tradition of CLOS, OpenAda defines a root metaclass named "Class". Instances of (subclasses of) Class represent reified classes in the Ada idiom and provide the means to translate them. It is the primary abstraction of the package OpenAda.Meta that provides a number of introspection routines oriented around the way Ada represents classes (i.e., tagged types declared within a package along with primitive operations). For a reified class, there are functions that, for example, return the following:

- references to the objects representing the components explicitly declared in the type declaration
- references to the visible primitive operations for the type
- references to the hidden primitives for the type
- a reference to the name of the direct ancestor for the type (if applicable)

The Class interface also provides access to the parameters passed to the instance of pragma Metaclass applied to the input source code. Metaclasses largely define the content and interpretation of these parameters.

The OpenAda compiler automatically reifies the unit or class specified to pragma Metaclass. In addition, any arbitrary class can be reified upon demand via function Class_For. This function takes as inputs both the name of the requested type and the name of the enclosing package. The class-specific operations above may then be applied to the designated result.

4.2 Reifying Language Constructs

Every syntactic construct is individually represented by a specific type declaration; each is visibly derived (directly or indirectly) from the base type Node declared in package OpenAda.Syntax. The interface defined by Node is minimal; specific facilities are defined in the concrete subclasses declared in package OpenAda.Syntax.Constructs and are based on the details of the constructs represented.

5 Intercession

In a compile-time reflective facility, intercession involves translating the baselevel code into new source code that meets some "non-functional" requirements. Metaclass programmers define the translation specified by a given metaclass by overriding the translation primitives of type OpenAda.Meta.Class. These overridden primitives make use of introspection primitives to interrogate the existing code, as necessary. We describe these translation primitives and the auxiliary facilities available to them in the following sections.

5.1   Translating the Baselevel

The metaclass Class supports intercession by means of a large number of primitive translating operations corresponding to the syntax of Ada. Operations to translate every concrete syntactic category are provided. Metalevel programmers override these translating operations in subclasses of Class to define a metaclass-specific translation. The base class methods are all concrete; derivatives only override those necessary. They do nothing unless overridden.

Each translating primitive is a procedure with a name formed by the prefix "Translate_" followed by the name of the syntactic category. For example, the following declaration is for the primitive operation translating Name constructs:

```
procedure Translate_Name
  ( This    : in out Class;
    Input   : in out Name;
    Control : in out Visitation_Controls );
```

These translating procedures are called automatically by the compiler as the program graph is traversed. Metaclass programmers are never expected to call them directly. The procedures are called in the order in which the corresponding nodes are encountered in the graph, using a depth-first traversal.

Although the compiler calls the translation routines automatically, metaclass programmers can control the traversal via the formal Control parameter of type Visitation_Controls if necessary.

New graphs can be constructed from other graphs and primitive values (e.g., Wide_String) using additional facility-defined "factory" functions declared in package OpenAda.Syntax.Constructs.Factory. They are used both by the internal parsers and by metaclass programmers. The name of any such function is "Make_" followed by the name of the syntactic constructs created. For example:

```
function Make_Requeue_Statement
  ( Entry_Name : Name_Reference; With_Abort : Boolean )
  return Requeue_Statement_Reference;
```

The value for the first parameter is a reference to a Name node previously created. This value could be provided using a functional programming style by calling Make_Name.

For relatively shallow graphs these factory functions are sufficient and convenient. However, their use would be a burden for complicated or deep graphs. For constructing deeper graphs OpenAda provides a memory-resident "text" abstraction that can be passed to yet another set of factory functions. These functions parse the text and return the resulting program graph.

6   Full Example

We illustrate using OpenAda by a complete version of the Verbose metaclass that causes any call to a primitive subprogram of the type to print the name of the subprogram before executing the body. Consider the main program:

```
with Ada.Text_IO;  use Ada.Text_IO;
with Aging;        use Aging;
procedure Demo is
```

```
   Me : Person( Initial_Age => 45 );
begin
   Put_Line( "I am" & Integer' Image(Current_Age(Me)) &
            " years old. " );
   Aging. Birthday_Arrives( Me );
   Put_Line( "I am" & Integer' Image(Current_Age(Me)) &
            " years old. " );
end Demo;
```

When executed, the intended effect is illustrated by the following console display:

```
Current_Age is called.
I am 45 years old.
Birthday_Arrives is called.
Current_Age is called.
I am 46 years old.
```

Given the Verbose.Class metaclass (shown momentarily), the metalevel programmer could apply it to the class Aging.Person as follows:

```
pragma Metaclass( Aging. Person, Verbose. Class );

package Aging is

   type Person( Initial_Age : Positive ) is tagged private;

   function Current_Age( This : Person ) return Positive;

   procedure Birthday_Arrives( This : in out Person );

private

   type Person( Initial_Age : Positive ) is tagged
      record
         Age : Natural := Initial_Age;
      end record;

end Aging;
```

The pragma indicates that the class Aging.Person is to be translated by the metaclass Verbose.Class. Prior to translation, the body of the package (shown below) meets the functional requirements using standard Ada.

```
package body Aging is

   function Current_Age( This : Person ) return Positive is
   begin
      return This. Age;
   end Current_Age;

   procedure Birthday_Arrives( This : in out Person ) is
   begin
      This. Age := This. Age + 1;
   end Birthday_Arrives;

end Aging;
```

After translation the package declaration has had the pragma removed but is the same in all other respects. In contrast, the Verbose.Class metaclass alters the primitive subprogram bodies after first adding a with_clause to the compilation unit (if not already present).

```
with Ada.Text_IO;

package body Aging is

  function Current_Age( This : in Person ) return Positive is
  begin
    Ada.Text_IO.Put_Line( "Current_Age is called." );
    return This.Age;
  end Current_Age;

  procedure Birthday_Arrives( This : in out Person ) is
  begin
    Ada.Text_IO.Put_Line("Birthday_Arrives is called.");
    This.Age := This.Age + 1;
  end Birthday_Arrives;

end Aging;
```

The Verbose metaclass thus has the following implementation:

```
pragma Metaclass( Verbose.Class );

with OpenAda.Meta;
with OpenAda.Syntax.Constructs;
use OpenAda.Syntax.Constructs;

package Verbose is

  use OpenAda.Syntax;

  type Class is new OpenAda.Meta.Class with private;

  procedure Translate_Compilation_Unit
    ( This    : in out Class;
      Input   : in out Compilation_Unit;
      Control : in out Visitation_Controls );

  procedure Translate_Subprogram_Body
    ( This    : in out Class;
      Input   : in out Subprogram_Body;
      Control : in out Visitation_Controls );

private
  type Class is new OpenAda.Meta.Class with null record;
end Verbose;
```

No additional components are required for Verbose.Class so a null extension suffices. The code will translate compilation units because only those can have with-clauses and we must insert a clause for Ada.Text_IO.

The body of Translate_Compilation_Unit goes to some lengths to mimic a manual production. This effort is purely for the sake of illustrating the introspection capability. In particular, the translator only places the with-clause on the package body, rather than the declaration, and then only if there is no clause for that package already present. Absent these niceties, the procedure body would require just the two assignment statements to the variable Clauses. (We justify the use of tag equality and other aspects in place of membership tests in [10].)

```ada
with OpenAda.DLL_Utilities;
use  OpenAda.DLL_Utilities;
with OpenAda.Syntax.Constructs.Factory;
use  OpenAda.Syntax.Constructs.Factory;

package body Verbose is

  procedure Translate_Compilation_Unit
    ( This    : in out Class;
      Input   : in out Compilation_Unit;
      Control : in out Visitation_Controls )
  is
    Clauses       : Sequence_Reference;
    Iteration     : Parsed_Content.List_Iterator;
    Next_Item     : Any_Node;
    Package_Names : Name_List_Reference;
    Found         : Boolean := False;
  begin
    if Associated_Unit(Input'Access).all'Tag /=
       Package_Body'Tag
    then
      Control := Abandon_Children;
      return;
    end if;
    Clauses := Context_Clause(Input'Access);
    Iteration :=
      Parsed_Content.Make_Iterator(Clauses.Content);
    while Parsed_Content.More(Iteration) loop
      Parsed_Content.Next( Iteration, Next_Item );
      if Next_Item.all'Tag = With_Clause'Tag then
        Package_Names :=
          Unit_Names(As_Any_With_Clause(Next_Item));
        if Includes( Package_Names, "Ada.Text_IO" ) then
          Found := True;
          exit;
        end if;
      end if;
    end loop;
    if not Found then
      Clauses := Clauses &
        Make_With_Clause("Ada.Text_IO");
    end if;
  end Translate_Compilation_Unit;

  procedure Translate_Subprogram_Body
    ( This    : in out Class;
      Input   : in out Subprogram_Body;
      Control : in out Visitation_Controls )
  is
    New_Statement   : Procedure_Call_Reference;
    Handled         : Handled_Statements_Reference;
    Statements_Part : Sequence_Reference;
    The_Unit_Name   : constant Wide_String :=
      Image(
        Unit_Name(Subprogram_Body'Class(Input)'Access));
  begin
    New_Statement := Make_Procedure_Call
      ( "Ada.Text_IO.Put_Line(""" &
        The_Unit_Name & " is called."");" );
    Handled :=
```

```
       Statements(Subprogram_Body'Class(Input)'Access);
    Statements_Part := Sequence_of_Statements(Handled);
    Parsed_Content.Attach( Any_Node(New_Statement),
                             Statements_Part.Content );
    Control := Abandon_Children;
  end Translate_Subprogram_Body;

end Verbose;
```

The procedure Translate_Subprogram_Body determines the name of the translated subprogram and creates a call to Ada.Text_IO to print the name and associated verbage. (Subprogram_Body is an abstract type so any primitive calls must be dispatching calls.) Once created, the new statement is inserted at the front of the subprogram's sequence of statements. There is no further processing required – we have no requirement to distinguish procedures from functions, for example – so we set Control accordingly.

7 Reification Limitations

Typically not all of the language is reified and, as a result, there are semantics that cannot be altered. Different languages exhibit this fact in differing ways. For example, Smalltalk – a very open programming language – does not reify method lookup, method return, or method execution because they are implemented by the underlying Smalltalk Virtual Machine. Those activities are implementation details performed by the VM for the sake of performance. In CLOS, however, they are explicit functions that can be overridden, thereby altering the semantics of methods. Similarly, any market-viable Java implementation provides garbage collection (GC). The Java language provides methods to influence the execution of GC but GC itself cannot be reified in a vendor-independent manner because it is implemented by the underlying Java Virtual Machine.

Note that this is not just a problem for syntax-based (i.e., compile-time) reflection, as the Smalltalk instance proves. Syntax is just how the issue is exposed for these implementations and OpenAda is no exception. Elaboration is a prime example; it is a critical part of the language but has no representational syntax. We discuss this general issue with two concrete examples: object creation and tasking.

7.1 Object Creation

C++ and Java have constructors representing object creation so there is a syntactic "hook" available for reification in both languages. This hook makes syntax-based translation support simple compared to Ada, which has no corresponding constructor syntax. In Ada, object elaboration (for a declared object) is an implicit operation performed upon entry to the declarative region containing the object declarations and may, depending on the objects in question, involve little more than incrementing a stack pointer. The object declarations themselves are not a substitute for constructors because the objects do not exist until *after* the corresponding object declarations are elaborated. Only the "controlled" types offer a partial hook – initialization – but the capability is not fully general: only *limited* controlled types guarantee that procedure Initialize will be called.

7.2 Tasking Activation, Completion, and Termination

Another example of partial reification concerns the Ada tasking facility. All the tasking constructs are reified in OpenAda and may be translated like any other construct. However, like the Smalltalk method call implementation, there are Ada tasking semantics that are not reified in OpenAda and cannot be reified in a vendor-independent manner. Task activation, completion and termination are not reified, for example.

In contrast, Java uses methods to invoke these operations and so OpenJava supports their translation [12]. One can argue that although Java's method-oriented concurrency interface is less expressive than the Ada statement-oriented approach, the method-based interface does facilitate somewhat more comprehensive concurrency reflection. On the other hand, the Java concurrency model is also only partially reified. For example, one cannot get access to the implicit lock associated with classes containing synchronized methods and so cannot change how the lock is managed. Nor are the other implementation aspects reified, such as the "ready queue".

One approach to dealing with partial reification would be to model the threading support portion of the underlying system software. Any such model would not be complete without also reifying the internal aspects of the concurrency implementation, such as the queues and locks, but the result for Ada or Java would be highly vendor-specific. A more general approach would be to provide a set of objects like that of CodA to represent Ada tasking semantics and use the vendor's facility to implement them. CodA takes a "bottom-up" approach by defining an extensible set of language-independent metacomponents that abstractly describe how objects interact, including message queuing, sending, receiving, execution, and so forth [8]. This approach would provide access to the queues and other implementation aspects without tying the model to a specific vendor.

8 Summary

We have introduced a compile-time reflective compiler supporting full Ada 95, explaining how such a compiler can be dynamically extended to perform user-defined translations. We have also described the introspection and intercession capabilities of the compiler and demonstrated their use in a complete example. More detailed discussion of the compiler, including limitations and application to software fault tolerance, are available elsewhere [10].

The source code and a Windows binary for the present version of OpenAda are currently available at http:\\www.classwide.com\OpenAda. (Note that the URL is case-sensitive.)

References

[1]   S. Chiba, "A Metaobject Protocol for C++," Proc. Object-Oriented Programming Systems Languages and Applications (OOPSLA'95), Austin, Texas, 1995, pp. 285-299.

[2]   S. Chiba, "A Study of Compile-time Metaobject Protocol," in *Department of Information Science, Graduate School of Science*, Toyko: University of Tokyo, 1996.

[3]   G. Kiczales, J. des Rivières, and D. Bobrow, *The Art of the Metaobject Protocol*, Cambridge, Massachusetts: MIT Press, 1991.

[4]   J. Lamping, G. Kiczales, L. Rodriguez, and E. Ruf, "An Architecture for An Open Compiler," Proc. International Workshop on New Models for Software Architecture '92 (IMSA'92) Workshop on Reflection and Meta-level Architectures, Tokyo, 1992, pp. 95-106.

[5]   P. Maes, "Concepts and Experiments In Computational Reflection," *ACM SIGPLAN Notices*, vol. 22, no. 12, pp. 147-155, 1987.

[6]   J. Malenfant, M. Jacques, and F.-N. Demers, "A Tutorial on Behavioral Reflection and its Implementation," Proc. Reflection'96, San Francisco, California, 1996, pp. 1-20.

[7]   H. Masuhara and A. Yonezawa, "An Object-Oriented Concurrent Reflective Language ABCL/R3" in *Object-Oriented Parallel and Distributed Programming*, T. B. Jean-Paul Bahsoun, Jean-Pierre Briot, Akinori Yonezawa, Ed., Paris: HERMES Science Publications, 2000, pp. 151--165.

[8]   J. McAffer, "Meta-level Programming with CodA" in *ECOOP'95 -- Object-Oriented Programming*, vol. 952, *Lecture Notes in Computer Science*, Åarhus, Denmark: Springer Verlag, 1995, pp. 190-214.

[9]   F. Rivard and P. Cointe, "From Envy-Classtalk to Ada'9X," 95-9-INFO, Ecole des Mines de Nantes, Nantes, France, January, 1995.

[10]   P. Rogers, "Reflection, Ada, and Software Fault Tolerance," in *Department of Computer Science*, York, UK: University of York, 2003.

[11]   B. C. Smith, "Reflection and Semantics in Lisp," Proc. 11th ACM Symposium on Principles of Programming Languages, 1984, pp. 23-35.

[12]   M. Tatsubori, S. Chiba, M.-O. Killijian, and K. Itano, "OpenJava: A Class-based Macro System for Java" in *Reflection and Software Engineering*, vol. 1826, *Lecture Notes in Computer Science*, W. Cazzola, R. Stroud, and F. Tisato, Eds.: Springer-Verlag, 2000, pp. 117-133.

XML4Ada95
Accessing XML Using the DOM in Ada95

Zdenko Vrandečić and Daniel Simon

Universität Stuttgart, Universitätsstraße 38, 70569 Stuttgart, Germany
denny@nodix.de, simon@informatik.uni-stuttgart.de

Abstract. This paper presents XML4Ada95, the implementation of an Ada binding to the XML parser library Xerces, offering for the first time a validating, general XML package in Ada95 with a complete access to XML the DOM Levels 1 and 2 Core. Xerces is written in C++, so patterns for interfacing Ada95 with C++ in a standardized fashion were developed in order to write XML4Ada95. Those patterns are described here, along with examples of how to use XML4Ada95 in your own application.

1 Introduction

This paper describes the *XML4Ada95* package[1], which was written at the University of Stuttgart. It offers access to XML documents at the level of the standardized DOM interface, thus enabling the user to parse and serialize XML-Documents, and further to validate the documents against DTDs and even XML Schemas from Ada95. XML4Ada95 is an implementation of an Ada binding to an XML parser library.

In recent discussions about the future of Ada [1] there are voices that request a direct support of XML in the language. But waiting until this becomes reality, if ever, would take too long for our purpose.

Although a native or even standard solution would be preferable, the effort of a native implementation is enormous in comparison to a language binding. Further, reusing the implementation of a parser in a wide-spread language such as C or C++ has a large number of users. The benefits of such a high activity can be exploited. Finally, it is not sure that there could be a similar XML user community for Ada95 that justifies the effort of a complete reimplementation.

When looking for a suitable parser for the binding, we intended to use a freely available implementation that is supported on a wide range of platforms. It should offer validation against DTD and XML Schema and a complete implementation of the DOM. Next, expecting some performance loss due to the binding, we opted for a reasonably fast implementation. And finally, we decided that the implementation should be in wide-spread use thus offering a well-tested solution with an established user base. Xerces [2] meets all of these requirements. The only drawback was Xerces being implemented in C++, which has

---

˙ Available at http://www.nodix.de/XML4Ada95.

A. Llamosí and A. Strohmeier (Eds.): Ada-Europe 2004, LNCS 3063, pp. 178–189, 2004.

```
<!ELEMENT Person    (Name, Birthday, Job*)>
<!ATTLIST Person    SizeOfShoe CDATA #IMPLIED>
<!ELEMENT Name      (First, Mid, Family)>
<!ELEMENT Birthday (Day, Month, Year?)>
<!ELEMENT Job    (#PCDATA)> <!ELEMENT First  (#PCDATA)>
<!ELEMENT Mid    (#PCDATA)> <!ELEMENT Family (#PCDATA)>
<!ELEMENT Day    (#PCDATA)> <!ELEMENT Month  (#PCDATA)>
<!ELEMENT Year (#PCDATA)>
```

Fig. 1. A simple DTD person.dtd.

no standardized interface to Ada95. Thus in creating this binding the problem of creating a standard-compatible way of interfacing to the C++-package had to be solved.

The rest of the paper is organized as follows. Section 2 gives a short introduction to XML. Then we describe XML4Ada95 from the application writer's point of view in Sect. 3. The design and implementation of the package as well as the description how we interfaced Ada and C++ via C is given in Sect. 4. Section 5 gives an overview of related work and in Sect. 6 we draw some conclusion from our experience with XML4Ada95.

2   XML and Co.

This section gives a short introduction to XML. After a quick glance at XML's roots, a simple example illustrates some of the facilities of XML. Finally, we present the two most used APIs for working with XML. You may safely skip this section if you already have the needed background knowledge.

2.1   History of XML

Since the mid-1990s, private web pages on the internet spreaded enormously. Today, there are more than 6.7 million internet domains registered in Germany. Even though almost all of the web pages are written in *Hypertext Markup Language* (HTML), most people are not aware of the background of that language.

HTML is based on SGML, and the roots can be followed back to the 1960s when Goldfarb, Mosher, and Lorie invented GML, a way of marking up technical documents with structural tags. SGML stands for *Standardized General Markup Language* and was adopted by ISO in 1986 [3]. SGML is a metalanguage, languages defined in SGML are called *applications*, documents written in such a language are called *documents*. In order to build an application, the user has to define a *document type definition* (DTD) by which the syntax of the documents is defined.

However, SGML has a significant draw-back: the complexity of the language makes it very flexible, but tools for SGML are therefore expensive. As a solution

```
<?xml version="1.0" encoding="UTF-8"?>
<!DOCTYPE Person SYSTEM "person.dtd">
<Person SizeOfShoe="12.5">
  <Name><First>John</First><Family>Doe</Family></Name>
  <Birthday><Day>23</Day><Month>May</Month></Birthday>
  <Job>Professor</Job>
</Person>
```

Fig. 2. An XML document `mydocument.xml` written for the DTD in Fig. 1.

to this problem the *eXtensible Markup Language* (XML) was proposed. XML is a restricted subset of SGML, where seldom used features from SGML are removed. In February 1998, XML became a W3C recommendation [4] (which corresponds to a standard in other organizations). Like SGML, XML is a metalanguage and an application language is defined by a DTD or an XML Schema. Schema aims to replace DTD eventually, offering a more powerful and flexible language and the advantage of being an XML application itself, whereas DTD defines an own, differing, although simple syntax. Today, XML has the status of a *lingua franca* for the definition of the syntax of markup languages.

2.2   A Simple Example

In Fig. 1, we define a simple language for the description of a person by a DTD. In this DTD, some simple elements with contents (that are elements themselves) are declared. An asterisk after the name of a content element means repetition, a question mark denotes an optional content element. The `#PCDATA` element stands for arbitrary data. Further, elements can define attributes. In our example, the element `Person` has the optional attribute `SizeOfShoe`.

Supposing the DTD file is named `person.dtd`, the document shown in Fig. 2 is an XML-document written in the "person" language. One of the benefits of XML is the syntactical verification that can be performed by any XML parser. An XML parser can verify the document in two respects: it can verify its *well-formedness* and its *validity*. In short, a document is well-formed if the following constraints are satisfied:

- The document has exactly one root element.
- The logical and physical structures must nest properly.
- Attributes are enclosed in quotation marks.

For a more precise definition of the term "well-formed", cf. [4]. If the document is well-formed, the parser can verify the document's validity by checking if the document complies with the constraints expressed in its DTD or the XML Schema. In our example in Fig. 2, the document is well-formed. However, the document is not valid because it lacks the non-optional content `Mid` of element `Name`. The example shows some of the disadvantages of XML: small amounts of data result in large documents. Further, everybody can define her own language and use

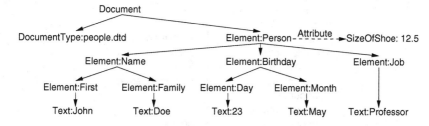

Fig. 3. The DOM tree resulting from the document in Fig. 2.

element names as meaningless as possible (just consider names such as p and n instead of Person and Name.

2.3 DOM and SAX Interfaces

In order to access XML documents, there are two well-used programming interfaces, SAX (*Simple API for XML*)[5] and DOM (*Document Object Model*)[6,7]. When using SAX, the programmer defines call-backs that are invoked whenever a certain event occurs during the sequential reading of the document. Because SAX does not provide access to the context of elements, it is fast. But if the programmer wants to look backward or forward in the documents, she has to care about that infrastructure herself.

The DOM interface presents the document as a tree and gives the programmer full access to traverse this tree and access the elements in any order. This comfortable way of accessing the document is usually achieved by significant performance loss (with respect to the much simpler SAX way of parsing). Figure 3 shows the tree resulting from the parsing of the document in Fig. 2.

3   The User's Point of View

XML4Ada95 consists of 25 packages organized as depicted in Fig. 4. The top-level package contains all necessary type declaration for using DOM in Ada. This is due to the facts discussed in Sect. 4. Basically, the package hierarchy directly corresponds to the DOM IDL specification.

3.1   Parsing a Document

From a user's point of view, reading and parsing a document like the one in Fig. 2 is simply

```
with org_w3c_dom;                        use org_w3c_dom;
with org_w3c_dom.Parser;
with org_w3c_dom.Document;
with org_w3c_dom.Util;
with org_w3c_dom.ImplementationLS;
```

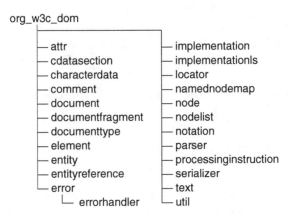

Fig. 4. The package hierarchy of XML4Ada95.

```
procedure Read is
  Reader : DOMParser;
  Doc    : DOMDocument;
begin
  Util.Initialize;
  Reader := ImplementationLS.CreateDOMParser (ImplementationLS.Fetch);

  Doc := Parser.ParseURI
            (Reader,
             From_Standard_String ("mydocument.xml"));
  -- here you can do with the document whatever you like
  Parser.Free (Reader);
  Util.Finalize;
end Read;
```

At first, the XML library needs some initialization. Afterwards, we create a
DOMParser that parses our document mydocument.xml by calling the corresponding parse function. The result of the call is the document's root.

3.2   Validating

Validating the XML document is likewise simple. After creating the parser, we
set some options for validation using the following code by calling the procedure
SetFeature.

```
Reader := ImplementationLS.CreateDOMParser (ImplementationLS.Fetch);
Parser.SetFeature (Reader, From_Standard_String ("validation"), True);
Parser.SetFeature (Reader, From_Standard_String ("validate-if-schema"),
                   True);
Doc := Parser.ParseURI (Reader,
                        From_Standard_String ("mydocument.xml"));
```

The semantics of the various features of the parser are defined by the Xerces library. The features required for validation are `validation` that reports all validation errors. If the feature `validate-if-schema` is set to `True` the parser will validate the document only if a grammar is specified.

3.3   Retrieving the Contents

After having parsed and validated the document we want to get access to the contents. As an example, we present the code required for analyzing John Doe's data. In the following example, the function `Return_SizeOfShoe` shows how to access an attribute, in our case the attribute `SizeOfShoe` of element `Person`.

```
function Return_SizeOfShoe (Doc : DOMDocument) return Standard.String is
   Person : DOMElement;
begin
   Person := Document.Get_DocumentElement (Doc);
   return To_Standard_String
            (Element.GetAttribute
               (Person, From_Standard_String ("SizeOfShoe")));
end Return_SizeOfShoe;
```

The procedure `Print_Name` below illustrates how to iterate over syntactical structures and how to access the contents of elements.

```
procedure Print_Name (Doc : DOMDocument) is
   Person, Child, Name, Text  : DOMNode;
   Names_List, Names_Children : DOMNodeList;
begin
   Person := Document.Get_DocumentElement (Doc);
   Names_List := Element.GetElementsByTagName
                    (From_Standard_String ("Name"));
   Name := NodeList.Item (Names_List, 0); -- must be exactly one (see DTD)
   Names_Children := Node.Get_ChildNodes (Name);
   for I in 0 .. NodeList.Get_Length (Names_Children) - 1 loop
      Child := NodeList.Item (Names_Children, I);
      Text  := Node.Get_FirstChild (Child);
      Put_Line (To_Standard_String (Node.Get_NodeValue (Text)));
   end loop;
end Print_Name;
```

Further information on the usage of XML4Ada95 can be found in the online documentation of the package.

4   Design and Implementation

When designing the package, we considered amongst others the following goals and constraints. First, the binding should provide an "Ada-look-and-feel". Second, to achieve high acceptance for the Ada package, we should keep as close to the DOM standard as possible. Although the W3C standard IDL specification could not be used as is (as showed in the next section), this can be a way leading to a *de facto*-standard binding for the DOM in Ada95. Additionally, the package should allow for an easy transition to a native implementation.

On the other side, having to use a low level language like C for the actual binding to Xerces had some impact on the actual code and disallowed us from using high level constructs, such as exceptions or inheritance, directly.

These points had to be balanced against each other and lead to a DOM interface that has a small number of changes with respect to the IDL specification, thus allowing to reuse big parts of the standard text for the documentation of XML4Ada95.

4.1   The Interface Definition

The World Wide Web Consortium offers standard bindings to the DOM written in IDL, Java, and ECMAScript, but not for any other language. Using the standard mappings from IDL to Ada95 [8] does not lead to acceptable results.

Obviously, Ada's inheritance mechanism was not taking into account when writing the DOM IDL specification. Using the standard mapping results in nonsense functions, e.g.,

```
function replaceChild (Self : DOMDocument; newChild : DOMDocument;
                       oldChild : DOMDocument)
   return DOMDocument;
```

This function of the *document* interface is inherited from the *node* interface. But according to the DOM specification, *document* can't have children of type *document*. Therefore, we cannot use inheritance when defining the interface in Ada.

Another example for a problem with the IDL are the forward declarations the IDL specifications use. These lead to circular dependencies and can't be reasonably translated to Ada95. We decided to resolve them by moving all type declarations to the root package. As inheritance does not work anyway, this did not cause further restrictions.

4.2   Interfacing Ada95 and C++ via C

Ada95 does not provide a standard way to interface with C++, but both Ada and C++ define a standardized interface to C, so we chose to use an intermediate C-binding for going from Ada to C++ and back. As a consequence, all C++-methods have to be wrapped in C-functions and then can be linked to the corresponding Ada95 functions or procedures.

High level language constructs of Ada and C++ like *object orientation, type safety, inheritance* or *exception handling* have to be translated into low level constructs that C can deal with. Arriving in the other language, the constructs have to be remapped onto the original constructs. Of course, all of this should be as efficient as possible.

The work in [9] describes the following patterns in detail.

Wrapping C++ in C. According to the *Ada Reference Manual* (ARM), we can access C functions by the following code. In Ada, we have

```
procedure CFunction (I : in Interfaces.C.Int);
pragma Import (C, cfuntion, "cfunction");
```

On the C side, the code looks like

```
void cfunction (int i) { ... }
```

We can now mask C++ as C by writing a file cpp1.h with

```
void cppfunction (int i) { ... }
```

cppwrap.cpp now masks the real function

```
#include "cpp1.h"
interface "C" void call_cppfunction (int i) { cppfunction (i); }
```

We implement the binding in two steps in order to be more independent from changes in the parser's header files. This was very useful when Xerces upgraded from Version 2.2.0 to Version 2.3.0. Indeed, not a single line of our code had to be changed.

Note that the developer of a binding is responsible for any type safety. Most compilers are not able to check types across language boundaries. Thus it is best to hide all implementation details arising from the binding from the client using the binding, and not allow him to work directly on the language binding level. The following patterns all adhere to this clear separation.

Wrapping Object Orientation. For wrapping object orientation in the C++ library, every single member function and member variable has to wrapped by using the following pattern.

```
#include "cppclass.cpp"
interface "C" void call_cppclass_memberfunction (CPPClass* this, int i) {
  this->memberfunction (i);
}

interface "C" void get_cppclass_member (CPPClass* this, int& i) {
  i = this->member;
}

interface "C" void set_cppclass_member (CPPClass* this, int i) {
  this->member = i;
}
```

The Ada specification file looks like

```
with System;
package CPP_Class is
  type CPP_Class is private;
  procedure Memberfunction (Self : in CPP_Class; I : in Integer);
```

```
  procedure Set_Member      (Self : in CPP_Class; I : in Integer);
  function  Get_Member      (Self : in CPP_Class) return Integer;

private
  subtype C_Pointer is System.Address;
  C_Null : constant C_Pointer := System.Null_Address;
  type CPP_Class is record This : C_Pointer := C_Null; end record;
end CPP_Class;
```

and the Ada implementation is

```
package body CPP_Class is
  procedure Memberfunction (Self : in CPP_Class; I : in Integer) is
    procedure Call_Memberfunction (This : in C_Pointer;
                                   I    : in Interfaces.C.Int);
    pragma Import (C, Call_Memberfunction,
                   "call_cppclass_memberfunction");
  begin
    Call_Memberfunction (Self.This, Interfaces.C.Int (I));
  end Memberfunction;

  function Get_Member (Self : in CPP_Class) return Integer is
    procedure Call_Get_Member (This : in C_Pointer;
                               I    : out Interfaces.C.Int);
    pragma Import(C, Call_Get_Member, "get_cppclass_member");
    Result : Interfaces.C.Int;
  begin
    Call_Get_Member (Self.This, Result);
    return Integer(Result);
  end Get_Member;

  procedure Set_Member (Self : in CPP_Class; I : in Integer) is
    procedure Call_Set_Member (This : in C_Pointer;
                               I    : in Interfaces.C.Int);
    pragma Import (C, Call_Set_Member, "set_cppclass_member");
  begin
    Call_Set_Member (Self.This, i);
  end Set_Member;
end CPP_Class;
```

Object construction and destruction are analogous and have to be performed explicitly on the Ada side of the program.

Inheritance. The DOM does not overwrite any inherited functions, and due to the design decisions as described in 4.1, no inheritance was used. In order to implement inheritance you must roll out all inherited functions (for further details refer to [9]).

Exceptions. C does not know about exceptions at all, and you cannot propagate exception through language boundaries. Therefore we have to deal with exceptions manually by the following patterns. On the C side, we define integer constants for the representation of the exceptions of C++.

```
const int OK = 0;
const int FUNCEXCEPTION = 1;
const int UNKNOWN_EXCEPTION = -1;

extern "C" void call_func(int& errorcode) {
  errorcode = OK;
  try {
    func();
  } catch (funcException x) {
    errorcode = FUNCEXCEPTION;
  } catch (...) {
    errorcode = UNKNOWN_EXCEPTION;
  }
}
```

In Ada, we can use corresponding constants to handle the error codes of the C side. The error codes are translated back to an adequate exception in Ada.

```
CPP_OK                 : constant :=  0;
CPP_Func_Exception     : constant :=  1;
CPP_Unknown_Exception  : constant := -1;
Func_Exception, Unknown_Exception : exception;

procedure Fun is
  procedure Call_Fun (Error_Code : out Interfaces.C.Int);
  pragma Import(C, Call_Fun, "call_fun");
  Error_Code : Interfaces.C.Int;
begin
  Call_Fun (Error_Code);
  case Error_Code is
      when CPP_OK             => null;
      when CPP_Func_Exception => raise Func_Exception;
      when others             => raise Unknown_Exception;
  end case;
end Fun;
```

Call-backs. In order to implement the error handler of the DOM, we have to allow the client of the binding to hook up a function he wrote for the XML package. So she is able to implement an arbitrary error handler with the following signature and register it.

```
type ErrorHandlerFunction is
    access function (E : DOMError) return Boolean;
procedure Set_ErrorHandler (Parser      : DOMParser;
                            ErrorHandler : ErrorHandlerFunction);
```

The implementation of the error handler looks like

```
Handler : ErrorHandlerFunction;
procedure Call_ErrorHandler (E : in C_Pointer; Rv : out Boolean);
pragma Export (C, Call_ErrorHandler, "call_errorhandler");

procedure Call_ErrorHandler (E : C_Pointer; Rv : out Boolean) is
  Error : DOMError;
begin
  Error.This := E;
  Rv := Handler (E);
end Call_ErrorHandler;

procedure Set_ErrorHandler (Parser       : DOMParser;
                            ErrorHandler : ErrorHandlerFunction) is
  procedure Call_Set_ErrorHandler;
  pragma Import (C, Call_Set_ErrorHandler,
                 "call_domparser_set_errorhandler");
  Error_Code : Interfaces.C.Int := 0;
begin
  Handler := ErrorHandler;
  Call_Set_ErrorHandler (Parser.This, Error_Code);
  Handle_Error (Error_Code);
end Set_ErrorHandler;
```

5 Related Work

The work presented in this paper is based on the Diploma thesis [9]. The discussion about what parser to use for the binding and the various design decisions is more elaborate.

The most promising work on XML access in Ada is XML/Ada [10] by Briot. However, XML/Ada is not able to validate documents and the DOM support is unsatisfactory.

The GUI toolkit *GtkAda* [11,12] contains a simple XML parser. This parser is not able to validate documents and does not support XML completely. Further, this work gives interesting insights in how to create a language binding to C.

A different approach to XML parsing is taken by *XMLBooster* [13]. XML-Booster is a XML parser generator that generates a parser according to a DTD or XML schema. Because there is no longer a general XML parsing involved, the parser is much faster than generic XML parsing. The parser generator is available for Windows platform only. Among a number of target languages there is also an Ada95 back-end.

Xerces is the Apache Group's popular and widely used XML parser [2]. Xerces is written in C++ and extensively documented. It allows validation against DTDs as well as XML schema. The parser supports DOM and SAX interfaces and is available on a great number of computer platforms. Further, the software is licensed under the Apache Software License [14], which makes it really free software. In particular, this license allows for using Xerces in commercial products.

6   Conclusion

In this paper, we reported on XML4Ada95, a Ada library to access XML at the level of the standardized DOM interface from Ada95. From the user's point of view, XML4Ada95 simply provides access to XML in the Ada language.

The implementation of the package leads to interesting issues when trying to integrate Ada95 to C++. By binding Ada95 to C++ via C, we achieved a well-performing solution to our initial XML parser problem.

If Wittgenstein was right when saying "Die Grenzen meiner Sprache sind die Grenzen meiner Welt." ("The limits of my language are the limits of my world."), then what we did was an adventure trip crossing several worlds. On our wishlist for Ada200Y, we'd like to see Ada having a standardized binding mechanism to C++, even though current scheme via C was sufficient for our task. Also, Ada should have native support for XML, or even better, a standardized interface. But until this is provided, XML4Ada95 offers a preliminary and useable solution.

References

1. Taft, S.T.: Ada 200Y—What and Why. Technical report, Available at http://anubis.dkuug.dk/JTC1/SC22/WG9/n420.pdf (2002)
2. Apache Software Foundation: Xerces C++ Parser. Available at http://xml.apache.org/xerces-c/ (2003)
3. ISO: ISO 8879—Standard Generalized Markup Language (SGML). (1986)
4. Bray, T., Paoli, J., Sperberg-McQueen, C., Maler, E.: Extensible Markup Language (XML) 1.0. Recommendation, W3C (World Wide Web Consortium) (2000) Available at http://www.w3.org/TR/REC-xml.
5. Brownell, D.: SAX2. O'Reilly, See also http://www.saxproject.org/ (2002)
6. Apparao, V., Byrne, S., Champion, M., Isaacs, S., Jacobs, I., Hors, A.L., Nicol, G., Robie, J., Sutor, R., Wilson, C., Wood, L.: Document Object Model (DOM) Level 1. Recommendation, W3C (1998) Available at http://www.w3.org/TR/REC-DOM-Level-1/.
7. Hors, A.L., Hegaret, P.L., Wood, L., Nicol, G., Robie, J., Champion, M., Byrne, S.: Document Object Model (DOM) Level 2 Core Specification. Recommendation, W3C (2000) Available at http://www.w3.org/TR/DOM-Level-2-Core/.
8. Object Management Group: Ada Language Mapping v1.2. Specification (2001) Available at http://www.omg.org/technology/documents/formal/ada_language_mapping.htm.
9. Vrandečić, Z.: XML4Ada95. Diplomarbeit, Universität Stuttgart, Stuttgart, Germany (2003)
10. Briot, E.: XML/Ada: a full XML suite. Available at http://libre.act-europe.fr/xmlada/ (2001)
11. Briot, E., Brobecker, J., Charlet, A., Setton, N.: GtkAda: a complete Ada95 graphical toolkit. Available at http://libre.act-europe.fr/GtkAda/ (2003)
12. Briot, E., Brobecker, J., Charlet, A.: GtkAda: Design and Implementation of a High Level Binding in Ada. In: 5th Ada-Europe International Conference. Volume 1845 of LNCS., Potsdam, Germany, Springer (2000) 112–124
13. RainCode: XMLBooster. Available at http://www.xmlbooster.com/ (2003)
14. Apache Software Foundation: The Apache Software License, Version 1.1. Available at http://xml.apache.org/LICENSE (1999)

A Randomised Test Approach to Testing Safety Critical Ada Code

Sukant K. Giri, Atit Mishra, Yogananda V. Jeppu, and Kundapur Karunakar

1 Aeronautical Development Agency
PO.Box-1718, Vimanapura Post, Bangalore
Pin 560017, India
{skgiri,yvj_2000}@yahoo.com

Abstract. The on board safety critical Ada code for the Indian Light Combat Aircraft, Tejas, has been tested in a Non Real Time (NRT) mode. This method of testing has a few drawbacks. The methodology suffers with certain deficiencies in areas such as coverage metrics, test case generation, and test case selection for regression testing. These drawbacks can be removed by using Randomised Test Approach to generate the test cases. This paper details the philosophy and presents some results of optimising test case generation using Genetic Algorithms.

1 Introduction

Testing is an essential part of any aircraft development program. The use of unstable airframe and fly-by-wire control and the stringent requirements on quality and mean time between failures has placed increased emphasis on testing, especially software. Combinations of flight and safety critical hardware and software are tested on various platforms before integrating on aircraft. Extensive flight tests are carried out to exercise the aircraft in various modes to ensure reliable performance.

The Indian Light Combat Aircraft, Tejas has flown numerous flights without encountering any critical software failure till date. This speaks volumes of the strict quality control in the software development process and the extensive testing carried out on the various platforms. Tejas is an unstable platform and has a Digital Flight Control Computer (DFCC) and advanced Control Laws for stabilisation and flight with good handling qualities [1]. The Control Laws are coded in Ada language by the Software House and extensively tested with the participation of the Independent Verification and Validation (IV&V) group. A new methodology was evolved to test the safety critical code in a Non Real Time Mode by the IV&V and Control Design group [2]. This method has given excellent results and has been accepted as a formal clearance methodology for onboard safety critical software. This method however has deficiencies mainly in the generation of test cases and giving a numerical metric for extent of software test.

A. Llamosí and A. Strohmeier (Eds.): Ada-Europe 2004, LNCS 3063, pp. 190–199, 2004.

2 Non Real Time Testing

The philosophy of the Non Real Time Testing (NRT) is to test the safety critical software in a non real time manner on a target board. The target board is a single board computer having the same processor as the final target. Test cases are generated to test each control system element manually. The test cases are executed on the target board and the results compared with a model code provided by the system designer. NRT is an end-to-end black box testing approach and thoroughly stresses the software under test.

The method however has a few drawbacks. The test cases are generated with an assumption that the software under test is a control system element. Adequacy of the test case is guaranteed by execution on a doctored code called Delta Model. This code has deliberately seeded errors and the test case has to bring out all the errors to qualify as a formal test case. Each case is manually generated and tested making this method time consuming. As the complexity of the control system increases with newer versions, more and more test cases are required to test the block completely. Increase in test cases reflects in an increase in the test time and adversely affects the project timing thus increasing pressure on the testers.

It is seen that many test cases test the same blocks over and over again as they come before the particular block under test. There is no metric available for each test case concerning adequacy of test cases, which can be used for optimisation. There is a definite scope for improvement in the NRT test case generation methodology.

3 Randomised Testing

Using randomised testing can reduce the drawbacks of NRT test case generation. The philosophy of randomised testing is to generate test cases randomly and automatically. Here the inputs to the software under test are not random numbers but sinusoidal waveforms, triangular waveforms or pulses with the properties of these waveforms like frequency, amplitude and bias selected randomly. Usage models are generally used to select random cases in software test practice. In case of flight system the signals, which go into the DFCC, are dictated by the aircraft's interaction with the outside world. This is mimicked in the test cases generation by using sinusoidal waveforms of various frequencies. A probability figure is associated with the frequency and amplitude. During normal flying the signals vary very slowly and therefore the lower frequencies are selected with a higher probability than higher frequency signals, which mimic sudden manoeuvres. The amplitude for the signal waveforms is also selected based on probability. Signal amplitudes within sensor range are selected with a higher probability than out of range signals.

Pilot inputs like under carriage lever and other modes are selected based on likelihood of selection. As an example, it is very unlikely that the pilot would raise undercarriage when on ground. But then this switch could fail giving a spurious signal. The safety critical software uses a number of transient switches, which are used to switch states with a specified, fade in time. This is to avoid sudden transients. The switching inputs are selected such that the switches toggle within the specified fade in time also to test the switch behaviour. Unlike in the case of NRT testing, all the input signals to the DFCC software are injected at once at the all input points. A test case is generated automatically using a front end developed in house. The test case has a description of the signal type and its characteristics rather than time histories. A driver, like in NRT, reads the test cases and generates and injects the test inputs to the software under test.

4 Software under Test (SUT)

Two safety critical items of the onboard software are the Control Laws and the Airdata System. The Control Laws have been considered as the software under test for the study. The Control Law consists of digital filters, rate limiters, switches, transient free switches, non-linearities and scheduled gains [1]. All these blocks are interconnected and this is given as a block diagram in the functionality document. The software group codes these blocks using Beacon Tools, which generates Ada code automatically. The Control Design group also provides a Fortran code, which is extensively tested on various platforms. This code is used to generate the adequacy criteria for each test case and to benchmark the Ada code.

5 Adequacy Criteria

A randomly generated test case is considered adequate if it excites several blocks of the SUT. The various blocks considered are the Control Law blocks like filters, non-

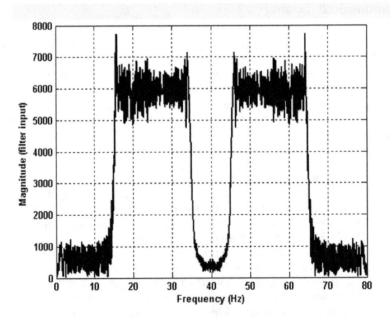

Fig. 1. Adequacy criteria for a filter. The frequency response of the input signal shows a number of points from 0 to 30 Hz which is "adequate" to excite the filter

linearities etc. Adequacy Criteria is defined for each block based on its functional description. The criteria are computed by executing the test cases on the Fortran Model provided by the Control Design group.

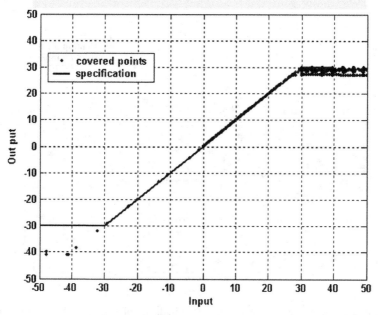

Fig. 2. Input Vs Output from a nonlinear block. The (*dots*) show the actual signal points against the specification for the non linearity block

Filters are control elements, which change the frequency characteristics of input signals. The filter transfer function is defined as the ratio of the output frequency response to the input frequency response. The adequacy criterion for a filter is based on this characteristic. The input signal to the filter is considered to be adequate if it has "enough" points greater than a threshold in the frequency range of interest. Figure 1 shows the plot of the Fast Fourier Transform (FFT) amplitude of the input signal to a filter block. The plot shows adequate signal strength in the frequency range 0 to 40 Hz. This is used to fix a score for the filter block.

A non-linear block modifies the input signal based on the characteristics specified as an input to output relation. Figure 2 shows the input output relation as a cross plot. The specified relation and the test case generated relation are shown in the figure. The adequacy criterion for the non-linear block is that there should be "sufficient" number of input signal points between two breakpoints.

Transient free switches are used to switch and fade between two input signals linearly. The fade time is specified for each switch. This property is used to fix the adequacy criterion for the switch. The output will be equal to one of the inputs. When the switch toggles the output will fade to the other input in the fade in time specified in seconds. After that it will be equal to the other signal. The gradient of the difference between the output and the two input signals is computed. In the zone where the output is equal to the one of the inputs the slope will be zero. In zones where the fading occurs the gradient will be constant and greater than zero. The test case is considered to be adequate if the gradient of the difference has adequate number of points and maximum time for the constant gradient is equal to the fade in time specified for the switch. Figure 3 shows the plot for a transient free switch with a fade in time of 1 second.

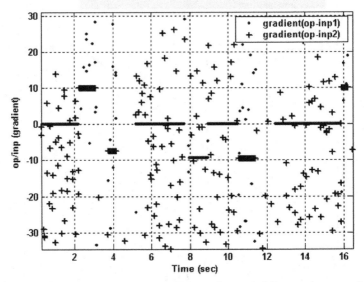

Fig. 3. Transient free switch characteristics. The gradients of difference between the switch output and the two inputs (*inp1 and inp2*) shows flat regions where the transient free switch is in operation. This is used to compute the adequacy criteria

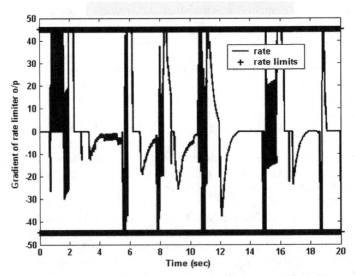

Fig. 4. Rate limiter block characteristics. The gradient of the output shows saturations at (*45*) the rate limits fixed for the block (+) showing that the input is "adequate" to excite the block.

Rate limiters are used in the Control Law to limit the rate of change of input to the specified limits. The gradient of the output of the rate limiter block should show saturation at the specified limits. This is shown in Figure 4. The adequacy criteria are computed for each and every control block as a score, which specifies the amount of coverage of the block. For example, if the rate limiter output shows saturation in only one limit it will have a score of 1.0, saturation in the positive and negative limits gives a score 2.0 and none 0.0.

These scores are computed for each and every block of the Control Law and specify the extent of test coverage of each test case. This will be used to select test cases during regression and to optimise test case generation using optimisation techniques.

6 Coverage Criteria

Another criterion associated with each test case is the coverage criteria. This is generated by executing the test case on Ada code on the target board or any other platform. This criterion specifies the extent of code coverage carried out by the test case. The Ada code is engineered with tap out points in each and every branch, subroutine or function of the code. The index is set to 1 if the particular portion of the code is executed.

An Ada code segment is provided below to illustrate this. Long_index variable contains the total number of code segments and the coverage achieved by the test case.

```
Procedure long_h1 is

Begin

     Long_index(1)  :=1 ;

End long_h1



Procedure long_h2 is

Begin

     Long_index(2)  :=1 ;

   If condition then

       Long_index(3)  :=1 ;

   Else

       Long_index(4)  :=1 ;

   endif

End long_h2
```

7 Test Results

A front end was developed using Matlab to generate the test case automatically. These cases were executed on the Model Code to compute the Adequacy Criteria and on the Ada code generate the Coverage Criteria. 174 cases were generated and tested for adequacy. It was found that the randomly generated test cases could give adequate Coverage Criteria as comparable to the manually generated 512 odd cases used in NRT test activity. The Adequacy Criterion was also met in the test cases thus drastically reducing the number of test cases by 65% required to test SUT. However, several cases gave poor Adequacy Criteria. This was because of the limits specified for the sensor inputs. It is felt that just randomly generating cases is a waste of time and effort. Random cases with optimisation have to be used to generate meaningful test cases.

The efficacy of a test methodology is finally measured in terms of its defect detection capability. Execution of the 174 cases on the Ada code and the Model unearthed three so far undetected defects. One of these was in the initialisation phase with multiple event switches and surprisingly found in the validated model! The other two were minor difference in the implementation logic of latched events. The error in the initialisation phase was detected because of the random combination of events during initialisation generated by the test case generator.

8 Optimisation

Genetic algorithm has been used extensively in software testing for generating test cases [3]. This method is used to generate optimal set of test cases to test components of Control Law. The Control Law uses gains scheduled as a function of the flight envelope [1]. The gains are a function of the speed and altitude of operation. 50 cases are used to test the scheduled gains in NRT. This has reduced to a set of 12 cases using randomised testing.

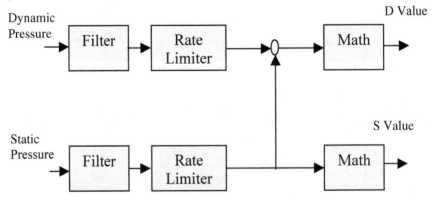

Fig. 5. Schematic of the gain scheduling parameter block. The two input signals (*Dynamic Pressure*) and (*Static Pressure*) pass through the blocks to give the (*D value*) and (*S Value*) used to schedule the gains of the controller

The selection of inputs for testing the gain tables is tricky because of nature of the system as shown in Figure 5. The static and dynamic pressures are heavily filtered and then rate limited before computing S and D values used for a two-dimensional table look up. The gains are given as an array of 23 x 9 elements. The selection of the inputs, the static and dynamic pressure should be such as to cover the complete grid. In generating the NRT test cases one value was kept constant and the other input changed slowly as a ramp signal so as to avoid rate saturation. The randomly selected cases tested various zones of the table and a set of 12 cases could be identified which covered the complete table. This is a clear case for optimisation.

The problem was formulated as an optimisation problem with three control parameters defining the two input signals, static and dynamic pressures. These were the frequency of the sinusoidal input signal, the amplitude and bias of the signal. The Adequacy Criteria defined was that each cell of the 23 x 9 array should have at least one point. The Matlab Genetic Algorithm toolbox GAOT was used to optimise the test case [4]. The number of cells covered by the test case had to be maximised by using GA.

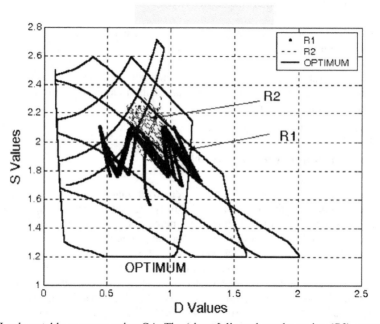

Fig. 6. Look up table coverage using GA. The (*dotted*) lines show the region (*R2*) covered by a set of random inputs. Region (R1) in the centre is for another set of randomly selected inputs. The (*Optimum*) curves cover the complete bottom left corner

The Genetic Algorithm could generate a test case which covered 89 cells for a 20 second execution time of test case. Increasing the test time to 30 seconds increased the number of cells covered to 115. It should be noted here that the NRT cases run for 90 seconds and more to cover the complete envelope. These figures do not cover the complete envelope of 207 cells. The grid was divided into 4 quarters and test cases generated using optimisation. It was possible to cover the complete envelope in 4 cases, a drastic reduction of 66% from randomised test case generation. Figure 6 shows the representation of the cell coverage. Random cases cover portions of the table, some even going beyond the table giving a score of 0. The optimised coverage shows 89 cells covered.

9 Testing Experiences

One build of the software was completely tested using randomised test cases generated automatically. Some of the experience and insights gained during the test activity are shared here.

1. Pure randomised test cases generation generates a lot of duplicate test cases, which have to be discarded. An optimisation is required to achieve useful test cases.

2. Optimisation is time consuming but as human intervention is not required the time can be utilised in some other fruitful activity.

3. Range of the sensors inputs have to be carefully selected to reflect real world scenarios to obtain meaningful test cases.

4. Autocode generators generate a lot of unreachable code especially in the initialisation phase. A code coverage analysis as part of the randomised test activity brings out these dead code efficiently.

10 Conclusion and Further Work

Randomised testing is a definite improvement over manually generated test cases. Optimisation algorithms like GA can be fruitfully utilised to generate optimal sets of test case thus saving a lot of test time. The metrics obtained during the test activity can be utilised for obtaining a useful metric for the test activity.

There is a lot of scope for further work in this field. Some of the possibilities that can be investigated are to optimise the test cases for Adequacy and Coverage Criteria together. Automatic test case selection for regression testing can be carried out based on a hierarchical model of each path of the software, which specifies the order of execution of the various blocks. Metrics on software reliability can be obtained for quality assurance.

Acknowledgement. The authors are grateful to Director, Aeronautical Development Agency, and Programme Director (Combat Aircrafts) for giving an opportunity to carry out and publish this work.

References

1. Shyam Chetty, Girish Deodhare, B.B. Misra: Design, Development and Flight Testing of Control Laws for the Indian Light Combat Aircraft, AIAA Guidance, Navigation and Control Conference, Monterey, CA, August 2002
2. Jeppu, Y.V., et al: Testing Safety Critical Ada Code Using Non Real Time Testing. In: Jean-Pierre Rosen, A Strohmeier (eds.): Reliable Software Technologies ADA-Europe 2003, Lecture Notes in Computer Science, Vol. 2655, Springer-Verlag, 382-393.
3. Ruofan Xu et al: Embedded Core Testing using Genetic Algorithms", Asian Test Symposium, 2000, 254-259.
4. Christopher R H et al: A Genetic Algorithm for Function Optimisation: A Matlab Implementation, available with the toolbox on the Internet.

Good Random Testing

Kwok Ping Chan[1*], Tsong Yueh Chen[2], and Dave Towey[1]

[1] Department of Computer Science and Information Systems,
University of Hong Kong, Hong Kong
{kpchan,dptowey}@csis.hku.hk
[2] School of Information Technology,
Swinburne University of Technology, Hawthorn 3122, Australia
tychen@it.swin.edu.au

Abstract. Software Testing is recognized as an essential part of the Software Development process. Random Testing (RT), the selection of test cases at random from the input domain, is a simple and efficient method of Software Testing. Previous research has indicated that, under certain circumstances, the performance of RT can be improved by enforcing a more even, well-spread distribution of test cases over the input domain. Test cases that contribute to this goal can be considered '*good*,' and are more desirable when choosing potential test cases than those that do not contribute. Fuzzy Set Theory enables a calculation of the degree of membership of the set of '*good*' test cases for any potential test case, in other words, a calculation of how '*good*' the test case is. This paper presents research in the area of improving on the failure finding efficiency of RT using Fuzzy Set Theory. An approach is proposed and evaluated according to simulation results and comparison with other testing methods.

1 Introduction

Although close to four decades have passed since the phrase "Software Engineering" (*SE*) came into common usage [13], it has been argued that, even now, some of its central challenges (e.g., "How not to make a mess of it"[8]) remain unresolved. Indeed "[t]he average customer of the computing industry has been served so poorly that he expects his system to crash all the time" [8].

Software Quality Assurance (*SQA*) refers to the branch of *SE* responsible for ensuring quality standards in produced software. Having high quality software is, of course, desirable; unfortunately however, quality may not be free [14], and, in unregulated industries, it has been asked: if clients do not demand better quality, why perform more than minimal *SQA* [15]?

A particularly simple, and cheap, approach to testing software is to draw test cases at random from the input domain. This technique, commonly referred to as Random Testing (*RT*), in addition to being both cheap and simple, offers several other attractions, including efficient test case generation algorithms, and easily calculated reli

---

* All correspondence should be addressed to: K. P. Chan, Department of Computer Science and Information Systems, University of Hong Kong, Hong Kong. Email: kpchan@csis.hku.hk

A. Llamosí and A. Strohmeier (Eds.): Ada-Europe 2004, LNCS 3063, pp. 200–212, 2004.

ability estimates [9]. It is particularly well suited to testing in the early stages of development [11].

In studies [4, 5, 6], it has been found that, under certain circumstances, by slightly modifying *RT* and requiring the test cases to be more widespread and evenly distributed over the input domain, the failure finding efficiency can be improved, on average by 40% to 50%. These methods, based on *RT*, but incorporating additional mechanisms to encourage a widespread distribution of test cases, are called Adaptive Random Testing (*ART*) methods.

Since the start of computer use, and going back perhaps as far as the Ancient Greeks, there has been an emphasis on precision, and a perceived bias against ambiguity. For computers, this has manifested itself in a need for people to think like computers in order to best use them; in scientific method and elsewhere, the analytical approach, which equates the understanding of the whole with an understanding of the smaller individual parts, has become dominant. Humans however, live and work in imprecise environments; ambiguity is the rule more often than the exception, and an ability to deal with the inherent fuzziness surrounding us is prerequisite to our survival. In 1965, Lotfi Zadeh introduced a theory of mathematical modeling incorporating fuzzy concepts [16]. This approach blurred the traditional crispness associated with mathematical methods and allowed for more vague and ill-defined concepts (e.g., tall, intelligent, etc) to be expressed. In Fuzzy Set Theory, instead of being either completely member or non-member of a set, elements are given a degree of membership, and can easily be compared with other elements.

From the insights gained in earlier studies [4, 5, 6], we are in a position where we can distinguish what might make a good test case from a less good one. In particular, given information about the *SUT*'s input domain, and the current set of executed test cases, we can evaluate which potential test cases will contribute more to the goal of having a well-distributed test case selection pattern than others. Fuzzy set theory offers a succinct methodology within which we can frame this. We refer to our proposed method as Fuzzy Adaptive Random Testing (*F-ART*).

In the next section, we introduce the background and motivation of this study, and describe some of the notation used in this paper. In Section 3, we explain the method employed for test case generation and selection. We carried out a simulation to examine the effectiveness of the proposed method, and also applied the method to several previously studied error-seeded programs. These empirical studies are explained in Section 4. In the final section (5), we examine the results and offer some conclusions and suggestions for future work.

2 Preliminaries

2.1 F-Measure

In this paper, as elsewhere [4, 5, 6], the performance of the testing strategies examined is evaluated according to the number of test cases required to find the first failure. This metric has been named the *F-measure*.

2.2 Background

When Random Testing is used as the strategy for testing, with the exception of avoiding repetition of test cases (points located in the input domain and used to test the software for failures), it is usual not to make use of previous test case information. Test cases are repeatedly generated and tested until one causes a failure (an input which reveals a failure region is referred to as a failure-causing input).

Given a program with an input domain of size d, if the total size of failure-causing input regions is m, then the failure rate of the program (the proportion of the entire input domain which is failure-causing) is m/d. For Random Testing with replacement of test cases [10], the expected number of test cases required to find the first failure (the *F-measure*) is the inverse of the failure rate: For example, when using Random Testing on an input domain with a failure rate of 0.1%, we expect the *F-measure* to be 1/(0.1%), 1000.

2.3 Failure Patterns

When the *SUT* contains an error, this error frequently manifests in the input domain in the form of a failure pattern, i.e., certain points (test cases), when selected and used as input to the *SUT*, reveal a failure. Previous research [3] has identified three major categories of such failure patterns: *point*, which is characterised by individual or small groups of failure-causing input patterns; *strip*, characterised by a narrow strip of failure-causing inputs; and *block*, characterised by the failure-causing inputs being concentrated in either one or a few regions. Figs. 1a-1c give example of these failure pattern types. (In the figures, the shaded areas represent the failure-causing regions, and the borders represent the outer boundaries of the input domain).

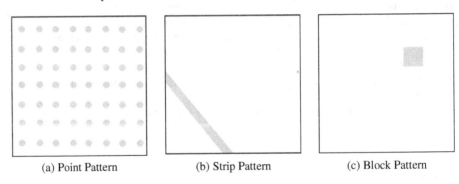

| (a) Point Pattern | (b) Strip Pattern | (c) Block Pattern |

Fig. 1. Types of Failure Patterns

2.4 Motivation

It has been suggested that, for non-point type failure patterns, the failure-finding efficiency of Random Testing (*RT*) methods could be greatly improved by ensuring an even and widespread distribution of test cases over the input domain [7]. Adaptive Random Testing (*ART*) refers to those approaches which are based on *RT*, but which incorporate some additional mechanism(s) to encourage this kind of distribution. Research using *ART* has, in empirical studies, demonstrated improvements averaging 50% over ordinary Random Testing methods [4, 5, 6].

There are many possible implementations of *ART*, Chen et al. proposed an *ART* strategy based on maximizing minimum distances between test cases [6]. Their method, Distance-based *ART* (*D-ART*), makes use of two sets of test cases: the executed set, a set of test cases which have been executed but without causing failure; and the candidate set, a set of test cases selected randomly from the input domain. Each time a new test case is required, the element in the candidate set with the maximum minimum distances from all the executed set elements is selected. One version of this method is the Fixed Size Candidate Set (*FSCS*) strategy, in which the candidate set is maintained with a constant number of elements. Each time an element is selected and executed, the element is added to the executed set, and the candidate set is completely reconstructed. Chen et al. report that the failure finding efficiency of *FSCS* improves as the size of the candidate set, k, increases, but that for k 10, there is little difference in the total number of test cases required to find the first failure (*F-measure*) [6].

An alternative implementation of *ART* involves the use of exclusion areas, and the restriction of test case selection to outside of these areas. This method is called the Restricted Random Testing (*RRT*) method [4, 5] (also known as Restricted *ART* (*R-ART*)). With *RRT*, the input domain from which test cases are generated is restricted to only those regions not close to previously executed test cases. This is implemented by creating an exclusion zone around each previously executed, but non failure-causing input. By correlating the size of the exclusion region around each input with the entire input domain size (targeting, for example, 50% of the input domain to be excluded), it is possible to ensure a minimum distance between each test case. The exclusion zone is the same size for each test case, but the area around each decreases with subsequent executions. Two versions of *RRT* exist: Ordinary Restricted Random Testing (*ORRT*) [5]; and Normalized Restricted Random Testing (*NRRT*) [4]. The *NRRT* version incorporates a scaling/homogenizing feature that reduces the effect that the input domain shape has on the efficacy of the algorithm.

Using insights gained from previous research, it has become possible to identify certain qualities in a potential test case that are desirable, and others that are not. This information enables us to define a fuzzy function that gives a measure of how good, or useful to the goal of achieving a widespread test case pattern, a potential test case is. This approach has been called Fuzzy Adaptive Random Testing (*F-ART*).

3   Method

In order to minimise the number of test cases required to find a failure in the software under test (*SUT*), it is desirable that we be able to select *good* test candidates. The definition of *good* here is restricted by the fact that we are conducting Black Box Testing, and hence know nothing about the internal workings of the *SUT*. What we do have however, is the information that, for certain types of failure patterns (non-point type), a widespread, even distribution of test cases is most efficient at finding failure. *Good* now becomes quantifiable in terms of how much a test case will contribute to the goal of a widespread and distributed test case pattern. Even in those cases where the failure pattern is of point type, the widespread distribution of test cases should not have any significant negative impact on the failure finding efficiency. This has been shown both through simulation and empirical analysis.

Fuzzy Set Theory [16] permits membership of a set to be defined in terms of a degree of belonging, and subsumes the crisp approach of discrete membership, or non-membership, found in traditional set theory. According to the theory, elements no longer need be classified as either "in" or "out," but can instead be given a grade of membership (usually between 0 and 1) of the set.

If we consider all the potential test cases within an input domain as a set, effectively an infinite set, then we can conceive of a subset containing elements that we consider *good*. The members of this *good* subset would change according to the pattern of executed test cases, but a function giving the degree of membership of this *good* subset can be designed. In particular, features that have been shown to encourage a widespread and even distribution of test cases over the input domain are evaluated and incorporated into the function.

3.1 Fuzzy Features

Several features are used to judge how good a potential test case is. As with the *NRRT* [4] version of Restricted Random Testing (*RRT*), a homogenizing feature is used to reduce the influence of the input domain's shape on the calculation of some of the fuzzy features.

Dynamic Minimum Separating Distance (DMSD): In the *RRT* method [4, 5], it was found that by restricting the regions of the input domain from which test cases may be drawn, a faster locating of the failure regions was obtained. Effectively, this restriction of the input domain was achieved by encouraging a minimum distance between each test case, this distance decreasing as the number of test cases increases. By incorporating a dynamic minimum separating distance into the membership function, we can help ensure the widespread and evenly distributed nature of the test case pattern over the input domain. Using a proportion of the entire input domain area/volume corresponding approximately to the optimum target exclusion ratio from *RRT*, a separating area/volume is calculated. This separating area/volume is divided by the number of executed test cases, and a distance equal to the radius of the circle/sphere with this area/volume is used as the **DMSD**.

Absolute Minimum Separating Distance (AMSD): The second feature to use distance to ensure the widespread selection of test cases is the **AMSD**, which encourages that, irrespective of the number of test cases, there should not be any 2 cases within this minimum distance of each other. Unlike the **DMSD** feature, **AMSD** does not change as the number of test cases increases.

Expected Quadrant Population (EQP): Independent of the number of test cases already executed, the input domain is divided into 2 equal regions per dimension. The expected number of test cases per region is calculated and compared with the actual number for the region into which the proposed test case would fall. If the region contains less than the expected number, then the proposed test case is favoured.

Proportion Close Test Cases (PCTC): The total number of test cases close to the proposed test case, relative to the proportion of area close to the test case, is calculated. If there is a significantly disproportionate number less points in the area, then the proposed test case is strongly favoured; conversely, if there is a significantly disproportionate number more points in the area, then the proposed test case is strongly disfavoured.

```
FOR (all test cases to date)
DO
        Count the total number of test cases close to the potential case
        Count the total number of test cases more than the absolute
            minimum separating distance (AMSD) from the potential case
        Count the total number of test cases more than the dynamic
            minimum separating distance (DMSD) from the potential case
END_FOR

IF (NOT all test cases are at last AMSD from the potential test case)
THEN Strongly disfavour the membership
END_IF

IF (all test cases are at least DMSD from the potential test case)
THEN Strongly favour the membership
END_IF

IF (there is significantly disproportionately MORE test cases close to potential test case)
THEN Strongly disfavour the membership
ELSEIF (there is significantly disproportionately LESS)
        THEN Strongly favour the membership
END_ELSEIF
END_IF

IF (there are less points in the quadrant of the potential test case than would be expected)
THEN Strongly favour the membership
END_IF

IF (there are significantly disproportionately MORE test cases close to the border area
    than would be expected) AND (the potential test case is NOT close)
THEN Favour the membership
ELSEIF (there are significantly disproportionately LESS test cases close to the border
        area than would be expected) AND (the potential test case IS close)
        THEN Favour the membership
END_ELSEIF
END_IF

IF (there are significantly disproportionately MORE test cases close to the central area
    than would be expected) AND (the potential test case is NOT close)
THEN Favour the membership
ELSEIF (there are significantly disproportionately LESS test cases close to the central
        area than would be expected) AND (the potential test case IS close)
        THEN Favour the membership
END_ELSEIF
END_IF
```

Algorithm 1. Outline of Membership Grade Evaluation Function

Threshold Selection method

IF (there have already been too many accepted points, on first try)
    THEN Increase the threshold
END_IF

WHILE (we haven't found an acceptable test case) AND
                (not yet tried more than maximum number of times to get a test case)
DO
        WHILE (we haven't found an acceptable test case) AND
                (not yet tried more than maximum number of times,
                for this threshold, to get a test case)
        DO
                Generate a random test case
                Determine the membership grade of this test case
                IF (the membership grade is above the threshold)
                THEN this test case is acceptable
                END_IF
        END_WHILE

        IF (we got an acceptable test case on first try)
        THEN increment the count for consecutive first try acceptable test cases
        ELSE reset the count to zero
        END_IF

        IF (we did not yet get an acceptable test case)
        THEN
                Reduce the threshold
                Reset the count for number of attempts to get an acceptable test case at a
                threshold
        ELSE OUTPUT the acceptable test case
        END_IF

END_WHILE

Algorithm 2. Outline of Threshold Selection (*TS*) Method

Random_Candidate_Set method

FOR (the total number of desired elements in the Candidate Set)
DO
        Generate a random test case
        Add this test case to the Candidate Set
        Determine the membership grade for this test case
END_FOR

OUTPUT the element of the candidate set with the highest membership grade

---

Algorithm 3. Outline of Random Candidate Set (*RCS*) Method

Proportion Close to Border (PCB): The total number of test cases close to the boundary of the input domain, relative to this area as a proportion of the entire input domain area, is calculated. If there is a significantly disproportionate number less points in the area, and the proposed test case is close to the border, then the proposed test case is strongly favoured. Likewise, if there is a significantly disproportionate number more points close to the border, and the proposed test case is not close, then the proposed test case is also strongly favoured.

Proportion Close to Centre (PCC): The total number of test cases close to the centre of the input domain, relative to this proportion of the area, is calculated. If there is a significantly disproportionate number less points in the area, and the proposed test case is close to the centre, then the proposed test case is strongly favoured. Likewise, if there is a significantly disproportionate number more points close to the centre, and the proposed test case is not close, then the proposed test case is also strongly favoured.

In all the above features, closeness is defined in terms of the Euclidean distance. An outline of the membership function is given in Algorithm 1

3.2 Selection

We have two methods of selecting test cases using the fuzzy membership function. In the first case, we use a dynamic threshold: when looking for a test case, as soon as one with a membership grade higher than the current threshold is found, we accept it, and use it to test the *SUT*. This version is referred to as the Threshold Selection (*TS*) method, and is outlined in Algorithm 2.

In the second method, we have a candidate set that holds a number (presently chosen as 10) of potential test candidates, all randomly generated. The membership grade for each of these candidates is calculated, and the test case with the highest grade is selected. This version is referred to as the Random Candidate Set (*RCS*) method, and is outlined in Algorithm 3.

4 Empirical Study

To investigate the effectiveness of the *F-ART* approach, we simulated a failure region within an input domain, and calculated how many test cases were required by each of the *F-ART* methods, and by ordinary *RT*, to find the failure (i.e., we calculated the *F-measure* for each method). In addition, we also applied the methods to several of the error-seeded programs previously studied by Chan et al. [4, 5] and Chen et al. [6].

4.1 Simulation

We conducted a simple simulation, in which a percentage of a square input domain was specified to be failure-causing (an input drawn from this region would cause the tested program to fail). This region was circular in shape, and its size was set at 0.01, 0.005, and 0.001 of the entire input area (= 1%, 0.5%, and 0.1%). By knowing what portion of the input domain is failure-causing ( ), we are able to calculate the expected *F-measure* by Random Testing (1/).

The simulation was conducted for both methods (Threshold Selection (*TS*) and Random Candidate Set (*RCS*)). The simulations were run to produce a sample size of 1,000 *F-measure* results for each method. The results are given in Table 1 below, included in which are the expected F-measure values for Random Testing (*RT*). As can be seen, the Fuzzy Adaptive Random Testing (*F-ART*) methods offer significant improvement over the expected value of *RT*.

Table 1. Average number of test cases required to find the first failure (*F*), and standard deviation (*STD*) for each method in the simulation. The results are averaged over 1,000 iterations

Method	= 1%		= 0.5%		= 0.1%	
	F	STD	F	STD	F	STD
Threshold Selection (*TS*)	91.0	84.6	168.8	148.1	807.9	664.9
Random Candidate Set (*RCS*)	79.6	64.0	152.5	123.9	690.2	539.1
Random Testing (Expected) (*RT*)	100.0	*	200.0	*	1000.0	*

4.2   Error-Seeded Programs

In our study, we tested the *F-ART* methods against seven error-seeded programs previously studied by Chan et al. [4, 5] and Chen et al. [6]. These programs [1, 12] all involve numerical calculations, were written in C (converted to C++ for our experiments) and vary in length from 30 to 200 statements.

Errors in the form of simple mutants [2] were seeded into the different programs. Four types of mutant operators were used: arithmetic operator replacement (*AOR*); relational operator replacement (*ROR*); scalar variable replacement (*SVR*) and constant replacement (*CR*). These mutant operators were chosen since they generate the most commonly occurring errors in numerical programs [2]. After the errors were seeded into the programs, the input domains for each program were set so that the overall failure rate would not be too large. Table 2 summarizes the details of the error-seeded programs.

Table 2. Program name, dimension (D), input domain, seeded error types, and total number of errors for each of the error-seeded programs. The error types are: arithmetic operator replacement (*AOR*); relational operator replacement (*ROR*); scalar variable replacement (*SVR*) and constant replacement (*CR*)

Program Name	D	Input Domain		Error Type				Total Errors
		From	To	AOR	ROR	SVR	CR	
bessj	2	(2.0, -1000.0)	(300.0, 15000.0)	2	1		1	4
bessj0	1	(-300000.0)	(300000.0)	2	1	1	1	5
cel	4	(0.001, 0.001, 0.001, 0.001)	(1.0, 300.0, 10000.0, 1000.0)	1	1		1	3
erfcc	1	(-300000.0)	(300000.0)	1	1	1	1	4
gammq	2	(0.0, 0.0)	(1700.0, 40.0)		3		1	4
plgndr	3	(10.0, 0.0, 0.0)	(500.0, 11.0, 1.0)	1	2		2	5
sncndn	2	(-5000.0, -5000.0)	(5000.0, 5000.0)			4	1	5

4.3 F-ART Applied to Seeded Programs

The results of the **F-ART** method when applied to the error-seeded programs are given below (Fig. 2). Also given are the best results for both the **ORRT** and **NRRT** versions of Restricted Random Testing (**RRT**), and the results for the **FSCS** version of Distance-based Adaptive Random Testing (**D-ART**). The figure shows the percentage improvement[1], for each method, over the **RT F-measure**.

From the figure, it can be seen that the results for the **F-ART** method show a significant improvement over **RT**, and are comparable with the results for the other methods. Only the **sncndn** program shows no significant improvement over **RT**. As discussed previously however, this program has a point-type failure pattern, and is therefore unlikely to show improvement with more evenly spread test cases [4, 5].

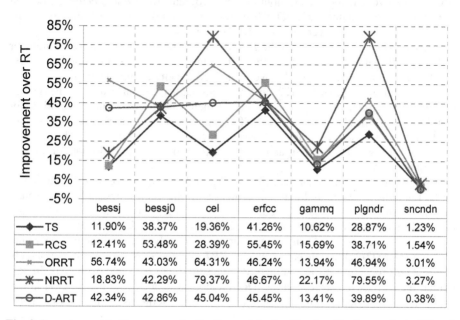

	bessj	bessj0	cel	erfcc	gammq	plgndr	sncndn
◆ TS	11.90%	38.37%	19.36%	41.26%	10.62%	28.87%	1.23%
■ RCS	12.41%	53.48%	28.39%	55.45%	15.69%	38.71%	1.54%
✳ ORRT	56.74%	43.03%	64.31%	46.24%	13.94%	46.94%	3.01%
✳ NRRT	18.83%	42.29%	79.37%	46.67%	22.17%	79.55%	3.27%
⊖ D-ART	42.34%	42.86%	45.04%	45.45%	13.41%	39.89%	0.38%

Fig. 2. Improvement in **F-measures** for the Fuzzy Adaptive Random Testing methods (**TS** and **RCS**), compared with the Random Testing F-measure. Ordinary Restricted Random Testing (**ORRT**), Normalized Restricted Random Testing (**NRRT**), and **FSCS** version of Distance-based Adaptive Random Testing (**D-ART**) results are also included. All figures refer to the improvement over the calculated **RT**

5 Discussion

$$\frac{(F-measure_{RT} - F-measure_{method})}{F-measure_{RT}} \times 100$$

In the simulations (section 4.1), the **F-ART** method showed improvement over the expected **F-measure** results for Random Testing (**RT**). When the method was applied

---

[1] Percentage improvement is calculated:

to several previously studied error-seeded programs (section 4.3), there was again universal improvement over *RT*.

As previously observed [4, 5], the *sncndn* program's performance was not expected to improve due to its failure pattern being of point type.

The *bessj* program, as with the *NRRT* method, shows less improvement with the *F-ART* method than with others. As suggested earlier [4], this is most likely linked to the failure pattern associated with this program, a narrow block, or incomplete strip type.

The improvement over *RT* for the *cel* program when using the *F-ART* method, although not as dramatic as for *NRRT* or *D-ART*, is significant. The *gammq* and *plgndr* programs also show good improvement under the *F-ART* approach, with improvements over *RT* comparable to those for *D-ART*, although not as significant as for *NRRT*. The two 1-Dimensional input domain programs (*bessj0* and *erfcc*) show best overall improvement under *F-ART* when compared against the other testing methods, with 53% and 55% improvement over *RT* respectively.

The overheads associated with the *F-ART* methods are determined by the number and nature of features used in the membership function. As the number and complexity of features increase, so does the overhead for the membership function.

In the Threshold Selection (*TS*) method, although potential test cases below the threshold are discarded, and their associated membership grade and calculation are therefore an overhead, the threshold itself is dynamic and decreases when the number of attempts to find an acceptable test case passes above a certain limit. This ensures that a test case will be selected, and that the execution overheads do not continue to grow unbounded.

Because the Random Candidate Set (*RCS*) method requires only that a candidate set be randomly created, and that the element with the highest threshold be selected, each iteration of the method is guaranteed to select a test case. The overhead is only that of the membership calculation of the discarded candidate set elements.

One of the features used in the current study, the dynamic minimum separating distance (*DMSD*), although based on the *RRT* method's exclusion zone approach, does not enforce a restriction and therefore does not incur the same overheads. In particular, the increased overhead in the *RRT* method associated with the increase in target exclusion rate does not have a similar increase in overheads for the *F-ART* methods.

The features used in the membership function presented here were chosen for their ability to encourage selection of test cases that help ensure an even distribution of test cases over the entire input domain. Research and identification of other features that also help ensure this distribution will enhance the proposed method.

The goal of achieving an even distribution of test cases was motivated by earlier findings suggesting that, for particular failure patterns, this was better than pure random methods at locating failure regions [4, 5, 6]. As alternative distributions become desirable, so too will alternative features and rules become necessary to best encourage the distribution. The proposed fuzzy membership method offers a particularly well-suited framework within which to develop these measures and rules.

6 Summary

In this paper we have presented a novel approach to Software Testing, Fuzzy Adaptive Random Testing (*F-ART*). The approach makes use of Fuzzy Set Theory to describe a membership function. The membership function evaluates a potential test case, and gives a degree of membership to the set of *good* test cases. Here we have defined *good* as those cases which contribute to the goal of achieving an evenly spread and well distributed test case pattern.

In a simulation, the proposed method has been shown to significantly outperform Random Testing, and compare well with Restricted Random Testing (*RRT*) [4, 5], and Distance-based Adaptive Random Testing (*D-ART*) [6], alternative testing strategies also based on *ART*.

The overheads associated with the method are determined mainly by the number and type of features employed in the membership rule. In most cases, because the features in the membership function are used to encourage particular types of test case, not restrict them, the overheads associated with wasted potential test case generation are low.

Acknowledgement. We should like to gratefully acknowledge the support given to this project by the Research Grants Council of the Hong Kong Special Administrative Region, China (Project No: HKU 7007/99E).

References

1. Association for Computer Machinery, 'Collected Algorithms from ACM, Vol. I, II, III', *Association for Computer Machinery*, 1980.
2. T. A. Budd, 'Mutation Analysis: Ideas, Examples, Problems and Prospects', *Computer Program Testing*, B. Chandrasekaran and S. Radicci (eds.), North-Holland, Amsterdam, pp. 129-148, 1981.
3. F. T. Chan, T. Y. Chen, I. K. Mak and Y. T. Yu, 'Proportional Sampling Strategy: Guidelines for Software Testing Practitioners', Information and Software Technology, Vol. 28, No. 12, pp. 775-782, December 1996.
4. K. P. Chan, T. Y. Chen and D. Towey, 'Normalized Restricted Random Testing', *8th Ada-Europe International Conference on Reliable Software Technologies*, Toulouse, France, June 16-20, 2003, Proceedings. LNCS 2655, pp. 368-381, Springer-Verlag Berlin Heidelberg 2003.
5. K. P. Chan, T. Y. Chen and D. Towey, 'Restricted Random Testing', *Software Quality - ECSQ 2002*, 7th European Conference, Helsinki, Finland, June 9-13, 2002, J. Kontio and R. Conradi (eds.), LNCS 2349, pp. 321-330, Springer-Verlag Berlin Heidelberg 2002.
6. T. Y. Chen, H. Leung and I. K. Mak, 'Adaptive Random Testing', submitted for publication.
7. T. Y. Chen, T. H. Tse, and Y. T. Yu, 'Proportional Sampling Strategy: A Compendium and Some Insights', *The Journal of Systems and Software*, 58, pp. 65-81, 2001.
8. E. W. Dijkstra, 'The End of Computing Science?' *Communications of the ACM*, Vol. 44, No. 3, p. 92, March 2001.
9. R. Hamlet, 'Random Testing', *Encyclopedia of Software Engineering*, edited by J. Marciniak, Wiley, pp. 970-978, 1984.

10. H. Leung, T. H. Tse, F. T. Chan and T. Y. Chen, 'Test Case Selection with and without Replacement', *Information Sciences*, 129 (1-4), pp. 81-103, 2000.

11. P. S. Loo and W. K. Tsai, 'Random Testing Revisited', *Information and Software Technology*, Vol. 30, No. 9, pp. 402-417, September 1988.

12. W. H. Press, B. P. Flannery, S. A. Teulolsky and W. T. Vetterling, *Numerical Recipes*, Cambridge University Press, 1986.

13. C.L. Simons, I.C. Parmee and P.D. Coward, '35 years on: to what extent has software engineering design achieved its goals?', *IEE Proc.-Softw.*, Vol. 150, No. 6, December 2003.

14. S. Slaughter, D. E. Harter, M. S. Krishnan, 'Evaluating the Cost of Software Quality', *Communications of the ACM*, Vol. 41, No. 8, pp. 67-73, August 1998.

15. J. M. Voas, 'Guest Editor's Introduction: Assuring Software Quality Assurance', *IEEE Software*, Vol. 20, No. 3, pp. 48-49, 2003.

16. L. A. Zadeh, 'Fuzzy Sets', *Information and Control*, Vol. 8, pp 338-353, 1965.

Teaching Real-Time Systems Around a Digital Model Railroad Platform Using Ada

Bárbara Álvarez, Juan A. Pastor, Francisco Ortiz, Pedro Sánchez, and
Pedro Navarro

Universidad Politécnica de Cartagena (Spain)
francisco.ortiz@upct.es

Abstract. This paper describes a laboratory equipped for the teaching of real-time systems. The laboratory has been built around a Digital Model Railroad Platform and it allows the development of different control applications for educational purposes. Because of the platform is a limited resource and the students can not test their programs simultaneously, a railroad platform simulator has been developed. The programming language used to implement the simulator has been Ada and the design and implementation of the system is described in this work. Ada is also selected in order to allow the students to carry out their practical exercises during the course[1].

Keywords: Education and training, real-time systems, object-oriented programming.

1 Introduction

Although many undergraduate courses in computer engineering acquaint students with the fundamental topics in real-time computing, many do not provide adequate laboratory platforms to exercise the software skills necessary to build physical real-time systems. The undergraduate real-time systems course at Technical University of Cartagena has been offered since 1999. The course is practical and it carries out in a laboratory with a Digital Model Railroad Platform. This laboratory is particularly useful for educational purposes in the control of physical real-time systems, where the characteristics of these systems can be put into practice. The environment allows the student to control concurrently several digital locomotives, the turnouts on the layout, etc.

Due to its possibilities, Ada [1][2] has been selected as a suitable programming language to learn the characteristics of real-time systems. During the course, classic programming techniques in Ada are studied. As the students can not test their programs simultaneously over the railroad platform, a simulator has been developed using Ada. In this way, all the students can implement and test their exercises in their

---

[1] This work was supported in part by Spanish Ministry of Education (with reference ACF2000-0037-IN) and the Regional Government of Murcia (Séneca Programmes with reference PB/5/FS/02)

A. Llamosí and A. Strohmeier (Eds.): Ada-Europe 2004, LNCS 3063, pp. 213–224, 2004.

computers. When the programs has been finished then they are tested over the real railroad mock-up.

In this paper, the Digital Model Railroad Platform and how the simulator has been developed are described. In particular, Section 2 gives a complete description of the Digital Model Railroad Platform. In section 3, the design and implementation of the simulator are reviewed. Section 4 contains the topics that the students learn during the real-time systems course and a model of a practical exercise. Finally, section 5 summarizes the benefits of this paper and outline future plans.

2 Laboratory Equipment: A Railroad System

The proposed railroad system has been developed around a commercial digital control system by Märklin [3]. In our railroad layout there are five digital locomotives, sixteen digital turnout switches (where two or more tracks are joined), six semaphores, and twenty-one reed contact sensors to manage and control. The reed contacts are placed before and after turnouts around the track in order to monitor the passing of locomotives. The total length of the track plus the turnouts results in a complex circuit in which several levels of difficulty (and risks) can be simulated. Because of the digital characteristics of the Märklin locomotives and tracks, all the information needed to control the railroad is run through the tracks. Several Märklin modules are used to connect (using a RS232 serial interface) the track to the computer.

Also, several video cameras are connected to the system. One of them shows users a video stream of the actual physical train system and provides the opportunity to carry out visual supervision of the locomotives. Other cameras are placed inside the locomotives for others control tasks (such as stopping before a semaphore, emergency stop before an obstacle, adjustment of train speed to the traffic conditions, etc.). Figure 1 shows a panoramic view of the railroad platform.

The laboratory equipment for controlling the digital model railroad platform is an Intel Pentium computer. As mentioned above, a serial connection is performed between the Märklin Digital Control System (see figure 2) and the computer that contains all tasks required to manage the railroad. The 6021 Control Unit is the core of the Märklin Digital System. This module receives the commands from the Interface Module and converts them to electric signals that are transmitted through the rails using only two wires. All the turnouts, semaphores, and locomotives carry a device to decode control commands. In this way, the number of wires is minimized to two. Each reed contact consists of two wires that indicate that some locomotive has travelled over it. Twenty reed contacts are installed to monitor the traffic on the railroad. The Märklin Track Detection Module includes three Märklin S88 decoders. Each one provides a reading of the status of the eight reed contacts.

In the Intel Pentium computer, a driver interface allows users to stop, reverse, and change the speed of each locomotive. Also, users are able to switch any of the sixteen connected turnouts on the layout. Each of these elements responds to computer commands. Because twenty students can not test at the same time they are code over the real platform, a simulator of such system has been developed using Ada. This simulator allows students to test their implementations as they were testing them using the physical railroad.

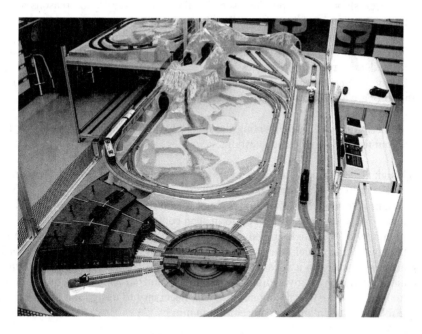

Fig. 1. Railroad platform.

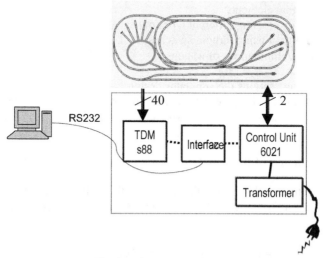

Fig. 2. Laboratory layout.

3   A Railroad Platform Simulator in Ada

As it has been shown in the previous sections there are several good reasons to provide students with a simulator of the railroad mock-up:

1. The mock-up is an expensive resource shared by all the students of the course. The students have a limited access to it.
2. In some circumstances (i.e. very expensive materials, ...) it is preferable to test the software against a simulator than against the real devices.

When designing and implementing the mock-up simulator it is necessary to take into account the following basic questions:

- Though it seems obvious, it is necessary to remark that it is not the same to model a railroad mock-up that a real railway.
- The aim is to model the mock-up and not to control the trains, but to provide the framework where students can perform such control.
- The model of the mock-up should be as flexible as possible. Every change that can occur in the actual mock-up should be easily translated to the model. For instance, in a mock-up it is easy to add and eliminate rail tracks, to put and remove trains, to modify a given train configuration and so on. These modifications should also be easy in the model. So, it is necessary to design the software with the following adaptability requirements in mind:

  ✓ Addition/elimination of rail tracks;
  ✓ Changes in the length of the rail tracks;
  ✓ Addition/modifications/elimination of reed contact sensors, semaphores and other signal elements;
  ✓ Possibility of using different types of sensors;
  ✓ Possibility of using turnout switches;
  ✓ Addition/eliminations of wagons.

In the following sections the simulator design is described. For space reasons only the most relevant issues have been explained. In particular, most of the aspects related to graphical representation of the mock-up have been omitted.

3.1   Static Structure of the Simulator

The static structure of the classes that represent the railway and trains are shown in the UML [4] diagram of figure 3. Only the most relevant methods are shown in the figure.

- Classes **Node**, **RailNode** and **TrainNode**.
  The basic constructive element of the trains and rails are the nodes of a double-linked list (class **Node**). The two subclasses of **Node** (**RailNode** and **Train-Node**) are respectively the constructive elements of **RailTrack** and **Wagon**

instances. In the same way, **RailTrack** and **Wagon** instances are the basic elements to build **RailWay** and **Train** instances. So, trains are simply double-linked lists that move over another double linked-list: the rail sections (see figure 4). Rail nodes and train nodes represent slices of rail and train of the same length and this length is the unit of granularity to consider the distances in the mock-up. In this way, the lengths of trains and rail sections should be clearly related between them and with the real dimensions of the mock-up.

RailNode has procedures for putting and removing **TrainNode** instances and for putting and removing a sensor. **TrainNode** has procedures for associating and dissociating it to a given **RailNode**. It is evident the strong coupling between **RailNodes** and **TrainNodes**, but this coupling also exists in the mock-up. Once started, the trains move along the railway autonomously and they can be stopped or accelerated, but their routes are completely determined by the railway configuration.

- Classes **RailTrack** and **Wagon**.

A **Wagon** instance is an aggregate of **TrainNode** instances (at least one). The length of a wagon is given by the number of **TrainNode** instances it comprises. **Wagon** provides a **concat** procedure that makes possible the union of wagons without being aware of the **TrainNode** instances.

In the same way, a **RailTrack** is an aggregate of **RailNode** instances (at least one). The length of a rail section is given by the number of **RailNode** instances it comprises. Newly, **RailTrack** provides a **concat** procedure that makes possible the union of rail sections without being aware of the **RailNode** instances. **RailTrack** instances may have one or more sensors (not more sensors than its length) and 0, 1 or 2 semaphores (one at each of its extremes). Finally, it is possible to associate a **RailTrack** with a given view through the procedure **setView**. The idea is to separate the logical behaviour of rail tracks from their graphic representations (as the pattern model-view-controller establishes [5]).

Finally, the procedure **subscribe** gives clients the possibility of being advertised when a collision happens in the **RailTrack**.

- Classes **Sensor, SwitchPoint** and **Semaphore**.

Class **Sensor** models the devices used for detecting the pass of trains. There are several types of sensors that are obtained by subclassing, whose interface is shown in Figure 3. Notice the presence of the procedure **subscribe**, that offers the possibility of subscribing clients to sensor changes (following an Observer pattern [5]). The clients that do not want to subscribe to sensor changes can simply poll the state of sensors through the function **isActive**.

Class **Semaphore** models the signalling devices that can be installed along the railway. For simplicity it is only allowed to attached them to the extreme of a given rail section.

SwitchPoint models the devices used for switching from one rail section to another. Given the inner representation of rail sections as doubled linked lists, the implementation of **SwitchPoint** is very simple.

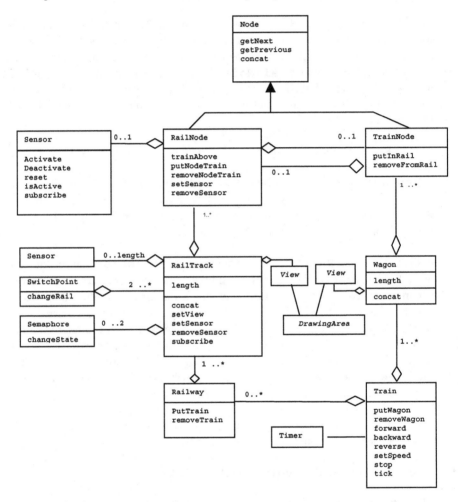

Fig. 3. Static structure of the simulator in UML

- Classes **View** and **DrawingArea**.

The views of **RailTrack** and **Wagon** instances can be drawn on a given **DrawingArea**. Classes **View** and **DrawingArea** are explicitly represented as abstract in the figure 3. Their implementations should be a *bridge* [5] between the application and a graphic framework that provides the functionality to define and manage the actual **DrawingArea** and **Views** (for example **GtkAda** [6]). In order to make easier the concatenation of views, **View** provides the procedure **concat** that allow programmers to draw two views (one after the other) without being care of the concrete coordinates of the views in the **DrawingArea**. Though it is not represented in Figure 3, it is also possible to associate views to **Sensor**, **SwitchPoints** and **Semaphore** instances.

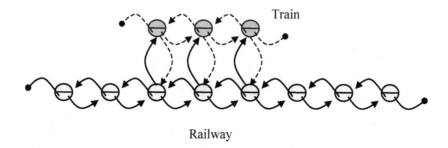

Railway

Fig. 4. Trains and rail sections as double-linked lists.

- Classes **Train** and **Railway**.

  A **Train** instance is an aggregate of **Wagon** instances that provides procedures to put and remove wagons, to start and stop the motion along the railway, to reverse the sense of the motion and to set the speed.

  RailWay is an aggregate of **RailTrack** instances that provides procedures to put trains on it and remove them from it.

- Class **Timer**.
  The **Timer** is the only active object of the mock-up. It invokes the train procedure that makes them to move along the railway. **Timer** provides the dynamic behaviour of the mock-up, so it is explained in the following section.

3.2 Behaviour of the Simulator

All the train actions are driven by an unique **Timer**. The relations between the **Train** instances and the **Timer** follow the *observer* pattern [5]. The **Timer** invokes the **tick** procedure of **Train** instances periodically. The **Timer** period defines the shortest time interval considered in the mock-up. When a train receives a tick, it may do two things:
- Nothing, or
- To move one unit of distance forward or backward (remember that the unit of distance is defined by the distance occupied by a **RailNode** or a **TrainNode**).

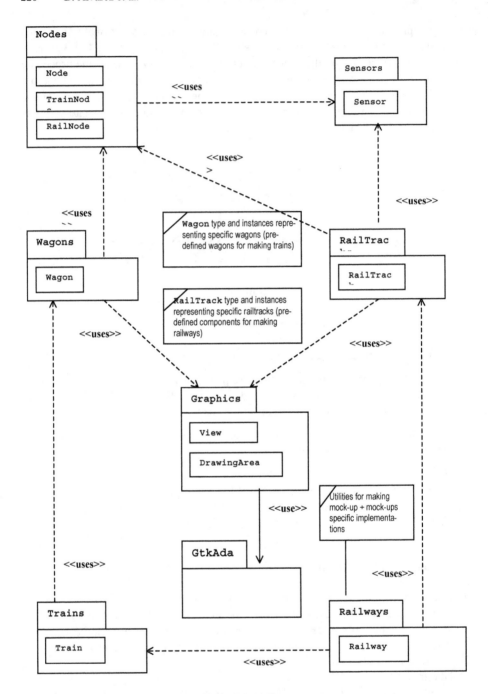

Fig. 5. Ada packages

A train reaches the maximum possible speed when it moves every time that **Timer** invokes its **tick** procedure. There is no speed lower limit, a train can decide to move every 1000 ticks or every one million. It is easy to deduce that a **Train** only can be in a position that is the initial plus a multiple of the unit of distance. There is an alternative approach: to make **Train** instances active objects, but although this approach have some advantages, lead us to significant concurrency problems that do not occur with the approach taken. If **RailTrack** and **Wagon** instances are constructed using **RailNodes** and **TrainNodes**, *the motion of a train consists in rearranging the mutual references between them* (see figure 4). As the rail sections are resources shared among all the trains that runs over them at a given instant, it is possible to question about synchronisation problems[2]. However, with the taken approach it is not possible that such problems arise, because the **Timer** invokes their **tick** procedures sequentially.

The implementations can choose to use real time or not. The **Timer** is not forced to generate a new *tick* until all the **tick** procedures have been executed. The implementation may choose a **Timer** driven by a real clock or not if it doesn't want to deal with scheduling issues and deadlines.

3.3 Ada Packages of the Simulator

The paradigm of *Object Oriented Programming* has been considered for implementing the simulator. All record types are extended on derivation provided they are marked as tagged. Record types also are private. So, we can extend from the type without knowing its details.

The structure of the application packages is described in Figure 5. Realize that such structure exhibits a three layered architecture. The **Railways** and **Trains** use the packages **RailTracks** and **Wagons** respectively, but they are not aware of the package **Nodes**. In this package, the type **Node** is the root of a tree of types and **RailNode** and **TrainNode** are derived from it. The primitive operations of **Node** are inherited by **RailNode** and **TrainNode** and some of them are redefined.

It would be possible to change the implementation details of **Wagons** and **Rail- Tracks** with a minimum impact over **Trains** and **Railways**. The packages **Wagons** and **RailTracks** include the types **Wagon** and **RailTrack** and specific implementations for specific wagons and rail tracks.

The package called **Trains** providing appropriate operations for creating trains, stopping, modifying speed, etc. The implementation has hidden away the inner workings from the user by making a record type **Train** as private.

4   The Real-Time Course: A Practical Exercise

The laboratory has been used in courses such as *Concurrent Programming* and *Real-Time Systems*. These courses are placed in the last year of the *Industrial Electronics*

---

[2] The railway is always a resource shared by all the trains (independently of the implementation).

and *Control Engineer* graduate curriculum, and they cover a good percent of ACM/IEEE-CS recommendations in computing technologies [7]. In particular, the course Real-Time Systems has seven lectures which concentrated on the following topics:

- Characteristics of real-time systems and introduction to Ada 95 language;
- Concurrent programming;
- Scheduling schemes (cyclic executive and priority-based models);
- Reliability, fault tolerance and low-level programming.

Although in the first topic *"Introduction to Ada"*, we consider basic Ada structures through discussions on programming in the small and programming in the large, other more advanced mechanisms of the language are introduced in the following lectures. As textbook, we recommend *"Real-Time Systems and Programming Languages"* by Burns and Welling [8].

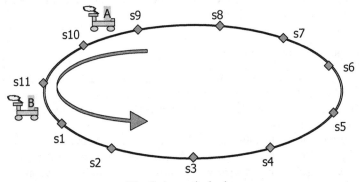

Fig. 6. A practical scheme.

The practical exercises must provide opportunities for these theoretical concepts testing. With the basic infrastructure described in the above sections, a highly comprehensive set of programming practices were developed. One of them is briefly described in this section, simply to give an overall idea of the laboratory's possibilities. The railroad platform simulator focuses on modularity. Students should be able to design an application module using simulator module interfaces. An example of practical exercise is carried out by the students starting from the following requirements specification. Once the students know the railroad platform, we fix the turnout switches in order to have a lineal problem as figure 6 shows.

It is necessary to avoid that a train collides with other train. Evidently, as turnout switches are fixed, we have one-way railroad and it is not possible that a train meets to other train in a turnout switch or two trains collide. In order to avoid accidents, it has always to have a "free stretch" between two trains[3]. In accordance with this idea, if a train (train A) has gone over a reed contact sensor which represents the beginning of a track and other train (train B) is on the following track then we have to stop the

---

[3] We define a "free stretch" as the space of tracks between two reed contacts.

first train (train A) until the second train (train B) leaves the occupied track. In this moment, the stopped train must recovery its initial speed.

As figure 6 describes, the train A is over a stretch between s9-s10 reed contacts and can go on towards the stretch delimited by s10-s11 reed contacts. However, this train must be stopped when standing on s11 reed contact if the train B has not stood on s1 reed contact.

To avoid the constant execution of stopping and starting procedures, it is recommended to increase the speed of the forward train (in our example train A) around 20% until having a "free stretch" between the trains again. From this moment, the forward train travels with its initial speed[4].

The students should implement in three phases a program that controls each train and supervises the behaviour of the mock-up. In a first phase, students should create a task to control each train by invoking its methods. In a second phase, students should implement a task that takes into account the global state of the mock-up and stop the trains to prevent collisions. This task has to monitor the state of the different sensors and modify the speed of the trains in order to avoid collisions between them. In the last phase, students should add some decision capacities in each train controller (for example, the train takes the decision of stopping because an obstacle is detected). Some real-time characteristics of the railroad platform are: critical safety operations need to have a very high priority (to stop a train, to stop the whole system, to change the state of a turnout switch, ...); the time needed to stop a train must be bounded; the detection of a possible collision between trains must be in certain limits, and so on. In addition, the times of standing on each reed contact sensor must be registered.

Finally, the student must take into account possible fails and manage them using the mechanism of exceptions that Ada offers. In this way, the exercise allows to practice the different topics reviewed during the course as concurrent programming, scheduling schemes, fault tolerance, etc.

6   Summary and Future Work

The platform described here requires students to utilize and exercise their knowledge of concurrent programming, real-time systems, control applications, and so on. The combining of physical environment with the simulator increase the motivation of the students and produce good learning results.

Obviously, the benefits of the laboratory do not end there. The railroad platform can be teleoperated via the Internet and remote users can view the current status of the real environment through a visual monitoring system, based on a webcam that shows the movements of each locomotive and its behaviour depending on the command sent from a remote web page. We have recently started up a number of activities addressing these objectives for teaching tasks at other courses.

---

[4] We suppose in this example that the students know the simulator and its interface to reading all sensorial information accurately.

References

1. *Ada 95 Reference Manual: Language and Standard Libraries*. International Standard ANSI/ISO/IEC-8652, 1995.
2. J. Barnes. *"Programming in Ada 95"*. Addison-Wesley, 1998.
3. http://www.marklin.com
4. OMG. (2001, September) UML reference manual v1.4. Object management group. [Online]. Available; http://www.omg.org/technology/documents/formal/uml.htm.
5. E. Gamma, R. Helm, R. Johnson, J. Vlissides. *"Design Patterns: Elements of Reusable Object Oriented Software"*, Addison Wesley, Reading Mass. 1995.
6. E. Briot, J. Brobecker, A. Charlet. GtkAda Reference Manual. Version 1.2.12. date 2001/03/13.
7. ACM and IEEE-CS. Year 2001 model curricula for computing (Computing curricula 2001). The joint IEEE computer society/ACM task force. [Online]. Available: http://www.acm.org/education/curricula.html.
8. Alan Burns, Andy Wellings. *"Real-Time Systems and Programming Languages"* Addison-Wesley, 2001.

High Integrity Ada in a UML and C World

Peter Amey and Neil White

Praxis Critical Systems, 20 Manvers St., Bath BA1 1PX, UK
{peter.amey,neil.white}@praxis-cs.co.uk

Abstract. The dictates of fashion and the desire to use "hot" technology not only affects software developers but also influences potential customers. Where once a client was just content to accept something that worked (actually, would be *delighted* to have something that worked) now they are concerned about the means by which it was constructed; not just in the sense of was it *well-enough* constructed but in the more malign sense of *was fashionable technology used.* This paper shows how the customer's desire to use de facto standards such as UML and their wish to use languages such as C— perhaps to support a small or unusual processor; to integrate with other subsystems; for the perceived comfort of future portability; or for other, non-technical reasons—can be aligned with the professional engineer's need to use those tools and languages which are truly appropriate for rigorous software development.

1 Introduction

From its inception, Praxis has espoused a *risk-based* approach to software development. This approach, described in [1], favours customizing the development process to mitigate identifiable project risks. So a project with a challenging certification hurdle to overcome would be structured to ensure that the necessary evidence was gathered during development, while one involving interfacing to novel and untried devices would favour early prototyping and strong abstraction of the interfaces from the rest of the system.

While we remain convinced that this approach is both rational and correct we find increasingly that the market comes with pre-programmed expectations of the tools and methods that should be used. Much of this trend has been generated by the evolution of heavyweight (and lucrative for tool vendors) processes such as the Rational Unified Process [2]. Increasingly it has become not only acceptable but *expected* to answer "we will use *industry-standard process X* and auto-generated *popular language Y*" in response to almost *any* software development challenge. So entrenched is this that an organization that responds "we will examine the risks and requirements of your problem and propose appropriate tools and processes to meet them" ends up looking as if they *don't have a process* (rather than being the only people who actually understood the question!).

Prevalent amongst the ingredients of the one-size-fits-all, universal process are the Unified Modelling Language (UML) [3] and the veteran low-level language C, the latter often now prefixed with feel-good qualifiers like "MISRA" [4] or "a safe subset of". For Ada practitioners, the latter is particularly puzzling. We know from experience and from overwhelming evidence (see for example [5,6]), that C is not suitable or at

A. Llamosí and A. Strohmeier (Eds.): Ada-Europe 2004, LNCS 3063, pp. 225–236, 2004.

least markedly less suitable than Ada, for the development of reliable software. Yet its perceived portability (actually less than Ada's) and apparently abundant supply of programmers (but of what quality?) keep it popular.

What, then, is the professional engineer to do when trying to do a principled job in the development of high-integrity software when he is constrained to deliver C (for whatever reason)? In the rest of this paper we describe a novel process, in use on a real project, involving:

- The *disciplined* use of UML and UML tools;
- the use of Ada to capture design abstractions implicit in the UML;
- the use of rigorous static analysis to bind Ada code to the design abstractions; and
- the auto-generation, from the validated Ada, of semantically-equivalent C source code.

2   The SPARK Language

We use SPARK as the "anchor" to which both our UML model and C code can be secured. SPARK [7,8] is an annotated sub-language of Ada. The combination of subsetting and the addition of annotations to strengthen the "contracts" between program components results in:

- A *semantically exact* and *unambiguous* language. SPARK is completely free from erroneous and implementation-defined behaviour. SPARK source code wholly predicts the behaviour of the machine code compiled from it.
- A language which allows a program written in it to be analysed to great depth, in a time and space efficient manner, without requiring access to a complete linkable closure of the entire program being checked.

The semantic precision of SPARK has a significant impact on both the construction of the UML model of the system to be developed and on the verification of the code generated from it.

3   The Disciplined Use of UML

3.1   Introducing UML

The UML is a drawing language. The language comprises nine types of diagram, which can be sub-divided into static and behavioural diagrams. A UML model can be viewed through an interwoven collection of diagrams. The UML definition gives no advice on the production of a model—you need a process to do that. Many vendors who sell UML tools are actually selling a process too. It is the correct application of a suitable process that ensures that the resulting model is complete and cohesive.

There is a syntax and a semantics associated with each of the UML diagrams. The problem lies with the details of the semantic descriptions; the semantics are not rich enough for the rigourous reasoning we require in the production of quality software.

We define a design approach which gives rich semantics, and the ability to reason, to a subset of UML. We do this by creating a mapping between the UML model and the (unambiguous) semantics of SPARK Ada; this has the inevitable effect of forcing exact semantics back into the model.

3.2 Defining a Design Approach

Before sitting down to construct the set of interwoven diagrams that will clearly convey the desired design, the author must have a clear conception of that design. In other words, the outline design must be known before trying to describe it in UML. Simply sitting in front of a UML tool and trying to draw design diagrams is basically the same activity as sitting in front of an editor and trying to write code. If you approach the problem that way, expect some rework down the line.

Praxis uses the INFORMED [9,10] design methodology, which was developed with the particular aim of producing designs which

- minimise information flow (and hence minimise coupling); and
- maximise cohesion.

Once an INFORMED design has been conceived, or an idea glimpsed, it can be described in the UML. Exactly which diagrams are selected from the UML is indicated by the nature of the system under design. The UML model needs to balance the static aspects of the system with the behavioural aspects. For example, we might use Class and Object diagrams to define the static structure of the system, with Statecharts and Object Sequence diagrams to express the behaviour of classes and operations.

Currently we have constructed a mapping between the *static* aspects of the UML and the *structural* aspects of SPARK Ada. In other words, we have a mapping between UML Class or Object diagrams, and SPARK Ada packages, subprograms, and state. "State" in this context means "persistent data stored at library package level", in SPARK these data are called "own variables" of the package.

We annotate the UML model operations with behavioural specifications sufficient to map to SPARK Ada contracts. When we finally come to write the subprogram bodies that meet individual contracts, we hand craft the code from the set of behavioural diagrams. We do *not* define a mapping between the UML behavioural diagrams and the behaviour of the code.

This means that our overall design approach is:

1. use INFORMED to design (part of) the system;
2. capture the design in UML, including component contracts (in the form of SPARK annotations);
3. use SPARK Ada semantics to get early validation of the (partial) system design; and
4. complete components, using SPARK Ada semantics to ensure contracts are met.

Before we move on to explain the mapping between UML and SPARK Ada, we take a short but enlightening detour into documentation. It is an interesting observation that many clients, despite being adamant in their need for UML, cannot actually understand an interwoven UML model. The lack of a clear beginning, middle, and end can cause confusion. This is a feature of many UML models, however well written. Customers find it much easier, perhaps even essential, to have a linear document set produced. In keeping with the customer (or certification authority) needs, we automatically generate requirements analysis, high- and low-level designs, interface descriptions, and all the other design documentation that you expect from a development process, direct from the UML model.

As a soundness check, anything in the UML model should go towards documentation or code generation. If there is anything in the model which is not involved with either, then the designer should reflect "what is this giving to me". Often the information is either a duplication, or should be contained in the document set.

3.3 Defining Semantics

The UML description of the design is only meaningful if everybody understands it in the same way. An ambiguous design description is worse than no design, because it leads to a misplaced feeling of trust. We define unambiguous semantics in UML by creating a one-to-one mapping between the static aspects of our UML model and SPARK Ada. (Technically we could achieve rich UML semantics with a many-to-one mapping onto SPARK Ada, but this gives no real benefit.) The SPARK Ada representation allows us to reason about the design and check contracts are being met.

We have already said that a UML model needs to balance static and behavioural aspects, so you can see that we have not given rich semantics to all of our UML model, just a sub-set of it. Indeed, the UML model may also contain static diagrams that fall outside the remit of the mapping—perhaps an architecture diagram showing how the (sub-) system under development fits into the larger project.

3.4 Extending UML with Stereotypes

In order to facilitate this semantic mapping, we need to add detail to our UML model. UML can be extended with *Stereotypes* and augmented with *Tagged Values* or *Constraints*.

Stereotypes allow new UML elements to be defined. These new elements *must* be based on an existing element. For example, a specialist class can be produced. Stereotypes are generally application or domain specific.

Tagged Values are simple "name = value" pairs that can be added to any element to give extra information.

Constraints are semantic restrictions represented by a text expression. The use of a mathematical expression can clearly be rigorous in this context. It should be noted, however, that there is nothing in the UML that demands that a constraint is unambiguous.

We use a combination of Stereotypes and Tagged Values. These were chosen for pragmatic reasons involving Artisan Real Time Studio [11], the UML tool that we are currently working with, but the approach would be suitable for other UML tools.

Stereotypes allow new UML elements to be produced. We define a new element *SPARK Ada package*, based on a UML class. Similarly, we define *SPARK Ada Subprogram* based on a UML operation and *SPARK Ada State* based on an attribute. This allows us to draw an object diagram with a named SPARK package containing subprograms and state. We use Tagged Values to include SPARK Ada annotations (contracts) on the package and subprograms. We also use Tagged Values to annotate state as "abstract" or as an "external variable" (these SPARK concepts are described in [12]).

We also define the Ada "with" and SPARK Ada "inherit" relationships between packages. These are based on the UML association relationship between classes. Again, Tagged Values add more detail to the "with" relationship by indicating package specification or package body. It should be noted that in SPARK Ada, a "with" relationship implies an "inherit" relationship (but not the reverse). We do not create work for ourselves, and so our UML "with" relationship implies the SPARK "inherit" relationship.

A collection of related stereotypes is called a *Profile*. Some tool vendors provide pre-defined profiles for common domains, for example an Ada profile and a real-time profile. We have placed our SPARK Ada Semantics stereotypes in a SPARK Ada profile and are working with Artisan to make it as widely available as possible.

3.5   Strengthening Contracts

The ability to express a contract for an operation at the UML level is limited, by most tools, to expressing a type and parameter signature for it. In principle we could strengthen the contract using the Object Constraint Language (OCL) but this is neither well suported by tools nor sufficiently well defined for our purposes. Instead we have extended the UML model to include SPARK annotations and used these to tighten the specification of the operation contracts.

SPARK Ada provides a range of contract levels. The weakest is a data flow contract. As we get stronger, we move through an information flow contract to a pre- and post-condition contract.

We can annotate the UML operations in our model with design-time contract information. Using the SPARK Examiner we can start to verify the design components very early—we don't need to wait for operation bodies to be written. We don't even need to wait for the full system design to be complete.

When the design *is* complete and we start to write code (hand crafted from the information in the behavioural diagrams in the UML model) we can verify each subprogram against its contract.

3.6   Example: A UML Fragment

Figure 1 is a class diagram showing a single class—an abstract data type (ADT) representing a colour. The ADT has public operations to create, swap and extract colours. There is also a private function (indicated with a leading - sign, as opposed to a + sign.) The stereotypes are shown inside ≪ brackets ≫. The class diagram omits much of the information associated with this class. For example, type definitions are not shown, although the operation profiles hint that a type colour is exported. The contracts for the operations are not shown. With tool support, you can select a class on a class diagram and see this information in a dialog box. When we generate documentation—maybe a low-level design for the class—we pull this information out from the data dictionary which supports the diagrams in the model. This example will be further developed in sections 3.8 and 5.1.

«SPARK Class» UML Example::Types::Colour_ADT	
«SPARK Operation»	+ Create (in ...)
«SPARK Operation»	+ Swap (inout Colour A, inout Colour B)
«SPARK Operation»	+ Extract (out ...)
«SPARK Operation»	- Split (...)

Fig. 1. An Example Class Diagram

3.7   Tool Support and SPARK Ada Code Generation

Tool support is essential for industrial use of UML. This paper leaves the choice of tool open, but it is worth remembering the earlier comments about distinguishing the UML from the process which leads to a model. A good UML tool will not enforce a specific process upon the user. Having described our design in an unambiguous notation, we can actually generate the SPARK Ada code from the model. Indeed, since we have an unambiguous mapping between two equivalent representations, we could also generate a UML model from SPARK Ada code.

We generate the code *structure*, but not the *behaviour*. In other words, we generate packages, procedures, types, variables, etc. We do not produce the code between the "begin" and the "end" of subprograms. The generation of behaviour from state diagrams and sequence diagrams is possible, but outside the scope of this paper. We do generate the SPARK contracts which define behaviour. If we have e.g. an information flow contract, then the behaviour is constrained but not fully defined—and the behaviour diagrams in the model should (informally) fill the gaps. If we have a pre- and post-condition contract, then the behaviour is much more fully (or *formally*) defined. The subprogram body still needs to be written by hand, and ultimately validated against its contract by the SPARK Examiner, and against the behavioural diagrams by code review, dynamic testing or proof as appropriate.

Actually, we do physically enter the bodies of SPARK subprograms directly into our UML model, because we want to keep everything maintained in one place. We do this by writing the code directly into a box attached to the UML operation. The code generation mechanism pulls this code out for us, but it is not *generated* in the strict sense of the word.

We have already explained the benefits of starting analysis when the program is only partially complete. Our code generation techniques allow us to generate package specifications for use by the Examiner when no part of the corresponding package body has been produced. This allows us to start checking contracts and consistency before package bodies are implemented.

When fully populated with bodies, the UML model is a complete description of the system from which complete and fully executable code can be generated.

3.8   Example: SPARK

The following code relates to the UML model from Section 3.6. The SPARK *structure* is auto-generated from the UML; the contract, in the form of annotations, is automatically extracted from the model; and the executable statements are hand written (but stored within the model for later code regeneration).

```
package Colour_ADT
is
    type RGB_Value is range 0 .. 500;

    type Colour is private;

    procedure Swap (A : in out Colour; B : in out Colour);
    --# derives A from B & B from A ; -- information flow contract

    -- Other operations here ...
private
    type Colour_Components is (
       Red,
       Green,
       Blue);

    type Colour is array (Colour_Components) of RGB_Value;
end Colour_ADT;

package body Colour_ADT
is
    procedure Swap (A : in out Colour; B : in out Colour);
    is
       Temp : Colour;
    begin -- hand-written implementation
       Temp := A;
       A := B;
       B := Temp;
    end Swap;

    Other operations here ...
end Colour_ADT;
```

In the package specification, note that the type RGB_Value is constrained, and the type Colour is private. The type Colour_Components is private, and only used in the definition of Colour.

4   Validation of the Ada Model

4.1   Static Analysis

Static analysis allows us to confirm two important properties of a program:

1. The program is *well-formed*. That is, the program *could be* a correct implementation of some useful specification because it is free from egregious errors such as data flow errors (e.g. use of uninitialized variables) and run-time errors (e.g. array bounds violations)
2. Furthermore, the program *actually is* a correct implementation of its specification.

This conceptual separation is quite deliberate: the first condition provides the logically-consistent framework which makes the second feasible. The idea that we should ensure a program *could* be correct before trying to establish whether it *is* correct was a major motivator for the development of information flow analysis. See for example [13] which noted that: "most programs presented to verifiers are actually wrong; considerable time can be wasted looking for proofs of incorrect programs before discovering that debugging is still needed".

In the context of the development process being described, static analysis works as follows. The custom templates for the UML support tool produce a skeletal framework for the design expressed in UML. This framework is ensured to be syntactically legal SPARK by careful design of the templates. Furthermore, the generated packages and subprogram specifications are annotated with a chosen level of SPARK annotations obtained from information embedded in the UML model. It is now possible to populate this model with executable code, written in SPARK, and to use the SPARK Examiner repeatedly to check it against the embedded annotations. The result is semantically well-formed SPARK which meets (apart from the possibility of run-time errors) the first of our two static analysis objectives.

The next step is to use the facilities of the SPARK Examiner to prove that the code, both auto-generated and hand-crafted, is free from predefined exceptions. The technology for this is well-proven, see for example [14]. After this step we have fully met our first objective: the SPARK code is unambiguous, free from run-time errors and free from other obstacles to rigorous reasoning such as would result from data flow errors. This code, because of its lack of ambiguity, is a suitable starting point for C code generation as described in Section 5.

4.2   Formal Verification

Either before C generation, or in parallel with it, we can now start to address the second of our objectives, correctness. There are a number of complementary strategies available. To gain the highest level of confidence possible, we could strengthen the contracts embedded in UML model still further by providing formal pre and post-condition predicates for the operations contained therein and use the proof capabilities of the Examiner to show that the UML specification and intermediate SPARK Ada model correspond. (For an example of a project employing SPARK proof see [15]). This process gives us two artefacts: a UML model annotated with a formal statement of required behaviour and unambiguous SPARK source code guaranteed to be a correct implementation of that model.

4.3 Dynamic Testing

We have a number of options for the dynamic testing of our generated code. As well as the obvious option of generating C, compiling and testing it we have another interesting possibility: direct compilation of the SPARK model, with an Ada compiler, for host-based testing. Again the lack of implementation dependencies and lack of ambiguity of SPARK come to our aid because it give us grounds for expecting the eventual target C code will behave in the same way as the host Ada.

Having established confidence in the SPARK Ada model derived from the augmented UML, we are ready for the final stage: producing deliverable C.

5   Generating C

In general, the generation of C from Ada is not without complications. C code that captures *all* the required semantics of Ada involves more than just translating Ada statements to C. We must, in addition, add in the run-time checks required by Ada and provide an exception raising and propagating mechanism should one of these checks fail. There are also issues such as evaluation order dependencies and parameter passing dependencies to consider: a faithful C model must capture the same semantic behaviour as would an Ada compiler. For these reasons, an Ada to C translator is best seen as a form of Ada compiler, with all the complexity that implies. In fact our approach makes use of exactly that: the AdaMagic compiler from SofCheck Inc (see [16]).

Fortunately, the development process thus far described results in a much simpler problem than the general translation of Ada to C. Our intermediate model is known to be semantically legal Ada; to have an exact, unambiguous meaning; and to be free from run-time errors. Furthermore, since it also uses only a subset of the Ada language, it avoids features that would make constructing a C model unnecessarily complex. An obvious example is the lack of tasking, a more subtle one is the prohibition of constructs leading to implicit heap use such as functions that return unconstrained types (including dynamic use of the "&" operator). Generating C from a rigorous SPARK model is therefore much more a question of the line-by-line transliteration of Ada statements (after telling the translator some properties of the eventual C compiler to be used). The translation is therefore very transparent and very traceable. Furthermore, we can ensure that the generated code meets standards such as MISRA-C much more readily than we can tell whether arbitrarily-produced C code meets those standards. We are currently working with SofCheck to exploit these inherent benefits of SPARK to C translation.

We can satisfy ourselves that proof of exception freedom at the SPARK level implies freedom from overflow and other run-time misbehaviour at the C level by ensuring that the underlying C types used to represent the base types of user-defined Ada ranges are large enough. Furthermore, we can supply the Examiner with this information by means of *type assertions* and a *target configuration file* to automate this part of the assurance process.

As a final bonus, the C code provides an intermediate representation between Ada and machine code. It will, for example, have "unwrapped" large aggregate or other structured assignments into simpler sequences of statements. This "flattened" code therefore provides a useful stepping stone for object code verification.

5.1   Example: The Generated C Code

The C automatically generated from the SPARK model of Section 3.8 is as follows:

```
typedef unsigned short uint16;

typedef uint16 Colour_ADT_RGB_Value;

typedef enum {
    Colour_ADT_Red,
    Colour_ADT_Blue,
    Colour_ADT_Green} Colour_ADT_Colour_Components;

typedef Colour_ADT_RGB_Value Colour_ADT_Colour[3];

void Colour_ADT_Swap(
    Colour_ADT_Colour *A,
    Colour_ADT_Colour *B)
{
    Colour_ADT_Colour Temp;

    memmove((void*)Temp,(void*)A,6);
    memmove((void*)A,(void*)B,6);
    memmove((void*)B,(void*)Temp,6);
}
```

Things to note include:

- The flat name space requires that the SPARK Ada package name is used as a prefix; this is done automatically by the code generator.
- All types are equally visible, because C has no concept of a private type; but we know from the Ada semantics of the intermediate model that the types are not being mis-used.
- The constrained type RGB_Value is now an unsigned short, but static analysis (exception freedom proof) has told us that the value never goes outside the legal range of 0 .. 500 and an unsigned short is large enough to hold this range.
- The array index type is an enumeration in the Ada, but needs to be converted to a natural here, again this is handled automatically.
- The exported parameters are passed as pointers; however, we know from the rules of SPARK that no aliasing effects are possible and that we actually have pass-by-copy semantics.
- The array assignments in the body of Swap have become lower level memory moves, because C doesn't support whole-array assignment.

6   Deliverables and Traceability

Deliverables are ultimately a contractual issue. However, we have available:

- A UML model, in a tool-supported form, annotated with rigorous descriptions of the required behaviour and populated with SPARK subprogram bodies that implement that behaviour.
- An intermediate SPARK Ada model with evidence that it is well-formed and free from run-time errors.
- Proof-based evidence that the SPARK implements the required behaviour.
- Host testing results obtained by compiling the SPARK directly (or by compiling translated C with a suitable host compiler).
- Target-based test results obtained by compiling and testing the generated C.
- Object code verification based on tracing the SPARK to the C and the C to the object code (which, if not easy, is at least *easier* than direct object code verification of the Ada).
- "Linear" documentation generated from the UML model.
- Deliverable C source code which is easily traceable to the intermediate SPARK model.

7   Conclusions

It is not always easy to accommodate the diverse expectations and requirements of all the stakeholders in a project. Where one set of requirements, in this case to use UML and C, runs directly counter to another, the need to produce demonstrably correct software at an acceptable cost, then that challenge is greater still. In the situation postulated, the developer can either alienate the customer by insisting on the use of the most *appropriate* rather than the most *fashionable* technology, or abandon their engineering principles and use techniques they know to be inadequate (or, we suppose, walk away and look for a different line of business).

With care, however, it *is* possible to reconcile these diverse expectations. Overall, the process described above meets the market expectations requiring a UML model of the delivered software together with C source code that can be traced to that model yet, simultaneously, allows the use of appropriate tools to ensure the accuracy and quality of the finished product.

The crucial and novel elements are:

1. The use of Ada (or in this case SPARK) as an *exact* intermediate representation between UML and C. This imposes semantics on the UML model and makes its validation much more straightforward.
2. The recognition that it is much easier to generate "safe" and accurate C from a semantically exact and error-free SPARK model than it is to write C and then demonstrate that it has the necessary properties of safety and accuracy.

The insertion of an *exact* SPARK representation between the UML and C means that we have replaced the generation of (potentially ambiguous) C from (potentially semantic-free) UML with a *precise* process.

As well as dealing with the "soft" issues of fashion emphasised throughout this paper, the approach is also useful when targeting small and specialised processors for which Ada support may be unavailable.

In summary the process exploits the fact that Ada can be seen as a *compilable design language* rather than just a plain and simple *programming* language.

References

1. Martyn A. Ould: *Strategies for Software Engineering.* 1990, John Wiley & Sons.
2. Rational Unified Process See: `http://www-3.ibm.com/software/awdtools/rup/`
3. Unified Modelling Language See: `http://www.uml.org/`
4. Motor Industry Software Reliability Association
   See: `http://www.misra.org.uk/index.htm`
5. Amey, Peter: *Correctness by Construction: Better Can Also Be Cheaper.* CrossTalk Journal, March 2002.[2]
6. German, Andy: *Software Static Code Analysis Lessons Learned* Crosstalk Journal Vol. 16 No. 11.
7. Barnes, John: *High Integrity Software - the SPARK Approach to Safety and Security.* Addison Wesley Longman, ISBN 0-321-13616-0. 2003
8. Finnie, Gavin et al: *SPARK 95 - The SPADE Ada 95 Kernel — Edition 3.1.* 2002, Praxis Critical Systems[1].
9. Amey, Peter: *The INFORMED Design Method for SPARK.* Praxis Critical Systems 1999, 2001[1]
10. Amey, Peter: *Closing the loop - The Influence of Code Analysis on Design.* Lecture Notes in Computer Science 2361 J. Bliebergerand A. Strohmeier (Eds.): Reliable Software Technologies - Ada-Europe 2002 7th Ada-Europe International Conference, Vienna, June 2002
11. Artisan Real Time Studio See: `http://www.artisansw.com/`
12. Amey, Peter: *A Language for Systems not Just Software.* Proceedings of ACM SIGAda 2001[2].
13. Bergeretti and Carré: *Information-flow and data-flow analysis of while-programs.* ACM Transactions on Programming Languages and Systems 1985[1], pp37-61.
14. Chapman, Rod; Amey, Peter: *Industrial Strength Exception Freedom.* Proceedings of ACM SIGAda 2002[2]
15. Steve King, Jonathan Hammond, Rod Chapman and Andy Pryor. *Is Proof More Cost Effective Than Testing?.* IEEE Transactions on Software Engineering Vol 26, No 8, August 2000, pp 675-686[2]
16. SofCheck Inc. See: `www.sofcheck.com`

---

[1] Also available from Praxis Critical Systems
[2] Also downloadable from `www.sparkada.com`

Ada Meets Giotto

Helge Hagenauer, Norbert Martinek, and Werner Pohlmann

Institut für Computerwissenschaften
Universität Salzburg
Jakob-Haringer-Straße 2
A-5020 Salzburg
Austria
{hagenau,nmartin,pohlmann}@cosy.sbg.ac.at

Abstract. Giotto is a new language for embedded software. It is time-triggered, with temporally fixed communication events and computations occurring in between. We give some motivation and then describe a framework that supports the Giotto programming model in Ada.

1 Introduction

Hard real-time systems must be predictable: one needs a guarantee that timing constraints are met. Predictability is affected by several factors in the hardware-software hierarchy, see e.g. [1], ch. 1.3. For programming, the choice of the language and/or judicious use of its elements are important. Concurrency, which introduces nondeterminism, does not necessarily preclude predictability on the relevant level of abstraction, but composing a system from tasks notoriously confronts the programmer with complications like race conditions, deadlocks or underspecified queueing policies.

In the Ada world, the Ravenscar Profile [2,3] is a major step forward. It supports preemptive-priority ceiling-locking scheduling as a well-understood basis for predictability and defines an appropriately restricted tasking model. Ravenscar will be included in the next Ada standard, and there are lean and efficient implementations. As the report [3] describes (see also [4]), Ravenscar programs allow static analysis of much more than temporal correctness.

A remaining problem is Ada's lack of real-time programming abstractions; concurrency has called forth much more thought and linguistic effort than this important subject. The effect of the single delay-until statement, which just sets a lower bound for the start of some activity, rarely is what one really wants. Consequently, programmers build implicit and sometimes obscure constructions which in some way or other rely on the scheduler as the ultimate semantic resort. Burns and Wellings name some desirable features like a deadline attribute in ch. 12.6 of [5], and the Ravenscar guide [3] offers recipes for typical situations. Let us consider one of these, [3], ch. 5.3, to illustrate the difficulty:

The problem is that two tasks, A and B, have a common period, but the second, B, shall execute only after the first, A, has completed. The solution is to release B later than A, with an offset t. This is easy enough with delay-untils,

A. Llamosí and A. Strohmeier (Eds.): Ada-Europe 2004, LNCS 3063, pp. 237–248, 2004.
© Springer-Verlag Berlin Heidelberg 2004

but does not relate B's start to A's actual completion time. So responsibility is shifted to scheduling: the authors require that it ensures A's completion within t. This introduction of a separating point between A and B is a natural solution indeed; the drawback is that it cannot be adequately expressed in the program text: now A has a deadline (smaller than its period) that is in no way syntactically connected with it, and B contains a magic number that should be a reasonable bound on A's completion time. It is easy to overlook this hidden relationship when modifying the program or moving it to another platform. Furthermore, a reader of this program may form a completely different idea of its mechanics: equal task priorities together with FIFO-within-priorities (as in Ravenscar) should do the job, so rather choose a small value for t and do schedulability analysis for deadlines = periods! In this second interpretation, the offset t is a meaningless number just to trick the scheduler into the desired behavior. – The report indicates an alternative solution which does not use an offset but simply gives different priorities to the tasks. Like the second interpretation of the first solution, this is programming by scheduler instead of making temporal relationships explicit. – As an aside, note that the example points to a more profound dilemma with concurrent real-time programming: to ensure some order of events or activities, one can use a wait-signal synchronisation technique or explicitly refer to the time axis. The latter alternative, as an overspecification, reduces flexibility, whereas the first tends to complicate analysis. (One can avoid the problem by simply concatenating the two tasks into one. The report [3] does not give any background information, but general software engineering considerations seem to speak against task fusion.)

Real-time programming must become much more declarative. This is an obvious corollary of predictability: you cannot prove that temporal constraints are satisfied if you are not aware of them. So what can we do with Ada as it is? One idea is to define an annotation language and use it to complement Ada syntax; this improves understandability and provides a basis for automated tools. See [6] and [7] for this approach. (The title of the first of these papers – "The Deadline Command" – is ironic; as the authors point out, there cannot be a deadline command in the usual sense of imperative programming since there is no effective mechanism that makes an arbitrary job complete within an arbitrary time limit.) Another way is to build software frameworks that raise the level of abstraction and enable sufficiently explicit solutions for certain application domains; we try this way here. Rather than invent something new just for illustration, we model our framework after the recent real-time language Giotto, which Henzinger, Horowitz and Kirsch designed for control software with periodic behavior ([8]; see also [9], [10] for additional information). We essentially represent Giotto's language elements by datatype definitions, which the user instantiates and then passes to a likewise predefined executive component to get the specified behavior. We built the framework within Ravenscar.

The Giotto programming model aims at determinism in the sense that a sequence of sensor readings gives a unique sequence of actuator settings, both in the value and the time domain, with low jitter. This is hard to achieve when working with interacting tasks and delay-until/deadline pairs. Giotto therefore distinguishes communications and computations. Communications occur at predefined times and are virtually instantaneous; they move values between sensors, computations and actuators. Computations, in contrast, take time and live in the intervals between the communications; computations use and produce values to realise control laws. – It may help to compare this layout with synchronous languages like Esterel, cf. e.g. [11], and with static clock-driven scheduling. In contrast to the first, Giotto's synchronous parts do not contain cyclic dependencies and therefore avoid problems with fixed points and consistency; furthermore Giotto realistically complements synchrony with non-zero-time computations. As regards static scheduling, note that a Giotto program defines a time-table for input/output events and not a schedule for the computational work; the former reflects the temporal needs of the control problem, whereas the latter is indirectly constrained but not actually fixed by the communication instants: any scheduling scheme – clock-driven, preemptive fixed priority, earliest-deadline-first etc – is welcome to try to map computational work to processor time so that the specified input/output times are kept. Giotto thus returns scheduling to its proper role: scheduling, which has to juggle with resources, execution times etc., is a question of implementation and not of giving meaning to a program. – A related semantic model appears in the TCEL language by Gerber and Hong [12], which features a distinction of temporally constrained "observable" events and "unobservable" computations, which, as far as causal dependencies allow, can be placed anywhere on the time axis. This approach is somewhat more expressive and more complicated than Giotto; the main impetus of TCEL is to have a smart compiler rearrange code portions to improve feasibility.

We shall tell more about Giotto in Sect. 2. Section 3 will describe our framework building, and Sect. 4 will sum up and indicate future work.

2 A Short Description of Giotto

To make our paper reasonably self-contained, this section recapitulates the main points about Giotto. Still, the reader may wish to consult [8] as the authoritative description. – Giotto is not a complete programming language but meant to define organisational skeletons that must be fleshed out with the help of some host language, e.g. with subroutines written in C for the computational work.

The principal elements of a Giotto program are ports, tasks, drivers and modes, which, loosely speaking, represent communication infrastructure, work to be done, communication & control and configuration.

Ports function like shared variables, with write and read operations and persistency between writes. There are sensor ports, whose values come from the environment, and task ports and actuator ports for computed content.

Tasks compute values for their output ports from values of their input ports and then terminate. Giotto tasks must not be confused with Ada tasks but should be viewed as subroutines, or, even better, functions - without side effects, internal synchronisation points etc.. Tasks are invoked periodically, and privately used ports can give a notion of state across invocations; so there results some similarity to processes.

Drivers are responsible for task invocations. They load the input ports with values which may be constants or, as the general case, readings from sensor ports or task output ports. In addition, drivers can be guarded, i.e. evaluate a predicate on current port values and thus decide whether the task in question shall be actually executed or not. (So drivers can e.g. be used for the approximative technique of dealing with events in a time-driven context by polling.) Similarly, drivers are used for writing values to actuators.

A Giotto program consists of a nonempty set of modes, which represent distinct ways of system operation like e.g. take-off, cruising or landing for aircrafts. A mode definition names the tasks that shall be invoked and associates frequencies and drivers with them. Actuator updates are specified similarly. All frequencies are interpreted relative to a period which is assigned to the mode. – Mode switches are specified by a target mode and, again, a frequency and a driver for the decision making. There is one designated start mode.

Figure 1 shows a (meaningless) example similar to [8], p. 91 (concrete syntax for Giotto seems to be not fixed yet). Note that the definitions of driver-, guard- and task-functions are missing as they are programmed in some other language.

```
sensor
  port s1 type float
actuator
  port a1 type float
input
  port i1 type float
  port i2 type float
output
  port o1 type float
  port o2 type float

task t1 input i1 output o1 function f1
task t2 input i1 output o2 function f2

driver d1 source o2 guard g1 destination i1 function h1
driver d2 source s1 guard g1 destination i2 function h1
driver d3 source o1 guard g1 destination a1 function h2

mode m1 period 200 ports o1,o2
  frequency 1 invoke t1 driver d1
  frequency 2 invoke t2 driver d2
  frequency 1 update d3

start m1
```

Fig. 1. Example Giotto program

Next we describe the semantics of a Giotto program. For readability and brevity, we use a semi-algorithmic style rather than give a mathematical definition based on sequences of states (but see [8]), and we leave out mode switching, i.e. assume that there is just one mode.

Let p be the period of the mode, and let task T be invoked with frequency f. Then the sequence $t_0 = 0, t_{i+1} = t_i + p/f$ defines the relevant times for task T; for actuators, the relevant times are defined in the same way. The ordered merge of all such sequences gives the relevant times of the mode. At any relevant time instant, several things must be done, stepwise and in a fixed order. The synchrony hypothesis here is that this work is not interrupted, and that the next relevant time is far enough in the future. As a further descriptive aid, we say that a task always is either active or not. A task, if active, ceases to be so at (the beginning of) its next relevant time; conversely, a task may become active only at (the end of) its relevant times. At the beginning, time $t = 0$, all tasks are inactive, and all ports are suitably initialised. Now for all relevant times t of the mode, Fig. 2 describes the appropriate activities.

```
for all tasks T
   if t is relevant for T and T is active
      set T not active;
      write the result of T to its output ports;
   end if,
end for;
for all sensor ports S
   update S according to environment;
end for;
for all actuators A
   if t is relevant for A
      update A according to driver,
   end if;
end for;
for all tasks T
   if t is relevant for T and driver guard is true
      set T active;
      update input ports according to driver;
      arrange for T to be executed after t;
   end if,
end for;
```

Fig. 2. General Mode activities

Let us emphasize two points. First, Giotto semantics prescribes when the input ports for a task invocation shall be loaded and when its results shall become available through its output ports. Second, Giotto semantics does not prescribe exactly when an invoked task must be executed, but only implies that execution must happen in a certain time interval, between the parameter passing at some relevant time t_i and the request for results at the next (for the task) relevant time t_{i+1}. There are several consequences:

- By the first remark, a Giotto program is outwardly deterministic. Depending on input values, processor load, platform characteristics etc., an invoked task will take more or less time to compute its results, but these results are made public for use always after the same period. Note that Giotto makes it easy to modify programs; since tasks are just functions without internal synchronisation points, the addition e.g. of some more tasks to a mode cannot lead to complications like deadlock that would make the specified temporal behavior logically impossible.
- By the second remark, there is much freedom for implementation, including internal nondeterminism. An obvious and easy scheme, which we use for our first go, is to have a maximum-priority Ada task that, as an executive, deals with the relevant times, and to furthermore use rate-monotonic scheduling on Ada tasks that implement Giotto tasks. If worst case execution times are known (and, again, mode changes ignored), schedulability analysis then is a standard procedure and easily automated, with task periods (= deadlines) explicitly given by the quotients of mode periods and task invocation frequencies in the program.
- Finally note that Giotto, like any language that allows to set temporal bounds for some activity, cannot on its own make the intended semantics come true: there must be a feasibility proof that combines program and platform characteristics. Even when such a proof is given, it may be wise to provide for deadlines that were missed because of exceptional conditions. Giotto, like the time-driven paradigm in general (cf. Kopetz' Time Triggered Architecture, [13]), provides an excellent basis for fault tolerance, esp. for error detection and containment: at the beginning of each relevant time, check that all task executions which should have finished did so indeed and produced acceptable results.

3   The Framework

To enable Giotto-like programming in Ada, we define Ada data types that represent the relevant Giotto language elements, i.e. the constructs in the abstract syntax. This essentially requires us to define a series of aggregates (a program is a set of modes, a mode consists of task invocations etc etc), which are naturally implemented by records and arrays but, for ease and safety of manipulation, should come along with appropriate interface operations. Use of these data types may be subdivided into several groups. Obviously, one must be able to first set up a quasi-Giotto program and then execute it; we therefore organise our definitions into two main packages, giottoconstructs and giottoexecutor, which we describe below. Other facilities may be wanted, too. Giotto, like other programming languages, has a number of contextual rules which range from the usual requirement that entities must be declared before used to more Giotto-specific principles like that two tasks must not use the same port to output results. Some of these restrictions are immanent in the program building methods of our `giottoconstructs` package, and some additional checks are done by procedures contained in the same module, but we shall possibly move such checks into a separate unit that, in addition, could provide other "syntax"-related services like producing various forms of program documentation. On the other hand, a constructed program needs a pre-run test on temporal feasability (relative to implementation strategy and platform characteristics), and consequently, the `giottoexecutor` package should be complemented with a corresponding analysis tool (which we did not yet build for our execution method).

Figure 3 shows the general structure of the involved packages.

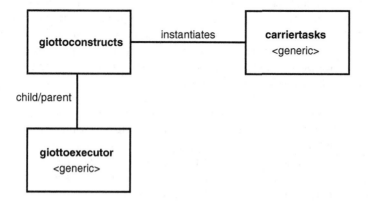

Fig. 3. Package structure

(*Remark:* We relied on the classic data abstraction facilities of Ada and did not use the flexibility offered by object-oriented techniques because these can lead to greater run-time costs and insecurities that are intolerable for hard real-time applications. Consequently, some of our constructions are less elegant, neat or general than they could have been otherwise. Strong typing sometimes comes into one's way, esp. by preventing heterogeneous collection classes. For Giotto ports for example, we decided to allow just one value type, float, to facilitate the management of sets of ports; a similar decision for Giotto task functions, drivers and so on followed . . .)

3.1   Package `giottoconstructs`

A Giotto program contains ports, tasks, drivers, task-invocations, actuator-updates, mode-switches and modes; the top-level notion, i.e. the proper program, is the set of modes together with an indication of the start mode. (Recall our informal explanation in Sect. 2 or consult [8] for more details.) Our package declares types for all these program elements but keeps the concrete representation private; it furthermore declares the corresponding access types and array types. – The above list of program elements is written so that each construct depends only on constructs listed to the left of it (with the single exception of modes which contain mode switches which in turn refer to target modes). This non-cyclic dependency suggests a bottom-up approach for program construction, which starts with port declarations and ends with the program as a set of modes; we support this kind of proceeding by supplying, for each type, constructor functions which take the components for an object as parameters. The constructor for Giotto tasks e.g. requires a name (for documentation and bookkeeping purposes), arrays of input/output/private ports and a function (for the intended value transformation) as parameters; a task invocation then has a constructor that requires a frequency (a positive number), the to-be-invoked task and the driver that should be used for the invocation. These constructors do not only return the desired object so that the programmer can go on but, as a side effect, create or add to some internal tables which are used for the above mentioned consistency checks and for quick referencing on program execution. – Naturally, we provide get/set operations wherever they appear necessary (for the mode/modeswitch problem) or convenient.

The definition of task functions and of drivers with their guards and value transfer functions is done outside Giotto in a host language, which, in our case, of course means Ada. Such subprograms deal with port values; but we decided to not offer read/write operations on ports but rather let the programmer work with in/out parameter sets of type float that are automatically matched with the respective ports when the subprogram is called by the executor. Similarly, a Giotto task, driver or guard should have an operation like "call" or "evaluate" when we consider the task etc as an element of a datatype. We again choose to not define public operations for these purposes but rather make the executor module a child package of `giottoconstructs` and let it work directly on the representation. This arrangement can provide all the necessary access, is safe enough, simpler for the user and at the same time economises on procedure calls. So, as regards operations, our data-type approach to Giotto reduces to offering constructors and, via an additional unit, a facility for execution.

Figure 4 shows the small example of Fig. 1 in Sect. 2 formulated in terms of the definitions in `giottoconstructs`:

3.2   Package `giottoexecutor`

With the help of this package, one can run a Giotto program that was set up using `giottoconstructs`. The specification of the executor package contains a single procedure start, with no parameters; the to-be-executed program is passed as a generic parameter into the package. By this arrangement, necessary initialisations (including object creation) can be done at elaboration time, prior to the actual start.

Giotto semantics, as we already pointed out, is abstract enough to allow very different implementation strategies. One could e.g. try static scheduling

```
mode1Ports: G_PortVec(1..2):= (newG_Port("OutPort  1", OPType),
             newG_Port("OutPort  2",OPType));

iPortsTask1: G_PortVec(1..1):= (others=>newG_Port("InpPort  1",IPType));
oPortsTask1: G_PortVec(1..1):= (others=>mode1Ports(1));
srcPorts1: G_PortVec(1..1):= (others=>mode1Ports(2));
t1: G_TaskPtr:= newG_Task("Task 1", iPortsTask1, oPortsTask1, f1'access);
invocT1: G_TInvocPtr:= newG_TInvoc(1, t1, newG_Driver("InvocTask1",
                 srcPorts1, iPortsTask1, g1'access, h1'access));

iPortsTask2: G_PortVec(1..1):= (others=>newG_Port("InpPort  2", IPType));
oPortsTask2: G_PortVec(1..1):= (others=>mode1Ports(2));
srcPorts2: G_PortVec(1..1):= (others=>newG_Port("SensPort 1", SPType,
                 updateS1'access));
t2: G_TaskPtr:= newG_Task("Task 2", iPortsTask2, oPortsTask2, f2'access);
invocT2: G_TInvocPtr:= newG_TInvoc(2, t2, newG_Driver("InvocTask2",
                 srcPorts2, iPortsTask2, g1'access, h1'access));

srcPorts3: G_PortVec(1..1):= (others=>mode1Ports(1));
dPortsAct1: G_PortVec(1..1):= (others=>newG_Port("ActPort  1", APType));
actUpdts1: G_ActUpdatePtr:= newG_ActUpdate(1,newG_Driver("Actuator 1",
                 srcPorts3, dPortsAct1, g1'access,h2'access));

m1Invocs: G_TInvocPtrVec(1..2):= (invocT1,invocT2);
m1ActUpdts: G_ActUpdatePtrVec(1..1):= (others=>actUpdts1);
m1: G_ModePtr:= newG_Mode("Mode 1",200, mode1Ports, m1Invocs,
                 m1ActUpdts,0);
```

Fig. 4. Ada solution of the example Giotto program

and therefore expand the program-defined time table for task invocations (in the Giotto sense) into a more finely grained schedule that additionally fixes the actual intervals in which each task function is evaluated. Or one can choose some form of dynamic scheduling. In an Ada/Ravenscar context, rate-monotonic fixed-priority scheduling seems an especially natural and easy choice; and so we built our first executor in this way.

Remember that Giotto tasks are functions together with ports for argument/result values, and that these functions are evaluated repeatedly according to the frequency specified in the invocation part of a mode. Naturally, we represent Giotto task functions by Ada subprograms, but to have the corresponding computational workload managed by a fixed-priority scheduler, we associate an Ada carrier task with each such subprogram (= Giotto task) so that the first periodically calls the latter. These carrier tasks are instances of the same discriminated task type, with discriminants for the task function (an access type) and the priority (a number correponding to task invocation frequency). This association of Giotto tasks with Ada tasks is done per mode, since a Giotto task may be invoked differently in different modes. Now to ensure Giotto semantics with its deterministic arrangement of data movements, one cannot simply realise the periodicity of carrier tasks by the usual delay-until in an infinite loop (see [3], 5.2) since this approach may let several tasks respond to the same clock event and thus makes it difficult to achieve the intended order of reads and writes. Instead, we introduce a further Ada task that directs the carrier tasks. This unique master task has highest priority and is the only clock-driven task. It interacts with the carrier tasks via protected objects that offer a wait/signal facility (see [3], 5.4/5.6 for this technique); these objects, one for each carrier task, are made known to the tasks via discriminants. The master task implements the operational Giotto semantics described in Sect. 2, i.e. at any relevant time of the current mode it moves data around, makes decisions and releases tasks. – Figure 5 shows our task structure.

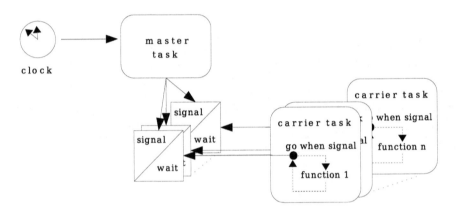

Fig. 5. Task Structure: time-triggered master task and carrier tasks

Since this kind of work, and, consequently, the master task itself, should conceptually not consume any time at all (and, in practice, should neither introduce much jitter nor turn out to be the performance bottleneck of the whole program), it is important to keep the inner loops small. In order to avoid that the master task on each execution must iterate over all Giotto tasks, actuators etc of the mode to see what activity is actually required (cf. the algorithm in Sect. 2), our implementation precomputes a kind of event list or agenda for the master task. I.e. we compute, for each mode of the Giotto program and one periodlength of it, what the relevant times of the mode are, i.e. at which times the master task must wake up, and precisely which Giotto tasks must then be deactivated, which actuators be written etc.. The construction of this agenda is not difficult; it can be done on a virtual tour through a mode period, where one uses the smallest common multiple of all frequencies as the finest possible time resolution, inspects all potential data movements and task invocations incident on these times and retains only those combinations of time and actions which are really necessary.

4   Conclusion

We described a framework that supports the Giotto programming model in Ada. This model is intended for periodic control applications, and, as far as this domain goes, has the virtue of combining the determinacy of the traditional cyclic executive with the flexibility of a tasking approach: the Giotto programmer specifies the timing of I/O events but leaves it to the implementation to accomodate the computational work that realises functionality. Our implementation, which has a cyclic master task supervise periodic worker tasks, nicely reflects this distinction.

Other implementation strategies are possible and possibly worthwhile. But before exploring such alternatives, we still have work to do for our present solution. As indicated above, we will complement our `giottoexecutor` package with a software component that checks schedulability via response-time analysis based on programmer-supplied WCET values. This tool, like `giottoexecutor`, makes use of the internal program representation as set up with `giottoconstructs` but naturally has to ask the programmer about worst case execution times of task functions as well as characteristic work portions of the execution method itself. - Furthermore, we want to integrate basic fault tolerance measures. If a carrier task fails to produce its results in time, a reasonable strategy for the master task is to use the most recent result vector instead. There are three possible causes for this failure situation: evaluation of the Giotto task function can produce a recognizably wrong result, stop because of a runtime error or take too much (possibly infinite) time. The first case requires some user-supplied healthiness test for results. In the second case the carrier task should catch the exception (i.e. not terminate but go on with its main loop!). The last case makes it necessary to abandon the current function evaluation; this is easily programmed with the ATC form of the select statement in the carrier task and the master task triggering the abort. Unfortunately, though for good reasons, Ravenscar excludes the select statement; we still look for a convincing solution. – As a deterministic programming abstraction, Giotto facilitates (or enables) verification of real-time systems; this was one of the motives of its designers. To secure this advantage, our implementation must be shown to be faithful to Giotto semantics and not introduce new insecurities. This is not an easy task, but an important obligation of framework builders; we shall start on this work when our software has stabilised and proved its usefulness.

Up to now, we have used our framework only in simulations (where the controlled object, the "plant", is a software mock-up) and cannot offer proper experience. Still, it is clear that we should spend some more effort on better performance and possibly re-do parts of our implementation. Our framework approach, though comfortable to the programmer, certainly tends to be somewhat heavy (with a lot of subprogram calls, data lookup etc.), and it may turn out that performance requirements make another way more attractive or mandatory. Possible alternatives are to reduce the whole thing to a programming idiom or pattern (with no or little predefined software support) to give the programmer better control on the specific example. Or, on the other hand, one could fall back on some translating or preprocessing strategy that results in code with less runtime costs. – Yet another direction of future work is to question some of Giotto's limitations and try to go beyond them. An obvious and easy extension is to allow more kinds of event times, e.g. deadlines smaller than periods, offsets etc.. (This would cover the example from [3], ch. 5.3, which we discussed in our introduction.) A more demanding question is whether and how other paradigms like event-driven computations or soft real time tasks can coexist with the Giotto model or be integrated.

References

1. Buttazzo, G.C.: Hard Real-Time Computing Systems. Kluwer, Boston (2000)
2. Burns, A., Dobbing, B., Romanski G.: The Ravenscar Tasking Profile for High Integrity Real-Time Programs. Proc. Ada Europe 1998. Lecture Notes in Computer Science, Vol. 1411. Springer (1998)
3. Burns, A., Dobbing, B., Vardanega T.: Guide for the Use of the Ravenscar Profile in High Integrity Systems. University of York Technical Reports YCS-2003-348 (2003)
4. Amey, P., Dobbing, B.: High Integrity Ravenscar. Proc. Ada Europe 2003. Lecture Notes in Computer Science, Vol. 2566. Springer (2003)
5. Burns, A., Wellings, A.: Real-Time Systems and Programming Languages. Addison Wesley (2001)
6. Fidge, C., Hayes, I., Watson, G.: The Deadline Command. IEEE Software, Special Issue on Real Time Systems, Vol. 146, No.2. IEEE (1999)
7. Burns, A., Lin, T.M.: Adding Temporal Annotations and Associated Verification to the Ravenscar Profile. Proc. Ada Europe 2003. Lecture Notes in Computer Science, Vol. 2655. Springer (2003)
8. Henzinger, T.A., Horowitz, B., Kirsch, C.M.: Giotto: A Time Triggered Language for Embedded Programming. Proc. IEEE, Vol 91, no. 1 (2003)
9. Kirsch, C.M.: Principles of Real-Time Programming. Proc. EMSOFT 2002. Lecture Notes in Computer Science, Vol. 2491. Springer (2002)
10. Kirsch, C.M., Sanvido, M.A.A., Henzinger, T.A., Pree, W.: A Giotto-Based Helicopter System. Proc. EMSOFT 2002. Lecture Notes in Computer Science, Vol. 2491. Springer (2002)
11. Halbwachs, N.: Synchronous Programming of Reactive Systems. Kluwer, Boston (1993)
12. Gerber, R., Hong, S.: Compiling Real-Time Programs With Timing Constraint Refinement and Structural Code Motion. IEEE Transactions on Software Engineering, Vol.21, No.5 (1995)
13. Kopetz, H.: Real-Time Systems. Kluwer, Boston (2001)

High-Integrity Interfacing to Programmable Logic with Ada

Adrian J. Hilton[1] and Jon G. Hall[2]

[1] Praxis Critical Systems, 20 Manvers Street, Bath BA1 1PX, England
Adrian.Hilton@praxis-cs.co.uk
[2] The Open University, Walton Hall, Milton Keynes MK7 6AA, England
J.G.Hall@open.ac.uk

Abstract. Programmable logic devices (PLDs) are now common components of safety-critical systems, and are increasingly used for safety-related or safety-critical functionality. Recent safety standards demand similar rigour in PLD specification, design and verification to that in critical software design. Existing PLD development tools and techniques are inadequate for the higher integrity levels.

In this paper we examine the use of Ada as a design language for PLDs. We analyse earlier work on Ada-to-HDL compilation and identify where it could be improved. We show how program fragments written in the SPARK Ada subset can be efficiently and rigorously translated into PLD programs, and how a SPARK Ada program can be effectively interfaced to a PLD program. The techniques discussed are then applied to a substantial case study and some preliminary conclusions are drawn from the results.

1 Introduction

Programmable Logic Devices (PLDs) are increasingly important components of safety-critical systems. By placing simple processing tasks within auxiliary hardware, the software load on a conventional CPU can be reduced, leading to improved system performance. They are also used to implement safety-specific functions that must be outside the direct address space of the main CPU. Technological improvements mean that PLD development has become more like software development in terms of program size, complexity, and the need to clarify a program's purpose and structure.

The airborne electronic hardware development guidance document RTCA DO-254 / EUROCAE ED-80[13] is the counterpart to the well-established civil avionics software standard RTCA DO-178B / EUROCAE ED-12B[12]. It provides a guide to the development of programs and hardware designs for electronic hardware in avionics. It covers PLDs as well as Application-Specific Integrated Circuits (ASICs), Line Replaceable Units (LRUs) and other electronic hardware. As well as being applied to systems aimed for Federal Aviation Authority acceptance, it may be used as a quality-related standard in non-FAA projects.

A. Llamosí and A. Strohmeier (Eds.): Ada-Europe 2004, LNCS 3063, pp. 249–260, 2004.
© Springer-Verlag Berlin Heidelberg 2004

This paper examines how the requirements of DO-254 for high-integrity PLD program development may be satisfied by the use of Ada, and in particular the SPARK subset. We do not address ASICs or other electronic hardware. We also consider how to analyse PLD program correctness in the context of its interface to an Ada program running on a conventional microprocessor.

The Ada compilation work to date has taken insufficient advantage of the properties of SPARK Ada programs; we address this. In Section 4.2 we outline an algorithm for compiling SPARK Ada code into hardware.

1.1   DO-254 Structure

DO-254 specifies the life cycle for PLD program development and provides guidance on how each step of the development should be done. It is not a prescriptive standard, providing instead recommendations on suitable general practice and allowing methods other than those described to be used. The emphasis is on choosing a pragmatic development process which nevertheless admits a clear argument to the certification authority (CA) that the developed system is of the required integrity.

DO-254 recommends a simple documentation structure with a set of planning documents that establish the design requirements, safety considerations, planned design and the verification that is to occur. This would typically be presented to the CA early in the project in order to agree that the process is suitable. This plan will depend heavily on the assessed *integrity level* of the component which may range from Level D (low criticality) to Level A (most critical). Note that the DO-254 recommendations differ very little for Levels A and B. We will focus on PLD programs of Level A and Level B integrity in this paper.

1.2   DO-254 High-Integrity Requirements

Appendix B of DO-254 specifies the verification recommended for Level A and Level B components in addition to that done for Levels C and D. This is based on a Functional Failure Path Analysis (FFPA) which decomposes the identified hazards related to the component into safety-related requirements for the design elements of the hardware program. The additional verification which DO-254 suggests may include some or all of:

architectural mitigation: changing the design to prevent, detect or correct hazardous conditions;

product service experience: arguing reliability based on the operational history of the component;

elemental analysis: applying detailed testing and / or manual analysis of safety-related design elements and their interconnections;

safety-specific analysis: relating the results of the FFPA to safety conditions on individual design elements and verifying that these conditions are not violated; and

formal methods: the application of rigorous notations and techniques to specify or analyse some or all of the design.

We show in this paper that using SPARK Ada supports the high-integrity verification methods of DO-254; specifically, elemental and safety-specific analysis, and is one way of using a formal notation and formal analysis techniques to increase confidence about PLD program design integrity.

2   Related Work

2.1   Other Standards

Within the United Kingdom, Interim Defence Standard 00-54[16] specifies safety-related hardware development in a similar way to DO-254. The main difference is that 00-54 is far more prescriptive than DO-254, and assumes that the development takes place within a safety management process as described in Defence Standard 00-56[15].

We have analysed the requirements of Defence Standard 00-54 and its implications for PLD program design in [8]. For the purposes of this paper it suffices to observe that 00-54 makes strict demands on the rigour and demonstrable correctness of PLD programs, and that these are significantly stricter than those in DO-254. Formal specification and analysis are *mandated* at the higher integrity levels.

IEC 61508 "Functional Safety of Electrical / Electronic / Programmable Electronic Safety-Related Systems"[10] is a standard which covers a wide range of systems and their components. Part 2 in particular gives requirements for the development and testing of electrical, electronic and programmable devices. Here the *programmable* part of the systems is not addressed in detail; there are requirements for aspects of the design to be analysed, but no real requirements for implementation language or related aspects. It is the experience of the authors that DO-254 is more directly usable for developers than IEC 61508 Part 2.

2.2   High-Level Imperative PLD Programming

The practical domain-agnostic choices for embedded system development are currently Ada, C, C++ and (to some extent) Java. Java in its existing form is unsuitable for real-time systems as it requires periodic garbage collection. The Xilinx Forge toolset[6] compiles Java byte-code to Verilog, but is at an early stage of development and it is not yet known what limits it places on the source Java program.

C has been the basis for PLD programming in a number of language/compiler sets including Sheraga's ANSI C to Behavioural VHDL Translator[14], System-C[5] and Handel-C[3]. Handel-C is the most promising approach and appears practical for efficient programming of low-criticality PLD applications. However the syntax and semantics of System-C and Handel-C are based on C and so they share C's fundamental problems with high integrity.

C's failings are described by Romanski in [11]. He makes the key comment "The [C] language attempts to hide the underlying machine so that programs become portable between different machines. Unfortunately, the target characteristics show through." The lack of strong typing, substantial unspecified or implementation-dependent behaviour, and language constructs such as unbracketed single clauses and admissibility of assignment into conditions in C are viewed by Romanski as some of the chief deficiencies that make it unsuitable for inclusion in safety-critical systems, even if a "safe" subset is used.

C++ is almost a strict superset of C, and its additional object-oriented language features are generally irrelevant to hardware-specific concerns.

Additionally, if we wish to abstract away as many target hardware details as possible then the use of a low-level language such as C appears to be going in the wrong direction. This leaves Ada as the sole remaining practical choice. The close relationship between the syntax of Ada and VHDL further suggests that this is an appropriate choice.

2.3   Ada as a HDL Design Language

Ada was compiled to Behavioural VHDL by Sheraga[14], but a more modern approach to compilation has been detailed by Audsley and Ward[17,19,20]. They have developed the York Ada Hardware Compiler which compiles sequential SPARK Ada 95 through a circuit graph form to EDIF netlist format. This is a practical demonstration that such compilation can be done. Their emphasis is on worst-case execution time analysis rather than support of a DO-254 process.

Audsley and Ward have outlined in [18] how the Ravenscar tasking profile may be implemented on PLDs. Their emphasis is on worst-case execution time and scheduling analysis, leveraging the known timings of a PLD program. They combine the Ravenscar profile with sequential SPARK; now that SPARK Ada incorporates Ravenscar[4] this combination is supported by the SPARK Examiner. Although they outline how the Ravenscar constructs may be represented on a PLD, they have not yet demonstrated compilation of a multi-task Ravenscar program onto a PLD.

The York Ada Hardware Compiler appears to be the most advanced hardware compiler of (SPARK) Ada available at the moment. It has not been assessed as a tool for critical systems use. It remains to be seen whether communicating Ravenscar tasks can be efficiently compiled onto and run on a PLD, and whether this is would be useful in PLD program design. The communication protocol between a PLD-based task and a software-based task must also be defined and analysed for correctness and efficiency.

3   Using Ada for High-Integrity Interfaces

Current PLD program development mainly uses the VHDL and Verilog hardware description languages (HDLs). Depending on the target domain there are a number of design tools available which generate an HDL description from a more abstract design specification. However, it is common for designs to be written directly in VHDL or Verilog.

As is the case in software, the larger a hardware program is, the harder it is to write. In software we deal with this initially by programming in a higher-level language, reverting to low-level only when required for performance reasons. When no appropriate higher-level language is available, we apply well-established programming techniques such as abstraction, encapsulation and refinement to divide the program into manageable units.

When developing a complex embedded system the exact hardware-software partitioning is often not known until late in the development cycle. Additionally, target hardware may not be available for early testing. For this reason it is necessary to be able to represent most of the program in software for the purpose of host-based testing. Developing the program design in a single high-level programming language is a practical interim solution. The language must however make it simple to extract a program fragment into PLD form.

[7] argues that the SPARK 95 annotated Ada subset[2] is useful in the role of a PLD design language. SPARK supports design and implementation of programs at the highest levels of integrity, including DO-178B Level A and UK Defence Standard 00-55 S4. Its annotations allow design specification of desired program properties (data and information flow, partial correctness and design hierarchy) which are then checked against the actual code by the SPARK Examiner and SPADE proof tools.

SPARK aids PLD program design and compilation in ways which include:

- the enforcing tool (the Examiner) has an established product service experience on high-integrity projects;
- data flow annotations require developers to specify all global variables read or modified by a subprogram, allowing a direct view of all input and output data flow in the subprogram;
- the information flow analyser knows the exact inputs and outputs of each program statement, allowing automatic detection of independent sequential statements which may execute in parallel;
- SPARK permits proofs of absence of run-time errors and expression overflows, which allow PLD arithmetic blocks to be designed without having to consider how to detect and handle overflow; and
- pre- and post- condition annotations on subprograms allow the developer to specify additional restrictions on parameter and global input values, and verify that those restrictions are always met.

In particular, the ability to specify and prove properties of SPARK programs is a powerful tool when we are applying elemental analysis and safety-specific analysis as per Appendix B of DO-254. Static analysis and partial program proof·are well-established formal methods with a history of use in industrial applications[1].

In Section 5 we give an example of the compilation of subprograms from a SPARK package body into VHDL.

4 The Design Options

When extracting a fragment of SPARK program code for execution on a PLD, the first task is to define the software-PLD interface. This is typically done with fully represented variables mapped onto memory locations corresponding to the PLD input and output pins, with additional variables to control asynchronous data sending and receiving. The developer must define and show correctness of this protocol before making any argument about the correctness of the software or the PLD.

To implement the extracted program fragment on the PLD there are three possible options: an interpreter, refinement and direct compilation. We reject an interpreter as impractical, given current PLD sizes. We now describe the other options.

4.1 Refinement

The pre- and post- condition annotations of SPARK allow the developer to specify the result of a subprogram computation. An example may be an integer square root routine:

```
procedure Sqrt(X : in Integer; Y : out Natural);
--# derives Y from X;
--# pre  X >= 0;
--# post (Y * Y <= X) and ((Y+1)*(Y+1) > X);
```

This defines the result Y as long as X is non-negative. The developer would then use the Examiner to generate proof conditions, and the SPADE tools to attempt to show that they are met. *As long as* any calling program only relies on the program meeting its specification, its implementation can be done in any way the developer likes.

This then allows us to replace the subprogram with an arbitrary PLD program, permitting the program to be optimised for minimum execution time outside the constraints imposed by the (essentially sequential) Ada language. However, to maintain integrity the developer is required to show somehow that the custom-designed PLD program meets the pre- and post-condition specification.

The authors have presented a formally defined specification and refinement system[9] suitable for designing parallel synchronous programs to run on programmable logic devices. The example developed in that article is a carry look-ahead adder optimised for execution time which it would make little sense to express in Ada. This then allows us to produce provably correct PLD program fragments as part of a larger Ada program design.

This can be combined with direct compilation, replacing one or more compiled subprogram logic blocks with the equivalent refined logic blocks.

4.2   Direct Compilation

This is the approach normally taken for Ada program compilation for PLDs, and appears to be the most practical for programs of substantial size.

We suggest that, in order to maximise traceability from program design to PLD program, we adopt a recursive composition of subprograms with a stateless flow of information through the subprogram. Each Ada subprogram is represented by a HDL block with input wires corresponding to the subprogram input parameters and SPARK global input variables, plus a "start computation" wire which is asserted when all the subprogram input data is valid. The output wires of the block correspond to the subprogram output parameters and SPARK global output variables, plus a "computation complete" wire which is asserted when the subprogram computation is complete. The internal subprogram HDL design uses the control flow constructs described by Audsley and Ward in [17].

5   A Case Study

The first author has developed a substantial Ada real-time control program as the base for PLD compilation work. This program controls a hypothetical safety-critical embedded system, and has been developed using extant safety-critical program development techniques and tools. The code is publically available at http://www.suslik.org/Simulator/ under the GNU General Public License.

5.1   The System

The system is the main control unit (MCU) for an endo-atmospheric interceptor missile, armed with a low-yield fission warhead. This system is clearly safety-critical; a detonation of the warhead at the launch site is a definite hazard to life. Of course, there are mission-critical requirements as well; if the warhead were never to go off, the missile targeted for interception would probably get through to its destination and be likewise a hazard.

The main hazard of the system will be detonation of the on-board warhead at an unsafe location (i.e., close to the launch point, or below a certain altitude). This dictates safety considerations such as having confidence in the estimated distance from launch point.

The control system itself consists of an interface to a standard 1553 bus, a number of packages monitoring system component data from the bus, and top-level packages reading data from these monitors and sending appropriate controls back onto the bus. The system components include a warhead, airspeed monitor and barometric sensor, supported by features such as a real-time clock and watchdog timer. An abbreviated system structure is shown in Figure 1.

5.2   The Implementation

The program was developed using SPARK Ada 95 with full information flow analysis and run-time checking. Initially it was developed to run entirely in

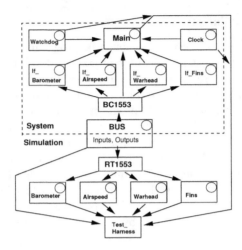

Fig. 1. Missile system design

software. Accompanying the main program is a set of simulation packages for the system components and an associated script-driven test harness for unit and system testing. The SPARK design boundary includes all packages but those directly related to testing.

The existing system code count is 504K of Ada files, with 16 800 lines. Of these, 2 500 lines are SPARK annotations, 2 900 are comments, 1 300 are blank, and the remaining 10 000 (forming 330K) are Ada code. 20K of this Ada was test-related code. There are 75 packages and public child packages, with 9 of those packages related to testing. This shows that the system is not trivial in size.

5.3   Identifying and Extracting a Fragment

We selected the Nav package as suitable for translation to hardware. This package provides subprograms for estimating the current missile heading, altitude and speed. It works by reading the barometer, compass, airspeed and INS sensor measurement and validity data, returning the data from the appropriate primary sensor if valid, and if invalid then estimating a result by combining data from the other (valid) sensors. There is a Maintain procedure which is called periodically from the main system polling loop and calculates updated sensor readings.

The original package has two SPARK abstract variables: location_state and sensor_state representing, respectively, histories of the recent sensor measurements and the sensors' validity states. The changes for PLD interfacing involved an extra abstract variable fpga_inputs representing the current sensor measurement and validity data output to the PLD. The location_state concrete variables were changed to be read-only variables memory-mapped to the PLD output pins and the new fpga_inputs concrete variables were write-only variables memory-mapped to the PLD output pins. The bodies of the estimation subprograms were essentially unchanged from the original, reading the same named variables.

The main change was in the polled procedure **Maintain** which originally called **Handle_XX** procedures to update each calculated measurement. This was replaced with direct writing of sensor data to the PLD inputs. It resulted in a simpler naive information flow for the subprogram, although there was some information loss in that the dependency of the PLD outputs on the PLD inputs was not expressed. To implement this, the two moded abstract state variables would be replaced by an single unmoded abstract state variable **State** which would be changed at each write or read of PLD information.

5.4 Transformation

The high-level structural steps of transformation of the selected **Handle_XX** subprograms into VHDL were:

1. replace global variables in the subprogram declaration and body with the appropriate PLD input and output vector names;
2. identify each subprogram's in and out argument and global data and create a VHDL architecture declaration for it;
3. add appropriate **Clock** and **Reset** inputs to the declaration;
4. connect the appropriate PLD input and output pins to the subprogram's inputs and outputs;
5. create the VHDL implementation for the subprogram by declaring architectures for the major Ada control flow elements;
6. add declarations for appropriate vectors to connect these architectures; and then
7. add the required connections between blocks and architecture inputs and outputs.

At the level of translating subprogram body code from SPARK Ada to VHDL, no initial effort was made to enable fine-grain parallelism. Instead, SPARK Ada program constructs (principally alternation and assignment) were mapped into the most directly corresponding VHDL representation (respectively, multiplexing from expression evaluation and data routing).

No compilation or simulation of the VHDL was done since it was a capability demonstration. A process for producing timing-robust VHDL from a SPARK design is clearly required for this transformation process to be practically useful. We must also compare execution time and PLD space usage for a benchmark set of Ada programs in order to form metrics-based arguments on the benefits of different compilation approaches.

5.5 DO-254 Considerations

Taking the main hazard of the system to be a detonation of the missile warhead in an unsafe altitude or distance, the **Nav** package is clearly safety-critical as it provides best-effort estimates of the missile position and associated confidence levels. As such it is plausibly of Level A criticality.

A functional failure path analysis would quickly identify the safety-related proof conditions that would need to be discharged for each major design element (in this case, the SPARK subprograms). The stages of the safety argument would be:

1. a demonstration that the Ada subprogram satisfied the safety conditions, by an appropriate combination of static analysis, proof and manual inspection;
2. an argument that the software-PLD communication protocol used did not contribute to any hazards;
3. a mapping of the compiled VHDL to the original Ada, combined with the safety argument for the Ada; and
4. an argument that the safety-related elements of the VHDL are preserved in form in the compiled netlist.

We do not, for brevity, complete this argument.

6   Discussion and Conclusions

We have described the requirements of RTCA DO-254 for high-integrity PLD programming. We have shown how Ada, and in particular SPARK Ada, is a suitable design language for high-integrity PLD programs. This has been done with the PLD programs forming part of a large hardware-software system. We have compared different approaches to translating Ada program fragments to an HDL, and concluded that a combination of refinement from formal specifications and direct compilation of SPARK Ada is effective and appropriate within the scope of RTCA DO-254.

We now examine what gaps in existing practice this work has revealed, and how these gaps may be filled.

6.1   Lessons from Extraction

The extraction process yielded the following data points:

- Relatively little of the package specification changed. The abstract state variables gained SPARK modes, and one extra output abstract variable was required, but the global and derives annotations did not change greatly.
- Most of the work in the package body involved mapping concrete state variables onto the correct area of memory. External global data (from the sensors) was passed directly onto the PLD inputs.
- The transformation was not quite automatic, but was effected quickly and was amenable to manual inspection for correctness.
- The SPARK annotations were very helpful in characterising the inputs and outputs quickly, making VHDL architecture declarations simple to write.

- Bit widths could be easily calculated manually, and minimised by use of `pragma Pack()` and Ada representation clauses. There seems no reason why these widths could not be estimated by a relatively simple tool, given a SPARK syntax tree.
- The guarantee of no expression overflow given by the Examiner `-exp` flag (and subsequent proof) would greatly simplify the process of writing VHDL to compute arithmetic expressions.

The recursive block-based compilation method proposed in Section 4.2 should be measured against the existing York compilation algorithm with respect to execution time, PLD space usage and ease of comparison of the compiled netlist with the original Ada. This will give a measure of what program forms are best suited to each compilation method.

6.2 Language

The existing Ada language appears adequate for non-specialised design of a class of PLD program. The SPARK Ada language improves on this by allowing static analysis of program structure and admitting formal proof of relevant program properties.

The lack of simple generics in SPARK Ada is likely to be cause developer pain on larger projects or when reuse is required. To implement a subprogram with an array argument, SPARK requires the type of the array be known statically at each point of subprogram call. Allowing parameterisation by an enumeration or numeric type would violate the existing SPARK subset but facilitate once-only declaration of the subprogram.

6.3 Summary

RTCA DO-254 is a new standard, and developers are now just starting to apply it in practice. The authors' experience with it to date is that it admits justification of PLD program safety at Level A with the exact approach defined by the developer. The range of verification methods proposed for Level A and Level B PLD programs allows a comprehensive multi-facetted argument for program safety.

SPARK Ada has been demonstrated to be a practical source language for PLD program compilation. We have shown how key features of SPARK Ada increase confidence that both the original and compiled program are correct. We have linked an existing rigorous parallel specification and refinement system with the specification and proof model of SPARK Ada, allowing provably correct PLD program fragments.

We and other developers have provided theory and tools to allow compilation of SPARK Ada programs onto PLDs at the highest level of integrity for DO-254. This work now requires a real-world case study to measure its practicality, susceptibility to verification, and computational efficiency.

References

1. Peter Amey and Rod Chapman. Industrial strength exception freedom. In *Proceedings of ACM SIGAda Annual International Conference*. ACM Press, December 2002.

2. John Barnes. *High Integrity Software: The SPARK Approach to Safety And Security*. Addison Wesley, April 2003.

3. Matthew Bowen. *Handel-C Language Reference Manual*. Embedded Solutions Ltd, 2.0 edition, October 1998.

4. Rod Chapman. SPARK Examiner release note - release 7.0. Technical report, Praxis Critical Systems Ltd., August 2003.

5. Jon Connell and Bruce Johnson. Early HW/SW integration using SystemC v2.0. In *Proceedings of the Embedded Systems Conference*. ARM and Synopsys Inc., 2002.

6. Don Davis. Forge: High performance hardware from high-level software. Technical report, Xilinx, September 2002.

7. Adrian J. Hilton. *High Integrity Hardware-Software Codesign*. PhD thesis, The Open University, December 2003.

8. Adrian J. Hilton and Jon G. Hall. Mandated requirements for hardware/software combination in safety-critical systems. In *Proceedings of the workshop on Requirements for High-Assurance Systems 2002*. Software Engineering Institute, Carnegie-Mellon University, September 2002.

9. Adrian J. Hilton and Jon G. Hall. Refining specifications to programmable logic. In John Derrick, Eerke Boiten, Jim Woodcock, and Joakim von Wright, editors, *Proceedings of REFINE 2002*, volume 30 of *Electronic Notes in Theoretical Computer Science*. Elsevier, November 2002.

10. International Electrotechnical Commission. *IEC Standard 61508, Functional Safety of Electrical / Electronic / Programmable Electronic Safety-Related Systems*, March 2000.

11. George Romanski. Review of 'Safer C' (by Les Hatton). Technical report, Thomson Software Products, January 1996.

12. RTCA / EUROCAE. *RTCA DO-178B / EUROCAE ED-12B: Software Considerations in Airborne Systems and Equipment Certification*, December 1992.

13. RTCA / EUROCAE. *RTCA DO-254 / EUROCAE ED-80: Design Assurance Guidance for Airborne Electronic Hardware*, April 2000.

14. R. J. Sheraga. ANSI C to behavioural VHDL translator, Ada to behavioural VHDL translator. *The RASSP Digest*, 3, September 1996.

15. UK Ministry of Defence. *Defence Standard 00-56 Issue 2*, December 1996. Safety Management Requirements for Defence Systems.

16. UK Ministry of Defence. *Interim Defence Standard 00-54 Issue 1*, March 1999. Requirements for Safety Related Electronic Hardware in Defence Equipment.

17. M. Ward and N. C. Audsley. Hardware implementation of programming languages for real-time. In *Proceedings of the Eighth IEEE Real-Time Embedded Technology and Applications Symposium (RTAS'02)*, pages 276–284. IEEE, September 2002.

18. M. Ward and N. C. Audsley. Hardware implementation of the Ravenscar Ada tasking profile. In *Proceedings of the International Conference on Compilers, Architectures and Synthesis for Embedded Systems*. ACM Press, 2002.

19. M. Ward and N. C. Audsley. Language issues of compiling Ada to hardware. In *11th International Real Time Ada Workshop*, April 2002.

20. M. Ward and N.C. Audsley. Hardware compilation of sequential Ada. In *Proceedings of CASES 2001*, pages 99–107, 2001.

Dynamic Ceiling Priorities: A Proposal for Ada0Y

Jorge Real[1], Alan Burns[2], Javier Miranda[3], Edmond Schonberg[4], and Alfons Crespo[1]

· Department of Computer Engineering (DISCA)
Universidad Politécnica de Valencia, Spain
{jorge,alfons}@disca.upv.es
· Department of Computer Science
University of York, UK
burns@cs.york.ac.uk
· Applied Microelectronics Research Institute (IUMA)
Universidad de Las Palmas de Gran Canaria, Spain
jmiranda@iuma.ulpgc.es
· Courant Institute of Mathematical Sciences
New York University, USA
schonberg@cs.nyu.edu

Abstract. In Ada 95, the ceiling priority of a protected object is a static value that can only be assigned once, when the protected object is declared. This restriction coexists with the ability to dynamically change the priorities of tasks, which indeed is a flexible mechanism for programming adaptable real-time systems. Ceiling priorities being static, it is not possible to adequately implement the dynamic nature of multi-moded systems or systems scheduled with dynamic priorities. It is possible to work around this problem (e.g, by using the so-called *ceiling of ceilings*) but there is an added cost in terms of blocking times.

The next revision of the Ada 95 Standard, known as Ada 0Y, is considering the inclusion of dynamic ceiling priorities in the language. This paper presents the arguments for dynamic ceilings and discusses the approach proposed by the International Real-Time Ada Workshop consensus group. An experimental implementation is also discussed in order to evaluate the impact of this feature on the GNAT Ada compiler and run-time system which, in a nutshell, has turned out to be very low.

1   Introduction

In Ada 83 [1], task priorities were static. A more flexible model was achieved in Ada 95 with the inclusion of dynamic priorities for tasks by means of the package Ada.Dynamic_Priorities.

The Ada 95 Standard also brought in protected objects (PO) —and protected types— as a means for implementing the notion of resources shared by several tasks, with the guarantee of consistent data sharing and inter-task communication. In addition, the locking policy Ceiling_Locking defined in Annex D of the Ada Reference Manual (ARM, for short) [2], provides the means to achieve a deterministic behaviour (in terms of blocking times) for the use of protected objects in Real-Time systems. Under this policy, a PO is assigned a priority, called the *ceiling priority*, that will be temporarily inherited by

A. Llamosí and A. Strohmeier (Eds.): Ada-Europe 2004, LNCS 3063, pp. 261–272, 2004.

a task while executing an operation provided in the PO's interface. The ceiling priority of a PO must be higher or equal to the base priority of any task that may use the PO. On a mono-processor system, this guarantees that a task using a shared resource may be blocked at most once by another lower priority task using the same resource [3,4].

Therefore, given a set of tasks sharing a resource (implemented via a PO), the ceiling priority of that PO must be assigned, at least, a ceiling priority equal to that of the highest-priority task in the set. The tasks in the set will normally run with their original priority (known as the *base* priority) but they will inherit the ceiling priority of a PO while running a protected operation inside it. To differentiate this temporary priority from the base priority of the task, the inherited priority is known as the *active* priority of the task.

In Ada 95, the ceiling priority of a PO can only be assigned once, by means of the pragma Priority, at the PO's creation time. This is sufficient for systems where the base priorities of all tasks remain unchanged during the lifetime of the system, but not for others where base priorities of the tasks may change, like systems with multiple operating modes and systems scheduled with dynamic priorities. For this reason, the next revision of the Ada 95 Standard is considering the inclusion of dynamic ceilings in the language. This paper presents the arguments for dynamic ceilings, discusses the approach proposed by the International Real-Time Ada Workshop consensus group, and shows the implementation details of this feature inside the GNAT Ada compiler (version 3.15p) [5].

The structure of the paper is as follows. Section 2 motivates the importance of dynamic ceilings. Section 3 reviews the possible implementation models for protected objects. Section 4 summarises the proposal of dynamic ceilings in its current state. In section 5 we show the details of an experimental implementation of the feature in the GNAT Ada compiler. Finally, Section 6 presents our conclusions.

2   Motivation for Dynamic Ceilings

The convenience of dynamic ceiling priorities in Ada arises mainly from the fact that task priorities are dynamic. Under the ceiling locking policy, the ceiling priority of a PO must be assigned a value not lower than the base priority of the highest-priority task using the object. This is simple in the case of systems where task priorities do not change during the life time of the system, but there exist systems where this is not so simple, for example:

- Systems scheduled with dynamic priorities (e.g., using the *Dynamic Priority Ceiling Protocol* [6] under the *Earliest Deadline First* scheduling policy [7]).
- Systems with multiple operating modes, each one with a possibly different priority assignment for certain tasks in different operating modes.
- Systems that are composed from existing subsystems. Some of these subsystems may define protected types that are imported (reused) to make them available to tasks belonging to other subsystems, with priorities that are unknown *a priori* and therefore can not be statically assigned.

A common workaround exists to these situations: to use the so-called *ceiling of ceilings* as the unique, static ceiling priority of a PO. In a system with dynamic task priorities, the ceiling of ceilings is defined as the highest priority a task using a particular PO *may be assigned* during its execution. To avoid violating the ceiling locking protocol, the ceiling of protected objects is initialised with the ceiling of ceilings. For example, in multi-moded systems, the ceiling of ceilings must consider the priorities of tasks across all the operating modes.

The use of ceiling of ceilings in multi-moded systems implies that a task running in a particular mode can be blocked by another one unnecessarily, due to an inflated ceiling priority resulting from the requirements of a different mode of operation. Consequently, the ceiling of ceilings produces an *excessive blocking* that reduces the schedulability of the task set. This approach is also error-prone during composition of sub-systems.

The problems imposed by the ceiling of ceilings in multi-moded systems have already been illustrated in [8], where two different solutions are proposed to eliminate its impact on blocking times, still using static ceilings. The first solution proposed is an algorithm to redistribute priorities of tasks across all operating modes. The new priority assignment preserves the relative priority ordering among tasks in their different modes, but eliminates the situation where a task may suffer excessive blocking due to using the ceiling of ceilings. This solution requires introducing priority gaps, i.e., levels of priority that can not be used in some modes. But its main drawback is the fact that it is not a general solution: it is not applicable to systems with circularities in the order relationship of ceilings across modes[1].

The second solution proposed in [8] consisted in separating the interface of protected objects from their internal state. Instead of declaring the state in the private part of the protected unit, the PO state would be accessible as a package, but the application should make the commitment to only access the state through calls to protected operations to an *interface* PO. For the same state, different interfaces should be used in different operating modes, each one with the ceiling priority needed for that mode. A deterministic mode change protocol should then be used to ensure the protection of the state, specially during the transition between modes. This alternative definitively eliminates the excessive blocking problem, and it is a general solution. But it obviously affects the design process of the system, that should be implemented according to these restrictions. For example, if a new mode is added to the system, then new interface protected objects should be implemented with the new ceiling assignments.

In summary, the existing methods for avoiding the excessive blocking caused by the ceiling of ceilings are mainly addressed to the case of multi-moded systems (not to the general problem of static ceilings) and present drawbacks that may be too onerous for certain applications. This motivates facing the problem from another perspective, by devising an adequate procedure for dynamically changing the ceiling priority of protected objects without losing the application's integrity.

---

[1] For example, given two protected objects PO1 and PO2, there exists a circularity in their ceiling ordering across modes if, given two operating modes M1 and M2, the ceiling of PO1 is higher than the ceiling of PO2 in mode M1, whereas in mode M2 the ceiling of PO2 is higher than the ceiling of PO1.

3   Implementation Models for Protected Objects

Before introducing the proposal for dynamic ceilings, it is convenient to recall the implementation models for protected objects in Ada. The proposal should take them into account, in order to minimise the impact on existing implementations[2].

Protected units provide three ways to access their internal state: protected functions, which allow concurrent, read-only access; protected procedures, for mutually exclusive read and write access; and protected entries, which also allow read/write access to the state. Furthermore, protected entries may be guarded with a boolean expression that is evaluated when the entry call is issued, before executing the instructions in the entry body. If the barrier evaluates to true (i.e., the barrier is *open*), then the body of the entry call is executed, like in a protected procedure call; but if the evaluation returns false (i.e., the barrier is *closed*), then the call is queued inside the PO until the associated barrier is opened.

A queued entry call whose barrier becomes open has precedence over other calls on the PO. This is often explained in terms of the *eggshell model*. The PO can be seen as if it was wrapped in an eggshell, which protects the object state from concurrent accesses. The lock on a PO is the eggshell.

Figure 1 graphically shows how this model works. The PO state is wrapped in the eggshell. The access to the state may be via a protected entry (the black small rectangle), a protected procedure (represented by a grey small rectangle) or a function (the white small rectangle). Grey circles represent tasks.

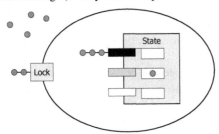

Fig. 1. The *eggshell* model

When a task issues a call to a protected operation, it first tries to get the lock of the PO, i.e., to *enter the eggshell*. The lock will be granted only if there are no tasks currently running a protected procedure or entry. If there are tasks running protected functions, then access to the PO may be granted only if the call is also a function call.

If the call is a protected entry call, then the calling task must enter the eggshell to evaluate the guard and, possibly, execute the entry body. If the evaluation of the guard results in an open barrier, then the entry call proceeds in mutual exclusion with other calls to the PO. But if the barrier is closed, then the call will be queued on that entry until the barrier becomes open. Meanwhile, other tasks may enter the eggshell, since tasks with queued calls are not active.

If the ceiling locking policy has been selected, a ceiling check is performed each time a task tries to enter the eggshell. If the task priority is higher than the ceiling, then the exception `Program_Error` is raised to the task. Other cases of bounded errors are (*i*) to raise the priority of a task with a call queued on a protected entry above the ceiling of the PO and (*ii*) the priority of a calling task being higher than the ceiling when an entry call from that task is cancelled (cf. [2] D-5(11)).

Finally, the ARM defines the concept of *protected actions*. This distinguishes between internal calls to protected subprograms (issued from within another protected

---

[2] A more extensive explanation of the implementation details of protected objects in GNAT can be found in [9].

subprogram in the same PO), and external calls issued from a different entity (PO or task). In the first case, the body of the subprogram is executed as for a normal subprogram call. If the call is an external call, then the body of the subprogram is executed as part of a new protected action on the target protected object; the protected action completes after the body of the subprogram is executed. The servicing of queued calls with open barriers is performed as part of the protected action.

3.1 Implementation Models for Servicing Queued Calls

We have reviewed the general implementation model of protected objects in Ada. This subsection deals with the existing implementation models for servicing queued calls on protected entries.

The Ada Standard does not specify which task should actually execute the entry body once the corresponding barrier gets open. There are two approaches to this issue, both compliant with the eggshell model:

- The *self-service* model. Before exiting the eggshell due to the end of a protected operation, the calling task selects a queued call whose barrier has become open as the effect of a change in the state of the PO, caused by the execution of the protected operation. The decision of which task to select is made according to the queuing policy in effect[3]. The selected task is awakened, thus making it the active task inside the eggshell. It will execute the entry body as soon as it is dispatched.
- The *proxy* model. In this model, it is the task leaving the eggshell who previously executes the re-evaluation of guards and also the entry bodies of all queued calls with open barriers on behalf of the calling tasks. After having executed the pending entry bodies, it wakes the affected tasks, making them eligible to run. The task exits the eggshell once it has serviced all pending tasks.

The advantages of the self-service model are enhanced parallelism (on multiprocessor platforms) and simpler schedulability analysis [9]. Nevertheless, the proxy model is generally the selected one due to its simplicity.

Note that in both models the ceiling violation check can be done once (when a calling task enters the eggshell) or twice (also when the barrier of a queued call gets open).

3.2 Priority-Driven, Mono-processor Implementation

On a mono-processor platform, if FIFO_Within_Priorities and Ceiling_Locking are selected as the task dispatching and locking policies, it is possible to implement the access to protected objects without the need for a lock. If a task gains access to a PO, it is because it was the highest-priority active task among those that may use the PO. Therefore, no other task was active inside it. Once the task enters the PO, its priority is raised to the ceiling, and thus no other tasks using the PO can start executing until the task inside the PO completes the execution of the call.

---

[3] The predefined queuing policies in Ada are FIFO_Queuing and Priority_Queuing (cf. [2], section D.4.)

This model of course precludes the possibility of having multiple threads executing protected functions, preventing the implementation of read/write optimisations. But the advantage is that no lock is needed, which removes the overhead of calling the OS to acquire it, and is perfectly suitable for bare-machine implementations of the run-time system.

4   Proposal for Dynamic Ceilings in Ada

The proposal for dynamic ceiling priorities in Ada is an active issue that is being discussed at the ISO/IEC JTC1/SC22/WG9 Ada Rapporteur Group (ARG). The ARG handles comments on the Ada Standard from the general public. These comments usually concern possible errors in the Standard or proposals for improving the language in future revisions. The ARG is tasked with resolving the errors and analysing the proposals. To do so, it creates *Ada Issues*. The proposal for dynamic ceilings has been assigned Ada Issue number 327 (AI327, for short) [10]. An AI has the form of a text document with sections to describe the problem they try to solve, explain the proposed solution, produce the wording to be reflected in the ARM and to further illustrate the proposal with examples. Discussion of a particular issue may produce changes in its contents. This section reflects the contents of the most up to date version of AI327 at the time of writing this paper.

AI327 proposes to define a new attribute `Priority` for protected objects. P'Priority represents a variable component of the enclosing protected object P (or current instance of the enclosing protected type P) of type `System.Any_Priority`, which denotes the priority of P. Its initial value is set by pragma `Priority` or `Interrupt_Priority` and can be changed by an assignment.

Use of this attribute is allowed only inside a protected body of P. Since the attribute is a part of the current instance of the PO, it is defined to be a constant within the body of a protected function, but a variable within the body of a protected procedure or an entry body.

Changing the ceiling priority of a PO P consists in assigning P'Priority the new ceiling value. In order not to cause any difficulties with respect to the relationship between the active priority of the running task and the ceiling priority of P, the effective change of the ceiling priority is postponed until the end of the protected action enclosing the assignment statement. Nevertheless, after a ceiling change, within the same protected body, the attribute P'Priority immediately reflects the new value.

With dynamic ceilings, it is necessary to define the errors that may occur due to using this feature. By reducing the scope of use of the attribute `Priority` to within the PO and by postponing the actual ceiling change until the end of the protected action, it is not possible for a task writing the attribute to violate the ceiling locking policy: if the task is able to assign P'Priority it is because it has already passed a ceiling check —when it entered the eggshell— and the value of the new ceiling does not affect the execution of the protected operation because that value will not be effective until the task has released the PO.

Nevertheless, it is possible that some other tasks are inside the eggshell, with pending calls queued on protected entries with closed barriers. Following any change of priority, it is a bounded error for the active priority of any task with a call queued on an entry of a protected object to be higher than the ceiling priority of the protected object. In this case one of the following applies:

1. Program_Error is raised in the calling task at any time prior to executing the entry body; or
2. when the entry opens, the entry body is executed at the new (lower) ceiling priority; or
3. when the entry opens, the entry body is executed at the new (lower) ceiling priority and Program_Error is raised in the calling task; or
4. when the entry opens, the entry body is executed with the ceiling priority that was in effect when they entry call was queued.

The previous four possibilities cover the cases where the PO is implemented with either the proxy or the self-service model, and where the ceiling violation is checked once (when entering the eggshell) or twice (also when opening a barrier). Case 1 is possible when the PO is implemented with self-service and re-check; Case 2 fits implementations following proxy and no re-check; Case 3 is suitable with proxy and re-check; Finally, case 4 accommodates self-service implementations with no second check.

4.1 Using Dynamic Ceilings

The following code defines a protected type that provides a protected procedure for the purpose of dynamically changing the ceiling priority:

```
protected type My_Protected is
  pragma Priority(Some_Initial_Value);
  procedure Set_My_Ceiling(Pr: in Any_Priority);
end My_Protected;

protected body My_Protected is
  procedure Set_My_Ceiling(Pr : in Any_Priority) is
  begin
    -- Code before setting the ceiling
    My_Protected'Priority := Pr;
    -- Code after setting the ceiling
  end Set_My_Ceiling;
end My_Protected;

P: My_Protected; -- Declaration of the PO
```

In this example, the caller to Set_My_Ceiling must know the name of the PO whose ceiling is to be changed—the call would have the form P.Set_My_Ceiling(Pr). A more flexible scheme can easily be obtained by means of an access-to-protected-subprogram, that could be used in the implementation of a general ceiling changer.

The proposal considers the possibility of using the Priority attribute in barrier expressions. Nevertheless, its use requires special care. For instance, using the attribute to form a barrier to keep tasks blocked on an entry until the ceiling equals a certain value is a dangerous programming practice, since just asking the value of P'Priority may produce Program_Error if the calling task has a priority higher than the ceiling in effect at the time of performing the entry call.

4.2   Discussion

This section summarises the grounds of this proposal. A more detailed discussion on this topic can be found in [11].

Two primary approaches have been considered to make this proposal: (1) to implement the ceiling change as a special operation on the PO, not necessarily as a protected operation under the ceiling locking protocol; and (2) to implement the ceiling change as a protected operation. We will now discuss the main problems with the first approach and later on, how the second solves them.

Implementation as a special operation. The motivation for the first approach was to be able to change a PO's ceiling from any priority, lower or higher than the ceiling, thus allowing to promptly change the ceilings from a high priority mode changer (in the mode change scenario). This approach was inspired by the use of ceilings in POSIX mutexes.

Three cases can be identified with respect to the relative priorities of tasks executing a protected operation, the task changing the ceiling —the *ceiling changer* hereafter— and the current and new ceiling priorities:

1. The ceiling changer has a lower or equal priority to the current ceiling and is changing the ceiling to a higher priority. In this situation the change can take place without problems and tasks with pending calls on entry queues are not affected. They may just inherit the new ceiling when they execute the protected operation, which will be higher or equal to their base priority.
2. The ceiling changer has a lower or equal priority to the current ceiling, as in case 1, but now it is changing the ceiling to a lower priority. Here, it is possible that calls queued on entries might have active priorities higher than the new ceiling. In this situation, the ceiling locking policy could be violated and it becomes necessary to bound the error in the language (eg, raising `Program_Error` to the tasks with queued calls.)
3. The ceiling changer has a higher priority than the current ceiling. Hence, the ceiling change cannot adhere the ceiling protocol. Note the POSIX 1003.1b Standard considers the same situation for the operation provided for changing the ceiling of a mutex [12]. Cases 1 or 2 still apply with respect to the relationship between the old and new ceilings.

The worst case is represented by the third situation, where data corruption may occur in the case of a purely priority-driven implementation on a mono-processor. Consider the case where a task with a priority 10 wants to lower the ceiling of a PO to 8. A task with a lower priority, say 5, could be executing a protected action (with an active priority 8) when it was preempted by the task with priority[4] 10. A third task with a medium priority, say 8, that uses the same PO, can be released while task 5 is preempted by task 10. When task 10 completes, the medium priority task 8 starts to run when task 5 is still in the middle of the protected operation. The risk of data corruption in the PO is clear.

Two possible solutions to this problem have been identified; unfortunately, both present important drawbacks. The first one is to use a lock on the PO that would prevent

---

[4] For short, a task with a priority P will be referred to as task P in this section.

task 8 in the example above to access the PO. The lock eliminates the risk for data corruption but the use of locks can cause well-known priority inversion problems. More importantly, the implementation of ceiling locking on a mono-processor does not require a lock. Hence this solution should also be rejected for efficiency reasons.

A second way to avoid the potential for data corruption is that the task executing the protected action when a ceiling change happens to occur, "immediately" inherits the new ceiling. In such case, no other task accessing the PO can preempt it, therefore the protected action will be normally completed even in the presence of a ceiling change. A problem with this approach is that the runtime needs to know the identity of the task running the protected action, something that is not needed in Ada but for this particular case. The approach was also rejected.

Implementation as a protected operation. The second approach —the one that is advocated in AI327— proposes to implement the ceiling change as a protected operation, thereby avoiding the problems described above.

With the current proposal, a task assigning the `Priority` attribute will be executed in mutual exclusion with other potential users of the PO, therefore ensuring that no other task is executing a protected action when the ceiling is changed. This approach avoids the situation described previously, where data consistency was at risk due to the asynchronous nature of the ceiling change when it is implemented as a special operation. It also makes it unnecessary to use a lock on the PO: the standard implementation of ceiling locking is sufficient to guarantee its execution in mutual exclusion with other users of the PO.

With respect to tasks with calls queued on protected entries, it could be the case that the ceiling of the PO is lowered below the active priority of the calling task, which represents a bounded error in Ada. According to the ARM, paragraph D.5(11): *If a task is blocked on a protected entry call, and the call is queued, it is a bounded error to raise its base priority above the ceiling priority of the corresponding protected object.*

In other words, if dynamic ceilings are considered, this rule would also apply to the case where a PO's ceiling is set below the active priority of tasks with calls queued on the PO's entries. The situation is already considered by the language, therefore no new problems are introduced in this sense.

Note that the proposal is that the new ceiling should take effect at the end of the protected action, instead of at the end of the protected operation that changes the ceiling. This is intended to reduce the risk of `Program_Error` for tasks with a queued call that have already successfully performed the initial entry call with respect to the ceiling check. Those tasks for whom the barrier becomes open as part of the same protected action as is changing the ceiling will be successfully executed at the old ceiling priority. Thus the only tasks that will be affected are those that remain blocked after the entire protected action has been completed.

5   Implementation on the GNAT Ada Compiler

A prototype implementation of dynamic ceilings has been done on the GNAT Ada compiler [13]. The implementation considered an earlier proposal to the one discussed in this paper, but with essentially the same semantics. Instead of using an attribute `Priority` for referring the ceiling priority of a PO, two attributes were defined to provide a differentiated read and write access to the PO's ceiling: `'Get_Ceiling` for reading and `'Set_Ceiling` for writing. The rest of the implementation follows practically the same semantics as explained in section 4.

The modifications to the compiler have included changes at two main levels: the front-end, to parse, analyse and expand the new attributes, and the run-time system. This section focuses on the changes to GNAT's run-time system.

In terms of new data structures to support dynamic ceilings, a new field was added to GNAT's `Protection` data type (the type used to represent protected objects). We call this field `New_Ceiling`, of type `System.Any_Priority`. An already existing field in type `Protection`, called `Ceiling`, is currently used by GNAT to represent the ceiling priority of the PO. Obviously, the run-time routine responsible for the initialization of protected objects has also been modified to set the initial value of `New_Ceiling` to the initial ceiling priority of the protected object.

In terms of new subprograms, we have added one function and two procedures:

```
function Get_Ceiling (Object: Protection) return Any_Priority is
begin
   return Object.Ceiling;
end Get_Ceiling;

procedure Set_Ceiling (Object: Protection_Access; Priority : Any_Priority) is
begin
   Object.New_Ceiling := Priority;
end Set_Ceiling;

procedure Adjust_Ceiling (Object: Protection_Access) is
begin
   Set_Prio_Ceiling (Object.L, Object.New_Ceiling);
   Object.Ceiling := Object.New_Ceiling;
end Adjust_Ceiling;
```

The function `Get_Ceiling` provides read access to the ceiling value. Note that it returns the current ceiling priority. The front-end generates a call to this function in replacement of a read access to the ceiling attribute (`Priority`, according to AI327).

The procedure `Set_Ceiling` just annotates the new value for the ceiling, to be applied at the end of the protected action. A call to this procedure is generated each time `Priority` is assigned a value.

Finally, the procedure `Adjust_Ceiling` will be used by the run-time system to effectively change the ceiling priority of the PO. The service `Set_Prio_Ceiling` is not available in the current versions of GNAT. Its implementation should call the corresponding POSIX service (ie., *pthread_mutex_setprioceiling()*) to update the ceiling of the PO's lock. Recall that a mono-processor, bare-machine implementation of the run-time system could avoid this call only by relying on priorities and the ceiling locking policy to achieve mutually exclusive access to the PO.

The run-time generates the call to `Adjust_Ceiling` at the right point, according to the semantics described in section 4. For that, we need to consider that the GNAT implementation of protected objects distinguishes two cases: (1) PO without entries, and (2) PO with entries. For brevity, we will only show the more complete case of protected objects with entries.

For each protected operation `proc`, the GNAT compiler generates two subprograms: `procP` and `procN`. The first one, `procP`, simply acquires the object lock and then invokes `procN`, which contains the final user code. If a call is internal, i.e. a call from within an operation of the same PO, then it directly invokes `procN`. If the call is external, it is implemented as a call to `procP`. One additional parameter is added by the compiler to the parameters profile of the protected subprograms: the object itself, designated `_object`.

Two cases must be considered here: protected procedures and protected entries. Since GNAT follows the proxy model for the implementation of protected objects (cf. [9]), after the code of a protected entry or procedure is executed, the run-time subprogram `Service_Entries` is called to service calls queued on entries of the PO. The desired semantics are to postpone the effective ceiling change until the end of the protected action, not just the protected operation. Therefore, the evaluation of guards and the execution of entry bodies with open barriers are performed at the old ceiling priority. The final code of a protected action is the following[5]:

```
 1: procedure procP (_object: in out poV; ... ) is
 2:
 3:    procedure Clean is
 4:    begin
 5:       GNARL.Service_Entries(_object._object'access);
 6:       GNARL.Adjust_Ceiling(_object._object'access);
 7:       GNARL.Unlock(_object._object'access);
 8:       GNARL.Abort_Undefer;
 9:    end Clean;
10:
11: begin
12:    GNARL.Abort_Defer;
13:    GNARL.Lock_Write(_object._object'access);
14:    procN(_object; ... );
15:    Clean;
16: exception
17:    when others =>
18:       declare
19:          E : Exception_Occurrence;
20:       begin
21:          GNARL.Save_Occurrence(E, GNARL.Get_Current_Exception);
22:          Clean;
23:          GNARL.Reraise (E);
24:       end;
25: end procP;
```

The final part of the execution of the protected action includes calling the `Clean` procedure, which is in charge of servicing blocked tasks (line 5) and after that, adjusting the ceiling (line 6) when the whole protected action has completed.

A slightly different code is needed to implement protected entries, but this example of protected procedure is complete enough to have an idea of the implementation complexity of dynamic ceilings on GNAT.

6 Conclusion

We have presented the current state of the proposal for including dynamic ceilings in the next revision of the Ada Standard. This feature is mainly motivated by the flexibility

---

[5] Readers with a deep knowledge of the GNAT run-time system will detect that this code fragment has minor differences with respect to the real code generated by the compiler. We have adapted the code expanded by GNAT to the Ada syntax to ease its reading.

required from dynamic systems, like EDF-scheduled or multi-moded systems. From the possible algorithms, the protected approach has turned out to be the preferred one, giving a good balance between flexibility and integrity. An implementation experiment has also been developed, showing the feasibility of the feature at a very low overhead.

Acknowledgements. The work presented in this paper is the result of several discussions in the scope of the International Real-Time Ada Workshop. Many thanks go to all the participants in the last editions of this Workshop for their contributions to the final proposal. Special thanks to Brian Dobbing for his contribution to the wording of AI327.

This work is partly funded by the Spanish Government's Ministry of Science and Technology projects number DPI2002–04432–C03–01 and TIC2001–1586–C03–03.

References

1. U.S. Department of Defense: Reference manual for the Ada programming language. ANSI/MIL-STD 1815 A, U.S. Department of Defense (1983)
2. T. Taft and R. Duff and R. Brukardt and E. Ploedereder (eds.): Consolidated Ada Reference Manual. Springer, Lecture Notes on Computer Science **2219** (2000)
3. Goodenough, J., Sha, L.: The Priority Ceiling Protocol: a method for minimising the blocking of high priority Ada tasks. In: Proceedings of the 2nd International Workshop on Real-Time Ada Issues, Devon (1988)
4. Sha, L., Rajkumar, R., Lehoczky, J.P.: Priority inheritance protocols: An approach to real-time synchronisation. IEEE Transactions on Computers **39** (1990) 1175–1185
5. Ada Core Technologies: GNAT Ada Compiler. http://www.gnat.com/ (2003)
6. Chen, M.I., Lin, K.J.: Dynamic Priority Ceilings: A Concurrency Control Protocol for Real-Time Systems. Real-Time Systems **2** (1990) 325–346
7. Liu, C., Layland, J.: Scheduling algorithms for multiprogramming in a hard real-time environment. Journal of the ACM **20** (1973) 46–61
8. Real, J., Wellings, A.: The ceiling protocol in multi-moded real-time systems. Reliable Software Technologies - Ada Europe 99, Lecture Notes in Computer Science **1622** (1999) 275–286
9. J. Miranda: A Detailed Description of the GNU Ada Run-Time. http://gnat.webhop.info and http://www.iuma.ulpgc.es/users/jmiranda (2002)
10. Ada Issue number AI-00327: Dynamic Ceiling Priorities. http://www.ada-auth.org/ais.html (2003)
11. Real, J., Crespo, A., Burns, A., Wellings, A.: Protected Ceiling Changes. Ada Letters **XXII** (2002) 66–71
12. IEEE: Portable Operating System Interface: Amendment 1: Realtime Extensions [C Language]. IEEE 1003.1b, IEEE (1993)
13. Miranda, J., Shonberg, E., Masmano, M., Real, J., Crespo, A.: Dynamic Ceiling Priorities in GNAT – Implementation Report. Ada Letters **XXIII** (2003) 20–23

Mixing Scheduling Policies in Ada*

Agustín Espinosa Minguet[1], Ana García-Fornes[1], Vicente Lorente Garcés[2], and
Andrés Terrasa Barrena[1]

. Departamento de Sistemas Informáticos y Computación
Universidad Politécnica de Valencia, Spain
{aespinos,agarcia,aterrasa}@dsic.upv.es
. Departamento de Informática de Sistemas y Computadoras
Universidad Politécnica de Valencia, Spain
vlorente@disca.upv.es

Abstract. Extending the real-time capabilities of the Ada language is a major
topic of the current review process of the Ada language. One of the alternatives
which is being considered for Ada is to introduce the possibility of using a mixture
of scheduling policies. Two approaches have been presented in previous works to
meet this objective: per-task policies and per-priority policies. In this paper, we
evaluate both of these approaches using them to define an interesting real-time
scheduling policy known as the Dual Priority Scheduling policy. As a result of
this evaluation, we also propose a hybrid approach.

1   Introduction

Extending the real-time capabilities of the Ada language is a major topic in the current
review process of the Ada language. One of the alternatives which is being considered
for Ada is to introduce the possibility of using a mixture of scheduling policies. Two
approaches have been presented in previous works in order to meet this objective: per-
task policies and per-priority policies.

Per-task policies were proposed by Aldea and González in [2]. In their work, the
POSIX Round Robin and Sporadic Server scheduling policies were incorporated into
the scheduling Ada model. Per-priority policies were proposed by Burns, González and
Wellings in [3]. In their work, a new Round Robin policy was proposed for Ada. The
key difference with respect to the first approach is that policies are associated to priority
levels, and not to tasks. In this case, a task is scheduled by the policy associated to its
base priority.

We are interested in evaluating both proposals, and to do this, in this paper we will try
to define another scheduling policy using both approaches, the Dual Priority scheduling
policy defined by Davis and Wellings in [5]. As a result of this evaluation an alternative
approach is proposed.

The rest of this paper is organised as follows. Section 2 reviews the per-task and
per-priority approaches. Section 3 reviews the Dual Priority policy which is used as a

---

* This work has been funded by the *Ministerio de Ciencia y Tecnologia* of the Spanish Government under grants DPI2002-04434-C04-02 and TIC2002-04123-C03-03 and by the Generalitat
Valenciana under grant CTIDIB/2002/61

A. Llamosí and A. Strohmeier (Eds.): Ada-Europe 2004, LNCS 3063, pp. 273–282, 2004.

test for these approaches. Section 4 presents the definition of the Dual Priority policy using the per-task approach. Section 5 presents the definition of the Dual Priority policy using the per-prio approach. Section 6 presents an alternative hybrid approach as a result of the evaluation performed. Conclusions are given in section 7.

2   Review of Proposals for Mixing Scheduling Policies in Ada

The Real-Time Systems Annex in Ada95 provides only one scheduling policy known as the `Fifo_Within_Priorities` policy, which is suitable for real-time applications . This policy requires preemptive, priority-based dispatching and can be established by using the pragma `Task_Dispatching_Policy`. When this policy is selected, all the tasks in an application must use it. However, in real-time applications that have a mixture of real-time and non real-time activities, it seems more appropriate to assign different scheduling policies to different kinds of tasks. In order to allow multiple scheduling policies in a real-time application written in Ada, two different approaches have recently emerged: per-task policies and per-priority policies. Both approaches are reviewed in this section.

In [2] the POSIX model was adopted and applied in Ada by means of a new scheduling policy called `Fixed_Priorities`. This policy can be used with the pragma `Task_Dispatching_Policy` as follows:

```
pragma Task_Dispatching_Policy (Fixed_Priorities);
```

This policy is the same as the standard `Fifo_Within_Priorities` policy, but a new pragma is allowed for specifying per-task policies:

```
pragma Individual_Task_Dispatching_Policy (Policy);
```

In [2], three values are defined for the parameter `Policy`: `Fifo_Within_Priorities` for the current standard policy, `Round_Robin_Within_Priorities` for the POSIX Round Robin scheduling policy and `Sporadic_Server` for the POSIX Sporadic Server scheduling policy. For the Sporadic Server policy, another pragma is provided in order to specify the required parameters for this policy:

```
pragma Sporadic_Server_Parameters (Low_Priority,
                                   Replenishment_Period,
                                   Max_Pending_Replenishments,
                                   Initial_Budget);
```

The Round Robin policy has no equivalent pragma, as the quantum is a system-wide value in POSIX. Therefore, no specific parameters are needed on a per-task basis.

A different approach was taken by Burns, González and Wellings in [3] in order to allow for different scheduling policies in an application. In their work, a new partition-wide policy was proposed called `Priority_Specific`. This policy can be used as follows:

```
pragma Task_Dispatching_Policy (Priority_Specific);
```

When this policy is used, each priority level can be assigned a different scheduling policy using a new pragma:

```
pragma Priority_Policy (Policy_Identifier, Priority
                        [, Policy_Argument_Definition]);
```

Two values are defined for Policy_Identifier: Fifo_Within_Priorities for the current Ada policy and Round_Robin for the Round Robin scheduling policy. For the Round Robin policy, the quantum can be assigned on a per-priority basis, using the Policy_Argument_Definition part. A new package Round_Robin_Dispatching is provided in order to check the quantum values available in the underlying system. In this approach, the Sporadic Server policy is not proposed.

As you can see, we have two different approaches which allow us to extend the scheduling model of the Ada language. In order to select the best approach, it seems reasonable to test the suitability of both approaches to other scheduling policies that are different from the ones that have been studied. Following this idea, we will try to define the Dual Priority scheduling policy using both approaches.

3   The Dual Priority Policy

The Dual Priority policy is a simple, elegant and effective scheduling algorithm proposed by Davis and Wellings in [5] that provides good response times to aperiodic tasks in real-time applications. This policy is defined as follows:

Each periodic task, which needs to meet a hard real time requirement, is assigned two priorities: a High priority and a Low priority. On the other hand, each aperiodic task, which has a soft real-time requirement, is assigned a Medium priority.

A periodic task uses its Low priority when it is released, and then, when a time called *promotion time* elapses, the task switches to its High priority. This promotion time can be calculated off-line and must be lower than the difference between the deadline and the worst-case response time of the task. Aperiodic tasks always use their Medium priority. The only requirement related to priority assignment is that any Medium and Low priority must be lower than any High priority. Medium and Low priorities may even overlap. As long as no periodic tasks are promoted, aperiodic tasks can be executed with preference over periodic tasks.

In [5], it is shown that, if a set of periodic tasks is schedulable when the usual fixed priority policy is used, then it is also schedulable when the Dual Priority policy is used. The Dual Priority policy can be used in a wide variety of situations. Periodic and aperiodic tasks can share resources when the Immediate Ceiling Protocol is used. Sporadic tasks can coexist with pure periodic tasks. Tasks can exhibit release jitter. Arbitrary deadlines, which may be greater than the periods, can also be used.

Figure 1 shows the typical priority assignment used in the Dual Priority policy. In this figure, there are three tasks. C1 and C2 are periodic tasks and AP1 is an aperiodic task. The High priorities for C1 and C2 are 6 and 5, respectively. The Low priorities for these tasks are 3 and 2. Task AP1 uses priority 4. In case a), both periodic tasks have been released and promoted. Therefore, they are using their High priority. In case b), both periodic tasks have been released but not promoted yet, and their priorities are Low.

In case c), only task C2 is promoted. As you can see, when no periodic task is promoted, the aperiodic task AP1 is executed in preference. This way, task AP1 can get a better response time than in a normal fixed priority policy, where task AP1 only executes when C1 and C2 are not ready.

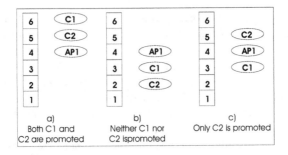

Fig. 1. Priority Assignment in the Dual Priority Policy

The Dual Priority policy is very flexible with respect to the priority assignment used and with respect to the scheduling policies that can be applied to these priorities, providing several interesting scheduling schemes. Let's look at examples.

The promotion time can be set to zero for any periodic task, and it is equivalent to using the normal fixed priority policy for these tasks. Figure 2 shows a system in which only a range of priorities is reserved for the Dual Priority policy. In this example, tasks that use priorities 7 and 8 are not interfered with by the execution of aperiodic tasks.

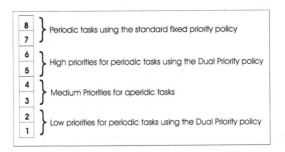

Fig. 2. Priority Assignment in the Dual Priority Policy

Another possibility is to use the same Low priority for all the periodic tasks. In this case, periodic tasks are executed in FIFO ordering when they are not promoted and, thus, only one extra priority level is needed to be able to use the Dual Priority policy. This scheme is shown in Figure 3 in which priority 1 is shared as the Low priority for all the periodic tasks.

Finally, any scheduling policy is applicable to tasks that execute in the Low or Medium priorities. Figure 4 shows a system in which aperiodic tasks and periodic tasks

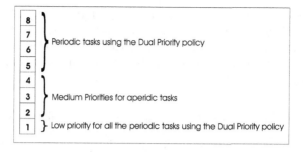

Fig. 3. Priority Assignment in the Dual Priority Policy

that are not promoted are scheduled using a Round Robin policy. Using this approach, when the system load is low, all tasks are scheduled using the Round Robin policy, and only when the load is high, periodic tasks use their High priorities in order to meet their deadlines. Round Robin policies, like this one, are useful for reducing the output jitter of real-time tasks, as it has been recently pointed out in [3].

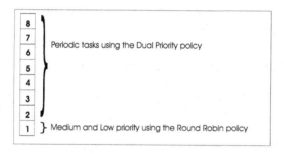

Fig. 4. Priority Assignment in the Dual Priority Policy

The Dual Priority policy can be implemented at the application level, using the services available in both Ada and POSIX, as shown by Burns and Wellings in [4]. Even though this is an interesting advantage, this approach has two main disadvantages. Coding the application is difficult, because scheduling operations must be mixed with the normal application code. In addition, system overhead is notably high. A system level implementation is simpler for the programmer and system overhead is lower.

We have implemented this policy at the system level in the MaRTE OS operating system [1] in order to measure the overhead introduced by this policy. The results obtained are shown in Table 1. In this table, the usual Fixed priorities policy is compared to the Dual Priority policy. The first row shows how much time the system wastes when a task suspends its execution using the Ada *delay until* statement. The second row shows how much time the system uses to awaken a task which is sleeping in a emphdelay until statement and to preempt a lower priority task. The third row shows how much time is consumed by the system in order to promote a task (this result is not applicable to the Fixed policy). As you can see, the system wastes 120 μs in the release, promotion and suspension of a task, which represents an increase in overhead of 36.4%. When the promotion operation does not take effect, the increase in overhead is 13.6%. Taking into account that promotion operations are not always performed, the system overhead of this policy is reasonably low.

Table 1. Dual Priority Policy Overheads (μs). Pentium 200Mhz processor

	Fixed Priorities	Dual Priorities	Overhead (%)
delay until sleep	44	47	6.8
delay until wakeup	44	53	20.0
promotion operation	-	20	-
total with promotion	88	120	36.4
total without promotion	88	100	13.6

The Dual Priority policy has a lot of useful features and introduces reasonably low overhead. Therefore, it is an interesting policy to use in real-time applications. Since this policy obviously requires mixing several scheduling policies in the same application, in the following sections, we will discuss how to introduce this policy in Ada using the approaches described in section 2.

4   The Dual Priority Policy as a Per-Task Policy

By using per-task policies, we can define the Dual Priority policy in Ada as follows:
As in the proposal of Aldea y González [2], we set the general fixed priority policy:

```
pragma Task_Dispatching_Policy (Fixed_Priorities)
```

A new per-task policy called Dual_Priority is defined. This policy can be set for any task using the Individual_Task_Dispatching_Policy.

```
pragma Individual_Task_Dispatching_Policy (Dual_Priority)
```

A task using this policy needs three scheduling parameters: High priority, Low priority and Promotion time. The High priority used by each task is the one specified via pragma Priority and possibly changed via Ada.Dynamic_Priorities.Set_Priority. Low priority and Promotion time can be assigned using this new pragma:

```
pragma Dual_Priority_Parameters (Low_Priority, Promotion_Time)
```

For the Dual Priorities policy, the same rules for FIFO_Within_Priorities apply with the following additional rules:

– When a task that uses the Dual_Priority policy becomes a blocked task, its base priority is changed to Low_Priority. Thus, when the task become ready later, it will be inserted at the tail of the ready queue associated with its Low_Priority priority. If a promotion operation for this task is pending (see below), this promotion operation is cancelled.

- Each time a task that uses the Dual_Priority policy is inserted at the tail of the ready queue associated to its Low_Priority priority, a promotion operation for this task is scheduled to occur at current time plus Promotion_Time.
- A promotion operation consists of changing the base priority for the associated task to its High priority. The semantics of this priority change is equivalent to the task executing Set_Priority (High).

It is important to note that, in this definition, it is assumed that a periodic task only suspends itself in order to wait for its next release, as is usual in real-time applications. Therefore, the first rule applies when a task ends its current release and, the second rule applies when a task starts a new release. If a task suspends itself while it is executing a release, this definition is not valid for the Dual Priority policy. To deal with this case, a subprogram should be provided so that a task can notify the system that the next time it becomes blocked, it is due to the end of the current release. This consideration applies to the definitions of the Dual Priority policy given in the followings sections as well.

The Dual Priority policy fits the per-task approach quite well. Defining this policy is relatively simple, and we get a high level of flexibility. Most of the scheduling schemes discussed in section 3 can be accomplished. Only the scheme proposed in Figure 4 cannot be applied when per-task policies are used, since we cannot set two scheduling policies to the same task, i.e., the Dual Priority policy and the Round Robin policy.

5 The Dual Priority Policy as a Per-Priority Policy

The definition of the Dual Priority policy using per-priority policies is addressed in this section. This policy requires a task to use two priorities, and scheduling actions are different when a task is executing at its High priority than when it is executing at its Low priority. Given this situation, defining the Dual Priority policy requires two related scheduling policies when the per-priority approach is used. Let us call these policies Dual_High and Dual_Low, respectively.

In accordance with the work presented in [3], these policies can be defined using the pragma Priority_Policy as:

```
pragma Priority_Policy (Dual_High, HP,
                        Low_Priority);

pragma Priority_Policy (Dual_Low, LP,
                        Promotion_Time, High_Priority);
```

For the Dual_High policy, the same rules for FIFO_Within_Priorities apply with the following additional rule:

- When a task becomes a blocked task and the policy for the base priority of this task is Dual_High, its base priority is changed to Low_Priority. Therefore, when the task becomes ready later, it will be inserted at the tail of the ready queue associated with the Low_Priority priority.

For the Dual_Low policy, the same rules for FIFO_Within_Priorities apply with the following additional rules:

- Each time a task is inserted at the tail of a ready queue for a priority level with Dual_Low policy, a promotion operation for this task is scheduled to occur at current time plus Promotion_Time.
- When a task leaves a ready queue for a priority level with Dual_Low policy, the promotion operation for this task is cancelled.
- A promotion operation consists of changing the base priority for the associated task to High_Priority. The semantics of this priority change is equivalent to the task executing Set_Priority (High_Priority).

This definition of the Dual Priority policy is relatively complex. It has been necessary to split this policy into two priority policies because different scheduling actions are needed depending on the current base priority of task. Another disadvantage of this definition is that tasks with different High priorities cannot share the same Low priority, as depicted in the scheduling schema in Figure 3. With this definition, if two tasks share the same Low priority, the same High priority must also be shared. The scheme shown in Figure 4 cannot be applied as happens with the per-task policies approach.

6   An Alternative Approach

In section 3, a scheduling scheme mixing the Dual Priority and Round Robin policies was introduced (see Figure 4). In this scheme, tasks which are executing at their Low priority are scheduled by a Round Robin policy, while the standard Fixed policy is used when tasks execute at their High priority. This scheme cannot be applied with any of the approaches that are evaluated in this paper. However, this scheme can be applied if a hybrid approach is adopted, as shown in this section. This hybrid approach is the following:

First, a general fixed priority policy called Fixed_Priorities can be used with the pragma Task_Dispatching_Policy.

```
pragma Task_Dispatching_Policy (Fixed_Priorities)
```

This general policy allows the definition of specific task policies and specific priority policies. These specific policies can be defined by using the following pragmas:

```
pragma Task_Specific_Policy (Policy
                        [,Policy_Parameters] );
```

```
pragma Priority_Specific_Policy (Policy, Priority
                        [,Policy_Parameters] );
```

The pragma Task_Specific_Policy can be used only within a task definition or in the declarative part of the main subprogram. Pragma Priority_Specific_Policy is a configuration pragma.

The allowable values for the Policy parameter when the pragma Task_Specific_Policy is used are: None and Dual_Priority. The allowable values for the Policy parameter when the pragma Priority_Specific_Policy is used are: Fifo and Round_Robin.

The task-specific None policy does not have policy parameters or additional rules, and it is set by default when the pragma Task_Specific_Policy is not used for a given task. The priority specific Fifo policy requires no policy parameters and its rules are the same as the standard Fifo_Within_Priorities policy. It is also the default policy when the pragma Priority_Specific_Policy is not used for a given priority. In this way, the general policy Fixed_Priorities is equivalent to the standard policy Fifo_Within_Priorities when no specific policies are declared.

The priority-specific Round_Robin policy requires one parameter in its definition, the quantum associated to the specified priority level. The semantics of this policy is the same as in [3].

```
pragma Priority_Specific_Policy (Round_Robin,
                                 Some_Priority, Some_Quantum);
```

The task specific Dual_Priority policy requires two parameters in its definition, the Low priority used by the task when it is not promoted and the task promotion time.

```
pragma Task_Specific_Policy (Dual_Priority,
                             High_Priority,
                             Low_Priority, Promotion_Time);
```

The semantics of this policy is equivalent to the one described in section 4.

By using this approach, the scheme in Figure 4 can be easily applied. In order to do this, we can define the Fifo priority specific policy to priority levels 2 to 8, and the Round_Robin policy for the priority level 1. Periodic tasks are assigned the task-specific policy Dual_Priority. The initial base priority for these tasks is set to some priority between 2 and 8, and the Low_Priority parameter is set to 1. The base priority of the aperiodic tasks is set to 1 and these tasks are not assigned any task-specific policy. In this way, all the application tasks execute under the Round Robin policy when no periodic tasks are promoted. The rest of the scheduling schemes depicted in section 3 can also be easily applied.

This approach is more complex than the other ones, but it provides greater flexibility since a task may be scheduled by two simultaneous scheduling policies: the task-specific policy and the priority-specific policy associated to the current base priority of the task.

7   Conclusions

This paper analyzes the problem of mixing scheduling policies in Ada. The suitability of two emerging approaches related to this topic, per-task policies and per-priority policies, has been evaluated using the Dual Priority policy as a test. The main conclusions of this work are the following:

The per-priority approach proposed in [3] is a very elegant solution and fits very well with the design principles of the Ada language. However, scheduling policies whose actions are closely related to task attributes are difficult to define with this approach. This is the case of the Dual Priority policy. We had to split this policy in two and only a limited set of the possibilities of this policy can be applied. We can expect a similar situation with other scheduling policies, such as the POSIX Sporadic Server, in which scheduling parameters and actions are closer to the task than its base priority level.

The per-task priority approach proposed in [2] follows the scheduling model of the POSIX system interface. It is a very important feature because this is a well-known and widely-used model. Any scheduling policy that can be defined with the per-priority approach can also be defined with the per-task approach, because this approach is more general. The Dual Priority policy fits very well in the Ada language when this approach is used, and a wide range of the possibilities of this policy can be applied. The major disadvantage is that it is mainly an operating system approach and not a language level approach, so incompatible combinations of scheduling policies may arise.

In this paper, a more general approach has been proposed by combining both of these approaches. The possibility of applying two scheduling policies to the same task is the most interesting feature of this approach. By using this feature, all the possibilities of the Dual Priority policy can be used. The Sporadic Sever policy can be applied in conjunction with this feature. For example, it could allow all the sporadic server tasks of an application to share the same Low priority, and be scheduled in this priority using a Round Robin policy. However, the complexity of this approach is higher, and incompatible scheduling situations can arise.

Selecting the best approach is not an easy decision and really depends on the needs of the Ada real-time community. The trade-off is between extending the Ada scheduling model toward a convenient but limited framework or extending it to a more general framework that offers a greater set of possibilities.

References

1. M. Aldea and M. González (2001) "MaRTE OS: An Ada Kernel for Real-Time Embedded Applications". International Conference on Reliable Software Technologies, Ada-Europe-2001. Springer-Verlag, 2001.
2. M. Aldea and M. González (2001) "Extending Ada's Real-Time System Annex with the POSIX Scheduling Services". 10th International Real-Time Ada Workshop, Las Navas del Marqués (Ávila), Spain, ACM Ada Letters.
3. A. Burns, M. González amd A.J. Wellings "A round robin scheduling policy' for Ada". International Conference on Reliable Software Technologies, Ada-Europe-2003, pp 334-343. Springer-Verlag, 2003.
4. A. Burns, A. and A.J. Wellings. (1996) "Dual Priority Scheduling in Ada 95 and Real-Time POSIX". 21st IFAC/IFIP Workshop on Real-Time Programming, pp. 45-50.
5. Davis. R.I. y Wellings, A.J. (1995) "Dual Priority Scheduling". Proceedings of the 16th IEEE Real-Time Systems Symposium, pp. 100-109.

Implementing an Application-Defined Scheduling Framework for Ada Tasking[*]

Mario Aldea[1], Javier Miranda[2], and Michael González Harbour[1]

[1]Departamento de Electrónica y Computadores, Universidad de Cantabria,
39005-Santander, SPAIN,
{aldeam, mgh}@unican.es

[2]Applied Microelectronics Research Institute, Univ. Las Palmas de Gran Canaria,
35017 Las Palmas de Gran Canaria, SPAIN
jmiranda@iuma.ulpgc.es

Abstract. A framework for application-defined scheduling and its corresponding application program interface (API) were defined during the last International Real-Time Ada Workshop, and are being proposed for standardization in the future revision of the Ada language. The framework allows applications to install one or more task schedulers capable of implementing a large variety of scheduling algorithms. This paper describes the implementation of this framework, both at the compiler and the run-time system levels. The objective of this work is to serve as a reference implementation in which the API can be evaluated and tested, and its performance can be assessed. We show that the amount of changes to the compiler is relatively small, and that the application scheduling capability can be supported with a small level of complexity.

Keywords: Real-Time, Kernel, Scheduling, Compilers, Ada 95, POSIX

1   Introduction

Real-time applications have evolved towards more complex systems in which there is a mixture of different kinds of timing requirements. It is common to see that in the same system the traditional hard real-time requirements, related for instance with the control part of the application, are mixed with more flexible requirements, related for instance with multimedia processing which requires the capability of reclaiming unused capacity to be able to fully utilize all the available system resources. A mixture of different quality of service requirements is therefore common, and these mixed requirements can only be met by using very flexible scheduling mechanisms.

The fixed priority scheduling policy currently specified in Ada 95's Real-Time annex is adequate for handling the traditional hard real-time requirements, or even soft real-time requirements when the application resources do not need to be fully utilized. However, it is well known that with dynamic priority mechanisms it is possible to achieve a higher degree of utilization of the system resources. But because the timing requirements in current applications are so diverse, it is not possible to pick a dynamic priority scheduling policy that satisfies all [2]. This makes it difficult to standardize on

---

* This work has been funded by the *Comisión Interministerial de Ciencia y Tecnología* of the Spanish Government under grants TIC 2001-1586-C03-03 and TIC 2002-04123-C03 and by the *Commission of the European Communities* under contract IST-2001-34140 (FIRST project).

A. Llamosí and A. Strohmeier (Eds.): Ada-Europe 2004, LNCS 3063, pp. 283–296, 2004.

just one, or even a few, because whichever set is picked, it will not satisfy all application developers.

For this reason, we prefer a more general solution in which application developers could install their own schedulers for Ada tasks. The past International Real-Time Ada Workshop (IRTAW) discussed and approved a framework and associated application program interface (API) for being able to install one or more application-defined schedulers inside the Ada run-time system [8]. This framework is being proposed for the next revision of the Ada language [10].

Before the application-defined scheduling API described in [8] can be standardized, it is necessary to build a reference implementation in which the design can be evaluated and tested. In this paper we present the details of this implementation. The designed API requires compiler, run-time system, and underlying kernel support, so we will describe the implementation at these three levels. In the compiler level we need to implement a few pragmas that enable the application to specify the schedulers, associate tasks to these schedulers, and specify their timing parameters. In the run-time system level we need to implement a new support package and change some internal operations. The implementation will be based on the GNAT compiler and on our application-defined scheduling facilities [6] implemented on top of our MaRTE OS [1], which is an operating system for embedded real-time systems that conforms to the POSIX Minimal Real-Time System Profile [3][4]. The application-defined scheduling facilities available in MaRTE OS are also being proposed for standardization under the POSIX standard [3]. When this scheduling framework is not available, many kernels allow installation of kernel modules that could enable programming the required hooks to implement the functionality. It is also possible to implement the application-defined scheduling services for Ada in a run-time system running on a bare machine. The Real-Time Specification for Java [15] provides a framework in which an implementer, but not the application developer, can plug in a new scheduler.

The paper is organized as follows. Section 2 gives an overview of the application-defined scheduling framework that has been proposed for the next revision of the Ada language. Section 3 describes a high-level view of the architecture of the implementation of the application-defined scheduling framework using GNAT and MaRTE OS. Section 4 gives an overview of the changes to the compiler and run-time system that were needed for that implementation. Section 5 describes the Ada.Application_Scheduling support package, as well as the changes that we had to make to the underlying MaRTE OS kernel. Section 6 briefly describes the changes made to the compiler's front-end. Section 7 evaluates the implementation both from the point of view of its complexity and of its performance. Finally, Section 8 gives our conclusions.

2   Overview of the Application-Defined Scheduling Proposal

Fig. 1 shows the proposed approach for application-defined scheduling. Each application scheduler is a special software module that can be implemented inside the run-time system or as a special user task, and that is responsible of scheduling a set of tasks that have been attached to it. According to the way a task is scheduled, we can categorize the tasks as:

- *System-scheduled tasks*: these tasks are scheduled directly by the underlying run-time system and/or the operating system.

- *Application-scheduled tasks*: these tasks are also scheduled by the run-time system and/or the operating system, but before they can be scheduled, they need to be made ready by their application-defined scheduler.

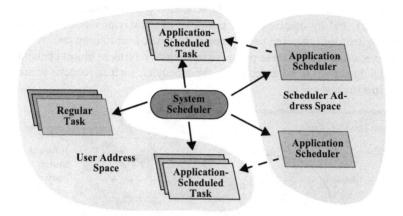

Fig. 1. Model for Application Scheduling

Because the scheduler may execute in an environment different than that of the application tasks, it is an error to share information between the scheduler and the rest of the application. An API is provided for exchanging information when needed. Application schedulers may share information among themselves.

Because the use of protected resources may cause priority inversions or similar delay effects, it is necessary to provide a general mechanism that can bound the delays caused by synchronization when using different kinds of scheduling techniques, and also when several schedulers are being used at the same time. We have chosen the Stack Resource Policy (SRP) [5] because it is applicable to a large variety of policies, including both fixed and deadline-based priority policies. The SRP is also being proposed for Ada 0Y with the name "preemption level locking policy" [13].

The scheduling API presented in [8] is designed to be compatible with the new Round_Robin policy described in [7] and proposed for Ada 0Y [14]. In that proposal, compatible scheduling policies are allowed in the system under the Priority_Specific Task_Dispatching_Policy, and the desired policy is assigned to each particular priority level, with the Priority_Policy pragma; two values are allowed: Fifo_Within_Priorities, or Round_Robin. At each priority level, only one policy is available, thus avoiding the potentially unpredictable effects of mixing tasks of different policies at the same level.

We propose adding one more value that could be used with the `Priority_Policy` pragma: `Application_Defined`; it represents tasks that are application scheduled. If the scheduler is implemented as a special task, its base priority must be at least equal to that of its scheduled tasks.

Application schedulers have the structure shown in Fig. 2 and are defined by extending the `Scheduler` abstract tagged type defined in the new package `Ada.Application_Scheduling`. This type contains primitive operations that are invoked by the system when a scheduling event occurs. The type is extended by adding the data structures required by the scheduler (for example, a ready queue and a delay queue), and by overriding the primitive operations of interest to perform the scheduling decisions required to implement the desired scheduling policy. As a result of their execution, each of these primitive operations returns an object containing a list of scheduling actions to be executed by the scheduler, such as requests to suspend or resume specific tasks

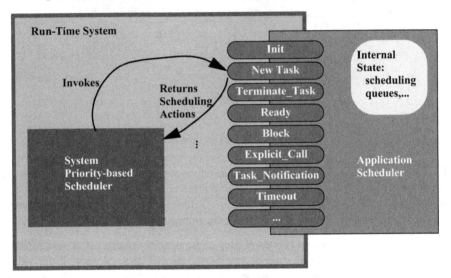

Fig. 2. Structure of an Application Scheduler

When defining an application scheduler we also need to extend the `Scheduling_Parameters` abstract tagged type defined in `Ada.Application_Scheduling`, to contain all the information that is necessary to specify the scheduling parameters of each task (such as its deadline, execution-time budget, period, and similar parameters).

3   Architecture of This Implementation

The implementation is based on the GNAT compiler together with the application-scheduling services described in [6], available in MaRTE OS [1], and extended with some new services that are necessary to support mutual exclusive synchronization using the SRP protocol [5]. Because group budget timers are not yet implemented in

MaRTE OS, we will leave this functionality unimplemented in this version. For a discussion on group budget timers see the Ada Issue generated at the last IRTAW [12].

Fig. 3 shows the high-level architecture of MaRTE OS from the perspective of an Ada application. Although in the future we plan on having implementations of application schedulers that do not require an additional task, the current kernel supports application scheduling by implementing the schedulers inside special user tasks. These tasks execute all the event handling actions at the priority specified by the application. This makes it possible to limit the overhead that a complex application scheduler could cause to critical tasks that might need to execute at a higher priority level. It also serializes the handling of scheduling events, which is a requirement imposed on the operations of the application scheduler to avoid having to program internal data synchronization.

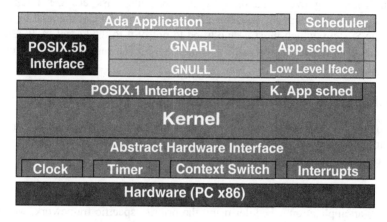

Fig. 3. Architecture of MaRTE OS from the perspective of Ada Applications

The application schedulers defined in [8] are specified as instances of an abstract tagged type. Our implementation uses a user task to implement the application scheduler. The scheduler task has a class-wide access discriminant that is used to pass the scheduler object to it. The task will serve as a driver for the scheduler object, by implementing the following pseudocode. Types `Scheduler` and `Scheduler_Actions` are defined in the `Ada.Application_Scheduling` package defined in [8]:

```
task type App_Sched_Task (Sched : access Scheduler'Class)
is
    Sched_Actions : Scheduling_Actions := Null_Actions;
begin
    Init(Sched);
    loop
        begin
            Execute_Scheduling_Actions (Sched_Actions);
            Wait_For_Sched_Event(Event);
            Sched_Actions:=Null_Actions;
```

```
      exception
         when Sched_Action_Error =>
               Error(Sched,Error_Code);
      end;
      case Event.Kind is
         when Ready =>
               Ready(Sched,Event.Task_Id,Sched_Actions);
         when Block =>
               Block(Sched,Event.Task_Id,Sched_Actions);
            . . .
      end case;
   end loop;
end App_Sched_Task;
```

All the scheduling events handled by the scheduler task are generated by the underlying kernel, except for one: `Abort_Task`. This event is generated by the Ada Run-Time System, which must be modified to notify it to the kernel. A POSIX real-time signal can be used to notify this event, because it can carry the task Id along with the signal.

4   Changes to the Compiler and the Run-Time System

The compiler needs modifications to add the various pragmas on which the application-defined scheduling API is based. The implementation of the changes to the compiler is described in Section 6.

4.1. Configuration Pragmas

To install an application scheduler using the priority-specific framework, we need to specify that the desired priority level, P, will be using an application-defined scheduler. We do so with the following configuration pragmas:

```
pragma Task_Dispatching_Policy (Priority_Specific);
pragma Priority_Policy (Application_Defined, P);
pragma Locking_Policy (Preemption_Level_Locking);
```

Therefore, we need to define a new value for the `Task_Dispatching_Policy` pragma. The effect of the pragma is to set the overall policy to the new value, and enable the use of the new pragmas defined to implement the application schedulers.

`Priority_Policy` is a new pragma that is only valid under the `Priority_Specific` dispatching policy. In our implementation there are two values allowed for the first argument of this pragma: `Application_Defined`, and `FIFO_Within_Priorities`; the latter is the default value and has the scheduling behaviour described in the Ada Reference Manual.

The effect of setting the `Priority_Policy` pragma to `Application_Defined` is to store this value associated with the specified priority level. This will later enable installation of the scheduler for that priority level, as described in subclause 4.2.

The `Locking_Policy` pragma is used to define the synchronization policy to be used for systems with application-defined schedulers. If the `Preemption_Level_Locking` value is chosen, this enables use of the `Preemption_Level` pragma for tasks and protected objects, as described in subclause 4.4. Under this locking policy, all protected objects will be implemented using preemption-level mutexes, instead of the regular priority ceiling mutexes.

4.2. Application Scheduler Pragma

We use the following pragma to attach the scheduler to the chosen priority level:

pragma Application_Scheduler (My_Scheduler, P, Parameters_Type);

where `My_Scheduler` is the scheduler type, specified as an extension of the type `Scheduler`, `P` is the desired priority level, and `Parameters_Type` is the type of the scheduling parameters, derived from the `Scheduling_Parameters` tagged type defined in package `Ada.Application_Scheduling`. This pragma should appear after the definition of the scheduler type, in a library-level unit. We have modified this pragma relative to the one proposed in [8], by adding the scheduling parameters type to enable us a run-time check that verifies the correctness of the specific scheduling parameters supplied for a given task when attached to this application scheduler. A new exception, `Wrong_Parameters_Type`, is added to notify failure of this check.

The effect of this pragma is to install, at elaboration time, a scheduler of the specified type for priority level P. A scheduler object is created and the corresponding scheduler task is also created with a pointer to the scheduler object as its discriminant, and with the tag for the specified scheduling parameters type. After the scheduler is created, all tasks that have their base priority equal to the value of P are attached to the new scheduler. Any task that is created in the future with that priority level, or that is switched to that priority level, will also become associated with the scheduler, after checking that its scheduling parameters are of the correct type.

4.3. Pragma for the Application-Scheduled Tasks

Application-scheduled tasks may choose to be scheduled by an application-defined scheduler just by setting their priority to the appropriate value. In addition, they must specify their own scheduling parameters, that will be used by the scheduler to schedule that task contending with the other tasks attached to the same application scheduler. We set the scheduling parameters through the following pragma:

pragma Application_Defined_Sched_Parameters
    (My_Parameters'**Access**);

where `My_Parameters` is an object of a type that extends the `Scheduling_Parameters` tagged type defined in package `Ada.Application_Scheduling`, and contains specific values for each parameter. These parameters may be changed dynamically with the `Set_Parameters` call. The application scheduling parameters have no effects in tasks with scheduling policies other than `Application_Defined`.

The effect of this pragma is to store a copy of the application-defined scheduling parameters in the task's control block, for future use by the corresponding application-defined scheduler.

4.4. Synchronization Pragma

As described above, a new `Locking_Policy` is defined for the SRP, identified with the `Preemption_Level_Locking` name. This is a configuration pragma that affects the whole partition. Under this locking policy, the priority ceilings of the protected objects continue to exist, and are assigned via the usual `pragma   Priority`. In addition, a new pragma may be used to assign a preemption level to each task and protected object:

```
pragma Preemption_Level (Level);
```

This pragma specifies the preemption level relative to tasks or protected objects of the same priority level.

The effect of this pragma when appearing in a protected object is to set the preemption level of the mutex associated with that protected object. Similarly, if the pragma appears within a task, the effect is to set the preemption level of the underlying thread in the kernel.

5   Support Package and Changes to the Underlying Operating System

Implementation of the `Ada.Application_Scheduling` package defined in [8] is trivial, because this is mostly a set of kernel data structures plus a nearly empty framework for the `Scheduler` tagged type. The main types defined in the package are:

- *Scheduler*. This is an abstract tagged type that represents the skeleton of a scheduler. The `Init` and `Error` primitive operations are abstract. The remaining primitive operations are all null, because if they are not overridden the default behaviour is to do nothing.

- *Event masks*. The type is the one provided by the kernel, and the operations are simple renames or wrappers of the corresponding kernel functions.

- *Scheduling parameters*. The type is abstract tagged, and the operations are wrappers for accessing the internal kernel operations that set and get the application-defined scheduling parameters.

- *Scheduling actions*. All of the scheduling actions are directly supported by the kernel, except for the use of timeouts and execution time timers. Because the single timeout and the execution-time timer actions do not need any special ordering relative to the rest of the actions, the scheduling actions type is designed as a record with three fields. The first one has the type of the kernel's internal scheduling actions. The second one is a single absolute time value (relative to the clock defined in the `Ada.Real_Time` package). The third field is a fixed-length array of execution-time timer actions.

The behaviour of the execution-time timers is described in the "Execution-Time Timers" Ada Issue developed at the last IRTAW [11]. In [8] we proposed an interface to set a scheduling action corresponding to the expiration of an execution-time timer. The interface had a parameter that was a handler to a protected object that would be signalled by the timer upon expiration. The problem with this approach is that the application scheduler task cannot wait simultaneously for a scheduling event and for the protected object to be signalled. A service task would need to be created, thus increasing complexity and overhead.

In this paper we propose changing the approach, by defining a new interface for setting a execution-time timer expiration scheduling action, with versions for absolute and relative time:

```
procedure Add_Timer_Expiration
   (Sched_Actions : in out Scheduling_Actions;
    T             : in out Timer;
    Abs_Time      : in Ada.Real_Time.Execution_Time.CPU_Time);
procedure Add_Timer_Expiration
   (Sched_Actions : in out Scheduling_Actions;
    T             : in out Timer;
    Interval      : in Ada.Real_Time.Time_Span);
```

Each of these actions is implemented in the scheduler task by arming the kernel timer associated with T to expire at the desired time and send a signal to the application scheduler upon its expiration. With the current kernel interface for application-defined scheduling [6] it is possible to simultaneously wait for a scheduling event and a kernel signal, and thus the new interface allows a much more efficient implementation. A similar interface would be required to specify a scheduling action to wait for the expiration of the budget of a group of timers.

A second change that we want to propose for the API specified in [8] is derived from our further experience with implementing application-level schedulers. We found that for some particular scheduling policies it is useful to be able to add a task at the head of the queue corresponding to its priority in the system scheduler, in addition to the normal "ready" scheduling action that adds the task at the tail of its queue. This implies adding a new parameter to the operation that adds the "ready" action, to specify whether the task is added at the back or the front of the queue; it has a default value that causes the task to be added at the back of the queue:

```
type Queue_Place is (Tail, Head);
procedure Add_Ready
   (Sched_Actions : in out Scheduling_Actions;
    Tid           : in Ada.Task_Identification.Task_Id;
    Place         : in Queue_Place:=Tail);
```

To implement the application-defined scheduling framework specified in [8] we had to modify the kernel interface and implementation in MaRTE OS. First of all, we had to add the new SRP synchronization protocol for the mutexes, together with the introduction of preemption level attributes both for mutexes and threads. Associated with this synchronization protocol, we had to add the mask of scheduling events that are deferred while a protected operation is in progress. This mask allows an efficient implementation of the SRP rules within the application-defined scheduler.

In addition, we had to implement a new kind of scheduling action, to support the "timed task notification" scheduling actions. This notification is useful to let the kernel manage the scheduler delay queue, and thus allow integrating this management with the operation of SRP mutexes, by deferring the notification until the end of the protected operations.

6   Compiler Support

This section presents the modifications carried out in the front-end to give support to the new pragmas. We will start with the compiler support for the basic pragmas required to install an application scheduler:

- Pragma `Task_Dispatching_Policy`: In case of the `Priority_Specific` policy, the semantic analyser enables the use of the new pragmas defined to implement application schedulers. In addition, it implicitly enables `Fifo_Within_Priorities` as the default dispatching policy to be used in priority levels without application schedulers (this is the default dispatching policy in MaRTE OS).

- Pragma `Priority_Policy`: In case of the `Application_Defined` policy, the semantic analyser checks that the `Priority_Specific` dispatching policy is enabled, evaluates the static expression found in the second argument (the priority level) and enables setting an application scheduler for that priority level.

- Pragma `Application_Scheduler`: The semantic analyser verifies that the `Priority_Specific` policy has been enabled, checks that the current compilation unit is a library-level unit, checks that the first argument is a valid extension of the abstract `Scheduler` type defined for this purpose in package `Ada.Application_Scheduling`, evaluates the static expression found in the second argument (the priority level), and checks that the third argument is a valid extension of the `Scheduling_Parameters` type and gets its tag (of the type `Ada.Tags.Tag`). The expander uses this scheduler type to generate an object and activate it with the specified priority level and tag. The following code is generated inside the elaboration code of the library unit where the application scheduler type is defined:

```
...  << default variables for the elaboration code>>
    I28b : aliased <<application scheduler type>>;
begin
    ...  << default elaboration code >>
    GNARL.Install_Scheduler
        (I28b'access, <<Priority>>, <<Params'Tag>>);
end library_unit_name;
```

Note that with this approach that there is no need to dynamically create the scheduler.

After the scheduler is created, all tasks that have their base priority equal to the value of the application scheduler must be attached to it. For this purpose, the front-end adds code to the elaboration of all tasks that checks if some application scheduler has been enabled for its priority, and attaches the task to it.

Referring to the pragmas related with the scheduling parameters, the front-end provides the following support:

- Pragma Application_Defined_Sched_Parameters: The semantic analyser verifies that the Priority_Specific policy has been enabled, checks that the pragma has been found inside a task definition, and checks that the argument is an access to an object of a type that extends the Scheduling_Parameters tagged type defined in package Ada.Application_Scheduling for this purpose. The expander uses this argument to generate code in the elaboration of the task that calls a run-time subprogram that checks the tag of the argument and passes that argument to the corresponding application scheduler.

Finally, referring to the pragmas related with the preemption level, the front-end does the following work:

- Pragma Locking_Policy: In case of Preemption_Level_Locking, the semantic analyser checks that the Priority_Specific policy is enabled, and enables the use of the Preemption_Level pragma for tasks and protected objects. In addition, it implicitly enables the Ceiling_Locking_Policy as the default locking policy for tasks and protected objects without the Preemption_Level_Locking policy (this is the default locking policy in MaRTE OS).

- Pragma Preemption_Level: The actions carried out are: verify that the Preemption_Level_Locking policy has been enabled, check that the pragma is placed inside a task definition or a protected type definition, and evaluate the static expression found in the argument (the preemption level). The expander uses this argument to generate code in the elaboration of the task or protected object to set the preemption-level of its mutex.

All the pragmas mentioned above have been implemented as changes to the latest public version (3.15p) of the GNAT compiler, and are available in the MaRTE OS web page [9]. We still need to implement support in the front-end for dynamically changing the priority of a task, and therefore changing the application scheduler. We also want to explore in a future implementation the possibility of assigning the same application scheduler to two or more priority levels, thus making it possible to implement scheduling algorithms in which tasks need two priorities, such as the posix Sporadic Server policy. With the current implementation this is only possible if there are no tasks between the two priorities that are scheduled outside the application scheduler. It is expected that these changes will be available soon.

7   Evaluation

At the compiler level the implementation with GNAT has been quite immediate because:

1. At the semantics level, the current support for the analysis of pragmas is enough to analyse the new pragmas.

2. At the expansion level, the compiler must add some simple code to the elaboration code associated with tasks, protected objects, and library-level packages.

3. At the run-time level, if the POSIX services required for application schedulers are   available,   the   implementation   of   the   new   package `Ada.Application_Scheduling` adds no special complexity.

The changes required in the run-time level are also rather small if an application-defined scheduling framework is supported by the underlying kernel, as was the case with our MaRTE OS implementation. When this support is not available, the amount of effort required to implement it is certainly more complex, but our experience with implementing this support in the kernel shows that it is relatively straightforward and does not require fundamental changes to the kernel data structures. We just need to add the necessary actions to notify the scheduling events, and then execute the scheduling actions with the functionality for suspending and resuming tasks already available in the kernel. This is possible in Ada implementations on a bare machine, or based on operating systems that have a modifiable kernel or that support installing kernel modules that could implement the required extensions.

In addition to this qualitative evaluation, we have made some experiments with the implementation to make a quantitative evaluation of its overhead. Table 1 shows some of the results of this evaluation as measured on a 1.1 GHz Pentium III processor.

Table 1. Results of overhead measurements

Metric	Time (μs)
Timed task notification event (from execution of a user task, until execution of the application scheduler)	1.3
Explicit scheduler invocation (from the call to the invoke operation, until the application scheduler executes)	0.9
Execute scheduling actions (one task suspended, one resumed, from scheduler execution until a new user task executes)	2.0
Delay execution (from invocation of delay, until a new user task is executing)	1.6
Rendezvous (from calling task invoking the entry, until it executes again after execution of a null accept)	6.9

The shaded metrics are for the implementation with no application scheduling, and serve as a comparison. We can see that a common context switch time with the current implementation is the sum of the scheduler invocation time (either the first or the second row) plus the execution time of the scheduling algorithm instructions (which varies with the algorithm chosen and is not shown in the table) plus the execution of the scheduling actions (row 3). So for the case of a timed task notification the overhead of the implementation (not counting the scheduling algorithm itself) would be 3.3 µs, just twice the time of a context switch due to a delay instruction, and half of the time needed to do a simple rendezvous. This kind of overhead is more than acceptable for common real-time applications which usually have timing requirements in the range of milliseconds or tens of milliseconds.

In the near future we plan to reduce this already small overhead by eliminating the need to have the application scheduler inside a user task. The proposed API allows implementing the scheduler operations as operations executed directly by the regular application tasks or by kernel.

8 Conclusion

The application-defined scheduling framework defined in [8] represents an opportunity for the Ada language to continue to be the reference language for real-time systems, by supporting the new application requirements for more flexible and resource-efficient scheduling. Before such a framework can be standardized it is necessary to build a reference implementation that can serve to test and evaluate the API and provide a guide for future implementations.

The implementation presented in this paper has shown that the API, with some minor changes described in the paper, is viable and provides an efficient and flexible way of installing and using application-defined schedulers for the Ada tasks. The integrated operation with preemption-level-based synchronization allows a large variety of scheduling policies to be implemented, and gives the application developers the degree of flexibility that is needed to support the requirements of today's applications with their evolving complexity.

The implementation has required a small amount of changes to the compiler and the run-time system. These changes are well localized and do not represent major changes to the existing parts of the implementation. If the underlying kernel does not support application-defined scheduling, our experience with its implementation in MaRTE shows that it is possible to make the implementation with only a moderate effort, without affecting the main kernel data structures and operations.

Performance measurements show moderate overheads that are perfectly acceptable for the majority of real-time requirements that can be found in common applications. In future implementations we plan to eliminate the need for the application scheduler to be implemented in a special user task. This will allow us to lower the overheads even further.

As a final conclusion, the results of the implementation presented in this paper allow us to recommend adoption of the application-defined scheduling services in the next revision of the Ada Language.

References

[1]   M. Aldea and M. González. "MaRTE OS: An Ada Kernel for Real-Time Embedded Applications". Proceedings of the International Conference on Reliable Software Technologies, Ada-Europe-2001, Leuven, Belgium, *Lecture Notes in Computer Science, LNCS 2043*, May, 2001.

[2]   ARTIST. *Roadmap on Advanced Real-Time Systems for Quality of Service Management.* http://artist-embedded.org/Roadmaps/A3-roadmap.pdf

[3]   IEEE Std 1003.1-2003. *Information Technology -Portable Operating System Interface (POSIX).* Institute of Electrical and electronic Engineers.

[4]   IEEE Std. 1003.13-2003. *Information Technology -Standardized Application Environment Profile- POSIX Realtime and Embedded Application Support (AEP).* The Institute of Electrical and Electronics Engineers.

[5]   Baker T.P., "Stack-Based Scheduling of Realtime Processes", Journal of Real-Time Systems, Volume 3, Issue 1 (March 1991), pp. 67–99.

[6]   Mario Aldea Rivas and Michael González Harbour. "POSIX-Compatible Application-Defined Scheduling in MaRTE OS" Proceedings of 14th Euromicro Conference on Real-Time Systems, Vienna, Austria, IEEE Computer Society Press, pp. 67-75, June 2002.

[7]   A. Burns, M. González Harbour and A.J. Wellings. "A Round Robin Scheduling Policy for Ada". Proceedings of the International Conference on Reliable Software Technologies, Ada-Europe-2003, Toulouse, France, in Lecture Notes in Computer Science, LNCS 2655, June, 2003, ISBN 3-540-40376-0.

[8]   Mario Aldea Rivas and Michael González Harbour. "Application-Defined Scheduling in Ada". Proceedings of the International Real-Time Ada Workshop (IRTAW-2003), Viana do Castelo, Portugal, September 2003.

[9]   MaRTE OS home page: http://marte.unican.es/

[10]   Pascal Leroy. "An Invitation to Ada 2005". International Conference on Reliable Software TEchnologies, Toulouse, France, in Lecture Notes on Computer Science, LNCS 2655, Springer, June 2003.

[11]   Ada Issue AI95-00307-01/05 "Execution-Time Clocks". http://www.ada-auth.org/~acats/AI-SUMMARY.HTML

[12]   Ada Issue AI95-00354-01/01 "Group Execution-Time Timers". http://www.ada-auth.org/~acats/AI-SUMMARY.HTML

[13]   Ada Issue AI95-00356-01/01 "Support for Preemption Level Locking Policy". http://www.ada-auth.org/~acats/AI-SUMMARY.HTML

[14]   Ada Issue AI95-00355-01/01 "Priority Specific Dispatching including Round Robin". http://www.ada-auth.org/~acats/AI-SUMMARY.HTML

[15]   The Real-Time specification for Java. http://www.rtj.org/rtsj-V1.0.pdf

A Theory of Persistent Containers
and Its Application to Ada

Mário Amado Alves

LIACC[1], University of Porto
maa@liacc.up.pt

Abstract. I argue for a standard container library for Ada featuring indefinite elements and persistence. I present a theory of persistent containers as a systematization of the motivations and technical issues involved in creating the library. I hope to show that having such a library represents a major improvement of the language.

1 Summary and Aims

In this paper I argue for a standard or conventional container library for Ada featuring indefinite elements[2] and persistence.

Standard means included in the reference of the next revision of the language (Ada 2005), as proposed in AI-302. *Conventional* means included in an separate reference, for example the Conventional/Common Ada Library (CAL) recently discussed on Ada Letters and CLA.

When one of these two targets is a concern, I default to the former. This is is part because the principal aspects of the current theory are already represented in AI-302—and so one aim of this paper is to strengthen that proposal, and eventually support the ensuing work.

With this in mind I try to provide a systematization of the motivations as well as of the technical aspects involved in creating the library, focusing on indefinite elements and persistence.

I hope to be able to show that such a library, in one of the forms explicitly or implicitly proposed here and in AI-302, represents an excellent opportunity to make the next revision of Ada a better language by a large leap.

2 Containers

In this section I present a general theory of containers upon which the remainder of the discussion draws. I define the general concept of container—focusing on what is *common* to all containers—, and introduce an abstract container space where container varieties are defined—representing the *differences* between containers.

---

[1] Laboratório de Inteligência Artificial e Ciências da Computação (www.liacc.up.pt).
[2] I.e. elements of indefinite *type*. In this paper I say "so and so things" meaning to qualify the type of the things when that meaning is obvious.

A. Llamosí and A. Strohmeier (Eds.): Ada-Europe 2004, LNCS 3063, pp. 297–308, 2004.
© Springer-Verlag Berlin Heidelberg 2004

2.1 Containers in General

A container is an object that contains a possibly multiple number of user data items—its *elements*.[3] A container has associated operations to consult and update the underlying collection of elements, including navigating or traversing the collection, and possibly (depending on the container variety) adding and removing elements. Examples of container: arrays, vectors, matrices, files, trees, lists, tables, stacks, queues, graphs, elementary containers.

A container is an abstract data type, realized in Ada as a private, definite, by-reference, controlled, possibly constrained, and possibly limited type. The controlled behaviour of a container includes memory magic (see below).

2.2 Container Varieties

Each container variety is defined as a region or point in the abstract container space defined by the following axes:

Structural axis. As in "data structures" (cf. e.g. AI302/1[4]). For example, it is along this axis that a vector is differentiated from a linked list, and a doubly linked list is differentiated from a singly linked one. This axis is usually the most visible—if not the only one—in container libraries.

Size axis. The number of elements. For example: fixed, bounded, unbounded. Some libraries represent this axis as (sub-values in) the structural axis. At a theoretic level, though, it is convenient to separate.

Element type axis. The type, or class, of contained elements. Example: definite, indefinite, String.

Persistence axis. A small number (circa 10) of persistence degrees. See corresponding sections in this paper. Some libraries have only one persistence degree (usually core-core), so this axis is omitted in their representation.

3 Desired Features of Ada 2005 Containers

The desire for a standard container library for Ada 2005 with specific features has been amply expressed in Ada fora e.g. comp.lang.ada—by both experienced Adaists and newcomers to the language. Table 1 summarizes the main such items along with the principal reasons why they are wanted.

---

[3] Note the word "data". I am assuming a vocation of containers for this "kind" of elements—as opposed to more "procedural" kinds like tasks and protected objects. This assumption rests simply on a first impression that it is uninteresting, problematic, or even impossible, to have elements of the latter kinds. That is, I have not fully researched this subject. So I accept that lifting the "data" restriction is an option left open—pending such research.

[4] I use this notation to refer to the numbered alternatives of AI-302. Note that alternative n corresponds to file number m0302 in the ARG database, with $m = n - 1$.

Table 1. Standard container library requirements

Item	Reasons
1. Standard library	most applications need containers; many other standard libraries (e.g. Directory_Operations, ASIS) also need containers: a standard container library makes intra-standard reference possible; in sum: more cohesion both in applications and in the standard; see also AI-302/1
2. Generic units	compile-time type checking; less restricted (than tagged) container types; cf. Heaney 2003; see also item 6
3. Indefinite elements	true containers (see below); class-wide element types; unconstrained element types; value semantics; pointerless programming (pointers are evil)
4. Persistence	long term persistence is a required item of most applications; large elements e.g. pictures are best kept on file; ditto for large number of elements; standard file containers facilitate data interchange
5. Uniform specifications	ease of use and understanding
6. Signature packages	ditto; also, provides a uniform specification for Ada 95 containers (arrays and files)
7. Implementation in Ada	ease of implementation, understanding and reference

3.1   True Containers = Indefinite Elements + Memory Magic

The container metaphor is fully realised only if the container truly contains the elements—and not just some kind of pointers to them. Most Ada 95 containers, namely arrays and direct and sequential files, meet this requirement only for indefinite elements. This is a rather trivial accomplishment, one should say, and in fact nothing more than a straightforward realisation of the general *hardware-orientedness* of Ada 95 (particularly in the case of arrays).

For Ada 2005 we want true containers, i.e. a full realisation of the container metaphor—as this represents a big step towards *application-orientedness*.

"A library should stay out of the programmer's way" (Heaney 2003). I would extend Heaney's motto here: a *language* should stay out of the programmer's way. Containers of indefinite elements help to achieve that. When you want an array of strings you want an array of strings not an array of pointers to string. You should not be forced to do memory management just because your element type is indefinite.

Before I said *most* Ada 95 containers allow only definite element types. The worthy exception is Unbounded_String.[5] This type has the most wonderful feature that "no storage associated with an Unbounded_String object shall be lost upon assignment or scope exit" §A.4.5 (88)[6]. Let us call this behaviour *memory magic*. The usefulness of Unbounded_String is indisputable—and it is a reasonable conjecture that this usefulness is due in great part to the featured memory magic. Therefore we want the same behaviour for all containers.

---

[5] Unbounded_String can be viewed either as an unbounded vector container of *definite* elements (characters) or as an *elementary container* (see corresponding section) of unconstrained strings (an indefinite type). Clearly it is the latter view that I adopt here.
[6] I use this notation to refer to parts of the ARM.

Currently the "Ada way" features an tension between *value semantics* (e.g. unconstrained parameter and return types) and *pointer programming* (i.e. the utilization of access types and values). Containers of indefinite elements with memory magic help to resolve this tension—admittedly in favour of the former force.

4 Persistence

In this paper the general concept of *persistence* means the duration of the *value* of an object with respect to the parts of the program in which the object is active. A specific such duration is called a *degree* of persistence.

This paper draws on two basic mono-state persistence degrees, called *core* and *file*, and combinations thereof, including the basic dual-state degree *cache*.

As indicated by their names, the basic persistence degrees relate closely to the *storage media* where the values are stored, but, more importantly, they relate *exactly* to the corresponding foundations provided by the language, namely objects and external files.[7]

A mono-state value is *always* stored in the corresponding storage medium, whereas a cache value *changes* from file to core upon creation, and back to file upon finalization, of the corresponding object.[8]

This theory clearly subsumes a concept of *working* vs. *backup* memory. Also, interestingly enough, the three basic persistence degrees defined here are perfectly aligned with those provided by a most respectable existing Ada container library: the Ada Booch Components (BC) with the persistent extensions by Bond & Barnes 2000. Table 2 represents the corresponding mappings. I hope this helps understand the current theory. Furthermore, I regard the perfect alignment with the extended BC library as an independent confirmation of the practical interest of the current theory.

Table 2. Basic degrees at work and backup, and in the extended BC library

Degree	Working memory	Backup memory	BC + Bond & Barnes 2000
core	core	core[9]	unextended BC
file	file	file	"external" extension
cache	core	file	"persistent" extension

5 Persistent Containers

In this context the terms *persistence*, *persistent* mean the extension of the persistence axis, i.e, the persistence degrees exhibited by the container varieties.

---

[7] The special case of objects stored in non-volatile storage pools (e.g. ROM and "flash" memory) was not specifically researched. My first impression is that it can be treated as a persistence degree not distinct from core.

[8] Most operating systems already provide a similar form of cache in association with files—in an automatic, "transparent" manner. Therefore in such systems an *explicit* cache degree for objects might be of no interest (the simpler file degree can be used instead). This issue has not been specifically researched. But note an explicit cache degree is still obviously necessary to attain it on run-time systems not providing such automatic cache.

[9] Backup core can be ROM or flash memory. As I said in a previous note this pends further research.

5.1 Combined Degrees

Containers have elements and possibly auxiliary data, e.g. nodes. In persistent containers, each of the two data types might be subject to a basic persistence degree. Therefore, the persistence degree of a container is a *combination* of basic persistent degrees.

Although some structural varieties might feature more that one type of auxiliary data (e.g. graphs have *nodes* and *edges*), the current theory does not consider such complexity with respect to the possible combinations of persistence degrees. Instead, a single concept of auxiliary data is posited—on the assumption that the same basic principles are applicable to an eventual version of the theory dealing explicitly with multiple types of auxiliary data.

The notation *elements_degree-auxiliary_data_degree* denotes a combined degree, where each side of the pair identifies the basic persistence degree of the indicated data type. For example *file-core* denotes elements on file, auxiliary data on core. This notation is extended freely to combinations of other things, when the meaning is obvious.

Note that core-core is usually the single degree offered by non-persistent libraries.

5.2 Estimated Applicability

The applicability of a basic degree to a data type depends greatly on the corresponding memory footprint, i.e. the quantity of space occupied by all data. In general core and cache degrees are associated with small memory footprints, and file degrees with big ones.

Let us try to generate a better idea of the applicability of core vs. file, that is traceable back to the basic pieces of the theory. The memory footprint is well approximated by a product of the number of items by their size. Because the number of auxiliary data items is usually equal to the number of elements, the two corresponding memory footprints are correlated. Table 3 shows this correlation for indicative values of item number and size in (small, big) and footprint values in (small, big, huge), with small being the neutral element, and big times big yielding huge.

Table 3. Indicative memory footprints

Number of elements	Element size	Auxiliary data item size	Elements footprint	Auxiliary data footprint
small	small	small	small	small
small	small	big	small	big
small	big	small	big	small
small	big	big	big	big
big	small	small	big	big
big	small	big	big	huge
big	big	small	huge	big
big	big	big	huge	huge

Let us try to estimate the probability P_1 that one data component (elements or auxiliary data) fits in core. Let us assume that each line in Table 3 has the same probability (12.5%). Normally small footprints fit in core and huge ones don't. Because they are in the same number in the list, they cancel each other out. As to big foot-prints it depends on exactly how big they and the available core are. Let us think they fit in a percentage X of the cases. Then $P_1 = X$.

Other interesting estimates that can be derived from these assumptions are the probability P_C that one container has (at least) one core-fitting component, i.e. that the component can be of core or cache degree, and the converse probability P_F that a container *must* have at least one file component. The formulae and a plot follow (see the Appendix for the mathematical deduction).

$$P_C = (3 + 6X - 2X^2) / 8$$
$$P_F = (7 - 2X - 2X^2) / 8$$

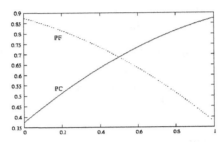

Remember that X is the percentage of cases that a big component fits in core, which is proportional to the available core. So naturally P_C rises with X, and P_F de-creases. The bounds are 37.5% and 87.5%, meaning that at least 37.5% of containers (in table 3) can have a core or cache component (clearly the three classes with a small component when X = 0), and at least 12.5% (100% − 87.5%) cannot (obviously the one huge-huge class when X = 100%); and conversely that at least 37.5% of contain-ers must have a file component (the three classes with a huge component) and 12.5% are never obliged to (the small-small class).[10]

6   Getting Real with Persistent Stores

It is desirable that the standard container library be implemented as much inside the language as possible. Already baseline, proof-of-concept and reference implementa-tions in Ada 95 exist for parts of the AI-302 library specification (see AI-302, ASCLWG, Heaney 2003, Charles, PragmARC). In this section I mainly discuss the implementation of persistent container varieties; along the way, because some intro-duced concepts have an impact on the *usage* of the library, I also touch on that.

6.1   Persistent Stores

The implementation of persistent containers is greatly facilitated if their logic can be written in a way that is independent of the persistence degree. I propose the *persistent store* abstraction for effecting this design.

---

[10] For expressing values of relative probability I shift freely between rational numbers and percentage notation.

Persistent stores—henceforth simply *stores*—are essentially a generalization of storage pools with respect to the storage medium. Whereas Ada storage pools are restricted to core memory, stores can also be file-based.

Here when I speak of storage pools I am referring more to their *essential* operations than to the Storage_Pool type. Namely, I am thinking of object creation, updating, and deletion—more than the lower level of allocation and deallocation of storage elements. That is, I am putting memory management completely *inside* the store capsule—and so, I am thinking of a store as a container. And, in fact, a certain container variety is a very convenient realisation of this abstraction.

6.2 Elementary Containers[11]

Elementary containers are containers of exactly one element. This is a very simple and yet very useful abstraction. Particularly if the element type is indefinite—which we will assume in this discussion.

Like any container, an elementary container is an abstract data type, realized in Ada as a private, definite, by-reference, controlled, possibly constrained, and possibly limited type—and featuring memory magic.

The realization of memory magic in Ada requires a significant amount of "clerical" work for every type (and sometimes for every object) requiring it. Thus the use of elementary containers relieves the programmer of that shore. That is: basically, elementary containers encapsulate that behaviour.

This has been done many times in dedicated forms e.g. "handles" and "smart pointers" (Kasakov 2003). What elementary containers bring anew is putting the abstraction in line with containers. This has rather useful consequences, as we shall see.

One interesting consequence is that an elementary container can be equated with a vector container of fixed or bounded size 1. In particular, if all index parameters are defaulted to 1, the interface can be exactly the same. The bounded variety gives a natural way to express the empty condition of the elementary container, namely as a logical size of zero.

Another important consequence regards implementation of persistent containers. If the logic of a container X is implemented using (directly or indirectly) persistent elementary containers—instead of access types and values—, then many persistent varieties of X can be realised simply by changing the actual elementary containers used.

This approach has been tested and used in developing proof-of-concept and reference implementations of persistent varieties of AI-302/2 containers—including adding indefinite elements to it. This process is fully recorded in the ASCLWG archives (see messages from September 2003). Its smoothness and speed is impressive. Once the persistent elementary containers package is in place, and the test container variety rewritten in terms of it, it takes just a few man-minutes to create each new persistent variety.

Browsing the source code, it is interesting to note how the "master" structural variety is written in a pointerless programming idiom. And also that the persistent varieties are created with just package specifications. This has big advantages, including

---

[11] Also called "uni-elementary containers" or "cells".

restricting code verification to the declarations, and reducing the semantics reference documentation.

Furthermore, with this approach, checking the correctness of the always tricky memory management component is highly facilitated—and therefore confidence in the software is augmented—, because the memory management component is strictly localized in the elementary containers package. A caveat though: this design might not transpose completely unmodified to *cache* components, which are likely to require adjustment between core and file positions on initialization and finalization of the container.

Yet another useful consequence of elementary containers regards a certain idiosyncrasy of Ada 95 (and expectedly Ada 2005). A natural way to implement memory magic is with controlled types. Therefore the corresponding objects must be defined at library level §3.9.1 (3). This is often considered a nuisance, for example when programming in the small. Fortunately standard generic packages are required not to have that restriction (AI-115). So, an Ada.Containers library with memory magic would provide users with a *standard* escape path to the restriction.[12]

7   Final Notes

7.1   A View of AI-302

Ada Issue 302 is a big Issue, and includes relations to external work. Not withstanding the official Ada Issue format, a more conceptual view, consisting of the following components, might help understanding this particular Ada Issue, both in general and in the context of the current paper:

PragmARC-for-ARG. Library specifications by Jeffrey Carter, based on his PragmARC library. The structural axis of the library in AI-302/1.

Charles-for-ARG. Library specifications by Matthew Heaney, based on his Charles library (which in turn is based on the C++ Standard Template Library). The structural axis of the library in AI-302/2.

Annexes <IE>, <PC> by myself. The element type and persistence axes of the library. Contained in alternative AI-302/2 merely for historical reasons: it is applicable to both PragmARC-for-ARG and Charles-for-ARG. The current paper relates to this component as it expounds the theory behind it.

Bases for the Design of a Standard Container Library for Ada, by myself. A proposed complete and consistent set of design decisions for the library. Contained in alternative AI-302/1 merely for historical reasons. This component was found wanting higher level definitions, namely rationalia for the decisions. The current paper meets this need partially.

---

[12] It is understood that a compiler must go a little bit outside the language here, i.e. if it implements memory magic via controlledness. I would expect compilers to be able to extend easily whatever means they have already setup for Ada 95.

ASCLWG. Most debate and proofs-of-concept were carried out in this working group, particularly for Charles-for-ARG and Annexes `<IE>`, `<PC>`. The archives are publicly available. The current paper also distils some parts of it.

Naturally this view is dependent on the *current state* of AI-302. This AI is classed *amendment* and it is hopefully an evolving item.[13]

7.2 No Code

I realise that in this paper I have discussed some usage and implementation issues without showing a single line of source code. This is in part due to the existing experiments requiring sanitization for proper presentation.[14] I simply did not had the chance to do that yet—and actually I find it wise to wait for reactions to the current ideas before engaging in that kind of work. Should the reactions be positive, I expect myself and others to do that work gladly. In the meanwhile, the interested reader can consult AI-302 and the ASCLWG archives and discuss the issue in the corresponding fora.

My personal experiments were based on Charles version 20030813, modified versions thereof, and preliminary versions of SCOPE (Signatured Containers with Persistence), a developing container library by myself which will eventually reach "announce" status in 2004 or 2005.

7.3 No Persistent Languages

I find the idea of persistent programming languages extremely interesting, natural, logical, and useful. And I know many other computer scientists and engineers agree. But alas a standard, reliable persistent language is lacking in the landscape.

The reasons for this state of affairs are not very clear to me. There was some trepidation in the early 1990's regarding making Ada 95 a persistent language, culminating with Oudshoorn & Crawley 1996. As we all know, none of the proposals passed. I risk attribute this failure mainly to the proposals requiring changes to the language.

The proposals in the current paper and AI-302 do not require such changes. Strictly they do not turn Ada into a persistent language either. But they do add a standard means of achieving persistence to an already standard, reliable language.

7.4 No Databases

When asked what are the main features offered by database systems, most people would answer *long term persistence* and *speedy data retrieval*.

---

[13] And indeed by the time this paper went to press yet another burst of activity on the Issue had occurred, with the result of indefinite elements (but not yet persistence) being now more likely to be included in the final proposal.

[14] Another reason is lack of space in this paper, which has reached the 12-page limit as it is.

Well, they would be wrong. What database systems non-trivially bring into applications is *distribution, transactions, concurrent access.*[15]

Hence this vision: Ada already has excellent foundations for concurrency and distributed systems. A decent persistent container library provides for the rest. A standard such library would make Ada the absolute language of choice for database systems or systems requiring databaseing e.g. web services.

No more dependency on unreliable external database components.

100% Ada, 0% bugs.

Acknowledgments. My first and foremost thanks go to Doctors Alípio Jorge and José Paulo Leal, co-advisors of my ongoing PhD research on adaptive hypertext, for supporting my Ada-related work in that context. I'm also incredibly thankful to all "container types" at the ARG and elsewhere for helping pushing the Ada.Containers idea—and to the RST reviewers and organizers for supporting its dissemination. I'm also greatly indebted to the Foundation for Science and Technology of the Portuguese government for PhD grant SFRH/BD/11109/2002 and for partially supporting my attendance of RST 2004.

References

[AI-115] Ada Issue 115 : Controlled types in language-defined generic packages. www.ada-auth.org

[AI-302] Ada Issue 302 : Data structure components for Ada. www.ada-auth.org

[ARG] Ada Rapporteur Group. www.ada-auth.org, ada-comment@ada-auth.org

[ARM] Ada Reference Manual : ISO/IEC 8652:1995(E) with Technical Corrigendum 1 : Language and Standard Libraries. www.adaic.org, www.ada-auth.org

[ASCLWG] Ada Standard Container Library Working Group. yahoogroups.com/group/asclwg, consulted 2003

[BC] Ada 95 Booch Components. (Software and associated documents maintained by Simon Wright.) http://www.pogner.demon.co.uk/components/bc/, consulted 2003

[Bond & Barnes 2000] Library Packages for Ada 95 / Mark Stephen Bond ; supervised by Dr. Alan Barnes. CS380-IP Final Year Individual Project Report, B.Sc. Computing Science, School of Engineering and Applied Science, Aston University, Birmingham ; May 2000. (Persistent extension of BC.) http://www.pogner.demon.co.uk/components/bc/contrib/bond/, consulted 2003

[Charles] Charles Container Library. (Software and associated documents by Matthew Heaney.) http://home.earthlink.net/~matthewjheaney/charles/, consulted 2003

[Heaney 2003] Charles : A Data Structure Library for Ada95 / Matthew Heaney. In: RST 2003.

[Kasakov 2003] www.dmitri-kasakov.de, consulted 2003

---

[15] And, of course, usually also a *relational data model* and *query optimization*. These items must be properly discussed elsewhere. Let me just make a few loose notes here: the second item is mostly an implication of the first; alternate data models exist (e.g. network, hierarchical); an 100% Ada database system is likely to provide a fresh view on database system implementation, as indicated by the DADAISM project (Keller & Wiederhold 1991).

[Keller & Wiederhold 1991]   Modularization of the DADAISM Ada Database System
    Architecture / Arthur M. Keller ; Gio Wiederhold. Stanford University. Draft of May 21,
    1991. http://www-db.stanford.edu/pub/keller/1991/dadaism-print.pdf, consulted 2004
[Oudshoorn & Crawley 1996]   Beyond Ada95 : The Addition of Persistence and its
    Consequences / Michael J. Oudshoorn ; Stephen C. Crawley. In: RST 1996.
[PragmARC] PragmAda Reusable Components.
    http://home.earthlink.net/~jrcarter010/pragmarc.htm, consulted 2003
[RST ####] International Conference on Reliable Software Technologies : Ada-Europe. Year
    #### from 1996 to 2004. Proceedings published by Springer-Verlag, in their LNCS series.
    12-page articles. Conference websites indexed on www.ada-europe.org

Appendix: Deduction of the Formulae for P_C and P_F

By definition small components always fit in core, huge ones never do, and big ones fit in a percentage X of the cases.

So the non-trivial case is when both components are big. This case can be represented by the square figure below, whose sides represent the relative size of each component, and therefore the total area represent the total set of possible occurrences. Making each paired point in the sides correspond to a possible value of X, the identified areas represent the interesting occurrences: area A represents that both components are below X (and therefore fit in core), areas B and C that exactly one component is below X, and area D that no component at all is below X.

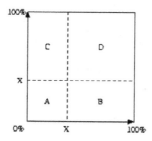

So the probability that at least one component fits in core is

$$A + B + C = 1 - D$$

and that at least one does not fit (and must therefore be of file degree) is

$$B + C + D = 1 - A.$$

So the absolute probabilities, for each container in table <footprints>, of having at least one core-fitting component, is, respectively (i.e. from top to bottom of the table),

$$1, 1, 1, 1 - D, 1 - D, X, X, 0.$$

And the absolute probabilities of having at least one component that does not fit and must therefore have file degree is

$$0, (1 - X), (1 - X), 1 - A, 1 - A, 1, 1, 1.$$

Because each container has the same probability the pursued formulae are the averages of these terms:

$$P_C = [1 + 1 + 1 + (1 - D) + (1 - D) + X + X + 0] / 8$$
$$P_F = [0 + (1 - X) + (1 - X) + (1 - A) + (1 - A) + 1 + 1 + 1] / 8$$

From the figure it is also clear that

$$A = X^2$$

and

$$D = (1 - X)^2.$$

These equations resolve trivially into the formulae given in the text.

Shortcuts: A Critical Look

Matthew Heaney

On2 Technologies, Inc.
matthewjheaney@earthlink.net
http://home.earthlink.net/~{}matthewjheaney/index.html

Abstract. Marco and Franch describe[1,2] a data structure implementation called a "shortcut" which they use to reengineer the Weller/Wright implementation[3] of the Booch Components library[4,5]. In this article I discuss the shortcomings of that library, and compare it to another library called Charles[6] based on the C++ STL[7]. I also analyze the shortcuts framework and demonstrate that the problems with the Booch Components it tries to solve are best solved other ways.

1 Introduction

The Booch Components library[4] was originally written by Grady Booch for Ada83. It comprises various containers including stacks, queues, lists, sets, and maps. Each kind of container has alternate forms with different storage semantics such as bounded vs. unbounded, implemented as uniquely-named library-level generic packages. (Note that only the storage dimension for a component varies. The library does not have a separate dimension for time semantics.)

Ada83 was of course an abstraction-oriented language, not an object-oriented one. As the software industry moved from simple abstract data types towards inheritance-oriented programming, Booch ported his library to C++, a language which had been gaining in popularity and which directly supported object-oriented programming. That version of the library (described in [8]) took advantage of C++ language features such as type extension, but the overall architecture of the library was the same.

When Ada95 was standardized and compilers became available, David Weller converted Booch's C++ implementation (which by then had undergone some moderate revision) to Ada95. This was a more or less faithful translation of the C++ design, not a mere port of the original Ada83 version. Simon Wright now maintains the latest version of the library (available at his web site [3]). It is the Weller/Wright implementation that I discuss here, and which Marco and Franch modified to use shortcuts.

A container library provides various abstractions for storing elements. Containers differ in their time and space properties. How fast is element insertion? Is it affected by how many elements are already in the container? How much storage overhead is there for each element? An important feature of a container is to provide a way to manipulate the elements once they're in the container. (After all, it's the elements that we really care about, not the container.) One common

A. Llamosí and A. Strohmeier (Eds.): Ada-Europe 2004, LNCS 3063, pp. 309–320, 2004.

technique is to provide a separate abstraction called an "iterator," analogous to a cursor or pointer, that can designate a specific element in the container. Typically the iterator type provides operations for navigating among container elements and indicating whether it still designates an element.

The containers in the Booch library come with an iterator type having the requisite functionality. Under certain conditions, however, some iterator operations can be inefficient. In order to correct these flaws, Marco and Franch augment the internal representation of the containers with a secondary data structure, and provide a "shortcut" abstraction as an alternative to iterators, that takes advantage of this new internal framework. Their shortcuts infrastructure is also intended to generalize behavior for types near the root of the container hierarchy.

2   List and Collection Containers

It is undeniable that Booch's writings have had a major influence on the programming community, especially among Ada programmers who learned Ada by reading his books and using his library. Modern attempts to either write a container library or simply specify a component taxonomy are often just deviations of his original design for the Booch Components. Given its pedigree, the Weller/Wright version of the Booch library was thus bound to have a certain popularity. However, in spite of being implemented in a superior language (Ada95 repaired a lot of Ada83 idiosyncracies), I argue that the new version of the library it not an improvement over the original.

Let's start with the basic List container. A linked-list is optimized for insertion at any position. Unlike for an array, insertion of an element into a list is a constant-time operation, because a new node can be simply linked onto the existing nodes. This is how things work in Charles and the STL:

```
List : List_Subtype;
...
procedure Insert
  (Posn : Iterator_Type;
   Item : Element_Subtype) is

   Iter : Iterator_Type;
begin
   Insert (List, Before => Posn, Item => Item, Iter => Iter);
   ...
```

Here Posn is an iterator that directly designates the internal node before which Item will be linked, and Iter is an iterator that directly designates the newly-inserted list node containing Item.

If list insertion were not constant then this would defeat the purpose of a list. However, insertion into a BC List container is in fact a linear time operation, because positions are specified using an integer index:

```
procedure Insert
  (Posn : Positive;
   Item : Element_Subtype) is
begin
   Insert (List, Item => Item, Before => Posn);
   ...
```

The reason why it's linear is that to find the internal node to which the new node is linked, Insert must walk the internal list of nodes until Posn number of nodes have been traversed. (Note that of course a search operation would be linear, but for a list this is acceptable because it is optimized for insertion and deletion, not searching.) The same inefficiency applies to other operations such as Replace. This is the case even for Append, which one would assume could be optimized by caching a pointer to the end of the list.

Ironically, the BC list has an explicit iterator type that does designate internal nodes, but it is only used for active iteration (manually walking the list to visit elements). Insert would be more efficient if it passed back an iterator that designates the newly-inserted node, since the iterator could then be used to directly specify a position in future insert operations. The insertion would be cheap because traversing the internal list would no longer be necessary.

Part of the problem is that the list container is a "polylithic" structure a la the list data structure in functional languages as LISP. This structure sharing allows elements to be on more than one list simultaneously, but it makes it hard to reason about elements in a list. For example, when is it safe to delete an element? This deficiency in the design is already understood, though. The library documentation admonishes users tempted by the List to use the Collection container instead. In fact the list package itself comes with this dire warning:

```
WARNING: If you just want a standard container to support
iteration, filtering and sorting, use Collections. The List
components are much more complex than you'll need.
```

The Collection abstraction appears to have been designed to remove the complexity associated with the List container. The container is monolithic, not polylithic, so there is no structure sharing and hence it's easier to use. In this respect the Charles list container more closely resembles the BC Collection rather than the BC List, since all containers in Charles are monolithic. However, even though Collection is easier to use than a List, and improves some things (the last node is cached, and so Append has constant time), the type is implemented similar to the List and therefore suffers from the same inefficiency. For example it uses an integer index to specify positions. This severely limits the usefulness of Collection, since containers that have linear time complexity do not scale well to large numbers of elements. This is especially the case in real-time programs that need fast and predictable execution behavior.[1]

---

[1] The priority queue container in Booch's original version had a similar problem, since it was implemented internally using a linked list. Elements of the list were

The problem in both cases is that the Iterator is only used to traverse the elements in the container, instead of having the more general function of designating elements, for whatever purpose. For example, instead of inserting an element into the container at a position specified using an integer, it would be more efficient to specify the position using an iterator. The list would not have to be traversed to find the internal node at that position because the iterator already designates the node directly. This is the technique used by both the STL and the Charles library.

The BC iterator abstraction has its own problems, however. The library is organized as a hierarchy of tagged types, with type Container as the root. It uses the Factory Method[9] design pattern to construct an iterator object for a container object in the hierarchy, which can then be used to visit elements in the container. Something like this:

```
procedure Op (C : in Container'Class) is
   I : Iterator'Class := New_Iterator (C);
begin
   while not Is_Done (I) loop
      E := Current_Item (I);
      -- do something with E
      Next (I);
   end loop;
end;
```

Since the New_Iterator constructor is primitive for the Container type, and a dispatching operation can only be primitive on one type, then the return type is Iterator'Class. This has several consequences. First of all, there is a space penalty because the iterator object must carry around a type tag. Second of all, the iterator object has a class-wide type, and therefore there's a performance penalty because all iterator operations are dispatching. In the typical case you know the container type statically, so the class-wide types add generality that you don't need and shouldn't have to pay for.

The worst problem, however, is that the type of an iterator object is indefinite (it's class-wide, remember), which means that the iterator can not be used anywhere where a definite type is required, such as a record component or a container element. This is most unfortunate, because it means the library cannot be used to implement some very nearly ubiquitous idioms.

For example, it is very common to use package state (i.e. some kind of container) to keep track of instances of an abstract data type. In the factory function for the type (or even in the Initialize procedure for a Controlled type) the object inserts a reference to itself into the container, and gets back an iterator that designates that container element. Something like this:

---

maintained in priority order, so to insert a new item required a linear traversal to find the correct insertion position. In Charles you can use a sorted set as a priority queue. It is implemented internally using a balanced tree, so insertions require only log time even in the worst case.

```
function New_T return T_Access is
   X : T_Access := new T;
begin
   Insert (Container, Item => X, Iterator => X.Iterator);
   return X;
end;
```

When the item is deleted, it uses its container iterator to remove itself from the container:

```
procedure Free (X : in out T_Access) is
begin
   Delete (Container, X.Iterator);
   ...
end;
```

This idiom allows us to do things with all extant items (send them all a shutdown message, for example), by simply iterating over the elements in the container. However, this isn't possible (at least not easily) using the BC library, since the iterator type cannot be stored as part of the instance state (because the iterator type is indefinite). But then again, Insert doesn't return an iterator anyway.

Another important idiom is to use a container of iterators to designate elements in another container. This is extremely useful especially when used with a sortable list. As we shall see this idiom largely obviates the need for shortcuts, which are implemented using a similar by less general technique.

In addition to how iterators are declared and used, there is also the issue of how Collection iterators are implemented. Recall that a Collection uses an integer index to designate positions (and hence items) in the container, and that finding an item requires a linear traversal of the internal list. It turns out that the Collection Iterator type is implemented using an index too, so a seemingly innocent function call like this

```
Item := Current_Item (Iterator);
```

might actually have linear time complexity. Instead of simply returning a value (which is what it *looks* like it does), it must traverse the internal list. In fact, the iteration loop above could actually have quadratic time complexity! To help ameliorate this problem the Collection type uses a cache to remember where it was the last time an iterator was dereferenced, so the next time a query occurs then that node or one of its nearest neighbors can be reused. However, if the dereferenced iterator isn't near the cached value then the list must be linearly traversed starting from the beginning. If the programmer deviates from the iteration idiom above then the caching mechanism will fail and he's going to incur a huge performance penalty without even realizing it.

Again these kinds of surprises are simply not acceptable in any program that has even modest performance needs. (Even non-realtime programs that run on the desktop must always service the window message queue in a timely manner.) If something looks like it's a constant time operation, then it should be.

The other problem is that using an index to implement an iterator breaks the model that an iterator designates an element in the container, not merely denoting a position. (If it were otherwise then why have both an iterator and an index?) If we have an iterator that we think designates element, and then another element is inserted anywhere in the list prior to that item, then the iterator will no longer designate that element. This is confusing and error-prone.

These kinds of issues seem to be what motivated Marco and Franch to create the shortcuts framework. For example, dereferencing an shortcut object to get an item is a constant time operation:

```
function Item_Of (The_Shortcut : Shortcut) return Item is
begin
   return SP.Value(SP.Pointer(The_Shortcut.Position)).all.Elem;
end;
```

Compare that with the BC deference operation, which must inspect an internal cache, and traverse a list if there's a miss. However, the code fragment above hints at the complexity of the shortcuts secondary store. Even though Charles doesn't use any extra storage infrastructure, it's just as efficient to query an item, and it's a lot simpler too:

```
function Element
    (Iterator : Iterator_Type) return Element_Type is
begin
    return Iterator.Node.Element;
end;
```

The whole problem with Collection could have been avoided by simply implementing Iterator as a pointer that designates the internal node of storage containing the item, instead of implementing it as an integer index. Then "dereferencing" an iterator would simply mean dereferencing the internal pointer. This would eliminate the need for the internal cache for the BC Collection type, and would obviate the need for the secondary index used by shortcuts.

Note also that in their modification of the Booch Components, Marco and Franch added the new shortcut abstraction, but still kept the Iterator type, which they reimplement as a private derivation from Shortcut. It's not immediately clear why both types are provided. Why not just keep type Iterator, implement it using the shortcut infrastructure, and then get rid of the Shortcut type?

3   Bag Containers and Hash Tables

The Booch Components library also has problems with its hash tables, which are used to implement the Bag containers. The hash table itself has a fixed bucket size, specified as a generic formal constant. When the hash table becomes full, it isn't resized and the elements are not rehashed onto a new larger buckets array. This means that as elements are inserted, the list at each bucket can grow without bound and thus lookup performance degrades. (Of course if the user knows the maximum number of elements in advance, then he can specify that as the buckets array length.[2])

Marco and Franch analyze the Bag subsystem and conclude that the implementation isn't general enough. Their argument is that the iterator type has a representation that requires derived types in the Bag class to be implemented using a hash table. To a certain extent this criticism is justified, since there's nothing in the Bags package that indicates that this is a hash-based implementation. They want to generalize the representation of the bag container and iterator types enough so that derived types in the class can have any implementation.

On the surface this seems like a good idea. However, we could justify the existing implementation as follows. Since the library doesn't have a separate dimension for time semantics (as it does for space semantics), you could argue there is no need to change implementations anyway. Under these circumstances it's very common to factor shared representation into the root type. The package could have been named "Bags_Hashed" instead of just "Bags" to make this explicit. Another possibility would be to declare the hash function and buckets count as generic formal parameters of the Bags package instead of in its children.

Alternatively the library could vary components along a time dimension too. The library could just provide a separate "Bags_Sorted" package and implement it using a balanced tree. It would have an interface identical to the hashed version (the generic formal region would be different, of course), and the user would then just instantiate the component that has the time semantics he requires for his application. This is how Charles and the STL both do it. You don't need a Bag parent type that has both hashed and sorted derived types, because the polymorphism happens already one level up in the Container class. (If that were not the case then why would all container types need to derive from Container?)

They argue that because the iterator type has a hashed representation, you're not able to implement one of the derived bag types as a binary search tree. However, even if it were possible to change the representation of the type from a hash table to a tree, this is hardly a hidden change because it would drastically alter the behavior of the abstraction. The issue is that the time complexity of a component is not an implementation detail – it is part and parcel of the specification. It is true that time behavior cannot be stated in the language itself, but nevertheless it is part of the specification of the component. Library designers don't have freedom that Marco and Franch imagine they have, because (among other reasons) library users choose a component based on its time behavior. So it would simply not be acceptable for a library designer to make such a radical change to a component behind the user's back. As a practical matter the library

---

[.] However, the hash table is still likely to perform badly for another reason. Hash values must be reduced modulo the buckets array length to compute the index. Unless care is taken in the selection of a hash table size, the hash function will produce poor scatter, leading to poor performance.

designer wouldn't be able to transparently make this change anyway, because a sorted implementation requires different things from the element type. The generic formal region would have to change to import an order relation instead of a hash function, and so all the instantiations would break.

4   Iterators

March and Franch characterize the implementation of the hashed bag iterator as inefficient, I think because the implementation of Reset requires that the buckets array be scanned in order to find the first non-empty bucket. But so what? The behavior of Reset is simply an artifact of active iteration over a hash table. There is nothing special about having to search for the *first* non-empty bucket, because such a search must occur for *every* non-empty bucket. In a well-performing hash function the keys are evenly distributed throughout the table, and so there is nothing special about the first key in the table – it's just the key that happens to be first. To iterate over the elements in a hash table you have to visit each bucket, and it doesn't matter whether some of the buckets happen to be empty. The properties of a hash table are such that an operation for "finding the first element" might not be as efficient as for other containers, but is precisely these properties which we wish to exploit because that's how the hash table is able to provide constant-time behavior even for large numbers of elements. We are interested in hash tables not because we want to iterate over all the elements, but rather because they provide fast insertion and lookup of items.

They claim that the shortcuts technique improves iterator efficiency (I assume because scanning to find the first element in the hash table is no longer necessary), but on closer inspection this is because they cache the first and last shortcuts as part of the representation of the root Container type. Even if we were to concede that this does improve efficiency, the gain is not due to shortcuts but rather to caching – something we can do even without shortcuts.

Note that even if finding the first element really were a problem, it would only be a problem for a hash table. To find the first element in a balanced tree, you could descend the tree from root to leaf, which is guaranteed to be a logarithmic-time operation even in the worst case. Or you could simply cache a pointer to the node containing the first element. (This is how the sorted sets and maps in Charles are implemented.) So again shortcuts are not necessary.

They also argue that the iterators "are strongly dependent on the concrete implementation," but again – so what? Iterators are intimately tied to their containers, so naturally they have knowledge of container representation. It is precisely this intimate knowledge that allows the iterator to iterate! They argue that a different derivation must declare an iterator type, but so what? The iterator is simply part of a larger abstraction that happens to be implemented using two separate types, and in all cases an iterator has a trivial implementation anyway.

5   Shortcuts Implementation

Marco and Franch want to define the root of the container type hierarchy in such a way that its representation does not depend on the representation of derived types in the class. They also want to implement iterators so that they have a container-independent representation. They do this using a two-level internal data structure. The "shortcuts" are on the upper level, which is basically a doubly-linked list of nodes; this is where the actual container elements are stored. The lower level is the data structure proper, which stores shortcuts instead of elements directly.

Whatever putative benefits shortcuts provide, you can see immediately that they come at a significant storage cost, since every container is now implemented as data structure *plus a doubly-linked list*. This penalty would be especially acute for array-based containers as a vector, which are otherwise very space efficient.

Another issue is that even though shortcuts were advertised as a technique to fix (what they perceive as) problems with the Bag container, they use shortcuts to implement Container type, the *parent* of Bag and indeed every other container type. This has some bizarre consequences, such as the fact that a linked list container is now implemented as *two* lists internally, one for the shortcuts and another for the actual list.

Shortcuts are a slight improvement over the BC iterator because type Shortcut is a definite type, which means you can use it as a record component, etc. However, as with the iterator, a shortcut is not only tagged but it is also controlled. This is a potential issue for clients because it adds space overhead and what may be prohibitive time overhead. Consider the case of a large number of iterator objects, such as in a container whose element type is the iterator type of some other container. Contrast this to the approach used in the Charles library, which implements iterators as a plain access type.

The Shortcuts infrastructure is quite invasive, because now every container has a secondary linked list internally. Users of the library pay this cost whether they want to or not. It would be better if the library provided simpler, more primitive components that could be easily combined. In this way the decision about whether and how best to combine components would then be made by the user, where the decision belongs.

To follow the example of Marco and Franch, we would like to be able to combine a linked list abstraction with a bag abstraction. Ideally these abstractions would be simple in the sense that the internally the linked list is only a linked list, and internally the bag is only a hash table (say). Assuming we had an iterator that designates elements (not simply a position), then we could implement something equivalent to the shortcuts schema either by instantiating a list on the element type and then instantiating a set on list iterator type, or by instantiating a set on the element type and then instantiating a list on the set iterator type.

It would be hard if not impossible to do this using the BC library. As we have seen the Iterator type is indefinite so it cannot be used to instantiate a component. But it wouldn't be very efficient anyway, because iterators are both tagged and controlled. This can be done very simply in Charles, however, because iterator types are always definite, and are always implemented as an access type that designates the node of internal storage. (The philosophy in Charles is that iterator types are designed to hide container representation, and be as efficient as possible. They do not confer any safety advantages beyond what the language provides for named access types.)

As an example, suppose we have a hashed set, and we want to display the elements in alphabetical order. Let's create a linked list of set iterators, and then sort the list. This is very similar to what shortcuts do internally, except that here we make it explicit:

```
package T_Sets is new Set_Types (T);
...
procedure Op (C : T_Sets.Container_Type) is
   package Iterator_Lists is
      new List_Types (T_Sets.Iterator_Type);

   L : Iterator_Lists.Container_Type (Length (C));

   procedure Append (I : T_Sets.Iterator_Type) is
   begin
      Append (L, New_Item => I);
   end;

   procedure Iterate is
      new T_Sets.Generic_Iteration (Append);

   procedure Process (LI : Iterator_Lists.Iterator_Type) is
      SI : T_Sets.Iterator_Type := Element (LI);
      E : T renames To_Access (SI).all;
   begin
      ... -- do something with E
   end;

   procedure Iterate is
      new Iterator_Lists.Generic_Iteration (Process);
begin
   Iterate (C);
   Sort (L); -- really, this is an instantiation
   Iterate (L);
end Op;
```

In this example the list is serving a function not unlike the shortcuts secondary store. We are manipulating the set elements, but only indirectly, through set iterators stored on the list. The point is to demonstrate that it's better for a library to provide primitives, that can be combined when and where the user chooses. No separate shortcuts framework is necessary.

6   Other Issues

There are other problems with the Weller/Wright implementation, some of which are already well-known. The fundamental flaw is that the library is designed as a hierarchy of tagged types declared in a hierarchy of generic packages. Each component therefore requires several instantiations just to create the type used to declare container objects. This turns out to be awkward and hence the library is hard to use. Programming is work, but it should be fun work, not drudgery. Shortcuts do not solve this problem. The real solution is to simply get rid of type hierarchy, since it's not needed anyway.

From Marco's and Franch's description of shortcuts, it's not clear who is supposed to benefit. Is it the library implementor or the library user? If the implementor, then at what level in the type hierarchy? Shortcuts allow the root package (the upper level of the data structure hierarchy) to be implemented without knowing how the lower level is implemented (e.g. as a hash table or a balanced tree), but the library implementor must still implement the lower level. A library user programs against a class-wide interface, so shortcuts don't appear to benefit him either since he can already manipulate the container object without knowing how it is implemented (indeed, that's what class-wide programming *is*).

They claim that by using shortcuts "many implementations can exist together for the same type of container," but this is true no matter how the library is implemented. Indeed, the Booch Components library is *already* implemented that way, because different instantiations of the same type of container can vary in their storage properties. They further claim that shortcuts make it possible to substitute old components for new ones, which I assume means that one set implementation can be substituted for another transparently. We have already seen, however, that different data structures have different time and space semantics, so even if the "functional behavior" remains unchanged, the "execution behavior" definitely will change, in a way that isn't necessarily favorable to a user. Furthermore, functional behavior is not really identical across implementations anyway. The most obvious difference between a sorted bag and a hashed bag (say) is that only the former allows in-order traversal of elements. It's also very common to have a few extra operations that are implementation-specific, to allow the user to gain some extra efficiency under certain circumstances. For example all the hashed containers in Charles have a Resize operation to specify the size of the buckets array in advance of insertion. This is useful if you know the number of elements a priori, because it eliminates the need to expand the buckets array and rehash existing elements as new elements inserted, and thus the time behavior of insert is more uniform.

7   Conclusion

The shortcuts technique is offered as a solution to problems with the Booch Components library, but I have argued that what Marco and Franch claim are problems aren't, and what they offer as a solution isn't. The Booch Components are flawed for many reasons, but those flaws cannot be corrected using shortcuts or indeed any other technique.

The library design problem has already been solved. In the case of needing to vary the time semantics of a component, the best technique is to simply provide separate components for each kind of implementation, and then leave it up to the library user to instantiate the most appropriate implementation for his application. It does not make sense for a library designer to provide only a single component with an implementation he chooses, because the library designer can't possibly know which implementation is "better."

The best thing for a library designer to do is provide flexible and efficient components, and then get out of the user's way. If a user needs to traverse elements in sort order, then a tree-based implementation is necessary and he can simply instantiate the sorted version of the component. Of course, the user pays for that luxury, because the time complexity is $O(\log N)$ instead of $O(1)$, but that's his choice to make. Otherwise if a user doesn't have any particular traversal needs, then perhaps a hashed set is adequate. It's up to him.

As for shortcuts, they aren't necessary since the efficiency improvements are better made by fixing the iterator type, not by introducing yet another access path to elements. The effect of the secondary storage layer of their shortcuts infrastructure can be achieved by explicitly using a list of iterators to designate elements in the original container.

References

1. Marco, J., Franch, X.: Reengineering the Booch Component Library. In Keller, H.B., Plödereder, E., eds.: Reliable Software Technologies Ada-Europe 2000. Volume 1845 of Lecture Notes in Computer Science., Springer (2000) 96–111
2. Marco, J., Franch, X.: A Framework for Designing and Implementing the Ada Standard Container Library. In: SIGAda '03, ACM (2003)
3. Weller, D., Wright, S.: Ada95 Booch Components. World Wide Web, http://www.pushface.org/ (1995)
4. Booch, G.: Software Components With Ada. The Benjamin/Cummings Publishing Company, Inc. (1987)
5. Booch, G.: Ada83 Booch Components. World Wide Web, http://www.adapower.com/original_booch/ (1986)
6. Heaney, M.: Charles: A Data Structure Library for Ada95. In Rosen, J.P., Strohmeier, A., eds.: Reliable Software Technologies Ada-Europe 2003. Volume 2655 of Lecture Notes in Computer Science., Springer (2003) 271–282
7. Musser, D.R., Derge, G.J., Saini, A.: STL Tutorial and Reference Guide. 2nd edn. Addison-Wesley Publishing Company (2001)
8. Booch, G., Vilot, M.: The Design of the C++ Booch Components. In: Proceedings of Conference on Object Oriented Programming: Systems, Languages, and Applications (OOPSLA). Volume 25 of SIGPLAN Notices., ACM (1990) 1–11
9. Gamma, E., Helm, R., Johnson, R., Vlissides, J.: Design Patterns. Addison-Wesley Publishing Company (1995)

Vector Processing in Ada

Franco Gasperoni

ACT Europe, 8 rue de Milan, 75009 Paris, France
gasperon@act-europe.com

Abstract. To handle signal processing algorithms such as the Fast Four-
rier Transform (FFT) or the Discrete Cosine Transform (DCT) system
designers have traditionally resorted to specialized hardware with built-
in vector-processing capabilities. With the advent of the Altivec vector
extensions for the general-purpose PowerPC processor, developers have
the ability to write efficient signal processing code in C and C++. Using
Altivec-enabled PowerPCs as an example, this paper explains what can
and should be done to write not only efficient, but also clean and reliable
vector processing code in Ada.

1   Introduction

In the 80s fast execution of signal processing algorithms such as the Fast Four-
rier Transform (FFT) [1] or the Discrete Cosine Transform (DCT) was relegated
to expensive vector supercomputers such as the Crays. The 90s have seen the
growth of specialized Digital Signal Processing (DSP) chips to lower the ac-
cessibility and cost of these algorithms in general-purpose embedded and non-
embedded systems. The advent of modern video/audio signal compression algorithms in MPEG-1, MP3, MPEG-2, and their ubiquitous use in general purpose
PCs have fostered the adjunction of vector-like capabilities in conventional general purpose processors such as the PowerPC which is used both in Apple Macs
and embedded systems. QuickTime, for instance, has been modified to take advantage of AltiVec extensions that come with the G4 PowerPC microprocessor
on the Mac.

To allow developers to code in high-level languages (instead of assembly),
Motorola has proposed a C/C++ language interface for Altivec-enabled Power-
PCs as well as an Altivec API (Application Programming Interface). With this
interface one can write efficient vector processing code in C/C++ but is rather
low-level and error-prone. Can Ada help? Can Ada provide an efficient, clean,
and reliable way to write vector processing software?

2   The Altivec PowerPC Vector Extensions

The Altivec extension adds Single-Instruction Multiple-Data (SIMD) computing
capabilities to the PowerPC, namely:

A. Llamosí and A. Strohmeier (Eds.): Ada-Europe 2004, LNCS 3063, pp. 321–331, 2004.

- 32 vector registers of 128-bits;
- Each vector register can be used as a vector of: 16 signed/unsigned 8-bit integers, or 8 signed/unsigned 16-bit integers, or 4 signed/unsigned 32-bit integers, or 4 IEEE-754 32-bit floats, plus a couple of additional data types such as pixel;
- Well over 70 generic vector processing instructions have been added to manipulate the above Altivec vectors.

The Altivec extensions are described in [2] and their C/C++ interface is summarized below.

3   Summary of Altivec C/C++ Language Interface

3.1   Altivec Data Types Available in C/C++

The Altivec data types that are made available in Motorola's C/C++ programming language extensions are descrived in the following table:

New C/C++ Type	Interpretation	Component Values
vector signed char	16 signed char	-128 .. 127
vector signed short	8 signed short	-32768 .. 32767
vector signed int	4 signed int	$-2^{**}31$ .. $2^{**}31$-1
vector unsigned char	16 unsigned char	0 .. 255
vector unsigned short	8 unsigned short	0 .. 65535
vector unsigned int	4 unsigned int	0 .. $2^{**}32$-1
vector bool char	16 unsigned char	0 (False), 255 (True)
vector bool short	8 unsigned short	0 (False), 65535 (True)
vector bool int	4 unsigned int	0 (False), $2^{**}32$-1 (True)
vector float	4 float	IEEE-754 values
vector pixel	8 unsigned short	1/5/5/5 pixel

3.2   Alignment Considerations

An Altivec vector object should be aligned on 16-byte boundaries. However, the Altivec technology does not generate alignment exceptions. If the address of an Altivec vector object does not align on a 16-byte boundary, a vector load/store ignores the low-order bits of the address. As a result developers must determine whether and when vector data becomes unaligned.

Fortunately, the Altivec extensions to the PowerPC ABI (Application Binary Interface) provide a number of guarantees to make developers' life easier.

The purpose of the PowerPC ABI is to establish a standard binary interface (register usage conventions, calling conventions, stack frame layout, setjmp(), longjmp(), etc.) for applications on PowerPC systems.

In the context of Altivec-enabled PowerPCs, some useful extensions to the core PowerPC ABI are:

- The compiler is responsible for aligning vector data types on 16-byte boundaries;
- Records, arrays and unions containing vector types must be aligned on a 16-byte boundaries and their internal organization padded, if necessary, so that each internal vector type is aligned on a 16-byte boundary.

Note that an array of components to be loaded into vector registers need not be aligned but will have to be accessed taking alignment into consideration. Special instructions in the Altivec API are provided to this end. As an example, suppose you have an arbitrary, and potentially non 16-byte aligned array called input of signed char (i.e. integers spanning -128 .. 127), that needs to be loaded into a vector v. That needs to be written as:

```
signed char *input;
// Possibly unaligned array of signed char

vector signed char v;
// Output vector containing input[0] through input[15]

vector signed char *temp;
vector signed char shift;
// Temporaries used to align input's data into v

// Figure out the alignment correction. 'vec_lvsl' below
// computes the number of bytes we need to shift the data
// pointed by 'temp' so that it becomes 16-byte aligned.

temp  = (vector signed char *) input;
shift = vec_lvsl (0, temp);

// Here 'shift' contains the permutation vector to do
// the appropriate shifting so that vector 'v' is
// 16-byte aligned and contains a copy of 'input'.
// 'vec_perm' does the actual permutation by taking two
// 16-byte memory chunks so that the actual vector is
// inside the union of the two memory chunks.

v = vec_perm (temp[0], temp[1], shift);
```

3.3   Motorola's Altivec C/C++ Language Extensions

Motorola has extended C/C++ as described below. In all the following cases the compiler is required to generate the appropriate Altivec vector handling instructions. Motorola's C/C++ extensions are:

- Assigning two vectors of the same type is allowed. For instance the following code snipet is valid:

```
vector signed int a, b;
a = b;
```

- The comparison operator (==), however, is not available for vector types.

- It is possible to initialize a vector with a vector literal. For instance in GCC one can write:

```
vector signed int a = (vector signed int) {1,2,3,4};
```

- One can take the address of a vector object (&a) and can dereference a pointer to a vector object. A vector pointer dereference *p implies a 128-bit vector load or store from the address obtained by clearing the low order bits of p. Access to unaligned memory must be carried out explicitly by the programmer using routines defined in the Altivec API.

- Casts between vector types are allowed. None of the casts performs a conversion: the bit pattern of the result is the same as the bit pattern of the argument that is cast. Casts between vector types and scalar types are illegal.

3.4   Motorola's Altivec API

Motorola has defined an intrinsic API to access all the functionalities provided by the Altivec architecture. There are about 70 generic functions defined in this API which give rise to over 200 unique function names and over 900 overloaded C++ functions once all possible parameter combinations are factored in.

The key point about this API is that although its routines look like regular function calls, in reality these operations are intrinsic to the compiler and generate direct Altivec processor instructions. The mapping is predominantly 1-to-1. As an example the following code snipet gives the profiles of the "Vector Absolute Value" routine available in the intrinsic Altivec API for C++:

```
inline vector signed char   vec_abs (vector signed char a1);
inline vector signed short vec_abs (vector signed short a1);
inline vector signed int    vec_abs (vector signed int a1);
inline vector float         vec_abs (vector float a1);
```

4   Programming the Altivec in Ada

The purpose of this section is to propose a semantic model to make the Altivec PowerPC extensions directly available to Ada developers. Several options are available:

1. Make available in Ada Motorola's C/C++ programming language extensions.

2. Have the compiler recognize computation-intensive loops involving arrays
   and by using the Altivec vector instructions implement optimizations found
   in vectorizing compilers as described, for instance, in [4].
3. Create a high-level Ada package that provides general vector processing functionalities such as vector add, multiply, permute, etc. with which developers
   could easily write FFTs, DCTs, ... that use the underlying vector processing
   hardware efficiently.

Given what is involved in vectorizing compilers and the amount of work and the
limitations involved in approach 2 we will discuss approach 1 in the following
sub-sections. Approach 3 will be addressed in the conclusion of this paper.

4.1   Altivec Data Types in Ada

It is tempting to define the Altivec data types as public array types in Ada.
This is not the model that is put forth by Motorola and it would mean that all
array operations, parameter passing, and attributes would have to be handled
explicitly in the Ada compiler which would, for instance, have to convert array
indexing operations into a sequence of Altivec calls. This would not only sprinkle
Ada front-ends with Altivec specific code, it would be a large undertaking that
would go beyond the programming model put forth by Motorola for C/C++.

Semantically Altivec vectors are really 128-bit "blobs" than can only be ma-
nipulated through the series of routines provided in the Motorola API. This
means that vector types should all be private types. For example:

```
type Vector_Float is private;
--  Corresponds to C/C++ "vector float"
```

These private vector types do not have to be limited since the Motorola spec
allows assignment. Direct vector equality could be made abstract to mimic Motorola spec.

For equality Motorola provides a number of vector comparaison routines that
should be used for equality depending on whether the vector comparison should
return a vector of booleans or a single boolean.

Because of C++'s inability to overload functions on the return type Motorola
has probably decided that it would be less confusing that all vector comparisons
appear explicitly by means of the corresponding function call in the Altivec
API. Thus, in Ada, we could have

```
type Vector_Float is private;
--  Corresponds to C/C++ "vector float"

function "=" (X, Y: Vector_Float) return Boolean is abstract;
```

It would, however, be perfectly reasonable and actually desireable to provide
"=" in a higher-level Altivec Ada package, where "=" would be implemented in
terms of the vector routines provided by Motorola. For instance one could write:

```
function "=" (X, Y: Vector_Float) return Boolean is
begin
   return Vec_All_Eq (X, Y);
   --      Vec_All_Eq is intrinsic. The compiler maps it
   --      directly to an Altivec machine instruction.
end "=";

function "=" (X, Y: Vector_Float) return Vector_4_Boolean is
begin
   return Vec_Cmpeq (X, Y);
end "=";
```

where Vector_4_Boolean corresponds to C/C++'s type "vector bool int". The above is a good example of how Ada's powerful semantic model offers a clear advantage over what is currently available in C/C++.

4.2   Alignment Considerations

Ada's alignment clauses provide a big help and relief to the programmer. Yet another area where, unlike their C/C++ colleagues, Ada programmers get help from the language. In the definition of each Ada vector type the alignment clause will be set to 16. For example we would have:

```
type Vector_Float is private;
for Vector_Float'Alignment use 16;
```

Furthermore every time an Ada developer desires to go back and forth betwen an Altivec vector and a corresponding array it can use a representation clause on the array type and be relieved from tedious alignment fiddling. As an example one could write:

```
type Arr_Float is array (Integer range 0 .. 3) of Float;
for Arr_Float'Alignment use 16;

function UC is new Ada.Unchecked_Conversion
                            (Arr_Float, Vector_Float);
VF : Vector_Float := UC (Arr_Float'(0 .. 3 => 3.141));
```

4.3   Motorola's Altivec API

Doing a clean Ada translation of Motorola's C/C++ API is not completely straightforward since, for instance, to load an array of components into an Altivec vector in C/C++ pointers are used systematically. As an example:

```
inline vector float vec_ld (int a1, float *a2);
```

is used in C++ to load an array of 4 single-precision floats into a vector which is then returned. a2 is a pointer to a stream of floats and a1 is an index in this stream from which the copy operation is started. Before doing the copy, address a2+a1 is 16 byte aligned, which means that if it is not, low-order bits are silently dropped. A similar function in Ada could look like:

```
function Vec_Ld (A1 : Integer; A2 : System.Address)
   return Vector_Float;
pragma Import (Intrinsic, Vec_Ld, "__builtin_altivec_lvx");
```

It would be helpful to also have a version with an array as a parameter, something like:

```
type Arr_Float is array (Integer range <>) of Float;
for Arr_Float'Alignment use 16;

function Vec_Ld (A : Arr_Float; I : Integer)
   return Vector_Float;
function Vec_Ld (A : Arr_Float) return Vector_Float;
pragma Inline (Vec_Ld);
```

In the second version the first parameter has been dropped because one can pass a slice. Of course when doing the above care must be taken that array bounds do not get in the way when making the actual call to the actual Altivec routine. The second routine could for instance be implemented as follows:

```
function Vec_Ld (A : Arr_Float) return Vector_Float is
begin
   pragma Assert (A'Address mod 16 = 0);
   --  No code is generated for this pragma when assertion
   --  checking is off.

   return Vec_Ld (0, A'Address);
   --     Vec_Ld is intrinsic. The compiler maps it
   --     directly to an Altivec machine instruction.
end Vec_Ld;
```

Note that Ada offers the opportunity to use explicit operators such as "+" or "<=" to define an alias for the corresponding routines in the API. Thus while the API will contain:

```
function Vec_Add (A1, A2: System.Address) return Vector_Float;
pragma Import (Intrinsic, Vec_Add, "__builtin_altivec_vaddfp");

function Vec_Add (A1, A2: Vector_Float) return Vector_Float;
pragma Inline (Vec_Add);
```

```
function Vec_Add (A1, A2: Vector_Float) return Vector_Float is
begin
   pragma Assert (A1'Address mod 16 = 0 and
                  A2'Address mod 16 = 0 );
   --  No code is generated for this pragma when assertion
   --  checking is off.

   return Vec_Add (A1'Address, A2'Address);
   --     Vec_Add is intrinsic. The compiler maps it
   --     directly to an Altivec machine instruction.
end Vec_Ld;
```

the Ada API should also contain:

```
function "+" renames Vec_Add;
```

The best way to organize the Ada implementation of the Altivec API would be to have a low-level Altivec package which is a one to one mapping to Motorola's API and have a higher-level package containing the Ada routines and renamings mentioned above that are not directly required by Motorola's API but are a convenient abstraction of the low-level Altivec routines provided by Motorola.

4.4   Ada 05 Unions

To have the ability to view a vector as both a vector and an array of components it is possible to use Ada unions. Unions are currently supported in GNAT and will probably be available in Ada's future revision: Ada 05. As an example a developer could write:

```
type Arr_Float is array (Integer range 0 .. 3) of Float;
for Arr_Float'Alignment use 16;

type Vector_Rec (Dont_Care : Boolean := False) is record
   case Dont_Care is
      when False =>
         A : Arr_Float;
      when True =>
         V : Vector_Float;
   end case;
end record;
pragma Unchecked_Union (Vector_Rec);

X : Vector_Rec := (A => (10.0, 11.0, 12.0, 13.0));

VF : Vector_Float := X.V;
```

Another way to achive the same effect would be to write something like:

```
A : Arr_Float;
V : Vector_Float;
for V'Address use A'Address;
```

Which is definitely in the clever-but-not-suggested category.

4.5   Vector Initialization

To initialize vector types we can either use the unchecked conversion approach demonstrated in a previous example, or the unchecked union, or directly provide an initialization routine. For instance we could have:

```
function Vec_Init (E1, E2, E3, E4: Float) return Vector_Float;
pragma Inline (Vec_Init);
```

and then write:

```
VF : Vector_Float := Vec_Init (10, 11, 12, 13);
```

4.6   Performance Issues

The main reason for using the Altivec extension in a PowerPC is to improve computational performance. As a result an Ada implementation of the PowerPC API must preserve efficiency. The mapping described above achieves that since the Altivec primitives are wrapped in a layer of Ada code that performs alignment checks only when assertions are enabled and otherwise maps the routine directly to the corresponding Altivec machine instruction. For example when a programmer writes:

```
procedure Proc (A, B : Vector_Float) is
  C : Vector_Float;
begin
  if not A = B then
    C = A + B;
    ...
  end if;
  ...
end Proc;
```

the comparison and the addition are compiled straight into Altivec machine instructions (when assertion cheks are off).

Thus programmers can objtain the same performance for the Altivec in Ada as they do in C, while retaining all of Ada's advantages mentioned in the previous sections.

5   Conclusion

The previous section explains how the Motorola Vector processing specification can be written in Ada to provide a safe and higher-level way to program Altivec-enabled PowerPCs which is as efficient as C.

However, depending on the signal procesing algorithm, the previous approach will still require a fairly low-level of coding for algorithms such as FFTs or DCTs which combine vector data in a non-local fashion. In the FFT, for instance, the famous butterfly permutation combines, in the first iteration, the 0-th element with the $n/2$-th element. Because vector processing hardware basically chops an n-element array into an array of n/s components, where each component fits into a vector register holding s elements, efficiently combining the 0-th array element with the $n/2$-th becomes a low-level programming feat. As an example the last two stages of an FFT must be handcrafted as follows [3]:

```
Data : array (0 .. N) of Vector_Float;

V_11, V_12, V_13, V_14, V_15 : Vector_Float;
V_21, V_22, V_23, V_24, V_25 : Vector_Float;
V_31, V_32, V_33, V_34, V_35 : Vector_Float;
V_41, V_42, V_43, V_44, V_45 : Vector_Float;

Permutation_0101 : constant Vector_Byte
  := Vec_Init (0,1,2,3,4,5,6,7, 0,1,2,3,4,5,6,7);
Permutation_2301 : constant Vector_Byte
  := Vec_Init (8,9,10,11,12,13,14,15, 0,1,2,3,4,5,6,7);
Permutation_3232 : constant Vector_Byte
  := Vec_Init (12,13,14,15,8,9,10,11, 12,13,14,15,8,9,10,11);

X : constant Vector_Float := Vec_Init (1.0,  1.0, -1.0, -1.0);
Y : constant Vector_Float := Vec_Init (1.0, -1.0, -1.0,  1.0);

Block : Unsigned_Integer := 0;
...
loop
    exit when Block >= (N + 1)/2;

    V_13 := Data (Block  ) - Data (Block+1);
    V_11 := Data (Block  ) + Data (Block+1);
    V_23 := Data (Block+2) - Data (Block+3);
    V_21 := Data (Block+2) + Data (Block+3);
    V_33 := Data (Block+4) - Data (Block+5);
    V_31 := Data (Block+4) + Data (Block+5);
    V_43 := Data (Block+6) - Data (Block+7);
    V_41 := Data (Block+6) + Data (Block+7);
```

```
V_15 := Vec_Permute (V_13, V_13, Permutation_3232);
V_14 := Vec_Permute (V_13, V_13, Permutation_0101);
V_12 := Vec_Permute (V_11, V_11, Permutation_2301);
V_25 := Vec_Permute (V_23, V_23, Permutation_3232);
V_24 := Vec_Permute (V_23, V_23, Permutation_0101);
V_22 := Vec_Permute (V_21, V_21, Permutation_2301);
V_35 := Vec_Permute (V_33, V_33, Permutation_3232);
V_34 := Vec_Permute (V_33, V_33, Permutation_0101);
V_32 := Vec_Permute (V_31, V_31, Permutation_2301);
V_45 := Vec_Permute (V_43, V_43, Permutation_3232);
V_44 := Vec_Permute (V_43, V_43, Permutation_0101);
V_42 := Vec_Permute (V_41, V_41, Permutation_2301);

Data (Block  ) := Vec_Multiply_Add (V_11, X, V_12);
Data (Block+1) := Vec_Multiply_Add (V_15, Y, V_14);
Data (Block+2) := Vec_Multiply_Add (V_21, X, V_22);
Data (Block+3) := Vec_Multiply_Add (V_25, Y, V_24);
Data (Block+4) := Vec_Multiply_Add (V_31, X, V_32);
Data (Block+5) := Vec_Multiply_Add (V_35, Y, V_34);
Data (Block+6) := Vec_Multiply_Add (V_41, X, V_42);
Data (Block+7) := Vec_Multiply_Add (V_45, Y, V_44);

Block := Block + 8;
end loop;
```

This code is more readable than the corresponding C code, but remains low-level. As a result an interesting research question is whether it is possible to write an Ada vector package with a number of high-level vector operators which, when combined, allow the simple writing of *efficient* signal processing algorithms such as FFTs, and DCTs on the Altivec.

References

1. Cormen, Leiserson, Rivest, *Introduction to Algorithms*, the MIT Press, 1990.
2. Motorola, *AltiVec Technology - Programming Interface Manual*,
   http://e-www.motorola.com/files/32bit/doc/ref_manual/ALTIVECPIM.pdf.
3. Motorola, *Complex Floating Point Fast Fourier Transform Optimization for AltiVec*,
   Application Note AN2115/D Rev. 2.1, 6/2003.
4. Wolfe, *Optimizing Supercompilers for Supercomputers*, the MIT Press, 1989.

Author Index

Aldea, Mario 283
Alonso, Alejandro 132
Álvarez, Bárbara 213
Alves, Mário Amado 297
Amey, Peter 225

Blieberger, Johann 78
Breuer, Peter T. 52
Burgstaller, Bernd 78
Burns, Alan 156, 261

Chan, Kwok Ping 200
Chen, Tsong Yueh 200
Crespo, Alfons 144, 261

Espinosa Minguet, Agustín 273

García-Fornes, Ana 273
García Valls, Marisol 52
Gasperoni, Franco 321
Giri, Sukant K. 190
Gogolla, Martin 1
González Harbour, Michael 91, 283
Gutiérrez, J. Javier 91

Hagenauer, Helge 237
Hall, Jon G. 249
Heaney, Matthew 309
Hilton, Adrian J. 249
Hugues, Jérôme 106

Jeppu, Yogananda V. 190

Karunakar, Kundapur 190
Kordon, Fabrice 106

López Campos, Juan 91
Lorente Garcés, Vicente 273

Martinek, Norbert 237
Masmano, Miguel 144
Miranda, Javier 261, 283
Mishra, Atit 190

Nadrchal, Stepan P. 120
Navarro, Pedro 213

Olivé, Antoni 16
Ortiz, Francisco 213

Pastor, Juan A. 213
Pautet, Laurent 106
Pohlmann, Werner 237
Puente, Juan Antonio de la 132
Pulido, José Antonio 132

Real, Jorge 144, 261
Ripoll, Ismael 144
Rogers, Patrick 166

Sánchez, Pedro 213
Scholz, Bernhard 78
Schonberg, Edmond 261
Simon, Daniel 178
Sward, Ricky E. 65

Taft, S. Tucker 156
Terrasa Barrena, Andrés 273
Towey, Dave 200

Vergnaud, Thomas 106
Vinoski, Steve 35
Vrandečić, Zdenko 178

Wellings, Andy J. 156, 166
White, Neil 225

Zamorano, Juan 132

Lecture Notes in Computer Science

For information about Vols. 1–2936

please contact your bookseller or Springer-Verlag

Vol. 3063: A. Llamosí, A. Strohmeier (Eds.), Reliable Software Technologies - Ada-Europe 2004. XIII, 333 pages. 2004.

Vol. 3060: A.Y. Tawfik, S.D. Goodwin (Eds.), Advances in Artificial Intelligence. XIII, 582 pages. 2004. (Subseries LNAI).

Vol. 3058: N. Sebe, M.S. Lew, T.S. Huang (Eds.), Computer Vision in Human-Computer Interaction. X, 233 pages. 2004.

Vol. 3053: J. Davies, D. Fensel, C. Bussler, R. Studer (Eds.), The Semantic Web: Research and Applications. XIII, 490 pages. 2004.

Vol. 3042: N. Mitrou, K. Kontovasilis, G.N. Rouskas, I. Iliadis, L. Merakos (Eds.), NETWORKING 2004, Networking Technologies, Services, and Protocols; Performance of Computer and Communication Networks; Mobile and Wireless Communications. XXXIII, 1519 pages. 2004.

Vol. 3034: J. Favela, E. Menasalvas, E. Chávez (Eds.), Advances in Web Intelligence. XIII, 227 pages. 2004. (Subseries LNAI).

Vol. 3033: M. Li, X.-H. Sun, Q. Deng, J. Ni (Eds.), Grid and Cooperative Computing. XXXVIII, 1076 pages. 2004.

Vol. 3032: M. Li, X.-H. Sun, Q. Deng, J. Ni (Eds.), Grid and Cooperative Computing. XXXVII, 1112 pages. 2004.

Vol. 3031: A. Butz, A. Krüger, P. Olivier (Eds.), Smart Graphics. X, 165 pages. 2004.

Vol. 3028: D. Neuenschwander, Probabilistic and Statistical Methods in Cryptology. X, 158 pages. 2004.

Vol. 3027: C. Cachin, J. Camenisch (Eds.), Advances in Cryptology - EUROCRYPT 2004. XI, 628 pages. 2004.

Vol. 3026: C. Ramamoorthy, R. Lee, K.W. Lee (Eds.), Software Engineering Research and Applications. XV, 377 pages. 2004.

Vol. 3025: G.A. Vouros, T. Panayiotopoulos (Eds.), Methods and Applications of Artificial Intelligence. XV, 546 pages. 2004. (Subseries LNAI).

Vol. 3024: T. Pajdla, J. Matas (Eds.), Computer Vision - ECCV 2004. XXVIII, 621 pages. 2004.

Vol. 3023: T. Pajdla, J. Matas (Eds.), Computer Vision - ECCV 2004. XXVIII, 611 pages. 2004.

Vol. 3022: T. Pajdla, J. Matas (Eds.), Computer Vision - ECCV 2004. XXVIII, 621 pages. 2004.

Vol. 3021: T. Pajdla, J. Matas (Eds.), Computer Vision - ECCV 2004. XXVIII, 633 pages. 2004.

Vol. 3019: R. Wyrzykowski, J. Dongarra, M. Paprzycki, J. Wasniewski (Eds.), Parallel Processing and Applied Mathematics. XIX, 1174 pages. 2004.

Vol. 3015: C. Barakat, I. Pratt (Eds.), Passive and Active Network Measurement. XI, 300 pages. 2004.

Vol. 3012: K. Kurumatani, S.-H. Chen, A. Ohuchi (Eds.), Multi-Agnets for Mass User Support. X, 217 pages. 2004. (Subseries LNAI).

Vol. 3011: J.-C. Régin, M. Rueher (Eds.), Integration of AI and OR Techniques in Constraint Programming for Combinatorial Optimization Problems. XI, 415 pages. 2004.

Vol. 3010: K.R. Apt, F. Fages, F. Rossi, P. Szeredi, J. Váncza (Eds.), Recent Advances in Constraints. VIII, 285 pages. 2004. (Subseries LNAI).

Vol. 3009: F. Bomarius, H. Iida (Eds.), Product Focused Software Process Improvement. XIV, 584 pages. 2004.

Vol. 3008: S. Heuel, Uncertain Projective Geometry. XVII, 205 pages. 2004.

Vol. 3007: J.X. Yu, X. Lin, H. Lu, Y. Zhang (Eds.), Advanced Web Technologies and Applications. XXII, 936 pages. 2004.

Vol. 3006: M. Matsui, R. Zuccherato (Eds.), Selected Areas in Cryptography. XI, 361 pages. 2004.

Vol. 3005: G.R. Raidl, S. Cagnoni, J. Branke, D.W. Corne, R. Drechsler, Y. Jin, C.G. Johnson, P. Machado, E. Marchiori, F. Rothlauf, G.D. Smith, G. Squillero (Eds.), Applications of Evolutionary Computing. XVII, 562 pages. 2004.

Vol. 3004: J. Gottlieb, G.R. Raidl (Eds.), Evolutionary Computation in Combinatorial Optimization. X, 241 pages. 2004.

Vol. 3003: M. Keijzer, U.-M. O'Reilly, S.M. Lucas, E. Costa, T. Soule (Eds.), Genetic Programming. XI, 410 pages. 2004.

Vol. 3002: D.L. Hicks (Ed.), Metainformatics. X, 213 pages. 2004.

Vol. 3001: A. Ferscha, F. Mattern (Eds.), Pervasive Computing. XVII, 358 pages. 2004.

Vol. 2999: E.A. Boiten, J. Derrick, G. Smith (Eds.), Integrated Formal Methods. XI, 541 pages. 2004.

Vol. 2998: Y. Kameyama, P.J. Stuckey (Eds.), Functional and Logic Programming. X, 307 pages. 2004.

Vol. 2997: S. McDonald, J. Tait (Eds.), Advances in Information Retrieval. XIII, 427 pages. 2004.

Vol. 2996: V. Diekert, M. Habib (Eds.), STACS 2004. XVI, 658 pages. 2004.

Vol. 2995: C. Jensen, S. Poslad, T. Dimitrakos (Eds.), Trust Management. XIII, 377 pages. 2004.

Vol. 2994: E. Rahm (Ed.), Data Integration in the Life Sciences. X, 221 pages. 2004. (Subseries LNBI).

Vol. 2993: R. Alur, G.J. Pappas (Eds.), Hybrid Systems: Computation and Control. XII, 674 pages. 2004.

Vol. 2992: E. Bertino, S. Christodoulakis, D. Plexousakis, V. Christophides, M. Koubarakis, K. Böhm, E. Ferrari (Eds.), Advances in Database Technology - EDBT 2004. XVIII, 877 pages. 2004.

Vol. 2991: R. Alt, A. Frommer, R.B. Kearfott, W. Luther (Eds.), Numerical Software with Result Verification. X, 315 pages. 2004.

Vol. 2989: S. Graf, L. Mounier (Eds.), Model Checking Software. X, 309 pages. 2004.

Vol. 2988: K. Jensen, A. Podelski (Eds.), Tools and Algorithms for the Construction and Analysis of Systems. XIV, 608 pages. 2004.

Vol. 2987: I. Walukiewicz (Ed.), Foundations of Software Science and Computation Structures. XIII, 529 pages. 2004.

Vol. 2986: D. Schmidt (Ed.), Programming Languages and Systems. XII, 417 pages. 2004.

Vol. 2985: E. Duesterwald (Ed.), Compiler Construction. X, 313 pages. 2004.

Vol. 2984: M. Wermelinger, T. Margaria-Steffen (Eds.), Fundamental Approaches to Software Engineering. XII, 389 pages. 2004.

Vol. 2983: S. Istrail, M.S. Waterman, A. Clark (Eds.), Computational Methods for SNPs and Haplotype Inference. IX, 153 pages. 2004. (Subseries LNBI).

Vol. 2982: N. Wakamiya, M. Solarski, J. Sterbenz (Eds.), Active Networks. XI, 308 pages. 2004.

Vol. 2981: C. Müller-Schloer, T. Ungerer, B. Bauer (Eds.), Organic and Pervasive Computing – ARCS 2004. XI, 339 pages. 2004.

Vol. 2980: A. Blackwell, K. Marriott, A. Shimojima (Eds.), Diagrammatic Representation and Inference. XV, 448 pages. 2004. (Subseries LNAI).

Vol. 2979: I. Stoica, Stateless Core: A Scalable Approach for Quality of Service in the Internet. XVI, 219 pages. 2004.

Vol. 2978: R. Groz, R.M. Hierons (Eds.), Testing of Communicating Systems. XII, 225 pages. 2004.

Vol. 2977: G. Di Marzo Serugendo, A. Karageorgos, O.F. Rana, F. Zambonelli (Eds.), Engineering Self-Organising Systems. X, 299 pages. 2004. (Subseries LNAI).

Vol. 2976: M. Farach-Colton (Ed.), LATIN 2004: Theoretical Informatics. XV, 626 pages. 2004.

Vol. 2973: Y. Lee, J. Li, K.-Y. Whang, D. Lee (Eds.), Database Systems for Advanced Applications. XXIV, 925 pages. 2004.

Vol. 2972: R. Monroy, G. Arroyo-Figueroa, L.E. Sucar, H. Sossa (Eds.), MICAI 2004: Advances in Artificial Intelligence. XVII, 923 pages. 2004. (Subseries LNAI).

Vol. 2971: J.I. Lim, D.H. Lee (Eds.), Information Security and Cryptology -ICISC 2003. XI, 458 pages. 2004.

Vol. 2970: F. Fernández Rivera, M. Bubak, A. Gómez Tato, R. Doallo (Eds.), Grid Computing. XI, 328 pages. 2004.

Vol. 2968: J. Chen, S. Hong (Eds.), Real-Time and Embedded Computing Systems and Applications. XIV, 620 pages. 2004.

Vol. 2967: S. Melnik, Generic Model Management. XX, 238 pages. 2004.

Vol. 2966: F.B. Sachse, Computational Cardiology. XVIII, 322 pages. 2004.

Vol. 2965: M.C. Calzarossa, E. Gelenbe, Performance Tools and Applications to Networked Systems. VIII, 385 pages. 2004.

Vol. 2964: T. Okamoto (Ed.), Topics in Cryptology – CT-RSA 2004. XI, 387 pages. 2004.

Vol. 2963: R. Sharp, Higher Level Hardware Synthesis. XVI, 195 pages. 2004.

Vol. 2962: S. Bistarelli, Semirings for Soft Constraint Solving and Programming. XII, 279 pages. 2004.

Vol. 2961: P. Eklund (Ed.), Concept Lattices. IX, 411 pages. 2004. (Subseries LNAI).

Vol. 2960: P.D. Mosses (Ed.), CASL Reference Manual. XVII, 528 pages. 2004.

Vol. 2959: R. Kazman, D. Port (Eds.), COTS-Based Software Systems. XIV, 219 pages. 2004.

Vol. 2958: L. Rauchwerger (Ed.), Languages and Compilers for Parallel Computing. XI, 556 pages. 2004.

Vol. 2957: P. Langendoerfer, M. Liu, I. Matta, V. Tsaousidis (Eds.), Wired/Wireless Internet Communications. XI, 307 pages. 2004.

Vol. 2956: A. Dengel, M. Junker, A. Weisbecker (Eds.), Reading and Learning. XII, 355 pages. 2004.

Vol. 2954: F. Crestani, M. Dunlop, S. Mizzaro (Eds.), Mobile and Ubiquitous Information Access. X, 299 pages. 2004.

Vol. 2953: K. Konrad, Model Generation for Natural Language Interpretation and Analysis. XIII, 166 pages. 2004. (Subseries LNAI).

Vol. 2952: N. Guelfi, E. Astesiano, G. Reggio (Eds.), Scientific Engineering of Distributed Java Applications. X, 157 pages. 2004.

Vol. 2951: M. Naor (Ed.), Theory of Cryptography. XI, 523 pages. 2004.

Vol. 2949: R. De Nicola, G. Ferrari, G. Meredith (Eds.), Coordination Models and Languages. X, 323 pages. 2004.

Vol. 2948: G.L. Mullen, A. Poli, H. Stichtenoth (Eds.), Finite Fields and Applications. VIII, 263 pages. 2004.

Vol. 2947: F. Bao, R. Deng, J. Zhou (Eds.), Public Key Cryptography – PKC 2004. XI, 455 pages. 2004.

Vol. 2946: R. Focardi, R. Gorrieri (Eds.), Foundations of Security Analysis and Design II. VII, 267 pages. 2004.

Vol. 2943: J. Chen, J. Reif (Eds.), DNA Computing. X, 225 pages. 2004.

Vol. 2941: M. Wirsing, A. Knapp, S. Balsamo (Eds.), Radical Innovations of Software and Systems Engineering in the Future. X, 359 pages. 2004.

Vol. 2940: C. Lucena, A. Garcia, A. Romanovsky, J. Castro, P.S. Alencar (Eds.), Software Engineering for Multi-Agent Systems II. XII, 279 pages. 2004.

Vol. 2939: T. Kalker, I.J. Cox, Y.M. Ro (Eds.), Digital Watermarking. XII, 602 pages. 2004.

Vol. 2937: B. Steffen, G. Levi (Eds.), Verification, Model Checking, and Abstract Interpretation. XI, 325 pages. 2004.